THE RHETORIC OF SEEING
IN ATTIC FORENSIC ORATORY

Ashley and Peter Larkin Series in Greek and Roman Culture

THE RHETORIC OF SEEING IN ATTIC FORENSIC ORATORY

PETER A. O'CONNELL

UNIVERSITY OF TEXAS PRESS
Austin

Copyright © 2017 by the University of Texas Press
All rights reserved
Printed in the United States of America
First edition, 2017

Requests for permission to reproduce material
from this work should be sent to:
Permissions
University of Texas Press
P.O. Box 7819
Austin, TX 78713-7819
http://utpress.utexas.edu/index.php/rp-form

♾ The paper used in this book meets the minimum requirements of
ANSI/NISO Z39.48-1992 (R1997) (Permanence of Paper).

LIBRARY OF CONGRESS CATALOGING-IN-PUBLICATION DATA
Names: O'Connell, Peter A., author.
Title: The rhetoric of seeing in Attic forensic oratory /
Peter A. O'Connell.
Other titles: Ashley and Peter Larkin series
in Greek and Roman culture.
Description: First edition. | Austin : University of Texas Press, 2017. |
Series: Ashley and Peter Larkin series in Greek and Roman culture |
Includes bibliographical references and index.
Identifiers: LCCN 2016030557 | ISBN 978-1-4773-1168-4
(cloth : alk. paper) | ISBN 978-1-4773-1169-1 (library e-book) |
ISBN 978-1-4773-1170-7 (non-library e-book)
Subjects: LCSH: Speeches, addresses, etc., Greek—History and
criticism. | Forensic orations—Greece—Athens—History
and criticism. | Rhetoric, Ancient. | Oratory, Ancient.
Classification: LCC PA3263 .O34 2017 | DDC 885/.0109—dc23
LC record available at https://lccn.loc.gov/2016030557

doi:10.7560/311684

For my parents

CONTENTS

ABBREVIATIONS OF ANCIENT AUTHORS ix

ABBREVIATIONS OF MODERN EDITIONS xi

NOTE ON TRANSLATIONS AND
THE SPELLING OF GREEK NAMES xv

ACKNOWLEDGMENTS xvii

INTRODUCTION: VISION AND PERFORMANCE
IN THE COURTS OF CLASSICAL ATHENS 1

PART ONE
PHYSICAL SIGHT
23

1. VISUAL RHETORIC AND VISUAL EVIDENCE 25

2. THE MEANINGS OF MOVEMENT 53

PART TWO
THE LANGUAGE OF DEMONSTRATION AND VISIBILITY
81

3. SHOWING AND SEEING 83
The Procedural Terminology of Witnessing

4. SAYING AS SHOWING, HEARING AS SEEING 105

CONTENTS

PART THREE
IMAGINARY SIGHT
119

5. VISUALIZING CIVIC SUFFERING 121

6. SHARED SPECTATORSHIP 141
Bridging the Gap between Past and Present and Here and There

CONCLUSION 169

APPENDIX OF SPEECHES 175

NOTES 191

BIBLIOGRAPHY 231

INDEX OF ANCIENT TEXTS 255

GENERAL INDEX 271

ABBREVIATIONS OF ANCIENT AUTHORS

Aeschin.	Aeschines
Ant.	Antiphon
Arist.	Aristotle
Rhet.	*Rhetoric*
Dem.	Demosthenes
Hyp.	Hyperides
Isae.	Isaeus
Isoc.	Isocrates
Lys.	Lysias
Pl.	Plato
Schol.	Scholia

NOTE ON SPEECH SUMMARIES

The reader may consult the "Appendix of Speeches" for summaries of every speech I discuss.

ABBREVIATIONS OF MODERN EDITIONS

Aujac	*Denys d'Halicarnasse: Opuscules rhétoriques*. 5 volumes. Edited by G. Aujac, 1978–1992. Paris: Les Belles Lettres.
Bernabé	*Poetae Epici Graeci testimonia et fragmenta, Pars II*. 3 volumes. Edited by A. Bernabé, 2004–2007. Munich: K. G. Saur/Berlin: Walter De Gruyter.
Carey	*Lysiae Orationes cum fragmentis*. Edited by C. Carey, 2007. Oxford: Clarendon Press.
Colin	*Hypéride: Discours*. Edited by G. Colin, 1946. Paris: Les Belles Lettres.
De Falco	*Demade oratore: Testimonianze e frammenti*. 2nd edition. Edited by V. De Falco, 1955. Naples: Libreria scientifica editrice.
Diehl	*Procli Diadochi in Platonis Timaeum commentaria*. 3 volumes. Edited by E. Diehl, 1903–1906. Leipzig: B. G. Teubner.
Diels-Kranz	*Die Fragmente der Vorsokratiker*. 6th edition. 3 volumes. Edited by H. Diels and W. Kranz, 1951–1952. Berlin: Weidmann.
Dilts	*Scholia Demosthenica*. 2 volumes. Edited by M. R. Dilts, 1983–1986. Leipzig: B. G. Teubner.
	Scholia in Aeschinem. Edited by M. R. Dilts, 1992. Stuttgart: B. G. Teubner.
Elice	*Romani Aquilae De figuris*. Edited by M. Elice, 2007. Hildesheim: Olms.
FGrH	*Die Fragmente der griechischen Historiker*. Edited by F. Jacoby and others, 1923–. Berlin: Weidmann/Leiden: E. J. Brill.

Fortenbaugh	*Theophrastus of Eresus: Sources for His Life, Writings, Thought, and Influence.* 2 volumes. Edited by W. W. Fortenbaugh and others, 1992. Leiden: E. J. Brill.
Gernet	*Antiphon: Discours, suivis des fragments d'Antiphon le sophiste.* Edited by L. Gernet, 1923. Paris: Les Belles Lettres.
GGM	*Geographi Graeci minores.* 2 volumes. Edited by K. Müller, 1855–1861. Paris: Didot.
Giannantoni	*Socratis et Socraticorum Reliquiae.* 4 volumes. Edited by G. Giannantoni, 1990. Naples: Bibliopolis.
Gigon	*Aristotelis Opera, Volumen 3: Librorum deperditorum fragmenta.* Edited by O. Gigon, 1987. Berlin: Walter de Gruyter.
Graham	*The Texts of Early Greek Philosophy: The Complete Fragments and Selected Testimonies of the Major Presocratics.* 2 volumes. Edited by D. W. Graham, 2010. Cambridge: Cambridge University Press.
Hajdú	*Ps.-Herodian: De figuris.* Edited by K. Hajdú, 1998. Berlin: Walter de Gruyter.
Halm	*Rhetores Latini minores.* Edited by K. Halm, 1863. Leipzig: B. G. Teubner.
IC	*Inscriptiones Creticae.* Edited by M. Guarducci, 1935–1950. Rome: Libreria dello Stato.
IE	*Eleusis: The Inscriptions on Stone. Documents of the Sanctuary of the Two Goddesses and the Public Documents of the Deme.* Edited by K. Clinton, 2005–2008. Athens: Archaeological Society at Athens.
IG I^3	*Inscriptiones Graecae I. Inscriptiones Atticae Euclidis anno anteriores.* 3rd edition. Edited by D. Lewis and others, 1981–1998. Berlin: Georg Reimer/Walter De Gruyter.
IG II^2	*Inscriptiones Graecae II et III. Inscriptiones Atticae Euclidis anno posteriores.* 2nd edition. Edited by J. Kirchner, 1913–1940. Berlin: Georg Reimer/Walter De Gruyter.
IG IX, 2	*Inscriptiones Graecae IX, 2. Corpus inscriptionum Graecarum Graeciae septentrionalis: Inscriptiones Thessaliae.* Edited by O. Kern, 1908. Berlin: Georg Reimer.
IG XI, 2	*Inscriptiones Graecae XI, 2. Inscriptiones Deli.* Edited by Félix Durrbach, 1912. Berlin: Georg Reimer.
IG XII, 6.1	*Inscriptiones Graecae, XII, 6.1. Inscriptiones insularum*

	maris Aegaei praeter Delum: Inscriptiones Chii et Sami cum Corassiis Icariaque. Part I. Edited by K. Hallof, 2000. Berlin: Walter De Gruyter.
Jensen	*Hyperidis Orationes sex cum ceterarum fragmentis*. Edited by C. Jensen, 1917. Leipzig: B. G. Teubner.
LSJ	*Greek-English Lexicon*. 9th edition. Compiled by H. G. Liddell and R. Scott and revised by H. S. Jones, 1940. Revised supplement 1996. Oxford: Clarendon Press.
Merkelbach-West	*Fragmenta Hesiodea*. Edited by R. Merkelbach and M. L. West, 1967. Oxford: Clarendon Press.
Patillon	*Aelius Theon: Progymnasmata*. Edited by M. Patillon, 1997. Paris: Les Belles Lettres.
Patillon *CR*	*Corpus Rhetoricum*. 5 volumes. Edited by M. Patillon, 2008–2014. Paris: Les Belles Lettres.
PCG	*Poetae Comici Graeci*. 8 volumes. Edited by R. Kassel and C. Austin, 1983–. Berlin: Walter de Gruyter.
P. Mil. Vogl. I	*Papiri della R. Università di Milano*. Edited by A. Vogliano, 1937. Milan: U. Hoepli.
POxy	*The Oxyrhynchus Papyri*. 1898–. London: The Egypt Exploration Society.
Rabe	*Prolegomenon Sylloge*. Edited by H. Rabe, 1931. Leipzig: B. G. Teubner.
	Hermogenis Opera. Edited by H. Rabe. 1913. Leipzig: B. G. Teubner.
Radermacher	*Artium scriptores (Reste der voraristotelischen Rhetorik)*, edited by L. Radermacher, 1951. Vienna: Rohrer.
Snell-Maehler	*Pindari Carmina cum fragmentis*. 2 volumes. Edited by B. Snell and H. Maehler, 1987–1989. Leipzig: B. G. Teubner.
Spengel	*Rhetores Graeci*. 3 volumes. Edited by L. Spengel, 1853–1856. Leipzig: B. G. Teubner.
Sudhaus	*Philodemi Volumina rhetorica*. 2 volumes and a supplement. Edited by S. Sudhaus, 1892–1896. Leipzig: B. G. Teubner.
Thalheim	*Antiphontis Orationes et fragmenta*. Edited by T. Thalheim, 1914. Leipzig: B. G. Teubner.
TrGF	*Tragicorum Graecorum Fragmenta*. 5 volumes. Edited by B. Snell, R. Kannicht and S. Radt, 1971–. Göttingen: Vandenhoeck & Ruprecht.

van der Valk	*Eustathii archiepiscopi Thessalonicensis Commentarii ad Homeri Iliadem pertinentes.* 4 volumes. Edited by M. van der Valk, 1971–1987. Leiden: E. J. Brill.
Walz	*Rhetores Graeci.* 9 volumes. Edited by C. Walz, 1832–1836. Stuttgart: J. G. Cotta.
West	*Iambi et elegi Graeci ante Alexandrum cantati.* 2nd edition. 2 volumes. Edited by M. L. West, 1989–1992. Oxford: Oxford University Press.

NOTE ON TRANSLATIONS AND THE SPELLING OF GREEK NAMES

Unless otherwise attributed, all translations are my own. I use Anglicized versions of the most familiar Greek names, including all the authors I discuss (e.g., Socrates, Clytemnestra, Isaeus, Aeschines), and of Greek places whose Anglicized names are customary (e.g., Athens, Thebes, Corinth). I have transliterated the names of other people and places.

ACKNOWLEDGMENTS

Many friends and colleagues have improved this book with formal and informal advice, including Karen Bassi, Nancy Felson, Edward Harris, Christopher Krebs, Richard Martin, Charles Platter, Harvey Yunis, and the two anonymous readers for University of Texas Press. David Elmer and Gregory Nagy read the original dissertation and helped me develop my central arguments. Albert Henrichs directed the dissertation and, many years before that, my senior thesis on the Eleusinian Mysteries. I have continued to benefit from his keen critical eye, his comprehensive knowledge of Greek and the Greeks, and the care he has for all of his students. Anastasia-Erasmia Peponi took a special interest in this book and in me, and I am grateful for her advice, friendship, and generosity.

I presented parts of my argument at Harvard, Stanford, the University of Georgia, the University of North Carolina, the University of Miami, the University of Notre Dame, the 2011 International Pragmatics Conference, the 2014 meeting of the American Philological Association, and the 2015 meeting of the Northeast Modern Language Association. I thank my hosts and audiences for their hospitality, questions, and criticism.

I wrote most of the book between 2011 and 2014, while I was an Andrew W. Mellon Fellow in the Humanities at Stanford. My colleagues in the Stanford Humanities Center and in the Mellon Fellowship greatly enriched my work by their cheerful company and their willingness to share insights from their own projects, especially ones unrelated to my own.

Finally, I am grateful to Jim Burr, Lynne Chapman, and Nancy Moore of University of Texas Press and to my research assistant Nicholas Gardner, who double-checked Greek references in the final stages of the project.

ACKNOWLEDGMENTS

A first book subvention grant from the Franklin College of the University of Georgia helped to pay for the indexing.

Any errors that remain are my own.

THE RHETORIC OF SEEING
IN ATTIC FORENSIC ORATORY

INTRODUCTION

VISION AND PERFORMANCE IN THE COURTS OF CLASSICAL ATHENS

The trial was drawing to a close. Hundreds of jurors were about to decide the fate of Phryne, one of the most beautiful courtesans in fourth-century Athens, and her advocate Hyperides realized that his arguments were falling on deaf ears. He stopped speaking and took Phryne's hand. Leading her to the front of the court where all the jurors could see her, he tore open her dress and revealed her breasts. Then he stood over Phryne and returned to his speech. Hyperides begged the jurors to have compassion on her naked beauty, turning their thoughts to the gods and filling them with reverence for Phryne, Aphrodite's oracle and servant. Giving in to pity, the jurors acquitted Phryne of impiety and voted not to execute her.

Athenaeus recounts this story in *The Scholars at Dinner* as a testament to Phryne's extraordinary beauty. It also shows the power of appearance to persuade. Hyperides' words alone were useless. Athenaeus writes, "He was accomplishing nothing by speaking." But that changed when Hyperides paired his words with a visual demonstration. Taking advantage of bared breasts' connections with ritual supplication and eroticism, he manipulated the jurors into acquitting Phryne for reasons that had nothing to do with the kinds of logical argument taught in Aristotle's *Rhetoric*. Athenaeus is careful to show that Hyperides crafted a unified persuasive strategy from what the jurors heard and what the jurors saw. "Based on her appearance," Athenaeus writes, "he made pleas for compassion appropriate for the end of a speech." Hearing words that complemented what they could see, the jurors were led to accept Phyrne's innocence.[1]

Few contemporary accounts of Phryne's trial survive. Since none of them mention her bare breasts, some modern scholars doubt that Hyperides really ripped her dress open and appealed to the jurors' eyes as well as their ears. Reliable records of Athenian trials mention visual effects nearly as sensational as Phryne's naked bosom, however. In one trial, the defendant proved his innocence by showing the jurors the woman he was accused of murdering, alive and well. In another, the defendant was said to have bitten off someone's nose in prison, and the prosecutor showed the jurors a man with no nose.[2] So, even if the Phryne story is apocryphal, there is no question that Athenian litigants could take advantage of what the jurors could see and use it to strengthen their cases.

Ancient rhetorical theorists were aware that oratorical persuasion required more than just words. In the *Orator*, Cicero writes that there are two components of giving a speech: speaking and doing. A speaker persuades not only through words but also through the tone of his voice, the movements of his body, and his visual appearance. The Romans refer to these features as *actio*, and the Greeks call them *hupokrisis*. In English, both terms can mean "delivery," "performance," or even "acting." Cicero insists that a speaker ignores these features at his peril: a good delivery can rescue a bad speech, and even a good speech can be undermined by a poor delivery.[3] The Romans developed an elaborate science of what features are appropriate for oratorical performance,[4] and they were conscious that earlier rhetorical theorists had neglected it. The anonymous author of the first-century BCE rhetorical treatise known as the *Rhetoric for Herennius* even tells us that no one had written carefully about it prior to him because it is difficult to express things like voice, appearance, and gesture in writing.[5] He echoes Aristotle, who three hundred years earlier said that no handbooks address delivery, even though it is a powerful rhetorical tool.[6]

Although Theophrastus, Aristotle's successor at the Lyceum in Athens, wrote a treatise *Peri hupokriseōs*, or *On Delivery*, which probably addressed oratorical and not theatrical performance,[7] it seems to be true that widespread systematic interest in the subject did not arise until the first century BCE. Philodemus, a slightly older contemporary of the author of the *Rhetoric for Herennius*, writes that formal instruction in oratorical delivery is a recent, and regrettable, development. He insists, however, that "many of the heroes and those who came after them were delivering their speeches in an admirable manner," even without handbooks to guide them. By "heroes," Philodemus seems to be thinking primarily of the Homeric heroes, since he cites "poets" in support of his claim. "Those who came after them" is a more expansive category, since Philodemus cites historians and speakers' own writings. Philodemus also maintains that the people he calls "statesmen" (*hoi politikoi*) already practice a method of delivery that enables them to seem respectable and

INTRODUCTION

noble, to exaggerate, and, most importantly, to mislead their audiences. Their method has always been a well-kept secret, but Philodemus says that his contemporaries are making it common knowledge with their handbooks.[8]

Even among modern scholars, however, the performance techniques of the Athenian orators remain far from common knowledge. Despite the emphasis on performance as a conceptual model for understanding the art, literature, and culture of Classical Athens during the last three decades, few scholars have attempted to study the speeches of Antiphon, Andocides, Lysias, Isocrates, Isaeus, Hyperides, Demosthenes, Aeschines, Dinarchus, and Lycurgus as, primarily, records of performances in the Athenian courts and assembly. With some notable exceptions, especially Edith Hall's work on "Lawcourt Dramas,"[9] modern scholars tend to study Attic oratory out of an interest in Athenian law, politics, or social history rather than in performance. *The Rhetoric of Seeing in Attic Forensic Oratory* recognizes that the oratory of the courts is one of the premier performance genres of Classical Athens. Following scholarly convention, I call this type of oratory "forensic," using the Latin term for activity connected with courts of law. My study is principally concerned with the interplay between visual and verbal features of forensic performances.

Before ending this introduction with an overview of the book's sections, I will investigate the place of forensic oratory within Athenian performance culture, explore the complex associations of vision and visuality in Classical Athens, briefly describe the settings of Athenian trials, and address the insights of modern studies of legal performance that have most influenced my study.

THE PERFORMANCE OF PERSUASION
IN THE COURTS OF CLASSICAL ATHENS

The modern discipline of performance studies reflects the many overlapping meanings of the verb "perform." It encompasses theories such as those of J. L. Austin, John Searle, and Judith Butler, which focus on how words or actions "do" things; anthropological studies of ritual and society; and the study of every kind of dramatic production.[10] The semantic range of "perform" is unmatched by any single word in Classical Greek. Depending on the context, it can be an appropriate translation for many Greek verbs, including *poieō* ("do, make"), *draō* ("do, accomplish"), *hu-*

pokrinomai ("play, act, deliver"), and *khoreuō* ("dance, sing and dance"). The concept of "performance," therefore, links many features of Greek society that the Greeks themselves may not have associated with each other. When we refer to Classical Athens as a "performance culture," we recognize that Athenian religion, politics, and entertainment all share features associated with carrying things out or making presentations before audiences.[11] Processions and sacrifices, dramatic and musical festivals, debates in the assembly, symposia, and competitive athletics are all performances in the modern sense of the term.

In what sense are defense and prosecution speeches performances? They are not performances in the sense of Searle's speech acts or Austin's performative utterances, where, in Austin's words, by "saying something we are doing something."[12] For instance, by saying "I now pronounce you man and wife," the presider at a wedding is not simply making a statement but performing the act of marrying the couple. In an Athenian trial, the principal speech act of this sort is the announcement of the jurors' verdict, which either convicts or acquits the defendant by being spoken. The speeches of the litigants are attempts to influence a speech act rather than speech acts in themselves.

Forensic speeches are performances in the sense that they are presentations before audiences. Litigants spoke before hundreds of jurors, and, often, like actors, they memorized speeches written for them by someone else, called a *logographos*, or "speechwriter."[13] The comparison to the theater is instructive, but it can be misleading.[14] Forensic speeches are performances not because they resemble dramas but because they are presentations before audiences. At the most basic level, then, the kind of performance this book addresses can be defined as "a communicative event before an audience." The slightly awkward "communicative event" indicates that a performance includes everything relevant to the performer's message to the audience, including but not limited to words and gestures. A performance can of course take place before an imaginary audience, or the performer can be his or her own audience, but such situations are irrelevant to this discussion.

The surviving texts of forensic speeches, therefore, are one aspect of a complex communicative event that would have included voice pitch and volume, pauses, gestures, movement, dress, and eye contact. Sometimes multiple speakers would take turns speaking. Sometimes the speaker would call witnesses or question his opponent. Sometimes the audience would heckle the speaker or the speaker would ask questions of the audience. We can think of each surviving forensic speech as a script for one part of a performance intended to convince a specific jury in a specific place on a specific occasion. From the outset, we must keep in mind that we are examining the works of professional speechwriters and not speeches delivered extemporaneously. Some litigants spoke without a speechwriter's aid and perhaps without even formally preparing a speech.[15] Systematic study of these performances is impossible. My study, therefore, shows how skilled authors deliberately composed speeches that exploited the performance conditions of the Athenian courts and the cultural biases of Athenian jurors to help their clients win their cases.

A forensic performance was a one-time event. Epic poetry and choral songs could be performed and re-performed at festivals and ritual occasions.[16] Dramas could be revived in deme theaters, the Theater of Dionysus, or outside Attica.[17] Most oratory, however, had no timeless quality.[18] Regardless of whether forensic speeches succeeded in convincing the jury, they were useless immediately after the trial except as advertisements of the speechwriter's skill, sources of information for politicians and partisans, examples of prose composition and rhetoric, and entertainment for connoisseurs.[19] There would never have been an occasion to perform them again in a context that mattered, although it is possible that they may have been used as rhetorical exercises or epideictic showpieces.[20] Plutarch reports a fictitious anecdote about Lysias that illustrates the one-time-only quality of forensic oratory:

> Lysias wrote a speech and gave it to a litigant. After he had read it many times, he came to Lysias because he was disappointed. He said that the speech had seemed wonderful to him the first time he had gone through it, but that it seemed completely dull and useless when he had read it a second and a third time. Lysias laughed and said, "You're not going to speak it more than once before the jurors, are you?"[21]

The ancient study of forensic oratory from at least the time of Aristotle took the form of theoretical analyses of organization and argumentation. Throughout antiquity, rhetorical theorists discussed the parts of speeches—prologue, narrative, proofs, and peroration—and the tasks of the orator—invention, arrangement, style, memory, and delivery.[22] This drive to categorize is fundamentally misleading.[23] Although Athenian forensic speeches followed a certain basic structure, the line between parts was fluid. A skillful speechwriter would use his entire speech to convince the jurors. Different parts of the speech might appeal to different jurors, but no Athenian speechwriter worried about maintaining a firm division between the narrative and the proofs.

In this book, I resist the urge to classify and categorize the parts of forensic speeches. Instead, I consider them as unified performances intended to persuade immediately, not after being analyzed by scholars. Forensic speeches are communicative events that happened in real time. The jurors could neither press rewind to hear the prologue again nor check a transcript for an argument they failed to understand. Talented speechwriters prepared unified compositions whose language and structure were designed solely to convince a single audience to vote in favor of the speaker a single time.[24] The connections between performance and persuasion, between speaker and audience,[25] are more significant than the divisions that later theorists make based on careful, and perhaps overly subtle, reading of the texts.

Most aspects of forensic performances are lost forever.[26] We can recover only the barest hints of how the speakers sounded, dressed, and moved. The language of the speeches, however, testifies to their origin as scripts for performances before live audiences. Literary critics in antiquity noticed stylistic differences between performative and nonperformative prose. Aristotle contrasts written and oral styles: "Leaving out conjunctions and saying the same thing again and again are rejected, appropriately, in writing [*en tēi graphikēi*] but not in a forensic context [*en agōnistikēi*]. Orators employ them because they are suited to performance [*hupokritikē*]."[27] Alcidamas, in his polemic against written speeches, maintains that precision (*akribeia*) and rhythm (*rhuthmos*) characterize written prose, while the oral improviser speaks "smoothly and with an appeal to human feelings" (*hugrōs kai philanthrōpōs*).[28] Furthermore, he claims that the best speechwriters imitate the extemporaneous style when they write forensic speeches.[29] Modern scholars also consider certain features of prose style characteristic of oral performance: Michael Gagarin identifies "signposts, ring-composition, parallelism, parataxis, relatively simplified sentence structure, and, of course, the notorious 'Gorgianic' verbal effects," and Rosalind Thomas, "excessive claims to have proved points, use of the first person, rhyming, rhetorical questions, and a lively awareness of the audience."[30]

This book studies for the first time another characteristic of performance in the Athenian courts: manipulation of the audience's seeing and hearing. Through examples from all forensic orators, but especially Demosthenes and Lysias, it demonstrates how litigants' words work together with their movements and physical appearance, how they exploit the Athenian preference for visual evidence through the language of demonstration and visibility, and how they plant images in their jurors' minds. Each chapter places persuasion in the courts within the network of concepts and images that contribute to Athenian notions of visuality. By focusing on references to seeing and hearing, the book also uncovers parallels among forensic, medical, and sophistic discourse that reflect a shared concern with how listeners come to know what they have not seen. Recognizing these parallels enables us to situate Attic forensic oratory more securely within the intellectual life of the Greek-speaking world in the late fifth and fourth centuries. The differences are just as important as the similarities, however. The rhetoric of seeing is a flexible category. Litigants and speechwriters shared some techniques with authors writing in other genres, but they adapted them to the circumstances of the Athenian courts and the expectations of their jurors. By recognizing the similarities and the differences, therefore, we can more fully appreciate what made the rhetoric of seeing in Attic forensic oratory unique and persuasive.

From the outset, it is important to note the methodological complication at the heart of this project. It depends on texts, the hundred or so surviving forensic speeches, to analyze fundamentally nontextual concepts: seeing, hearing, and performance. Almost all scholars of ancient Greek literature face this dilemma. The Greeks themselves experienced dramas, choral poetry, epic poetry, and oratory as performances, but we can access these performances primarily through texts. Vase paintings are a significant secondary source for drama, but very few images can be convincingly associated with the courts. Furthermore, the texts of forensic speeches are an imperfect record of the original performances, since authors may have modified their arguments after the trial.

The texts we have probably do substantially represent the performed versions of the speeches. While expansion or adjustment of arguments is possible, and perhaps even likely, there would have been little sense in publishing a speech that had no connection to the original performance. Even if the performative elements in published speeches were embellished in antiquity to add verisimilitude to a significantly altered work, they are still evidence for the kinds of things that Athenians would have considered appropriate for performances. As a result, even though it ultimately cannot be proven, I take it as axiomatic that surviving forensic speeches are records of and evidence for actual court performances.[31]

While forensic speeches themselves, as delivered, were one-time events, they have had, and continue to have, an enduring legacy as texts.

There was a market for them soon after they were first performed: Aristotle, according to Dionysius of Halicarnassus, said that very many bundles of Isocrates' forensic speeches were available from the booksellers.[32] Some of the features I study in this book, such as choice of words and appeals to the imagination, could have affected readers in similar ways to how they affected the original listening and looking audience of jurors. I argue, however, that these individual features can best be understood in their original context as part of a unified persuasive strategy that recognized the jurors as always both looking and listening. This is what I mean by "the performance of persuasion." Persuasion was not simply the result of argument or particular rhetorical and stylistic techniques. Rather, it was the result of multiple factors working together and reinforcing each other from the beginning of a speech until the end. Moreover, while texts give us an insight primarily into what jurors would have heard, their language attests to the central importance of vision and visuality to the performance of persuasion. Through carefully chosen verbal cues, Athenian litigants would simultaneously take advantage of what the jurors could actually see, of the images they pictured for themselves, and of the concepts and emotions they would have associated with their status as viewers.

Visuality is a complex and personal topic. Even within the same culture, individuals can respond to visual stimuli in different ways at different times, place varying and inconsistent emphases on the importance of seeing and the importance of hearing, and prefer sometimes to look and other times to be looked at. Throughout my discussion, I seek to avoid oversimplification and recognize the nuances and complexities inherent to what is always a personal experience. Even when hundreds of jurors were looking at the same litigants during a trial, each juror experienced his role as a viewer in a unique way. Since this is a study of forensic persuasion, the differences among individual jurors' experiences are ultimately less important than their similarities. Litigants succeeded in Athenian trials by convincing a majority of the jurors, and they designed their performances to take advantage of the visual biases, expectations, and susceptibilities that they anticipated most jurors would share. This book is a study of those techniques of persuasion. It discusses how litigants tried to manipulate their jurors' seeing and hearing and why they believed these attempts would help them win their trials. Since we rarely know the outcome of Athenian trials, it only occasionally addresses the success or failure of individual speeches.

INTRODUCTION

Among the many ways that Athenians could have experienced visuality, two are especially important for litigants and jurors in the courts: the connections between seeing and power, on the one hand, and seeing and knowledge, on the other. Starting from Simon Goldhill's conceptual model of a "civic gaze" that operates when large groups of Athenians look at and judge individual competitors, the next section of this introduction explores how a concern with power and knowledge would have influenced the behavior of jurors and litigants.

THE JURORS' GAZE

Goldhill argues that the "civic gaze" is at the heart of Athenian citizenship. The law courts, the assembly, and the theater provided an opportunity for issues and ideas to be debated before a mass audience of citizens. "To be in an audience was not just a thread in the city's social fabric, it was a fundamental political act. To sit as an evaluating, judging spectator was to participate as a political subject." For Goldhill, seeing and evaluating and being seen and being evaluated are a central aspect of what it meant to be an Athenian citizen. Competitive display before spectators undoubtedly had a central role in Classical Athens and in Greek culture generally, dating back to the Homeric epics and perhaps even to the boxing boys on a Theran fresco. As Goldhill shows, the term *agōn* applies to competitive public displays ranging from athletic competitions to jury trials to assembly debates to choral disputes in drama. All of these events featured some kind of competition before an audience who both listens and looks.[33]

The "civic gaze" would have posed a challenge to some, and perhaps most, Athenian litigants. The need to prove one's case before the eyes of hundreds of fellow citizens exposed a litigant to possible disgrace and shame.[34] As Aristotle writes, "Things done before people's eyes and in the open cause shame more than other things do; indeed, this gives rise to the proverb, 'Shame is in the eyes.' Therefore people feel greater shame before those who are going to be with them and those who are paying attention to them, because both situations are before their eyes."[35] The connection between shame and being seen, which is also explicit in tragedy and implied in Homer,[36] is the cornerstone of Jean-Paul Sartre's understanding of shame. Shame, he argues, "is the *recognition* of the fact that I *am* indeed the object which the Other is looking at and judging."

INTRODUCTION

An individual's sense of shame before a gazing spectator curtails his ability to act freely and forces him to tailor his behavior to the will of the one who looks.[37] In Sartre's formulation, then, an Athenian litigant falling prey to shame would be rendered nearly powerless by the gaze of the jurors. The jurors' consciousness of their own role as gazers may also have complemented the real voting power they held over the litigants. In another context, erotic vase paintings, men are sometimes shown gazing on sexually submissive, or even sexually abused, women,[38] underscoring a parallel between looking and dominating that, *mutatis mutandis*, may have operated in the courts as well.

Although these real or imagined, conscious or unconscious feelings of power and powerlessness may have influenced the behavior of jurors and litigants in Athenian trials, seeing and being seen can stir a range of emotions. The ancient Greeks did not experience a uniform emotional response as either subjects or objects of the gaze. On the contrary, seeing and being seen could incite love. They could bring glory. They could demonstrate moderation. They could even facilitate contact with the divine.[39] Indeed, the Athenians do not seem to have associated the gaze primarily with inducing shame and curtailing freedom.[40] Sometimes the gazer has power over the object of the gaze, and sometimes the object of the gaze has power over the gazer.[41] In Plato's *Phaedrus* and *Cratylus*, the one who is seen emits particles that affect the gazer, while in *Timaeus* the gazing eye emits fire from within the body.[42] Aristotle recognizes this double nature of sight, stating succinctly, "In the same way that the sense of sight is acted upon by what it sees, it also does something to it in return."[43] Finally, although Herodotus' Gyges states that the queen of Lydia is the property of her husband Kandaules and that the gaze is a privilege of his power, the queen who is seen ultimately decides the fate of her husband and her voyeur.[44]

Context and relationship, therefore, determine the effects of seeing and being seen. Individuals may also experience two contradictory responses at the same time. Just as in Plato's *Republic* the same man can simultaneously want to drink and want to abstain from drinking, so the same person can simultaneously feel a sense of power and a sense of powerlessness.[45] These tensions governed the experience of the "civic gaze" in the courts of Classical Athens. At the same time that litigants could experience the shame and powerlessness that arise from being under the jurors' gaze and subject to the power of their vote, they could also manipulate the jurors into accepting their cases by directing the jurors' impression of visual power and control. Similarly, impressionable jurors could have felt a sense of power as gazers while at the same time compromising their real power as voters by following the directives of a litigant who influences how they respond to what they see.

One of the main ways that litigants tried to influence the jurors' votes through visual display was by leading their friends, family members, and especially their children to the front of the court at the end of their speeches. In the *Apology*, Plato's Socrates criticizes this as a shameless, but very common, plea for pity. When speakers mention this tactic, they often describe the supporters weeping, begging, and supplicating. What the supporters, and especially the children, looked like could be just as important as these verbal pleas. In *On the Dishonest Embassy* (Aeschines 2), Aeschines notes that his children are not even old enough to understand what is going on, but they will be objects of pity if Aeschines is convicted. Wanting the jurors to respond to what they see as much as to what they hear, he draws their visual attention to the children by calling them "the ones right here [*touti*], the little children."[46] Edith Hall points out that Aeschylus' *Suppliants* seems to recognize the importance of children's appearance during supplication spectacles. Danaos instructs his daughters to supplicate Pelasgos with their voices and their appearances, saying, "First of all, no boldness should accompany your voice, and no wantonness should proceed from your faces, after you've gotten them under control, and from your quiet eyes."[47] The Danaids are teenagers, not small children, and the scene is Argos, not an Athenian court. Nonetheless, Danaos' emphasis on his daughters' faces, eyes, and voices indicates that an Athenian audience would expect pleas for pity to combine visual and verbal features.

By parading their children, family members, and other friends before the jurors as they were finishing their presentations, defendants made sure that this choreographed tableau was the last thing the jurors would have seen before they voted. Through a plea for pity that was partly visual and partly verbal, therefore, they tried to take advantage of the jurors' status as gazers. If the jurors followed the speaker's prompting, they would temper their anger in response to the spectacle they were seeing and wield their power in his favor, voting for mercy rather than for vengeance.

So far, I have been discussing the relationship between vision and power, or, even more generally, between vision and emotional response. But this narrow focus does not adequately address the range of Greek conceptions of visuality and their implications for the Attic courts. The connection between seeing and knowing is also fundamental. The verb "know" (*oida/eidenai*) is the perfect tense of the verb that in the aorist means "see" (*eidon/idein*). On a semantic level, knowledge is the state that results when someone has completed looking: to say that you know something is the same as to say that you have seen it. Aristotle exploits this verbal overlap at the beginning of the *Metaphysics*, when he explains that people love sight more than the other senses because it is through sight that we satisfy our hunger for knowledge.[48] Another verb of seeing, *theōreō*, is used to describe the process of gaining knowledge through speculative reasoning. Its nominal form, *theōria*, gives us the English word "theory." Since one of the main tasks of jurors is to determine which of two accounts of the same events is more likely to have happened, their status as viewers is closely connected to their special status as the designated "knowers" charged with resolving uncertainty into certainty.[49]

Within a single trial, therefore, jurors and litigants could experience the "civic gaze" in a variety of overlapping ways centering on feelings of power and knowledge. Since seeing and being seen are never simple, we should not be surprised that litigants take advantage of them in complex ways. The series of verbs that concludes Lysias' prosecution speech *Against Eratosthenes* (Lysias 12) illustrates how litigants could use references to the jurors' sight to appeal simultaneously to their sense of knowledge and sense of power. Lysias says, "I will end my accusation. You have heard. You have seen. You have suffered. You have him. Judge."[50] "You have seen" follows a reference to second-hand knowledge, "You have heard," and it precedes a reference to first-hand experience, "You have suffered." As a third way that the jurors might know about Eratosthenes, seeing occupies a middle ground between these two poles. But, at the same time, "you have seen" is also linked with another verb, "you have him." The verb "you have" (*ekhete*) has no direct object in Greek, but the context makes clear that Eratosthenes is the person the jurors have. He is present in the court, under the jurors' control. Throughout Lysias' speech, they have seen him sitting before them, a constant reminder that a self-proclaimed tyrant is now subordinate to a democratic jury. Now that Eratosthenes is about to begin his defense, Lysias wants the jurors to continue seeing him as their subject—the person they have—and not as an authoritative figure about to convince them of the justice of his case.

INTRODUCTION

THE SPACES AND AUDIENCES OF THE ATHENIAN COURTS

Assessing the precise force of phrases like "you have seen" in Athenian forensic speeches is a challenge, since we know little of what the Athenian courts actually looked like. Despite our ignorance of the visual details of specific trials, we can paint a reasonably accurate picture of their general performance conditions. References to the courts are common in both literature and inscriptions. Even though they are often contradictory and always difficult to link with the meager archaeological evidence, enough information survives for us to reconstruct something of what Athenian litigants and jurors must have experienced in the courts. This discussion of performance conditions focuses first on the types of people who probably composed Athenian juries, then on the courts' locations and physical features, and finally on the special features of the homicide courts.

The audience for forensic performances would have included jurors, called *dikastai* (singular, *dikastēs*), and interested observers, "the people standing around" who were welcome to attend trials except in rare circumstances.[51] A more accurate translation of *dikastai* would be "judges." Athenian courts had no official analogous to a modern judge, and the function of the *dikastai* combined the functions of a modern judge and jury. Following scholarly convention, I call the *dikastai* "jurors," but I ask the reader to bear in mind that this convenient translation only approximates their actual role in Athenian courts. In the 330s and 320s, trials required a minimum of 201 jurors, and important public cases could have multiples of 500 jurors, with an extra man to prevent ties.[52] At earlier periods, the numbers of jurors may have been slightly different, but these numbers are a reasonable approximation of jury sizes throughout the fifth and fourth centuries.[53] Jurors for individual trials were drawn from a group of 6,000 eligible men who swore a special oath every year.[54] They had to be at least thirty years old, and neither in debt to the state nor deprived of civic rights.[55]

Athenian courts tried cases between 175 and 225 days a year, and by the early fourth century, multiple courts could be in session simultaneously.[56] All 6,000 eligible jurors would not have reported for service every day, but more jurors had to be available than were necessary to staff all the trials. To ensure that litigants could not know who their jurors would be before the trial began, the Athenians allotted only some of the available jurors to trials.⁵⁷ Only jurors assigned to trials received payment for their service, originally two obols but raised to three by Kleon in the 420s.⁵⁸ This system, to be effective, probably relied on a core group of jurors who had sufficient leisure to present themselves for jury service on a regular basis and would not have been greatly inconvenienced if they were not selected for a panel. This core group of unemployed men would have lived close enough to the center of Athens to come to the courts easily, and a disproportionate number of them may have been elderly. If this is correct, the elderly urban jurors of Aristophanes' *Wasps* would represent a stereotype that reflects an underlying reality.⁵⁹ Apart from this core group, the demographic composition of individual juries would probably have varied widely. The Athenians would have needed different numbers of jurors on different days, and there is no reason to suppose that the same people, or even the same types of people, came every day. In addition, sensational trials involving public figures or scandalous disputes may have attracted curious jurors who avoided more mundane cases.⁶⁰

By the mid-fourth century, the Athenians had designed a complex of buildings used exclusively for trials.⁶¹ In earlier periods, they held trials in a variety of locations that served other functions as well, such as the Stoa Poikile and the Odeion. We also hear of court buildings called Parabyston and Trigonion, but we know almost nothing about them.⁶² In the ad hoc courts, and perhaps in the purpose-built ones as well, the jurors sat on wooden benches that could have been arranged in rows or as "inward-facing circles."⁶³ In front of the jurors' benches, there would have been at least one wooden platform called a *bēma* for the speakers.⁶⁴ The court would also have contained the water-clock, or *klepsudra*, and the voting urns, as well as seating for the presiding magistrate, the secretary, the litigants, their supporters, and their witnesses.⁶⁵ Since trials could have happened indoors, in partly enclosed stoas, and perhaps even outdoors, a variety of conditions could have affected how well the audience could see and hear the litigants. Unlike on the Pnyx, however, there is no reason to suppose that hearing or seeing was impossible, except perhaps for very large trials.⁶⁶

From this survey, a general picture of Athenian trials emerges. A litigant performing his speech would have looked out on hundreds of men, who would probably have represented a broad swath of Athenian society, aside from the group of regular jurors that I hypothesize formed the core of the court system. The jurors would have looked back, focusing on the speaker but also aware of the other participants in the trial and the apparatus of the court. While the details of this arrangement would have varied among the many places the Athenians held trials, the close visual relationship between the jurors and the performing litigant was probably a feature of every trial, and its importance should not be underestimated.

I have been describing the conditions and personnel of the trials judged by *dikastai*. The Athenians had other judicial procedures that resembled trials, including examinations of public officials (*dokimasiai*) that could be judged by the council (*boulē*) and impeachments of public officials (*eisangeliai*) that could be judged by the assembly. The personnel and locations of these procedures and others like them are beyond the scope of this overview. We are particularly well informed of the unique circumstances of Athenian homicide trials, however, and because their performance conditions differed significantly from the regular courts I discuss them here.

In cases of homicide, the Athenians employed special procedures in special locations to address the seriousness of the charge and the ritual pollution resulting from even justifiable murder.[67] All homicide trials had to be conducted under the open sky and, seemingly, within a sanctuary.[68] Cases of intentional homicide, intentional wounding, poisoning, or arson were tried on the hill called the Areopagos, where there was a cave sacred to the Semnai Theai. Cases of unintentional homicide and planning a death, as well as the murders of slaves, metics, and foreigners, were tried at the Palladion, a sanctuary of Pallas Athena. Cases of justifiable homicide were tried at the Delphinion, a sanctuary of Apollo Delphinios.[69] The location of the Palladion is unknown, but the Delphinion complex has been tentatively identified as a temple and another Archaic building south of the Olympeion.[70] Scholars generally agree that a case would be assigned to either the Areopagos or the Palladion based on whether the plaintiff charged intentional or unintentional homicide, and that it would go to the Delphinion only if the defendant pled justifiable homicide.[71] At the Areopagos and almost certainly in the other courts too, litigants and their witnesses swore special oaths while standing upon cut pieces of a boar, a ram, and a bull. Each litigant was also allowed to make a second speech responding to his opponent's arguments, although the defendant could go into voluntary exile before giving his second speech. In all three courts, the plaintiffs would have been close relatives of the victims.[72]

We also hear of two other homicide courts: the court called *en Phreattoi*, where cases were tried of intentional homicide committed by someone already in exile because of an earlier unintentional homicide, with the defendant making his speeches from a boat anchored offshore, and the Prytaneion, which judged cases of homicide committed by an inanimate object, an animal, or an unknown person. Since it is not clear that the hearings held by the Prytaneion were really trials or that the court *en Phreattoi* was convened except on very rare occasions, I do not address them here.[73]

The jurors at the Areopagos were the Areopagites, who, after the reforms of Ephialtes in the mid-fifth century, were all living former archons. Estimates of their numbers and average age vary, but there were probably at least 145 total Areopagites at any given time, and most of these would have been in their late forties or older. Attendance does not appear to have been mandatory or monetarily compensated, so the number of Areopagites at any given trial may have been well below the total membership of the body.[74] Their being former archons may have given them greater legal expertise and made them more competent than a regular jury.[75] According to Drakon's legislation, a group of 51 men known as *ephetai* judged homicide trials at the Palladion and the Delphinion. We do not know whether this special group continued to exist in the fifth and fourth centuries or if the Athenians appointed jurors to these courts in the regular manner for nonhomicide trials.[76]

The small number of Areopagites would have made the Areopagos a more intimate performance setting than a regular Athenian trial, even if murder cases could have attracted a greater number of curious spectators. Trials at the Palladion and Delphinion would have been even more intimate if they really were judged by 51 *ephetai*. Even aside from the number of jurors, homicide trials must have posed unique performance challenges to both litigants, thanks to the family tie between the plaintiff and the victim, the solemn oaths, the second speeches, and the ritual atmosphere.[77]

Although we have a wealth of specific details about the jurors, procedures, and locations of the Athenian courts, we have no decisive evidence about how they would have affected the litigants. This reflects a central challenge of any discussion of performance in antiquity. Anyone analyzing performance conditions today, either in theaters or in courts, would attend a performance and observe the way that space and audience affect it. They would consider the role of acoustics, lighting, and sight lines, as well as the voices, outfits, and movements of the performers themselves. To study a play from only the book or a trial from only a transcript might yield interesting results, but no one would confuse it with the study of the performance itself. For ancient forensic performances, however, this is the only option. Except for homicide trials, it is impossible even to match individual speeches with specific locations. So, I ask the reader to keep this general picture of the performance conditions of Athenian trials in his or her mind throughout the rest of this book. Although specific details would have varied among locations and dates, most litigants would have performed their speeches in a context like the ones I have described here.

Litigants and speechwriters would probably have prepared and rehearsed their speeches without knowing which location the trial would be assigned to or exactly what jurors would judge it, except in cases of homicide.[78] As a result, there would have been no way for them to make reference to specific visual details they could not safely predict ahead of time. This would explain why forensic speeches very rarely mention any visible features of the courts beyond general references to the speaker's platform and the water-clock. Since we are studying speeches designed, in all likelihood, to succeed across a range of possible locations and audiences, we should not despair excessively about our ignorance of where individual trials happened and who their jurors were.

While some significant details of the original performances are beyond recovery, the texts that survive represent the best attempts of litigants and speechwriters to prepare performances that would persuade a typical audience of Athenian jurors in a typical Athenian court. When we analyze these texts as performances with only a general knowledge of their performance contexts, therefore, we are in a position similar to their authors when they composed them. Even if we have no access to the actual moment of performance, we can examine how litigants and speechwriters planned their performances and what features they expected would persuade the jurors. Furthermore, even if some speeches underwent significant posttrial revision before being circulated as written texts, the core of even these speeches must reflect the versions that were prepared and rehearsed before the trial itself.

PERFORMANCE IN MODERN COURTROOMS

Law and legal procedure are a persistent theme in modern American plays, movies, and television shows. Dramas such as *Inherit the Wind*, *To Kill a Mockingbird*, *Perry Mason*, and *Law and Order* exploit the tension, suspense, and ultimate resolution of fictional trials, exploring the nature of justice and, just as importantly, entertaining their audiences. The line between law and popular entertainment is not always clear. Millions of Americans followed the trials of O. J. Simpson and Casey Anthony as though they were soap operas, and arbitration hearings on *The People's Court* and *Judge Judy* compete directly with afternoon talk shows every day of the week. Classical Athenian theatergoers shared our interest in trials. In the *Eumenides*, Aeschylus presented a meditation on justice and civilization through Orestes' trial on the Areopagos, and, at the other extreme, the parodic trial of the dog Labes in Aristophanes' *Wasps* poked fun at Athenian juries and legal procedure. Furthermore, some of "the people standing around" and watching Athenian trials may have been attracted by a similar kind of voyeuristic pleasure to what viewers of televised trials experience today.

The parallel between trials and dramas has led modern scholars to develop theories of "law as performance."[79] Many of these theories use performance as a metaphor for understanding the nature of law itself. For instance, Jack M. Balkin and Sanford Levinson argue that law is properly understood as an ongoing process of enforcement and interpretation—a performance—rather than as a series of unchanging statutes. Judges who interpret written laws in broad or narrow ways are like musicians who add to or excise from original written scores.[80] Similarly, Sara Ramshaw contends that judges in common law traditions resemble actors or jazz musicians who "jam," or collectively improvise in accordance with a basic structure they all agree to follow. Like jamming, which requires a single performer to cooperate with the other participants and to respond to the reactions of the audience, judicial decisions can be thought of as spontaneous improvisations that apply the predetermined structure of legal precedents to unique cases in light of the needs and expectations of a particular community.[81]

Arguments such as these, which posit that law exists in action rather than in texts, can help illuminate the nature of law and justice in the Athenian courts, where litigants regularly employed a range of arguments based on their particular characters and circumstances as well as on written laws.[82] This study, however, is not concerned with the nature of law but with the nature of persuasion during legal proceedings. Hence, it is more closely related to approaches to "law as performance" that consider strategies used by modern lawyers during courtroom arguments. Three foundational insights of these approaches inform the entire project.

First, forensic performances create *representations of reality*. Juries need to make decisions based on events they did not witness. Lacking first-hand knowledge, they depend on witnesses and advocates to present a coherent set of relevant facts that will enable them to render a just judgment. Even with procedural safeguards governing the types of evidence that are admissible, and even with complete good faith on the part of both parties to the lawsuit, there will always be a gap between the reality of what happened and how it is represented to the court.[83] Litigants, or their advocates, can take advantage of this gap by presenting cases that are like reality in ways that are favorable to themselves. This verisimilitude need not correspond to actual reality, as Tzvetan Todorov has shown. In a modern courtroom, verisimilitude in Todorov's sense refers to what the judge and jurors believe is like reality, to what the standards of legal discourse accept as like reality, or to what the litigant convinces the judge and jurors is actual reality and not mere adherence to the standards of legal discourse.[84]

A modern example nicely illustrates the concept of verisimilitude. Judges sometimes allow lawyers to present computer animations to jurors that purport to show how a contested event happened.[85] Such animations are by definition not reality, but, if they correspond to the jurors' conception of how the event could have happened, they are like reality. If they are allowed into court in the first place, they are recognized as adhering to the standards that legal discourse admits to be like reality. Finally, if the lawyer draws the jurors' attention to their very artificiality but insists that they still convey the truth, they are like reality. Computer animations, then, are persuasive only to the extent that the jurors accept them as an adequate representation of what really happened. Within the limits of their own time and place, Athenian litigants and speechwriters also represented reality with techniques that corresponded to what the jurors could accept as like reality. As with modern juries and computer animations, we should not ask ourselves whether the jurors were confused between representation and reality but to what extent litigants could exploit the recognized differences between representation and reality in their own favor.

Second, forensic performances are part of a *culturally determined system of legal discourse*. Communication in any formal legal setting depends upon three fundamental elements: acceptance of a set of procedural and legal norms; knowledge of the technical terminology necessary to discuss those norms; and familiarity with the nontechnical but customary language, actions, and ways of thinking that tend to accompany the technical terminology. In this context, "procedural and legal norms" is an umbrella term referring not only to codified laws and procedures but also to shared concepts that provide a framework for talking about law and justice. For the Athenians, these include religious belief, democratic ideology, and family duty, as well as a commitment to the power of the people to adjudicate disputes through jury trials. On a more mundane level, they also include the distinctions among Athenian procedures, many of which we can no longer appreciate. Technical terminology fits into this cultural framework, and, as a result, most Athenian legal terms have no exact equivalent in English. The most famous example is the charge of *hubris*, which modern scholars still struggle to define. Even seemingly pedestrian terms associated with inheritance like *diathēkē* and *klēros* can only be approximated in English by "will" and "estate." These partial overlaps in meaning can make Athenian legal discourse seem simultaneously familiar and exotic to modern readers.

My study is most concerned with the third element of communication in legal settings, nontechnical but customary features of legal discourse. Among the most important of these nontechnical but customary features is the nontechnical or semitechnical vocabulary that authors or speakers use to talk about the law or to make an argument more persuasive. As Bernard J. Hibbitts has shown in a study of American legal discourse, language can reflect cultural values shared, perhaps unconsciously, by authors or speakers and their audiences. In a 1994 article, he argues that an increase in legal metaphors based on hearing and speaking and a corresponding decrease in metaphors based on seeing reflect the increased participation in the American legal system of groups who tend to favor oral communication over visual communication, such as women and certain minorities.[86] The details of Hibbitts' sociological model that certain groups favor certain types of communication may be open to debate. However, his insight into the cultural resonance of metaphors in legal discourse illustrates a productive way of thinking about performance and persuasion in legal contexts. Words that reflect an audience's preconceptions or cultural biases can influence the way that they respond to arguments.

Anthony G. Amsterdam and Randy Hertz provide an example of how this can work in practice. In an analysis of the closing arguments of a 1991 homicide trial in New York City, they show that the defense attorney uses metaphors of speaking and looking to present "the jury's thinking processes as physical and active." First, by referring to the jurors' thoughts as though they are speech ("I can hear you all saying . . ."), the defense attorney encourages them to consider the trial as a dialogue between them and the lawyers and not to accept the prosecution's case as authoritative. Second, by telling them to "look" when he wants them to listen attentively to his words, the defense attorney encourages the jurors to focus on their responsibility to judge the person they are actually looking at in the court: he also directs them to "look" at him during his speech. The prosecutor avoids visual language of this sort, instead emphasizing the jurors as disinterested judges rather than active participants.[87]

The modern lawyer who chooses to integrate metaphors like these into his or her rhetorical strategy must be intimately familiar with the cultural preconceptions the jurors are likely to share. Athenian litigants and speechwriters would have faced a similar challenge when deciding the kind of language to use in their arguments. Vocabulary choice is always at the heart of the relationship between the performer and the audience. When we study the language of Athenian forensic speeches, we must consider both the underlying patterns of thought that repeated words or phrases represent and the specific reasons that speakers deploy them in their arguments. Just as "look" has a special resonance in the defense speech studied by Amsterdam and Hertz, words that refer to seeing and sight can play a central role in the rhetorical strategy of Athenian forensic speeches, even if their visual connotation is not always in the forefront of jurors' minds.

Third, forensic performances rely primarily upon words, and *every word is important*. The "law and literature" movement of the past thirty years has accustomed scholars to analyzing modern legal texts with techniques of literary criticism. One of the most productive approaches relies on a meticulous analysis of individual words and their function within sentences. For instance, Anthony G. Amsterdam and Jerome R. Bruner's study of nouns and verbs in decisions of the U.S. Supreme Court shows that lexical choice often plays a central role in argument. In Justice Story's decision in *Prigg v. Pennsylvania* (1842), which held that individual states could not pass laws interfering with slave owners' constitutional right to recover runaway slaves, nouns referring to government entities are the subjects of verbs more often than nouns referring to people. Nouns referring to people of African descent especially tend to be the objects of verbs or to appear in subordinate constructions. Story's vocabulary and grammar, then, present a world in which government is the prime actor, and people of African descent are particularly powerless. This reflects his reasoning, which presented the issue primarily as a conflict between states to be decided by the federal government rather than as a matter affecting individuals. There is a similar emphasis on

INTRODUCTION

government entities as actors in Justice Kennedy's decision in *Freeman v. Pitts* (1992), which held that federal supervision of segregated school districts is unnecessary if the segregation does not result from state policy but from demographic patterns. In Justice Warren's decision in *Brown v. Board of Education* (1954), in contrast, nouns referring to government entities are still the most frequent actors, but both whites and blacks are the subjects of verbs more frequently than in either *Prigg* or *Pitts*.[88]

This type of analysis reveals that word choice and grammatical construction can be integral to the construction of legal arguments. To paraphrase Amsterdam and Bruner, language creates a world.[89] Although Athenian forensic speeches differ from U.S. Supreme Court decisions in many ways, they can also use language to create a world that reinforces their core arguments. In approaching them, we should never dismiss attention to small details as pedantry. As Amsterdam and Bruner show, even the seemingly minor distinction between active and passive voice can contribute to the effectiveness of an argument. In a language as nuanced as Greek, we can anticipate that particles, verbal aspect, and word order can play similarly significant roles in persuading an audience.

AN OVERVIEW OF THE BOOK

These three insights have shaped my thinking about forensic persuasion in Classical Athens, and they provide a foundation for many of the interpretations I present in this book. My argument explores the ways that litigants and speechwriters in a wide variety of cases try to harness the power of the jurors' sight and use it against their opponents. It proceeds through three parts. The first part, "Physical Sight," considers how litigants' performances combine what the jurors can see with what they can hear. The second part, "The Language of Demonstration and Visibility," examines how litigants use words associated with sight to create a conceptual world where the jurors are encouraged to compare themselves to witnesses who have authoritative knowledge of the cases they have to judge. The third part, "Imaginary Sight," shows how litigants encourage jurors to imagine they are present at events they could never have seen. Jurors who respond to litigants' directives develop mental pictures that encourage them to accept the litigants' claims.

At the end of this book, an appendix includes short descriptions of every speech I discuss. Readers may wish to refer to this appendix to supplement the details provided in the chapters.

PART ONE

PHYSICAL SIGHT

ONE

VISUAL RHETORIC AND VISUAL EVIDENCE

Athenian litigants could exploit jurors' prejudices by directing their eyes towards visual features seemingly favorable to themselves and unfavorable to their opponents. Appearance played a central role in many trials and triallike hearings, especially the examinations of personal character known as *dokimasiai*. Either through direct references or subtle verbal cues, litigants could use what the jurors saw to reinforce their verbal arguments.

INTRODUCTION: THE RHETORIC OF APPEARANCE IN THE SWEET TRIAL

In Arthur Garfield Hays' opening statement in the murder trial of Ossian H. Sweet and his ten companions, Hays called the jurors' attention to the appearance of his clients. He said:

> Doctor Ossian H. Sweet—Doctor, stand up so the jury can look you over—was born in Orlando, Florida, in October, 1895. His father was a minister and farmer. His grandfather was a slave. There were six children, of whom three are before you now. Defendant Doctor Otis Sweet, a dentist highly respected among his people in the City of Detroit, and Henry Sweet, who is now a college student. Henry and Otis, stand up. The other member of the Sweet family before you today is Mrs. Sweet, whose name was Mitchell before her marriage. Mrs. Sweet, stand up.
> These are four of the defendants and the first fact in our case of which we shall expect you gentlemen to take notice is that they do not look like murderers.

It was 1925, and Dr. Sweet, his wife, his brothers, and seven of their friends were charged with murdering a white man during a mob attack on the Sweets' house in one of Detroit's white neighborhoods. Their defense lawyers, led by Hays and Clarence Darrow, tried to portray the Sweets and their friends as dignified, reasonable people who acted out of a rational fear for their lives. Throughout the trial, they encouraged the jurors to draw conclusions based on what they could see in the court and on the arguments they heard. In this excerpt from Hays' opening statement, he even calls the conclusion that the Sweets "do not look like murderers" a fact. Well-dressed and poised, they appeared to be a successful, refined American family, an appearance consistent with Hays' account of the physician's rise from poverty, his happy marriage, and his medical studies in Vienna and Paris.[1]

Since jurors conditioned to associate blackness with guilt could have condemned the Sweets even if the evidence favored them, it was crucial for Hays to influence the way the jurors responded to the Sweets' appearance. He tried to guide them to see a group of well-dressed, attractive people exhibiting the visual characteristics fitting for a successful physician, his family, and his social circle. For the jurors to accept the "fact" that the Sweets did not look like murderers, they had to make inferences based on the visual characteristics emphasized by Hays. If they instead made inferences based simply on the Sweets' skin color, any juror whose prejudice dominated his judgment would instead conclude that they did look like murderers. Indeed, eavesdroppers on the jurors' deliberations heard one juror say, "Two of you had these fellows convicted before you came here."[2] In the end, the Sweets' jury deadlocked, and the judge declared a mistrial. Only Ossian Sweet's brother Henry was tried a second time; he was acquitted, and the charges against the other ten original defendants were dismissed.

Hays' visual strategy, like the Sweet trial itself, was a product of the segregated United States, but its rhetorical roots lie in Classical Athens. Employing tactics similar to Hays', Athenian litigants could take advantage of visual characteristics favorable to themselves and unfavorable to their opponents, emphasizing that what the jurors could see seemed to confirm the arguments they heard. This is a significant aspect of Athenian forensic oratory. Even some arguments that seem incomplete or vague when we read them today would have been perfectly clear to the jurors, since their sight would have provided a context that the text alone does not preserve.

Although we cannot know exactly what Athenian jurors would have seen while they sat in court, we can follow cues in the texts to determine when litigants are appealing to what the jurors could see. Verbs such as *horaō* ("see") and *theaomai* ("watch" or "look") and nouns such as *ophthalmoi* ("eyes") and *opsis* ("appearance") often signal that litigants are directing the jurors to look at someone or something. These words tend to be used closely with forms of the demonstrative pronoun *houtos*, which, like "this" or "that" in English, points the jurors' eyes in a specific direction. Employing a term derived from *deiknumi*, the Greek word for pointing, I call this pronoun "deictic."[3] Through some or all of these verbal indicators, the speeches I examine in this chapter signal unambiguously the places where the litigants integrate into their verbal arguments what the jurors can see. I show how Athenian litigants both exploit their jurors' biases and try to use appearance as a form of proof. My discussion of visual display develops some of Edith Hall's insights. In "Lawcourt Dramas: Acting and Performance in Legal Oratory," a chapter in *The Theatrical Cast of Athens*, Hall focuses on the theatrical aspects of appearance in the courts. I instead emphasize the rhetorical aspects of appearance, especially when it works together with verbal argument. Our approaches are complementary, since rhetorical techniques that developed in response to the specific challenges and opportunities of courtroom persuasion can still resemble the practices of the theater. Hall calls this resemblance "isomorphism," a term that recognizes parallels without implying equivalency.[4]

VISUAL BIAS AND FORENSIC TACTICS

The racial issues of the Sweet trial would never have had an exact parallel in Classical Athens. Although people with non-Greek appearances could have appeared in the courts as resident aliens (*metoikoi* or "metics"), foreigners (*xenoi*), or, perhaps in rare cases, actual citizens,[5] there is no evidence that they would have suffered a disadvantage primarily because of the way they looked. Indeed, we learn in *On the Estate of Dikaiogenes* (Isaeus 5) that a panel of Athenian jurors in an earlier trial involving the same estate believed the testimony of an Egyptian named Melas, literally "Black," and determined that the younger Dikaiogenes had a stronger claim to the elder Dikaiogenes' estate than the speaker's mother and aunts did. Even though the speaker now accuses Melas and his friends of lying, the original jurors clearly concluded that a dark-skinned non-Athenian was more trustworthy than the witnesses for the speaker's father Polyaratos, who seems to have led the defense in that trial.[6] As a class, Egyptians may have had a bad reputation among some Athenians; this at least is the easiest explanation of Hyperides' description of Athenogenes as a "man who writes speeches and plies a trade in the agora and, worst of all, is an Egyptian."[7] Nonetheless, as the example of Melas shows, this reputation, even if widespread, did not lead jurors to disregard their testimony or presume their guilt in the way that many American jurors did in trials involving African Americans during much of the twentieth century.

That non-Greek visual characteristics did not cause an inherent disadvantage in the courts of Classical Athens should not surprise us. The extent to which the Athenians may have exhibited racism, in its modern sense, is a question beyond the scope of this chapter, but there is no evidence that any group suffered social, political, or legal mistreatment solely because of skin color or other visual characteristics.[8] Moreover, even if systemic prejudice based on appearance did exist in Classical Athens, it would have affected the outcome of relatively few trials. When both litigants were Athenian citizens, as they must have been in the majority of cases, they would usually have shared the same general appearance with the jurors and with each other, and so neither litigant would have faced an institutionalized disadvantage because a conspicuous visual trait marked him as other. Even many metics and slaves of Greek heritage must have looked virtually indistinguishable from Athenian citizens. The Old Oligarch claims there was no way to tell who was an Athenian citizen and who was a slave from a visual examination alone.[9] He exaggerates to make an antidemocratic point, but his polemical statement finds some confirmation in the many scenes on Athenian vases where it is impossible to determine whether someone is a slave or free person.[10] Furthermore, while litigants do not hesitate to attack their opponents for not being full-blooded Athenians, they base the attacks on questionable parentage rather than heritable visible characteristics.[11] Appearance alone, therefore, seems to have been a relatively unimportant factor in distinguishing between Athenian citizens and non-Athenian citizens in Athens.

Nonetheless, the Athenians had well-developed visual prejudices directed even against their fellow citizens. Dress, hairstyle, weight, or age could have biased some jurors against one litigant or in favor of another. Socrates' making fun of the short, bald coppersmith who acquired some money, got out of jail, bathed, and put on new clothes as though about to get married suggests an elite prejudice against the short, bald, and overdressed but also a sense among the laboring class that certain occasions required a special appearance.¹² At the other end of the class spectrum, Theophrastus caricatures the oligarch strutting around in a carefully draped cloak with hair of moderate length and precisely trimmed fingernails who is embarrassed to sit next to a thin man at the assembly who could not afford to anoint himself with oil.¹³

Biases such as these, even if Plato and Theophrastus exaggerate them for comic effect, could provide ammunition against an opponent. Hyperides, for example, attacked Philippides' weight, saying, "When it comes to his body, he's worthless on account of his thinness."¹⁴ Litigants also had to be prepared to defend themselves from attacks on their own visual characteristics, especially if they seemed to confirm a negative feature of their reputation and might have predisposed some of their jurors to vote against them. For example, Nikoboulos in *Against Pantainetos* (Demosthenes 37) asks the jurors to disregard his style of walking, along with his voice and his reputation as a moneylender.¹⁵ Many other litigants probably faced similar dilemmas and made no mention of them, and even litigants whose appearances were favorable may have chosen not to bring them up. Since looks often speak for themselves, it may often have been unnecessary, and perhaps even counterproductive, to overemphasize something all the jurors could see and interpret on their own.

Two Lysianic speeches illustrate how litigants sometimes tried to prevent appearances from influencing their jurors. First, in *For Mantitheos* (Lysias 16), Mantitheos tells the council members who are judging him, "It isn't appropriate to like or hate anybody on the basis of his appearance [*ap(o) opseōs*], but you should examine him on the basis of his actions."¹⁶ Since Mantitheos was visible in front of his judges, he had no need to explain what his appearance was or why it might have offended them.¹⁷ Such a vague reference allowed Mantitheos to respond to his detractors without planting specific ideas in the minds of men who were not already predisposed to judge him based on his looks. Second, the speaker of *Against Theomnestos* (Lysias 10) guards against the possibility that the impressive appearances of Theomnestos and his father would bias the jurors in their favor by saying, "They are more worthy of your anger in as much as they are pretty big and youthful as far as their appearances [*opseis*] are concerned. For it's clear that they're powerful in their bodies but depraved in their souls."¹⁸ Like Mantitheos, he uses a general reference to appearance and bodily strength that would have been immediately clear to a viewing audience. In this way, he tries to sway the jurors who were likely to be favorably influenced by the way Theomnestos and his father looked, while at the same time he avoids giving specific verbal details that might have drawn the other jurors' attention to something they may not have paid much attention to in the first place. The author of the *Rhetoric for Alexander* recognizes the importance of preemptive tactics such as this one, writing, "Whatever things you think the judges are going to call into question, anticipate their reaction and call them into question yourself."[19] Although the *Rhetoric for Alexander* emphasizes prejudices associated with reputation rather than appearance, the author's advice is relevant to prejudice in general, especially since appearance can prompt one of the prejudices that he says "arise from the present time against the person himself."[20]

In the *Rhetoric*, Aristotle recognizes that appearance has the potential to affect jurors' judgment. First, discussing in book 1 ways that criminals can escape suspicion, he notes that weak men will not seem guilty of assault and that poor and ugly men will not seem guilty of adultery. Aristotle's emphasis on ugliness indicates that he is thinking of looks and not just reputation, even though he does not explicitly mention appearance here.[21] Unlike the author of the *Rhetoric for Alexander*, who explains how litigants can counter prejudicial assumptions such as these,[22] Aristotle is proposing a reason why certain types of criminals are unlikely to be suspected, namely, because they expect assumptions based at least partly on visual prejudices to work in their favor. We can extend his logic to a general rule that everyone whose appearance can generate prejudices favorable to themselves ought to take advantage of them.

Second, in book 2, Aristotle notes that clothing can be a means of persuasion, since the clothes of those who have suffered can induce pity. His argument is complex. Aristotle maintains that pity is related to proximity, and so we are more likely to pity sufferings that are close to us, either in time or in space. He speaks of proximity in a specifically visual way: through various techniques, people "make the evil appear [*phainesthai*] near, placing it before the eyes [*pro ommatōn*] as either about to happen or having happened."[23] Aristotle uses the expression "before the eyes" to refer to things an audience can really see and to things that they picture in their minds. It has some aspects of the imaginary sense here, since Aristotle associates it with evils that have not happened yet.[24] Nonetheless, the discussion of clothing as one of the signs that leads to increased pity makes it clear that he is also thinking of an audience who actually see and react to a speaker's appearance: "The clothing of those who have suffered and as many things there are of a similar sort, the actions and words and as many other things as there are characteristic of those who are in the midst of suffering" make pity greater because "it appears [*phainesthai*] near, as when someone is unworthy and the suffering appears before the eyes [*en ophthalmois*]."[25] Aristotle's argument earlier in this section that gestures can also contribute to pity further establishes that he is thinking of an audience responding to the visual elements of a performance.[26]

Third, in book 3, Aristotle maintains that appearance can set a precedent. If one fastidious (*kathareios*) man was shown to be an adulterer, then another fastidious man must be an adulterer too.[27] Aristotle considers fastidiousness to be at least in part a visual quality, since in his earlier discussion of qualities that induce a friendly feeling, Aristotle mentions "those who are fastidious [*kathareious*] in their appearance [*opsin*], their dress, their whole life."[28]

Finally, also in book 3, Aristotle writes that speaking style must be appropriate to the speaker's *genos* and *hexis*. By *genos*, Aristotle means characteristics such as age or gender or nationality. By *hexis*, he means "the things according to which someone is the kind of person he or she is in his or her manner of living." George Kennedy defines *hexis* as "moral state."[29] Based on a survey of its use across the works of Aristotle, Nancy Worman defines it more precisely as "the dispositions that are formed over time by habitual action and that constitute different character types."[30] *Hexis* has had a fruitful reception in critical theory of the twentieth- and twenty-first centuries, especially as the term that Pierre Bourdieu uses for "political mythology realized, *em-bodied*, turned into a permanent disposition, a durable manner of standing, speaking, and thereby of *feeling* and *thinking*."[31] For our purposes, it will be sufficient to note that both *genos*, in the sense of age or gender, and *hexis*, in the sense of a disposition formed by habitual activity, have visual qualities. Since they also have nonvisual qualities, we should not overstate the importance of appearance to either *genos* or *hexis*. Once we acknowledge this caveat, however, we can reasonably conclude that Aristotle believes that appearance is one of several qualities that should be consistent with speaking style to be persuasive. When he says that a rustic person who hoped to persuade an audience would need to speak in the way they expected a rustic person to speak,[32] one of the reasons behind the audience's expectation would have been that the speaker looked like a country bumpkin and not like a student fresh from Isocrates' school.

From Aristotle's discussions of appearance, litigants can learn to manipulate jurors by appealing to their visual biases. Appearance in these cases is not proof; it merely implies innocence or guilt because of the cultural lens through which the jurors interpret it. Whether a man is guilty of adultery has nothing to do with how handsome he is, but jurors accustomed to think that ugly men would never attract women and that mutual attraction is necessary for adultery could be encouraged to jump to a conclusion and acquit an ugly defendant. The same is true in visual arguments based on precedent. Only cultural assumptions could lead jurors to draw the logically unsound conclusion that someone careful about his appearance and personal hygiene is an adulterer because similarly fastidious men have in the past been adulterers. Only jurors accustomed to associate speaking style with appearance would trust a farmer who looked like a farmer and spoke like a farmer more than a farmer who looked like a farmer but spoke like a sophist.

In the Sweet case, Hays took advantage of his jurors' cultural assumptions in a way that would have been familiar to Aristotle when he implicitly invoked the jurors' own sense of precedent by stressing that people who look like the Sweets do not look like murderers. Furthermore, Darrow seems to have emphasized that the *genos* and *hexis* of the Sweets' witnesses coincided with their speaking style, maintaining that they were "attractive," "good looking," and "intelligent."[33] The two defense lawyers, therefore, emphasized the visual characteristics of the Sweets and their supporters that were most likely to match the white jurors' illogical but culturally informed notions of what is nonthreatening and trustworthy.

Although this type of visual strategy does not take the form of an Aristotelian enthymeme, it employs the same general strategy as the first type of apparent enthymeme that Aristotle discusses, likening apparent enthymemes to false syllogisms. These state that "if so-and-so is not, then such-and-such must be," even if there is no connection between so-and-so and such-and-such. Referring to Isocrates' *Evagoras* (Isocrates 9), Aristotle explains that although Evagoras "saved some, avenged others and gave the Greeks freedom," these accomplishments do not lead logically to the conclusion they imply. He does not state what that conclusion is, but Isocrates uses them as proof of Evagoras' bravery, good sense, and virtue. Aristotle maintains that the compact and antithetical arrangement of the argument makes it seem that there is a logical connection between the premise, that Evagoras led military campaigns benefiting the Greeks, and the conclusion, that Evagoras has a good character, even though there is not.[34] Similarly, there is no real logical correlation between the way the Sweets look and whether they are murderers, but Hays presents their appearance as though it is evidence. Instead of a compact prose style that encourages the jurors to jump to unjustified conclusions, Hays relies on cultural assumptions that imply a connection between looks and innocence. In a similar way, Athenian forensic speeches can also appeal to the jurors' visual biases and urge them to draw conclusions favorable to the speakers, even if there is no logical connection between the appearance and the conclusion.

For Polystratos

As Hays insists that the Sweets are not murderers because they do not look like murderers, the speakers of *For Polystratos* (Lysias 20) insist that Polystratos, an admitted member of the oligarchic government known as the Four Hundred, is not an oligarch because he does not look like an oligarch. *For Polystratos* dates from soon after the restoration of the democracy in 410.[35] Although it is transmitted as a single speech in the manuscripts, it is actually two speeches spliced together without comment.[36] Someone who refers to Polystratos' sons in the third person speaks the first speech, paragraphs 1–10, and one of Polystratos' sons speaks the second speech, paragraphs 11–36.[37]

Athenian litigants were permitted to entrust some or all of their speaking time to supporters who were not directly involved in the lawsuit. A supporting speaker was called by the technical term *sunēgoros* (plural *sunēgoroi*), literally "someone speaking alongside." The practice was not uncommon in the Athenian courts, and Lykophron in Hyperides' *In Defense of Lykophron* (Hyperides 1) even maintains that allowing good speakers to speak for less talented speakers is an admirable democratic custom.[38] Using *sunēgoroi* was not without risks, however. Opponents could insinuate that the practice was irregular and perhaps corrupt,[39] and it also imposed a distance between the litigant and the jurors that would not have been there if he had spoken for himself. The speakers of *For Polystratos*, therefore, need to create a sympathetic character for a defendant who is present but not speaking and to build a connection between him and his jurors. One way they try to accomplish this is by asking the jurors to look at Polystratos and by integrating what the jurors see into their rhetorical strategy.

Near the beginning of the first speech, the speaker draws the jurors' eyes to Polystratos and urges them to accept that, based on his appearance, he could not have been a fervent oligarch. He says:

οὗτος δὲ τίνος ἂν ἕνεκα ὀλιγαρχίας ἐπεθύμησε; πότερον ὡς ἡλικίαν εἶχε λέγων τι διαπράττεσθαι παρ' ὑμῖν, ἢ τῷ σώματι πιστεύων, ἵνα ὑβρίζοι εἰς τῶν ὑμετέρων τινά; ἀλλ' ὁρᾶτε αὐτοῦ τὴν ἡλικίαν, ᾗ καὶ τοὺς ἄλλους ἱκανός ἐστιν ἀποτρέπειν τούτων. (Lys. 20.3)

This man here [*houtos*], why would he have desired an oligarchy? Was it because he was the right age to accomplish something among you by speaking? Or was it because he had enough confidence in his body to treat anyone of your people with *hubris*? But you are seeing [*horate*] how old he is: at his age, he has his hands full dissuading others from doing these kinds of things.

At the beginning of the first sentence I have quoted, the speaker points out Polystratos with the deictic pronoun *houtos*, "this man here." This is the second consecutive sentence to begin with *houtos*, and these two sentences immediately follow a sentence that ends by pointing out Polystratos with *houtosi*, a stronger form of *houtos* whose final *iota* is generally thought to be the verbal equivalent of a pointing finger.[40] Through these deictic pronouns, the speaker directs the jury's visual attention towards the defendant. Then, with "you are seeing," he narrows their focus to one aspect of what they see, Polystratos' age. *Horate*, which I have translated as "you are seeing," could also be translated as a direct command, since Greek does not distinguish between the indicative and imperative in second-person plural present verb forms. According to the speaker, Polystratos' age provides visual confirmation that he was unable to lead by his speaking and that he was too weak to mistreat the *dēmos*. Adding implicit credence to these two conclusions is that someone else is speaking for Polystratos.

By making this argument at the beginning of his speech, the speaker ensures that the advanced age of Polystratos is both lodged in the jury's mind and physically before the jury's eyes during the remainder of his speech and the second speech. The arguments of both speeches in Polystratos' defense, therefore, are supported by the initial visual argument. This is particularly true of the other six sentences that begin with *houtos* and detail Polystratos' goodwill towards the *dēmos*, implicitly associating his appearance and his behavior.[41]

There are reasons to doubt the connection between Polystratos' appearance and his supposed innocence. Would old age really have prevented Polystratos from having ambitions of power over the other Athenians? Moreover, since the family appears to be wealthy, might his involvement with the oligarchs have had nothing to do with power and everything to do with class? There is no real logical relationship between Polystratos' age and his loyalty to the *dēmos*, but the speaker suggests that there is a direct correlation. The argument relies on the conventional Greek belief that men grow more moderate as they age. According to Aristotle, old age is characterized by rational calculation rather than impetuous action. In *Rhetoric*, he even calls old men *sōphronikoi*, or "self-controlled,"[42] a term echoed in Antiphon's third tetralogy (Antiphon 4), where the prosecutor argues that the defendant is more likely to have struck the first blow than the dead man, who was older and therefore more self-controlled (*sōphronizei*).[43] Since Antiphon's tetralogies are model speeches, there are no references to the jury's sight. In a live performance, the speaker could have strengthened his argument by asking the jury to look at the defendant while calling their attention to his age, just like Polystratos' *sunēgoros* does.

The speaker of Lysias' *Against Simon* (Lysias 3) also calls attention to his age and urges his jurors to believe that Simon has prevented him from being like an especially self-controlled man (*sōphronestatos*) who is able to control his lust.[44] Even though he uses no explicitly visual vocabulary, the speaker's appearance may have subtly complemented the moderate personality he constructs for himself. Indeed, he seems to recognize that the jurors would be looking at him during this section of his speech, since he redirects their gazes to Simon in the next sentence by referring to him with the deictic pronoun *houtosi*. Since Simon has charged the speaker with assault, it would strengthen his defense if his visual appearance suggested a victim, not an instigator.[45]

Although there are no further direct requests that the jurors look at Polystratos in the two speeches that constitute *For Polystratos*, the rhetorical effectiveness of the second speech's conclusion depends on him being present and visible in the courtroom. Polystratos' son refers to other defendants, whom he has seen parading their weeping children before the jury in the hopes of inducing pity.[46] Then he notes that his family can display only themselves and their father:

> οἱ μὲν γὰρ ἄλλοι τοὺς παῖδας παραστησάμενοι ἐξαιτοῦνται ὑμᾶς, ἡμεῖς δὲ τὸν πατέρα τουτονὶ καὶ ἡμᾶς ἐξαιτούμεθα μὴ ἡμᾶς ἀντὶ μὲν ἐπιτίμων ἀτίμους ποιήσητε, ἀντὶ δὲ πολιτῶν ἀπόλιδας· ἀλλὰ ἐλεήσατε καὶ τὸν πατέρα γέροντα ὄντα καὶ ἡμᾶς.
> (Lys. 20.35)

Other people beseech you while they make their children stand up next to them; we make ourselves stand up, and our father, this man here [*toutoni*], and we beseech you not to make us unprivileged instead of privileged, noncitizens instead of citizens. Instead, pity our father, since he is an old man, and us.

If Polystratos' son is speaking literally, Polystratos and his adult sons must be standing on the *bēma* next to him, taking the place of the small children that other litigants display to their jurors. Even if he is speaking metaphorically, however, he is certainly drawing the jurors' eyes to Polystratos, since he points him out as "this man here" with the deictic pronoun *toutoni*. Just as in paragraph 3, the speaker again calls special attention to Polystratos' age. Here, he seeks the jurors' pity and does not repeat his argument that Polystratos is too old to be an oligarch. There is a kind of visual ring composition, however, in the way this final appeal to the jurors' sight matches the appeal at the beginning of the first speech.[47] As a result, the reference to Polystratos' age is not just an appeal to the jurors' pity but also implicitly a reminder of the connection between his age and his loyalty to the *dēmos*. The two speeches of *For Polystratos* are a single performance, marked by different prose styles but linked by a reliance on the rhetorical effect of Polystratos' visual age.

The speakers of *For Polystratos* were not alone in using this visual technique, and it may even have been an established feature of Athenian forensic strategy. For example, there is a less elaborate reference by a *sunēgoros* to a litigant's appearance in Demosthenes' *For Phormion* (Demosthenes 36). The speaker, who may be Demosthenes himself,[48] begins the speech by explaining why Phormion cannot speak for himself. The first words he says are:

τὴν μὲν ἀπειρίαν τοῦ λέγειν, καὶ ὡς ἀδυνάτως ἔχει Φορμίων, αὐτοὶ πάντες ὁρᾶτ', ὦ ἄνδρες Ἀθηναῖοι. (Dem. 36.1)

You are all seeing [*horat(e)*], gentlemen of Athens, Phormion's inexperience with speaking and how impaired he is.

With *horate*, the speaker directs the jurors' eyes to Phormion, using their sight to justify Phormion's silence and his own role as a *sunēgoros*. Although he does not link Phormion's appearance with his innocence, as the speaker of *For Polystratos* does, he subtly emphasizes Phormion's appearance throughout the speech, verbally pointing to him fifteen times with the deictic pronoun *houtosi* and once with *hodi*.[49] The way Phormion looked may have contributed to the contrast the speaker consistently draws between Phormion's care and honesty and his opponent Apollodoros' profligacy, malice, and greed. The person the jurors see—a weak and perhaps timid man with no experience in public speaking—would be the antithesis of the loud, brash, and melodramatic Apollodoros that the speaker describes.[50]

Near the end of the speech, the speaker even introduces witnesses to attest to each man's character.[51] In this section, he twice draws the jurors' eyes to Phormion with a form of *houtosi*. After the clerk reads the testimonies about Apollodoros' wickedness, the speaker asks rhetorically, "Is this man here [*houtosi*] like that?" After some further testimony about Phormion's character, he says, "And read as well in how many public ways this man here [*houtosi*] has been good to the *polis*."[52] Then, driving home that the jurors should be looking at Phormion and Apollodoros while they listen to evidence of their contrasting characters, he uses a form of *houtosi* for Apollodoros, declaring that Phormion "has never treated Apollodoros, the one here [*toutoni*], unjustly."[53] Furthermore, the final time the speaker refers to Phormion as *houtosi*, he pleads for the jurors to treat him justly despite the slanders, shouts, and shamelessness of Apollodoros.[54] By repeatedly drawing the jurors' eyes to Phormion, the speaker makes Phormion's appearance part of his argument. As in *For Polystratos*, appearance and words contribute to a unified forensic strategy.

Against Philon

In *For Polystratos*, the speakers draw the jurors' attention to one aspect of Polystratos' appearance, his advanced age, and use it to suggest his innocence by exploiting the jurors' assumptions about old men's moderate behavior. In *Against Philon* (Lysias 31),[55] the speaker employs a similar strategy in prosecution instead of in defense, maintaining that Philon's physical strength confirms the charges brought against him. The speech is from a meeting held to determine whether Philon was qualified to join the *boulē*, the council of five-hundred men selected each year to act as a kind of executive board for the Athenian assembly. The technical term for a meeting like this was *dokimasia*, or "scrutiny." It took the form of a trial before the outgoing members of the *boulē*, called *bouleutai*, with a prosecutor speaking against the candidate's qualifications and then the candidate defending himself.⁵⁶ Philon's *dokimasia* probably took place between 403 and 395.⁵⁷

The speaker of *Against Philon* argues that Philon is not qualified to join the *boulē* because he supported neither the democrats nor the oligarchs in the civil strife of 404/403 and therefore has forfeited his place in Athenian government. Since Philon showed no patriotism or interest in Athens but preferred to live as a metic in Oropos, the speaker can treat him as someone every member of the outgoing *boulē* can dislike, regardless of their political sympathies.⁵⁸ He emphasizes that Philon had no excuse for his behavior because of his physical vitality, which the *bouleutai* can see. By frequently repeating words and phrases that emphasize Philon's status as an able-bodied man, the speaker of *Against Philon* closely coordinates his verbal argument with Philon's appearance. *Dunatos* and other *dun-* words refer to ability. A prefixed alpha negates these terms, and so *adunatos* refers to a lack of ability, as do similar *dun-* words with an alpha prefix.

Employing this terminology, the speaker admits that the helpless and the poor were neutral by necessity in 404/403 and so deserve pardon. He stresses the relationship of physical ability to guilt, saying:

καθέστηκε δέ τι ἔθος δίκαιον πᾶσιν ἀνθρώποις τῶν αὐτῶν ἀδικημάτων μάλιστα ὀργίζεσθαι τοῖς μάλιστα δυναμένοις μὴ ἀδικεῖν, τοῖς δὲ πένησιν ἢ ἀδυνάτοις τῷ σώματι συγγνώμην ἔχειν διὰ τὸ ἡγεῖσθαι ἄκοντας αὐτοὺς ἁμαρτάνειν. (Lys. 31.11)

A just custom has been established among all men: if the crimes are the same, to be especially angry at those who are especially able to avoid committing them [*tois malista dunamenois mē adikein*], but to pardon those who are poor or lack bodily ability [*adunatois tōi sōmati*], since we assume they err unwillingly.

He then goes on to say in the next sentence that Philon was neither poor nor disabled, drawing the jurors' attention to his appearance:

οὗτος τοίνυν οὐδεμιᾶς συγγνώμης ἄξιός ἐστι τυχεῖν· οὔτε γὰρ τῷ σώματι ἀδύνατος ἦν ταλαιπωρεῖν, ὡς καὶ ὑμεῖς ὁρᾶτε, οὔτε τῇ οὐσίᾳ ἄπορος λῃτουργεῖν, ὡς ἐγὼ ἀποδείξω. (Lys. 31.12)

This man, therefore, hasn't earned any pardon: he didn't lack bodily ability [*tōi sōmati adunatos*] to endure hard work, as you are seeing [*horate*], nor was he too poor to undertake liturgies, as I am about to demonstrate.

There are two reasons for the *bouleutai* to conclude that Philon does not deserve pardon: the evidence of their eyes and the evidence of the speaker's presentation.[59] The two parallel "as" (*hōs*) clauses, which even have the same number of syllables, place these two reasons on the same logical level. The visual evidence of Philon's bodily strength may be even more important than the upcoming spoken argument about his wealth, however, since the repetition "lack bodily ability . . . lack bodily ability" (*adunatois tōi sōmati . . . tōi sōmati adunatos*) calls special attention to it. Moreover, this repetition of *dun-* words continues the theme of ability first introduced with "those who are especially able to avoid committing them" (*tois malista dunamenois mē adikein*) in paragraph 11.

The phrase "lacking bodily ability" (*tōi sōmati adunatos*) is a persistent motif in the speech's narrative, and every time the *bouleutai* hear it, it reminds them of what they see, namely, that Philon is not "lacking bodily ability." First, the speaker suggests that Philon may claim that bodily impairment prevented him from giving aid to the democrats in Peiraieus. He says:

> ὑπολείπεται τοίνυν αὐτῷ λέγειν ὡς τῷ μὲν σώματι δι' ἀσθένειάν τινα γενομένην ἀδύνατος κατέστη βοηθῆσαι εἰς τὸν Πειραιᾶ, ἀπὸ δὲ τῶν ὑπαρχόντων ἐπαγγειλάμενος αὐτὸς ἢ χρήματ' εἰσενεγκεῖν εἰς τὸ πλῆθος τὸ ὑμέτερον ἢ ὁπλίσαι τινὰς τῶν ἑαυτοῦ δημοτῶν, ὥσπερ καὶ ἄλλοι πολλοὶ τῶν πολιτῶν αὐτοὶ οὐ δυνάμενοι λῃτουργεῖν τοῖς σώμασιν. (Lys. 31.15)

> It remains for him, then, to say that he lacked the bodily ability [*tōi . . . sōmati . . . adunatos*] to bring help to Peiraieus because of the presence of some weakness, but that he promised either to bring money to you, the masses, or to arm some of his own demesmen, just as many other citizens did if they weren't able [*ou dunamenoi*] to perform a liturgy with their bodies [*tois sōmasin*].

The speaker calls a witness to prove that Philon did not spend any money arming his fellow demesmen, but the evidence of the *bouleutai*'s sight has already shown that he was among those who were eligible to give liturgies with their bodies rather than their incomes. Lysias' client uses Philon's appearance not to prove his guilt but to exaggerate the extent of his guilt. According to him, the *bouleutai* judging the *dokimasia* should feel particular anger at Philon because strong men ought to use their strength on behalf of the *polis*. The argument depends on assumptions about the greater responsibilities of strong men than of weak men, which the speaker laid out in paragraph 11 and which he expects the jurors to share. He frames Philon's appearance in terms of these assumptions, making it a sign of his bad character and unfitness to serve on the *boulē*.

Later in the speech, the speaker claims that Philon led a group of bandits who terrorized the elderly in the countryside around Oropos. These elderly were easy prey because of their physical weakness. He continues to repeat forms of *adunatos* to stress the difference between them and Philon. The speaker describes them as "favorable to the masses but unable [*adunatoi*] to help because of old age." Many of them cannot testify at the hearing, "for the same reason they were unable [*adunatoi*] to help the *polis* then." This *dokimasia* may be the second time Philon takes advantage of them, and the speaker warns the *bouleutai* that "my opponent must not doubly benefit from their inability [*adunamian*]."[60] The rhetorical effectiveness of this account, which lacks much support from its supposed victims, lies in the contrast between Philon's physical strength, which the *bouleutai* can see, and his victims' weakness, which they hear about. The repeated forms of *adunatos* and *adunamia* act as a constant verbal reminder of this contrast.

Near the end of *Against Philon* there is another reference to physical sight. The speaker refers to Philon's supporting speakers, whom he can see in the court: "I see [*horō*] some men who are now preparing to help him and to make requests of you, since they were unable to persuade me."[61] The reference to sight here lacks the rhetorical significance of the reference to Philon's vigorous appearance.[62] It sets up a temporal contrast between the willingness of Philon's friends to urge his approval as a *bouleutēs* now and their failure to urge him to fight for the *polis* in 404/403, rather than an explicitly visual argument.[63] Significantly, it also demonstrates the speaker's ability to integrate his surroundings into his performance. It thus gives further support to the conclusion that his rhetoric takes advantage of Philon's appearance. If the audience did not see a strong man in front of them, the argument that Philon chose to squander his strength on banditry instead of patriotism would lose most of its force.

Against Meidias

In *For Polystratos* and *Against Philon*, the speakers appeal to their jurors' biases by exploiting visual characteristics. Their tactics depend on what Polystratos and Philon look like, namely, an old man and a powerful man respectively. We now turn to *Against Meidias* (Demosthenes 21), a speech that employs the same basic strategy but introduces a new element to it. Instead of exploiting the appearance of one of the litigants, Demosthenes directs the jurors to look at an Athenian named Straton, whose silence seems to confirm his account of Meidias' treachery. The speech is from Demosthenes' prosecution of Meidias for punching him in the face at the Dionysia in 348, when Demosthenes was the financial sponsor, or *khorēgos*, of his tribe's men's dithyrambic chorus, a song-and-dance ensemble that performed in honor of Dionysus. Demosthenes may have settled with Meidias before the trial, since Aeschines claims that he "sold" the affront for thirty mnai.[64] Aeschines is almost certainly twisting the truth, but even if Demosthenes never actually performed *Against Meidias* before a jury, the speech still provides evidence for the kinds of tactics that he would have used in court.[65]

To support his argument that Meidias' violence poses a threat to the entire *polis*, Demosthenes summons Straton to the *bēma* and displays him to the jurors. Straton had acted as an arbitrator in an earlier quarrel between Demosthenes and Meidias. When Meidias failed to attend the arbitration, he lost the case by default and was fined 1,000 drachmas. Meidias then accused Straton of misconduct and succeeded in having him disenfranchised. As Demosthenes presents it, Meidias acted consistently with the *kakoētheia* ("bad character") he displays in all of his actions by trumping up the charge against Straton. Straton's punishment also points the jurors to how they should punish Meidias: if Meidias thinks that such an excessive penalty is fitting for an arbitrator's misconduct when only 1,000 drachmas were at stake, then by the same logic death is a barely adequate punishment for assaulting Demosthenes, a public official performing his duties.[66]

Having framed Straton's disenfranchisement as an indication of Meidias' insolence and as a benchmark for the jurors to follow when they give their sentence, Demosthenes calls Straton himself to the *bēma*. He uses the formulaic imperative *kalei* ("call"), as though he is calling a witness to confirm testimony that the clerk will read out.[67] But, because disenfranchised citizens cannot testify in court, Straton can appear only in silence. Demosthenes says:

κάλει δὴ καὶ τὸν Στράτωνα αὐτὸν τὸν τὰ τοιαῦτα πεπονθότα· ἑστάναι γὰρ ἐξέσται δήπουθεν αὐτῷ. οὗτος, ὦ ἄνδρες Ἀθηναῖοι, πένης μὲν ἴσως ἐστίν, οὐ πονηρὸς δέ γε. οὗτος μέντοι πολίτης ὤν, ἐστρατευμένος ἁπάσας τὰς ἐν ἡλικίᾳ στρατείας καὶ δεινὸν οὐδὲν εἰργασμένος, ἕστηκεν νυνὶ σιωπῇ, οὐ μόνον τῶν ἄλλων ἀγαθῶν τῶν κοινῶν ἀπεστερημένος, ἀλλὰ καὶ τοῦ φθέγξασθαι ἢ ὀδύρασθαι· καὶ οὐδ' εἰ δίκαι' ἢ ἄδικα πέπονθεν, οὐδὲ ταῦτ' ἔξεστιν αὐτῷ πρὸς ὑμᾶς εἰπεῖν. καὶ ταῦτα πέπονθεν ὑπὸ Μειδίου καὶ τοῦ Μειδίου πλούτου καὶ τῆς ὑπερηφανίας παρὰ τὴν πενίαν καὶ ἐρημίαν καὶ τὸ τῶν πολλῶν εἷς εἶναι. (Dem. 21.95–96)

Now call [*kalei*] Straton himself as well, the one who suffered such things. For I presume he will be permitted to stand. This man [*houtos*], Athenian gentlemen, is perhaps poor, but not wicked at all. This man [*houtos*], although he is a citizen, although he served on all the expeditions when he was of military age and did nothing terrible, stands at this moment [*nuni*] in silence, deprived not only of other common benefits but also of speaking or weeping. And he is not even allowed to tell you whether he has suffered justly or unjustly. Indeed, he suffered these things from Meidias and Meidias' wealth and arrogance because of his poverty and lack of supporters and status as one of the many.

Although Demosthenes does not use a verb of seeing to call the jury's attention to Straton, the repeated *houtos* directs their eyes to him; the deictic adverb *nuni* also indicates that he is standing in court while Demosthenes is speaking these words. Demosthenes provides the jurors with the necessary information to interpret Straton's silence in the way most favorable to himself. He describes Meidias' attack on Straton as though it had nothing to do with the arbitration or even with Demosthenes; instead, his Straton has suffered at the hand of a rich and arrogant man because he is poor, lacks a posse of supporters, and is "one of the many." Only a few minutes ago, Demosthenes claimed it was not safe for anyone even to walk in the same street as Meidias, since he deprived Straton, whom Demosthenes called simply "one of the Athenians," of his rights.[68] Now, by displaying Straton and equating him with "the many," Demosthenes gives what seems to be visual confirmation of this claim. Anyone of the jurors, he implies, could suffer the same fate as Straton if he has the misfortune to cross paths with Meidias.

The visual display, therefore, is designed to encourage the jurors to identify with the person they see and to recognize in his loss of citizenship the threat that Meidias poses also to them. It is not, on its own, proof that Meidias really does pose a threat to the *polis* and its citizens. We do not know what Straton looked like, although his appearance must have encouraged the jurors to imagine themselves in his place. Straton's silence was a more important part of the display than his looks, however, and Demosthenes may even have briefly stopped speaking to allow the jurors to focus their attention on the mute Straton.[69] A pause would be most effective after the sentence that explains how Straton has lost the right to speak and weep. Then, when Demosthenes says, "And he is not even allowed to tell you whether he has suffered justly or unjustly," the jurors would have just experienced a period of unnatural silence in court from someone like themselves who could not testify as a witness because, according to Demosthenes, he merely followed the laws and refused to accept a bribe to change his decision.

The scholia to *Against Meidias*, which compare Straton to a mute character in a drama,[70] maintain that his appearance will prompt pity from the jurors because he is similar to them,[71] noting further that Demosthenes emphasizes Straton's poverty and Meidias' wealth because Straton and the jurors are poor, and poor men pity each other and hate the wealthy.[72] These are generalizations, but the scholiasts' instincts are perceptive. Seeing Straton alone and mute would have prompted some jurors to pity him because they identified with him and not with Meidias. Part of Demosthenes' strategy in *Against Meidias* is to make Meidias seem like a brash and violent maniac who threatened the entire democracy by assaulting Demosthenes at the Dionysia.[73] Not all of the jurors will have identified with Demosthenes or cared about Meidias punching him, however. Straton, therefore, serves both as the antithesis of Meidias and as an alternative to Demosthenes. Through his visual demonstration, Demosthenes shows the jurors that someone like them, and not just someone like him, can be the victim of Meidias' cruelty.

The scholia are also sensitive to the way that the effectiveness of Straton's silence depends on and complements Demosthenes' words. One scholion, which explains the phrase "the one who suffered such things," reads:

τὸν τὰ τοιαῦτα πεπονθότα] οἷα ἠκούσατε. προδιατέθεικε δὲ ταῖς αὐξήσεσι τὸν ἀκροατήν, ἵνα μᾶλλον γένηται περιπαθὴς ὡς δεινοῦ πράγματος μέλλων γίγνεσθαι θεατής. (Schol. to Dem. 21.95 [322 Dilts])

"The one who suffered such things": Such things as you heard. Demosthenes has predisposed the hearer by his amplifications so that he may be more deeply moved, about to be a spectator, so to speak, of a terrible thing.

"Such things," glossed as "such things as you heard," refer to Straton's disenfranchisement, which, as the scholiast notes, the jurors have already heard Demosthenes describe. The tenses of the verbs in the next sentence are significant: Demosthenes has *already* predisposed the hearer to pity Straton so that he may be more deeply moved *now* when he is about to see him. "His amplifications" refers to the long and detailed description of the arbitration and its aftermath. Menander Rhetor instructs aspiring rhetoricians that "amplifications" in introductory sections prepare the hearer to pay more attention to the main point of a particular section of an oration.[74] The scholiast to *Against Meidias* suggests that Demosthenes has done something similar. By describing Straton's suffering, Demosthenes has prepared his jurors to become spectators of a visual display. Because they already know his history, the scholiast expects that the jurors will be moved when they see him. If Demosthenes had not described the sufferings, the visual demonstration would not have been as effective, since the jurors would not necessarily have interpreted Straton's silence as the punishment of an innocent person who happened to cross Meidias' path. As the scholia realize, Demosthenes' words work together with Straton's appearance to encourage the jurors to identify with Straton, to pity his sufferings, and to recognize Meidias as a danger to each of them.

Against Pantainetos

Other litigants call the jurors' attention to the appearance of people who cannot speak in court, but their visual strategies are more conventional than Demosthenes' elaborate mixture of words, appearance, and silence in *Against Meidias*. *Against Pantainetos* (Demosthenes 37) is a good example. Demosthenes' client Niokoboulos mocks Pantainetos' claim that a slave named Antigenes forcibly took money from one of Pantainetos' slaves and repossessed a silver refinery that Pantainetos was renting from Nikoboulos.[75] Referring to Antigenes' appearance, he says:

ἵνα δ' εἰδῆτε ὑφ' οὗ φησὶ καὶ τὰ δεινὰ πεπονθέναι, θεάσασθε. οὗτός ἐστιν ὁ Πανταίνετον ἐκβαλών, οὗτός ἐσθ' ὁ κρείττων τῶν φίλων τῶν Πανταινέτου καὶ τῶν νόμων. (Dem. 37.44)

So that you may know by what man he alleges he has suffered such horrible treatment, look [*theasasthe*]! This man [*houtos*] is the one who ejected Pantainetos, this man [*houtos*] is the one stronger than Pantainetos' friends and the laws!

The deictic pronoun *houtos* as the first word in two successive clauses recalls the similar repetition of *houtos* in Demosthenes' demonstration of Straton, but here Antigenes' silence is not at issue. As a slave, he could not testify in court, and in any event, the two litigants had not agreed on terms for his torture. Instead, Nikoboulos makes a more straightforward argument about Antigenes' appearance, emphasized by the imperative "look" at the end of the first sentence. The way Antigenes looked must have made Pantainetos' claims seem unlikely, perhaps because the slave was old or weak or just small.[76] The mention of Pantainetos' friends adds to the impression of Antigenes' weakness. Although Nikoboulos never says that Pantainetos' friends tried and failed to stop Antigenes when he describes the charge against Antigenes and quotes Pantainetos' indictment, he does say that a "factory of conspirators" accompanied Pantainetos when he first proposed terms for Antigenes' torture.[77] The unusual metaphor creates the impression that Pantainetos has the support of a huge group of men. These are the friends, Nikoboulos implies, that the jurors are supposed to believe Antigenes overcame.

Nikoboulos later strengthens the contrast between Antigenes and Pantainetos' friends. He argues conventionally that Pantainetos trusts words, witnesses, and emotional displays rather than facts. His witnesses include "the filthy and foul Prokles, this big guy here [*toutōi*], and Stratokles, the most persuasive of all men and also the most wicked."[78] The dative deictic *toutōi*, which is used only with Prokles and not with Stratokles and which appears in a marked position at the end of the clause, demonstrates that Nikoboulos is talking about, and perhaps pointing to, someone who is present in the court and visible to the jurors. Part of Nikoboulos' reason for pointing him out must have been to contrast him with Antigenes, whom he would have asked the jurors to look at only a few minutes earlier. This strong man, he implies, is one of the friends that Antigenes is alleged to have overpowered. Nikoboulos could even have paused after saying "this big guy here" and quickly glanced from Prokles to Antigenes; the visual comparison would have been effective without any more words.

Regardless of whether Nikoboulos emphasized the contrast between Prokles and Antigenes, it is clear that he expected the jurors to dismiss

Antigenes as a likely aggressor because of the way he looked. The visual argument is not decisive or even particularly convincing, since Antigenes may have been the leader of a group of stronger slaves. More importantly, his appearance does nothing to refute Pantainetos' claim that Antigenes was following Nikoboulos' orders.[79] It is not intended to convince, however, but merely to plant a doubt in the minds of the jurors who harbor assumptions about physical weakness. If Antigenes appears to be too weak to have taken money from Pantainetos' slave or to have guarded the confiscated workshop, then some of the jurors may infer that Pantainetos must be lying about Antigenes' involvement. If he is lying about that, perhaps he is lying about everything else too. Nikoboulos has already prepared the jurors to suspect Pantainetos' motives and character by describing how he abandons his friends after using them to achieve his own ends.[80] A clumsy lie about a powerless slave would be consistent with this persona.

VISUAL PROOF

So far, we have been examining visual strategies that take advantage of the jurors' assumptions and prejudices. Other types of visual strategies do not rely primarily on bias but instead present appearance as though it is actual evidence. We hear of some particularly sensational examples from the Athenian courts. In *Against Kallimakhos* (Isocrates 18), for example, the speaker tells the jury about a previous trial in which Kallimakhos' opponent Kratinos proved his innocence by displaying alive the slave woman Kallimakhos swore Kratinos had murdered.[81] Through this display, Kratinos presented the living woman as a direct visual refutation of Kallimakhos' sworn statement that she was dead, real proof rather than apparent proof based on the jurors' biases. Kratinos may have been perpetrating a fraud by presenting another woman in place of the dead slave woman, but his honesty has nothing to do with the visual aspect of the strategy. What the jurors saw appeared to be visual evidence confirming Kratinos' innocence without having to pass through a cultural filter. More gruesomely, in *The First Speech Against Aristogeiton* (Demosthenes 25), Demosthenes supports his account of Aristogeiton's misbehavior in prison by summoning the prisoner whose nose, he claims, Aristogeiton bit off.[82] The appearance of the noseless man is intended as visual evidence for Aristogeiton's violent tendencies, not as a visual detail whose meaning depended on the jurors' prejudices or assumptions about men without noses.

Wounded litigants often used their injuries as visual evidence against their assailants. The most detailed account of such a display comes in *Against Euergos and Mnesiboulos* (Demosthenes 47), which is usually attributed to Apollodoros. The anonymous speaker describes how he proved that a certain Theophemos had beaten him up by demonstrating his wounds to the *boulē*. "Since the *boulē* was angry about what I had suffered and since they saw [*idousa*] how I had been treated," the speaker says, they ordered him to bring an indictment against Theophemos.[83] The combined effect of the speaker's words and his wounds, along with Theophemos' neglect of the *boulē*'s authority, lead the *boulē* to decide in his favor. We may compare the scene in Xenophon's *Memorabilia* where Nikomakhides complains to Socrates that he was not chosen as a *stratēgos* despite having spent his entire life commanding soldiers and receiving many wounds from the enemy. A *stratēgos* was a military commander, similar to a modern general but with greater political responsibilities. Nikomakhides tries to strengthen his case by displaying the wounds to Socrates while he speaks; Xenophon uses the imperfect verb "he was demonstrating" (*epedeiknuen*) to stress that the visual display accompanies the verbal carping and complements it.[84]

Although neither of these examples refers to a display of wounds during a trial, the evidence of other forensic speeches suggests that similar demonstrations were common, especially in trials before the Areopagos for intentional wounding. Visual evidence of a wound or a scar must have been a valuable asset for someone bringing such a suit, since we even hear of plaintiffs injuring themselves.[85] Although a self-inflicted wound would have increased the notoriety of the alleged incident and perhaps made it easier to secure false witnesses, it must have been intended more for the jurors than the general public. Indeed, this is the implication of Mantitheos' account in *The Second Speech Against Boiotos* (Demosthenes 40). Mantitheos tells the jurors that he was acquitted in an earlier trial for intentional wounding only after a physician admitted cutting the plaintiff Boiotos' head to provide false evidence of the wound.[86] If the physician had not admitted to helping Boiotos fake the evidence, the wound would have been visual evidence of Mantitheos' guilt.

The most elaborate example of appearance as visual evidence that survives from Classical Athens comes in *For the Disabled Man* (Lysias 24),[87] whose speaker argues before the *boulē* that he should continue to receive a pension from the *polis* because a physical impairment prevents him from supporting himself.⁸⁸ The Greek word that I translate as "disabled" is *adunatos*, which we have already encountered in *Against Philon* (Lysias 31), and a more literal but less idiomatic translation would be *For the Man Who Lacks Ability*.⁸⁹ The opponent, whose speech does not survive, appears to have argued that the speaker is able-bodied, since he rides horses, and that his income is great enough to make the pension superfluous, since his shop attracts men who have money to spend.⁹⁰ Lysias' client presents neither evidence nor witnesses to counter these allegations.⁹¹ He merely asserts first that he must not be able-bodied, since he uses two crutches and relies on borrowed horses for long trips, and second that his shop, which he admits attracts unsavory characters, does not provide him with sufficient income to support himself or even to purchase a slave to help run it.⁹²

Regardless of whether these claims are true, the key to the speaker's strategy lies in the lack of witnesses. The case is self-evident, the speaker maintains, because of what the *bouleutai* can see. Mocking his opponent's fervent prosecution of what he frames as a frivolous charge, he says:

ὁ μὲν γὰρ ὥσπερ ἐπικλήρου τῆς συμφορᾶς οὔσης ἀμφισβητήσων ἥκει καὶ πειρᾶται πείθειν ὑμᾶς ὡς οὐκ εἰμὶ τοιοῦτος οἷον ὑμεῖς ὁρᾶτε πάντες· ὑμεῖς δὲ (ὃ τῶν εὖ φρονούντων ἔργον ἐστί) μᾶλλον πιστεύετε τοῖς ὑμετέροις αὐτῶν ὀφθαλμοῖς ἢ τοῖς τούτου λόγοις. (Lys. 24.14)

> He comes to challenge the validity of my misfortune like someone about to lay claim to an heiress, and he is trying to persuade you that I am not the kind of person that all of you are seeing [*horate*]. You, however, ought to trust your own eyes [*ophthalmois*] rather than my opponent's words. This is the duty of those who are in their right minds.

We can infer that the *bouleutai* see before them the speaker supporting himself with the two crutches he mentions a little earlier in the speech.⁹³ Martha Rose maintains that "the nature and severity of the defendant's physical impairment are not the issue in Lysias 24; the issue is his ability to make a living."⁹⁴ The speaker, however, is careful to blur the distinction between these two categories, emphasizing that what he looks like is proof that he deserves the pension. In paragraph 6, he even implies that his impairment directly affects his ability to work, saying of his trade, "Already I work at it with difficulty."

He also takes advantage of what the *bouleutai* can see to trivialize his opponent's case.[95] This is clearest when he mocks his attempt to accuse him of *hubris*:

> ὥστε μοι δοκεῖ ὁ κατήγορος εἰπεῖν περὶ τῆς ἐμῆς ὕβρεως οὐ σπουδάζων, ἀλλὰ παίζων, οὐδ' ὑμᾶς πεῖσαι βουλόμενος ὥς εἰμι τοιοῦτος, ἀλλ' ἐμὲ κωμῳδεῖν βουλόμενος, ὥσπερ τι καλὸν ποιῶν. (Lys. 24.18)

> Therefore it seems to me that my accuser is not being serious when he talks about my *hubris*, but is joking. He doesn't really want to persuade you that I am this kind of person, but he wants to treat me like a character in a comedy, as though he is being witty.

Only because his impairment is visible can the speaker get away with treating the prosecution as a joke. Pathos is never far from the humor, however. From the beginning of the speech, the speaker makes clear that he should be pitied,[96] and the last quarter of the speech is a sustained appeal to the *boulē*'s pity.[97] He speaks of his disability as a separation from the greatest things, and of his pension as the only share he has in his country.[98] Finally, the last words he says in the speech mention his weakness:

> οὗτος δὲ τοῦ λοιποῦ μαθήσεται μὴ τοῖς ἀσθενεστέροις ἐπιβουλεύειν ἀλλὰ τῶν ὁμοίων αὐτῷ περιγίγνεσθαι. (Lys. 24.27)

> From now on, my opponent will lose the habit of plotting against weaker men and will learn instead to overcome those who are like him.

This is not just a general statement but a specific reference to the *dokimasia* and to the speaker. He has consistently associated himself with weakness, contrasting in paragraph 7 his present impairment with his comparative strength when he was young, and in paragraphs 16–18 equating the weak with the physically impaired. Furthermore, although he has not directly referred to his appearance since paragraph 14, it has remained an integral part of his performance: the *bouleutai* cannot help looking at him and seeing that he is weaker than his opponent. This reference to the trial as a plot against the weak is therefore an effective way to end his argument. The speaker's last seconds before the jurors link a verbal claim of weakness to the visible evidence of his need for crutches, reminding them that, according to the speaker's logic, the case is self-evident. The speaker subtly emphasizes that he looks like someone who cannot generate sufficient income to support himself and so should continue to receive a pension from the *polis*. Cultural assumptions might make an ugly man seem innocent of adultery or a weak man of assault, but a man with crutches has visual evidence that he deserves a pension.

The case must not have been as self-evident as the speaker insists, however. Even if his opponent brought the lawsuit for malicious or political reasons, he must have had enough evidence to think he could win the case. Moreover, since the speaker presents no witnesses or evidence aside from his appearance, some of the *bouleutai* may have doubted that their eyes really perceived the full story. Yet the speaker did not have to convince everyone. Christopher Carey has shown that he introduces humor and pathos immediately after his weakest arguments as a "diversionary digression" to distract the *bouleutai* from analyzing them too carefully.[99] Just as the speaker tries to manipulate the *bouleutai* who are prone to laughter or sympathy, he also tries to manipulate the ones who tend to trust their eyes. If more than half of them were susceptible to these tactics, he would have succeeded in keeping his pension.

CONCLUSIONS

Arthur Garfield Hays called it a fact that the Sweets did not look like murderers, encouraging the jurors to focus on the visual characteristics they associated with law-abiding citizens. In this chapter, I have argued that this strategy was already familiar to Athenian litigants and speechwriters. By appealing to the jurors' visual prejudices or by treating appearance as though it is actual visual proof, speakers try to manipulate the jurors into accepting their arguments. Words and appearance work together. What the jurors hear leads them to interpret what they see in a way favorable to the speaker, and what they see reinforces or even seems to confirm the arguments they hear. Although tactics vary among individual speeches, ranging from the vague references in *For Mantitheos* to the complex combination of words, silence, and appearance in *Against Meidias* to the visual proof the speaker claims to provide in *For the Disabled Man*, the basic strategy remains the same. Jurors can be persuaded by what they see as well as by what they hear, and a successful forensic performance should address itself to both senses.

All of the speeches I have discussed in detail in this chapter are attributed to Demosthenes and Lysias. These two orators may have been the most skilled at integrating the jurors' sight into the spoken arguments of their clients, or, in Demosthenes' case, into their own arguments. It is more likely, however, that this is an accident of preservation, since most surviving forensic speeches are attributed to Demosthenes and Lysias. That all but one of the surviving speeches of Isaeus deal with inheritance adds plausibility to this argument. The inheritance speeches in the Demosthenic and Lysianic corpora do not refer to appearance either, so inheritance does not seem to have been a type of suit that lent itself to visual demonstration. If we had access to a greater range of Isaeus' speeches, we might find visual arguments similar to the ones in Lysias and Demosthenes.

There are hints of visual arguments in orators whose work has been preserved less fully than Lysias' and Demosthenes'. Hyperides may have been fond of them, if the story in Athenaeus' *Scholars at Dinner* of him tearing Phryne's *khitōn* and baring her breasts to the jurors preserves a seed of truth. As we saw earlier in this chapter, he also seems to have made fun of Philippides' excessive thinness. Furthermore, although the speaker's shock in Dinarchus' *Against Philokles* (Dinarchus 3) that Philokles has dared "to show [*deixai*] himself" to the jurors does not seem to have an especially visual force, the interest in demonstration may indicate that Dinarchus could exploit the jurors' visual prejudices if the occasion called for it.[100]

In conclusion, I return to *Against Theomnestos* (Lysias 10), which argues that Theomnestos and his father conceal corrupt and cowardly characters with their youthful and vigorous appearance. The danger of visual bias clouding the jury's judgment is relevant only to a live performance before an observing audience. If the section were omitted, readers would be no less likely to condemn or acquit Theomnestos. Although readers of Athenian forensic speeches are subject to biases and agendas, we cannot be influenced by what we cannot see.

The ancient editor who abridged *Against Theomnestos* seems to have appreciated that the reference to appearance would have less meaning for readers than it had for jurors in court. Modern editors designate the abridged version (called an "epitome") Lysias 11.[101] By comparing the epitome with *Against Theomnestos*, we can determine what parts of the original speech the epitomizer considered inessential for his audience. The epitome follows the contents and language of *Against Theomnestos* closely, but it omits the argument about the appearance of Theomnestos and his father in paragraph 29 and another reference to sight in paragraph 1.[102] The epitomizer seems to have concluded that these visual references were superfluous for an audience outside of the court that could not see what Theomnestos and his father actually looked like.

The epitomizer's choices give us an insight into the kinds of things that may have been excised when speeches were edited after trials. Even though most forensic speeches are not epitomes, they are also not exact transcripts of what the litigants said. Their first editors, who could have been the speechwriters themselves, may have had similar concerns to the later epitomizer of *Against Theomnestos*. In preparing the compositions for audiences outside the courts, they may have sought to remove things that no longer made sense, like references to what the jurors, but not the later audiences, could see. By analyzing some of the references to sight that do remain in the texts of forensic speeches, this chapter has shown that they are parts of unified performances intended to persuade the jurors through a combined appeal to their eyes and their ears. We should always remember, however, that our texts do not give us access to the experience of the original audiences and, like the epitome of *Against Theomnestos*, may not capture the essence of the original performance. Appearance and the prejudices it provoked probably played a much larger role in Athenian oratory than we can ever know.

———————— TWO ————————

THE MEANINGS OF MOVEMENT

Gestures were a vital part of performances in the Athenian courts, but unusual gestures could distract or annoy jurors. Litigants would generally have gestured in a way that called attention to themselves and their speeches without offending the jurors' sense of propriety or undermining their arguments.

INTRODUCTION: A LATE ANTIQUE ACCOUNT OF THE INVENTION OF RHETORIC

When Gelon and Hieron ruled Syracuse, an anonymous late antique account tells us, they banned speech among their subjects. The Syracusans could only use their feet, hands, and eyes to communicate and so they "devised a system for pointing out their business through gesture [*skhēmati*]." After Zeus heard their prayers for deliverance and freed them from tyranny, the Syracusans chose to live as a democracy. Life in the democracy was disorganized and chaotic until Korax, a former adviser to Hieron, realized that he could use speech to persuade the Syracusans to put their affairs in order. With a speech organized into formal parts, he "devised a system for persuading the people just as he used to persuade one man." Then, having invented rhetoric, Korax began to teach it to others.[1]

The author of this late antique fantasy recognizes the communicative potential of visual signs. Pointed fingers, nodding heads, raised eyebrows, shrugged shoulders, clapping hands, and bitten lips all have recognizable meanings that enable us to communicate without words. Strings of gestures can convey complex concepts in a way that resembles spoken language. Studies have shown that deaf and mute children who have not learned sign language use consistent gestures for individual concepts and organize their strings of gestures in consistent patterns. In other words, their gestures have both a lexicon and a grammar.[2] The sign system the anonymous author imagines must have worked in this way. Humans most often do not use gestures independently of spoken language, however. Rather, we gesture while we speak to reinforce or add nuance to our words. When speech alone is ambiguous, gestures can clarify it by showing, for instance, sincerity or irony, mockery or respect. In these cases, gesture and speech are part of a single system and combine to communicate a unified message to someone who both looks and listens.[3]

Korax's rhetoric does not allow for such a unified system of aural and visual persuasion; the story carefully distinguishes between gestures and speech. In fact, the meaning of *skhēma* changes after Korax's invention of rhetoric. At the beginning of the story, a *skhēma* is one of the gestures the Syracusans use to communicate when they are forbidden to speak. Later, after Korax's invention, a *skhēma* is a rhetorical figure: Korax's student Teisias uses the *dilēmmaton skhēma*, the rhetorical figure of two mutually contradictory propositions leading to the same conclusion,[4] in an attempt to convince a court to excuse him from his teacher's fees. "If you taught me persuasion," Teisias challenges Korax, "look, I persuade you to charge nothing, but if you did not teach me persuasion, I also owe you nothing because you did not teach me persuasion." Korax then turns the same *skhēma* against Teisias: "If you persuade me not to charge you because you were taught persuasion, you ought to give me my fee since you were taught persuasion, but on the contrary if you do not persuade me not to charge, you also ought to give me my fee, since you did not persuade me not to charge my fee." The verbal *skhēma*, represented by these types of logical arguments, has replaced the visual *skhēma*, which has no place in the formal rhetoric of the Syracusans' newly civilized democracy.

Although the details of this story reflect late antique and Byzantine rhetorical interests, it seems to preserve an authentic historical memory about the method of argumentation that Korax and Teisias taught and that enjoyed a vogue among intellectuals and litigants in the fifth century BCE.[5] The counterintuitive logic Teisias employs to avoid paying his teacher's fees also characterizes, for instance, Pheidippides' justification for beating his father, Strepsiades, in Aristophanes' *Clouds*.[6] Real litigants in democratic Athens did not limit themselves to logical arguments like the ones our story associates with Korax and Teisias, however. As I showed in chapter 1, they tried to persuade their jurors through both verbal and visual techniques. A skillful litigant would use his words, his appearance, and his gestures to appeal to as many jurors as he could.

Athenian litigants do not often mention their hands, arms, heads, and legs, but their bodies are unlikely to have been completely still at any point during their performances. As Plato writes in the *Laws*, "On the whole, no one at all is able to keep his body still while he makes sounds, whether in songs or in speeches."[7] Since there are very few references to words and gestures working side-by-side in the Attic forensic speeches that survive, it is impossible to give an overview of the repertoire of courtroom gestures or to draw even tentative conclusions about the specific roles they may have played in all but a handful of individual speeches. This chapter, therefore, approaches gestures from a cultural perspective, arguing that the gestures most likely to be effective in Athenian courts were ones corresponding to jurors' expectations about propriety and naturalness. Litigants whose gestures failed to meet these expectations could distract the jurors, expose themselves to ridicule, or even undermine their own cases.

APPROPRIATE AND INAPPROPRIATE GESTURES

Ambivalence about gesture's role in formal argumentation persists from antiquity to today. Khilon of Sparta, one of the Seven Sages, is supposed to have said, "Don't move your hands while you speak. It's a sign of madness."[8] Homer's Antenor, on the other hand, tells Helen that the Trojans underestimated Odysseus' intelligence because "he did not move his scepter back and forth," while he spoke, "but held it stiff like an ignorant man."[9] Homer does not tell us how good speakers usually gestured with the scepter, but we get a sense of its central role in rhetorical performance in Book One of the *Iliad*, when Achilles swears by it and then flings it to the ground.[10] Unknowingly echoing Khilon, Keene Trial Consultants' "Jury Room" blog advised trial lawyers in 2011, "Stand up straight! And stop talking so much with your hands! It's distracting."[11] Other modern handbooks of trial advocacy advise lawyers to use gestures and movements that correspond to their language and make their arguments easier to follow. They avoid specific suggestions and encourage lawyers to move their hands as they would in normal conversations, describing ideal gestures with words like "appropriate," "natural," "consistent," and "confident."[12]

Both Khilon and the "Jury Room" blog are concerned with the potentially distracting effects of gestures: they can cause an audience to draw unwarranted conclusions about the speaker's sanity or simply to stop paying attention to the argument. Antenor and the other trial handbooks, however, focus on the way that gestures can complement an argument in a natural way. For Antenor, the absence of appropriate gestures is a distraction in itself. Combining these seemingly contradictory recommendations, we can conclude that, properly used, gestures in antiquity and today ought to help the audience focus on the argument and not on the gestures, unless there is a specific reason to draw attention to the gestures themselves. Only particularly skilled speakers can manipulate their audiences through unexpected gestures or failures to gesture. Odysseus used his stiffness to lower his audience's expectations and then triumphantly transcend them, but a less talented performer would have risked alienating his audience and undermining his argument. In most situations, therefore, gestures should reinforce a verbal argument by meeting an audience's expectations about what is natural or appropriate.

Ancient rhetorical treatises emphasize the close connection between gestures and argument. In the *Brutus*, for instance, Cicero praises Marcus Antonius' oratorical performances for their internal consistency: "His gesturing was not expressing his words but was corresponding with his thoughts—his hands, his shoulders, his chest, the stamping of his foot, his posture, his pacing, his every movement consistent with his words and his thoughts."[13] Cicero insists that gestures should complement the entire subject of an oration, and not express the sense of individual words.[14] Quintilian similarly emphasizes that both body and voice work together to obey the dictates of the mind.[15] He anticipates the conclusion of modern scholars that gestures and speech are part of a single system and combine to communicate a unified message.[16] The unified nature of oratorical performances is also implicit in the five tasks traditionally assigned to orators: invention, arrangement, expression, memory, and delivery.[17] In *On the Orator*, Cicero describes these five items as encompassing what he calls *omnis oratoris vis ac facultas* ("all of an orator's power and skill").[18] Taken as a whole, then, they are meant to represent a unified account of speech-making, from preparation through performance. Language dominates the categories of invention, arrangement, and expression, but delivery includes both visual and verbal aspects.

Nowhere was unity of presentation more important than in the Athenian courts. Jurors had to decide between two competing accounts of the same events, and they often could not have confirmed the litigants' claims from their own personal knowledge. As a result, forensic speeches serve many related purposes: they tell stories, present evidence, make logical arguments, and create a credible and sympathetic character for the speaker. While different gestures may be appropriate for each part of a speech, they can never be inconsistent with the character the speaker crafts for himself.

Since litigants often try to convince the jurors that they have little experience either in rhetoric or in law,[19] most of them would seek to use the kinds of gestures that the jurors would associate with natural speech. Gestures that suggested professional training would have undermined their claims of inexperience and could have led them to lose an otherwise strong case.[20] This conclusion is consistent with Aristotle's remarks in the *Rhetoric* that a persuasive *lexis*, or speaking style, ought to be appropriate for a speaker's identity and the topic of the speech. Even in poetry, Aristotle maintains, "It would be rather inappropriate for a slave to use fine language, or for an excessively young man to use fine language, or for anyone to use fine language about excessively trivial things."[21] Consequently, he argues, "Those who compose speeches should not be noticed, and they should seem to speak naturally and not artificially. For the former is persuasive but the latter is not, since listeners are suspicious of those who are, as it were, trying to trick them, just as they are against wines that are mixed together."[22] If speaking artificially could hurt a litigant, gesturing artificially could too.

It is difficult to know what kinds of gestures were natural and appropriate for the Athenians. Cultures vary in the types of gestures speakers employ, their frequency, and their connotations. While pointing with the hand or the head is common across cultures and easily interpreted, nods, shoulder shrugs, eyebrow raises, finger movements, and subtle changes in posture often carry meanings unique to particular cultures and particular contexts. Quintilian has left us a detailed discussion of gestures and movement in Roman oratory,[23] but no Athenian seems to have written a comparable treatise. Analysis of Attic literature, sculpture, and vase paintings, however, has enabled scholars such as Andreas Katsouris and Alan Hughes to assemble catalogues of Athenian gestures and their possible meanings.[24] Taking a different approach, Alan Boegehold has argued that ambiguous or incomplete sentences in Greek literature indicate places where gestures would have complemented the language.[25] Although we can hypothesize about the kinds of gestures the Athenians used and the situations in which gestures were appropriate, we cannot match specific gestures with specific moments in surviving forensic orations. Furthermore, the Athenians were sensitive to registers of speech. Just as some kinds of speech acceptable in the agora would have been unacceptable in a court, so some gestures would have been as well, even if they were natural and appropriate in other places. The appropriate gestures for most forensic performances, therefore, would have been the ones the Athenians associated with formal registers of communication.

By formal registers of communication, I am not suggesting that all litigants would have strictly adhered to a defined standard of formal speaking and gesturing. Different people could have used different types of gestures effectively, but all litigants who thought seriously about their performance strategy would have tried to use gestures appropriate for their characters and for the courts, unless, like Odysseus in the *Iliad*, they had a strategic reason to violate propriety.

Litigants who prepared their speeches in advance, with or without the help of a speechwriter, may have practiced their gestures to ensure they were appropriate. The accounts of speech rehearsals in Aristophanes' *Knights*, Euripides' *Electra*, and Plato's *Phaedrus*, however, focus on language and content and make no mention of gestures.[26] Silence about gestures, even in three different sources, is not evidence that speakers did not practice them. Instead, it suggests that speakers may have associated gestures so closely with language and content that they did not single them out as a distinct subject for rehearsal. Additionally, a speaker who wished to stress his inexperience with litigation could have sabotaged himself if he practiced his gestures so much that they seemed artificial instead of spontaneous.

Dionysius of Halicarnassus, although he writes in the first century BCE, supports the conclusion that a speaker who closely engages with the language and content of a speech will instinctively gesture in an appropriate way. Dionysius advises the reader who wishes to understand the power of Demosthenes' speeches that Demosthenes' style dictates the proper tone of voice, facial expressions, and hand movements to the performer because it is full of moral and emotional qualities. He finds that an attentive reading of Demosthenes' words will stir certain emotions, such as anger, grief, indignation, contempt, and sympathy, and that the experience of these emotions will naturally lead to an effective delivery.[27]

Dionysius is talking about his contemporaries reading and performing Demosthenes' deliberative speeches, but his insight is just as relevant for Demosthenes' clients performing the forensic speeches he wrote for them, or perhaps helped them write. Since the emotions inspired by the language were the clients' own emotions, and since the language was at the very least inspired by their own descriptions and arguments, their gestures would have been even more instinctive than the gestures of later readers. By recognizing the instinctive nature of gestures, we can explain why the Athenians seem to have paid so little attention to them in accounts of rehearsals and in rhetorical handbooks.

While instinct may have been a reliable guide in many situations, it may also have led some litigants to gesture in ways inappropriate for the courts. To guard against this, litigants could have tempered their instinct with knowledge based on their observation of earlier trials. Victor Bers argues in *Genos Dikanikon* that professional speakers in court would have avoided features of language or style that had been used by amateur litigants who had lost in earlier trials. Bers focuses on language, but the same principle applies to gestures. Litigants who hoped to win and who paid attention to their performances would not have gestured like litigants whose gestures in earlier trials seemed to annoy the judges or distract them from favorable arguments. A speaker could have ensured that his gestures were appropriate by relying on a combination of instinct and observation.

Confident performers could have chosen to augment their arguments with unusual or complex gestures, poses, and facial expressions. Pleas for pity, for instance, probably called for specially rehearsed gestures. Aristotle, who rarely mentions gestures in the *Rhetoric*, theorizes that "those people who help the effect with gestures, sounds, display of feeling, and acting in general are necessarily more pitiable."[28] Although Aristotle is not explicitly recommending that litigants gesture to arouse pity in their jurors, this is the most logical way to understand this section, especially since he says they help to bring the suffering "before the eyes," which is a technical way he refers to vividness in poetry or oratory.[29] Public figures were probably more likely to risk making unusual gestures than litigants who claimed to have no experience with the courts or with speaking in public. Gestures implying practice or professional training would not have conflicted with their characters.

The assembly may have encouraged more expansive gestures than the courts, since the audience was much larger and many men were at a greater distance from the speaker. Exaggerated movements of hands and arms, as well as moments of complete, unnatural stillness, could help command their attention. Gestures would have played a particularly important role if some assemblymen had difficulty hearing the speaker.[30] Movement alone would not have communicated the content of the proposal, but forceful gestures and an upright posture could have projected an image of competence and power. If Plutarch's description of Kleon "stripping off his outer cloak and slapping his thigh and running while he spoke"[31] preserves an authentic memory of assembly performances, it would support the conclusion that gestures in the assembly differed from gestures in the courts. We nowhere hear of litigants employing gestures or movements like these. Along the same lines, Bers suggests Kleon's running may actually refer to the way that speakers on the Pnyx may have had to move around for the various sections of the Assembly to hear them.[32]

Further support that gestures in the assembly would have been more expansive than gestures in the courts comes from Aeschines' caricatured descriptions of Demosthenes' and Timarkhos' gestures. In *Against Ktesiphon* (Aeschines 3), Aeschines claims that Demosthenes whirled himself around in a circle as though he were moving against Alexander during one of his assembly speeches,[33] and in *On the Dishonest Embassy* (Aeschines 2), he mocks the way Demosthenes prepared to speak: "After he inspired awe with his gestures, as usual, and rubbed his head, he looked out on the applauding *dēmos* which had welcomed the words from me."[34] More sensationally, in *Against Timarkhos* (Aeschines 1), Aeschines compares Timarkhos' gestures to the *pankration*, a no-holds-barred fighting competition at Panhellenic festivals that featured kicks, punches, and wrestling holds.[35] Aeschines is not an impartial or even particularly truthful witness, and there is every reason not to take him at his word when he says anything about his opponents. Nonetheless, he could never have hoped that his criticisms would be plausible if there was not a grain of truth behind his caricatures. It is one thing to lie about something that most jurors could never have known, such as Demosthenes cutting his own head to fake a wound, or to insinuate that Demosthenes had made a deal with Meidias, but it is another thing to lie repeatedly about things that happened before thousands of Athenians on the Pnyx. Later in this chapter, I will address Aeschines' descriptions of Demosthenes and Timarkhos in more detail, but for now it is sufficient to recognize that, once we allow for hyperbole, they offer tentative support for concluding that a broader range of gestures was customary in the assembly than in the courts.

This discussion of gestures leads to three conclusions. First, most litigants would have followed their instincts and used appropriate gestures in court to complement their arguments, add credibility to their character, and not distract or annoy the jurors. Second, some litigants may have chosen to use unusual gestures if, like Odysseus before the Trojans, they felt particular confidence in their ability to manipulate the jurors by stymieing their expectations, or if their characters were well known enough that unusual gestures would not undermine their self-presentations. Third, the gestures appropriate for the courts may not have been the same as the gestures appropriate for the assembly. My discussion has borrowed vague words such as "appropriate," "natural," and "unusual" from modern trial handbooks and from Aristotle's *Rhetoric*, since we have no concrete examples of gestures in Athenian oratory other than Aeschines' caricatures and Demosthenes' responses to them. These vague terms are consistent with a discourse about gestural propriety that is reflected in Plato's *Republic* and Aristotle's *Poetics*.

THE ETHICS OF GESTURE IN PLATO AND ARISTOTLE

By the mid-fourth century, and probably earlier, Athenian elites seem to have developed an ethical interpretation of gesture. An individual's gestures were thought to reflect his moral worth, and therefore some gestures were thought to be unworthy of certain people. This kind of thinking about gestures is consistent with the elite Athenian tendency to connect appearance with moral qualities.[36] The fundamental sources for the ethical interpretation of gestures are book 3 of Plato's *Republic* and the end of our text of Aristotle's *Poetics*. Although this line of ethical analysis considers poetic performances, gestures in court should be interpreted against the same background. Before an audience accustomed to interpreting gestures in an ethical way, inappropriate gestures could hinder a litigant's case and his claims to social status.

Plato's discussion of mimesis in *Republic* 3, although not primarily about gestures, includes gestures among the behaviors of inferior people that the guardians should not imitate during poetic performances. While Plato is vague about which specific gestures ought to be avoided, he distinguishes appropriate gestures from inappropriate ones based on the type of people who employ them. A brief consideration of Plato's larger argument about mimesis, although it is not my central concern here, will place his statements about gestures in their context and enable us to interpret them correctly.

After Socrates and Adeimantos agree about the types of stories that ought to be excluded from their ideal city, they next consider the way the permissible stories should be told.[37] They conclude that the city's guardians should avoid mimetic performances, which require the performer to adopt the characteristics of someone else, since Socrates maintains that mimesis of any sort would distract the guardians from their central task, which is "to be craftsmen, in the very strict sense of the word, of the free *polis* and to practice nothing that does not pertain to this."[38] Although Socrates is mainly interested in verbal mimesis, he declares that mimesis involves both speech (*kata phōnēn*) and gesture (*kata skhēma*).[39] *Skhēma* here probably denotes a range of gestures, postures, and appearance; Penelope Murray's translation "bearing" is therefore more accurate than "gesture" alone.[40] Since Plato later uses the dative plural *skhēmasin* to refer principally to gestures, however, I translate *skhēma* as "gesture" to make clear the connection between the two passages that "bearing" would obscure.

The guardians, according to Socrates, should prefer to perform not through mimesis but through *diēgēsis*, usually translated "narrative," where they tell a story without pretending to be someone else. If the guardians do choose to practice mimesis, however, they should imitate only men who exhibit bravery, moderation, piety, and freedom. "They should not do things characteristic of a lack of freedom, nor should they be good at imitating them, nor anything else shameful," Socrates says.[41] Since frequent imitation accustoms the imitator to the things he imitates, the person who imitates shameful behavior will come to enjoy it. Socrates makes clear that sustained imitations will "establish themselves as habits and nature in body and voice [*kata sōma kai phōnas*] and in mind [*kata dianoian*]."[42] So, if we follow Socrates' logic, we can conclude that, since gestures are features of the body, there must therefore be certain gestures "characteristic of a lack of freedom," and, if someone imitates these gestures, he will become accustomed to them and so begin to behave like someone who lacks freedom.

After this theoretical preface about the dangers of mimesis, Socrates proceeds to outline a series of characters that the guardians should not adopt, including women, slaves, men who practice an assortment of vices, craftsmen, rowers, and their commanders.[43] He says of the moderate man, "He will not wish to make himself like someone inferior in a serious way."[44] Only a person who is already inferior will "undertake to imitate everything in a serious way and in front of many people."[45] Here, Socrates moves from imitation of people to imitation of sounds: thunder, wind, hail, axes, pulleys, instruments, and animal noises.[46] This kind of mimesis is as bad as the imitation of inferior characters for the reasons Socrates has already stated: it distracts the imitator from his real tasks, and it accustoms him to acting like someone or something unworthy of his place in society. Although all the examples Socrates gives here are of sound, he includes gesture among the methods of mimesis practiced by the inferior person. He rhetorically asks Adeimantos, "Will the entire speaking style [*lexis*] of this man be through mimesis by means of vocal sounds [*phōnais*] and gestures [*skhēmasin*], or perhaps having some tiny amount of narrative [*diēgēseōs*]?"[47] Although *skhēmasin* here probably encompasses a range of visual attributes, as an aspect of *lexis* ("speaking style") it must refer principally to gestures as the counterpart of voice.[48]

The pairing of sound and gesture recalls the habits of body, voice, and mind that Socrates has already said become customary through frequent imitation. In the ideal city, therefore, gesture ought to be avoided like any other type of mimesis. Nonetheless, Socrates leaves open the possibility that some forms of gesture may be admirable. When he ironically describes how the citizens would honor the performer of poetry who "is able to become adaptable through wisdom and to imitate all things" but would also escort him from their city, he contrasts him with the useful performer that the city admits: "the sort of person who imitates for us the speaking style [*lexin*] of the good man and says the things he says in those forms which we established from the beginning when we were undertaking to educate the soldiers."[49]

Socrates' conception of speaking style, or *lexis*, in this section of the *Republic* includes both voice and gestures, as we saw in his criticism of the inferior man whose *lexis* is "through mimesis by means of vocal sounds [*phōnais*] and gestures [*skhēmasin*]."[50] Socrates therefore seems implicitly to grant that the gestures of the good man are worthy of imitation because they are beneficial to the educational process, just like the kind of stories he has already admitted to his city, the ones that portray the gods and heroes in only a positive light. Based on what he has already said about the superiority of *diēgēsis* to mimesis, we are supposed to imagine that this good performer tells stories without adopting the personae of any of his characters except the good men: "He will wish to declaim as though he is that person, and he will feel no shame about such a mimesis."[51] When he does adopt the good man's persona, therefore, the performer will imitate not only his sounds but also his bodily movements.

According to Socrates' reasoning, there exist two types of gestures: those of good men and those of inferior people, including women. There are two overlapping dangers of gesturing, and they are the same as the dangers Socrates assigns in this section to mimesis in general. First, practicing the gestures of bad or inferior people encourages the gesturer to accustom himself to acting like those people. Second, practicing the varied gestures of an assortment of people, both good and bad, throughout a performance distracts the performer from doing what he ought to do. This is the problem with the performer that Socrates imagines the residents escorting out of the city: he "imitates all things."[52]

Although Plato presents his concerns about mimesis in general, and gestures in particular, within a discussion about the rules of an ideal city, they must at a basic level reflect the sentiments of elite Athenians. Plato's insistence that there are recognizably inferior people whose vocal patterns and gestures should not be imitated indicates that some Athenians either perceived or imagined they perceived distinctions among the ways that Athenians spoke and gestured. If these distinctions were invented by Plato, Socrates' argument about mimesis would be nonsensical: it would be impossible to link social status with habits of voice and body, even as a purely theoretical model, if everyone was thought to speak and move in equivalent ways.

The discussion in *Republic* 3, therefore, supports the conclusion that elite Athenians associated certain gestures with elites and others with nonelites, although Plato may be exaggerating the differences for the sake of making his point. There is some evidence that elite Athenians were expected to show restraint in their movements and their gestures, including the way that Polemarkhos in Plato's *Republic* sends his slaves to run after Socrates rather than running himself and the images of tragic performances that show upper-class characters dressed in heavy cloaks (*himatia*) with their left hands covered and slaves with uncovered hands.[53] But whether different classes of Athenians actually used discernibly different gestures is less important than that elite Athenians thought that they did and that gestures, like other visual characteristics, manifested internal worth.

Aristotle develops Plato's discussion of mimesis and gesture near the end of our text of the *Poetics*.[54] He argues that tragic mimesis is superior to epic mimesis, despite what he considers the inappropriate gestures often associated with tragic performances. His initial proposition links these gestures, which he calls "moving a great movement," with the demands of vulgar audiences. Recalling Plato's Socrates' criticism of the performer who "imitates all things," Aristotle writes:

εἰ γὰρ ἡ ἧττον φορτικὴ βελτίων, τοιαύτη δ' ἡ πρὸς βελτίους θεατάς ἐστιν ἀεί, λίαν δῆλον ὅτι ἡ ἅπαντα μιμουμένη φορτική· ὡς γὰρ οὐκ αἰσθανομένων ἂν μὴ αὐτὸς προσθῇ, πολλὴν κίνησιν κινοῦνται, οἷον οἱ φαῦλοι αὐληταὶ κυλιόμενοι ἂν δίσκον δέῃ μιμεῖσθαι, καὶ ἕλκοντες τὸν κορυφαῖον ἂν Σκύλλαν αὐλῶσιν. (Arist. *Poetics* 26 1461b27–32)

If the less vulgar form of mimesis is better, and if this is the kind that is always before better spectators, it is completely evident that the form of mimesis that imitates everything is vulgar. For, since they [the performers] believe that the audience does not notice anything unless he [the performer] sets it before them, they [the performers] move a great movement, like inferior *auletai* who spin themselves around [*kuliomenoi*] whenever they have to imitate a discus and who drag around [*helkontes*] the *koruphaios* whenever they play "Skylla."

In this section, Aristotle employs technical terms of Greek musical production that have no English equivalent. *Auletai* (singular, *auletēs*) are musicians who played the double-piped reed instrument called an *aulos* as an accompaniment to the chorus, a song-and-dance ensemble whose lead performer was the *koruphaios*. Aristotle in these two sentences moves from a general principle, that the more vulgar form of mimesis imitates everything, to a specific example that demonstrates the principle's validity, the case of the inferior *auletai*. Whether Aristotle is criticizing *auletai* who perform for dithyrambs or dramas is unimportant, but it is clear that "great movements" by *auletai* were familiar enough for him to use them as a characteristic example of gestural excess.[55]

It is hard to know precisely what kind of movements Aristotle is criticizing. The middle participle *kuliomenoi*, which I have translated "spin themselves around" must mean that the *auletai* are mimicking the spinning flight of a discus by twisting or spinning their bodies. The verb *kuliō* usually means "roll" rather than "spin," but it is difficult to believe that an *auletēs* could have rolled on the ground while holding his instrument. More puzzling is the active participle *helkontes*, which I have translated "drag around." Again because of his instrument, it is hard to envision an *auletēs* actually dragging the *koruphaios* around, even if the performance conventions would have allowed this. Aristotle may be using the word to refer to a pantomime of dragging, but I think it most likely that he is exaggerating the actual gestures of the *auletai* with a metaphor, much as we might use the word "maul" today even in the absence of physical contact. Liddell, Scott, and Jones' lexicon gives "tear in pieces" as a possible rendering of *helkō*, and this kind of violent movement probably lies behind Aristotle's metaphor.[56]

Aristotle introduces the gestures of the *aulētai* not to attack them directly but as examples of the kind of gestures he disapproves of in tragic actors. He proceeds to associate these sorts of gestures with the performance of the fifth-century actor Kallippides. Kallippides' older colleague Mynniskos is said to have called him an ape "because he was overdoing it so much."[57] Since Aristotle's criticism is rooted in the tastes of the audience, we can conclude that Kallippides "was overdoing it so much" because he believed that his audience would "not notice anything" unless he accompanied it with mimetic gestures, just like the *aulētai* who spin themselves around or make violent gestures at the *koruphaios*. In other words, he was doing what his audiences wanted and therefore employing what Aristotle considers a vulgar form of mimesis.

Aristotle maintains, however, that those people who believe that epic mimesis is less vulgar than tragic mimesis because it is "before better spectators who have no need of gestures" are incorrect. Rhapsodes can "overdo it with gestural signals" just as much as tragic actors.[58] What matters, Aristotle says, is not whether a performance includes gestures, but whether the gestures are of the right sort. He concludes his discussion of gesture by saying:

> εἶτα οὐδὲ κίνησις ἅπασα ἀποδοκιμαστέα, εἴπερ μηδ' ὄρχησις, ἀλλ' ἡ φαύλων, ὅπερ καὶ Καλλιππίδῃ ἐπετιμᾶτο καὶ νῦν ἄλλοις ὡς οὐκ ἐλευθέρας γυναῖκας μιμουμένων. (Arist. *Poetics* 26 1462a8–11)

> Second, not every movement ought to be censured, unless dance is as well, but only the movement of inferior people, which is why both Kallippides and other current performers are criticized, since they make a mimesis of women who are not free.

Aristotle again echoes Plato's terminology here. In *Republic* 3, Socrates says that the guardians should never imitate people or things that are not free, and Aristotle criticizes the movements of Kallippides and his ilk because they are an imitation of "women who are not free." In the part of the *Republic* we examined, Plato is concerned primarily with the harmful effects of mimesis on individuals who practice it, while Aristotle is using it here as a standard for judging performances. Despite these different focuses, both discussions turn on the existence of good and bad gestures, and they equate the bad gestures with inferior people who are not free. Aristotle believed that some gestures were not only acceptable but necessary in tragic performances, since he envisions the playwright working out his plots with both language and gestures to make sure his story is internally consistent and his characters' emotions are plausible.[59] Moreover, as he makes clear here, he has no objection to the movements employed by dancers. His objection to the gestures of Kallippides seems to be, as Eric Csapo has argued, that Kallippides was "overdoing it so much" by "imitating everything." He made too many gestures, including ones associated with lower-class people.[60]

For Aristotle, then, just as for Plato, there are two categories of gestures, ones associated with good people and ones associated with inferior people. Unlike Plato, however, Aristotle gives us two specific examples of the kinds of gestures that ought to be avoided: spinning like a discus and whatever violent movements could be described metaphorically as dragging the *koruphaios* around. Following the interpretation of Csapo, I conclude that these actions are inappropriate not because they are somehow too exuberant but because they are the kind of thing that Athenian elites should never do. Aristotle's criticism of these gestures, therefore, attests to his own social status and aesthetic tastes. By reading between the lines, however, we find that gestures like these must have received a generally positive reaction from Athenian audiences. What Aristotle takes as a sign of the audience's vulgarity is also a sign of their preference. There is every reason to believe that audiences, or at least a significant number of audience members, liked it when the *aulētai* spun like a discus or made violent gestures towards the *koruphaios*, since, if they agreed with Aristotle's condemnation of these movements, no *auletai* would have continued performing them.

The *Poetics*, therefore, attests to a tension between the way Aristotle interpreted gestures and the way some members of the Athenian public interpreted gestures. The movements that Aristotle condemns seem to have found favor with audiences dating back at least to the 420s, the height of Kallippides' career. Following Plato's lead, however, Aristotle associates these popular gestures with inferior people and so finds them indicative of an inferior form of mimesis. While Aristotle's judgments about performance are not evidence for anyone's opinion other than his own, both he and Plato seem to be relying on assumptions that reflect a tendency among Athenian elites to equate gesture with social status. It makes sense to criticize people who imitate the gestures of inferior people only if there actually were gestures that elites believed characterized the people they considered inferior.

Speakers, especially elite speakers, had to contend with these biases when they chose their gestures in court or in the assembly. Speakers who employed the oratorical equivalent of spinning like a discus may have impressed some of their audience, the ones Aristotle would label vulgar, but alienated others. For a tradesman to gesture in court like he gestures in the agora or like his wife when she fetches water from the fountain would be a faux pas, a potentially embarrassing breach of decorum. For an elite citizen to make similar gestures, however, could be a public declaration of social inferiority. At best, he would look ridiculous; at worst, especially in a trial against another elite observed by other elites, he would look inferior to his opponent.

One of the scholia to Demosthenes, which may partly depend on Peripatetic sources,[61] seems to base its analysis of a section of *Against Androtion* (Demosthenes 22) on an ethical interpretation of *skhēma*. Demosthenes' client Diodoros describes an indebted Athenian who tries to escape the debt collectors who have invaded his home by climbing over his roof or hiding under his bed or by "disgracing himself in other ways that are the actions of slaves, not free men."[62] The word for "disgracing himself" is a form of the verb *askhēmoneō*, literally, "have a bad *skhēma*," in the general sense of "bearing" or "deportment." The scholion explains this phrase in the following way: "Think of everything that people do when they are afraid of being caught in the act: they imitate the voice and the deportment [*skhēma*] of women, they seem to be servants, they put their hands to things associated with slaves and to other things in an unsophisticated way."[63] For our purposes, it is significant that the scholion interprets *askhēmoneō* in a manner consistent with the Platonic and Aristotelian tradition, directly linking "having a bad *skhēma*" with imitating women and slaves. This scholion does not, of course, address oratorical gestures. It does, however, serve to situate the next section of this chapter within a long tradition of interpreting references to *skhēma* in forensic oratory through an ethical model influenced by Plato and Aristotle.

PHYSIOGNOMIC ARGUMENTS

We cannot directly study the ways that ethical interpretations of gestures would have affected actual performances in the courts, since, as I have already noted, we usually cannot match particular gestures with particular moments in speeches. When litigants do refer to gestures, they are almost always criticizing what their opponents did in the past or defending what they did themselves. The gestures are narrative details that are visual only in the sense that the audience could have seen them in the past and would associate them with sight. Litigants use gestures and other visual details they describe to support arguments based on what Jon Hesk has termed "physiognomic interpretation," or matching certain physical traits to character types.[64] This is what Apollodoros does in the *First Speech against Stephanos* (Demosthenes 45), when he associates Stephanos' grave countenance with antisocial tendencies,[65] and what Demosthenes does in *Against Meidias* (Demosthenes 21), when he claims that even people who do not know Meidias are irritated by his deportment.[66] Aeschines and Demosthenes are especially fond of physiognomic interpretation. Even more than other orators, they use descriptions of their opponents' visual attributes, including their bodies and their clothing, to lead the jurors to conclusions about their characters and, hence, their guilt.[67] Unlike actual gestures, however, physiognomic interpretation is not dependent upon live performance. Texts that were not written to be performed before specific audiences on specific occasions, like Theophrastus' *Characters*, also use reported visual appearance as a reflection of inner character.[68]

Aristotle recognizes the effectiveness of physiognomic arguments in the *Rhetoric*. He advises litigants to "speak from the emotions, narrating both things that follow from them and things that the audience knows and things that are personally characteristic of yourself or your opponent."[69] After giving an example of his own, "And he went away scowling at me," and recounting how Aeschines of Sphettos (a different Aeschines from Aeschines the orator) described Cratylus hissing and energetically shaking his hands, Aristotle notes that "these are convincing, because things that the audience knows are signs of things they do not know."[70] Aristotle's argument depends on an audience who can decode facial expressions, sounds, and gestures. To interpret Aeschines' description of Cratylus, they must know what energetic handshaking represents. Similarly, litigants who describe gestures employed in the past rely on jurors who can draw on their own knowledge of gestural practice to infer the kind of character or emotional state represented by those gestures. If the gestures described do not enable the jurors to draw immediate conclusions based on past experience, a litigant can try to influence them to respond to the gestures in the ways that he wants. In *Against Ktesiphon* and *Against Timarkhos*, Aeschines the orator tries to lead his jurors to particular physiognomic interpretations of the ways that Demosthenes and Timarkhos had gestured in the assembly by linking descriptions of their gestures with judgments about their characters.

Gesture, Character, and Social Status in Against Ktesiphon

Although Aeschines' account of Demosthenes' gestures in *Against Ktesiphon* (Aeschines 3) is rhetorical rather than theoretical, it reflects the same ethical concerns that lie behind Plato's and Aristotle's discussions of gestures in *Republic* 3 and the *Poetics*. Aeschines even mocks Demosthenes' gestures with words similar to the ones Aristotle uses to describe the vulgar *aulētai*. Just as there were audience members who enjoyed the spinning *aulētai*, however, there would also have been Athenians who enjoyed Demosthenes' performances. As a result, Aeschines' criticisms and Demosthenes' response attest not only an ethical interpretation of gestures as a rhetorical strategy in the courts but also the challenge facing elite orators who wanted to convince as many Athenians as possible with all the tools at their disposal, including those scorned by other elites.

Aeschines' criticism of Demosthenes' gestures is part of a more general attack on the way he performs in the assembly. Throughout *Against Ktesiphon*, Aeschines mocks Demosthenes' attitude on the *bēma*. During one assembly, Demosthenes comes forward "with much gravity," preparing to extol the imaginary Peloponnesian and Akarnanian forces arrayed against Philip in order to conceal his real purpose, that monies be diverted from the Athenians to Kallias of Khalkis, who Aeschines claims bribed Demosthenes; at another assembly, he leaps up to threaten anyone proposing peace, a subject not even under discussion, to signal to the Thebans that they should give him a share of any money they receive from Philip for making peace themselves; at another, shaking with fear and half-dead after deserting Athens and commandeering a ship to extort money from other Greeks, he begs to be appointed an *eirēnophulax*, or "peace guardian."[71] In these three examples, Aeschines interprets Demosthenes' demeanor before the assembly primarily from an ethical perspective. It reflects the flaws of his character and is never appropriate to what the occasion actually demands.

Aeschines' ethical interpretation of Demosthenes' performances extends to his choice of words. He condemns Demosthenes for using the phrase "not tear the alliance away from the peace" in a speech urging the immediate passage of the Peace of Philokrates. The phrase stuck with Aeschines for sixteen years because "of the unpleasantness of the speaker and of the word coinciding."[72] He specifically objects to *aporrhēxai* (from *aporrhēgnumi*, "tear away"), which appears nowhere else in the surviving corpus of Attic oratory.[73] This is one of the earliest examples of stylistic criticism of oratorical language, and Aeschines links it with an ethical judgment. By judging both Demosthenes' character and his language "unpleasant," he implies that inappropriate expressions correlate to a bad character.

Aeschines must have expected that his stylistic judgment would strengthen his case against Demosthenes, since he employs it in the middle of an argument he admits some jurors will find "rather implausible,"[74] that Demosthenes and Philokrates had been bribed by Philip to convince the assembly to accept peace and an alliance on Philip's terms. Therefore, regardless of whether Demosthenes actually said "not tear the alliance away from the peace,"[75] Aeschines must have expected some, if not most, of his audience to share his condemnation of the phrase and to link Demosthenes' bad prose style with his bad character. He also relies on the power of suggestion. By claiming that Demosthenes used an inappropriate expression, he presents himself as an authoritative arbiter of propriety. Any juror who finds nothing objectionable in *aporrhēxai* or in other aspects of Demosthenes' performances now has to reconsider his own judgments. Part of Aeschines' strategy is to shame these jurors into agreeing with him, convincing them to suppress their own opinions of Demosthenes' style as ill informed and indicative of their own inadequate sense of propriety.[76]

Aeschines' discussion of gestures continues the same rhetorical strategy he employed in his criticism of *aporrhēxai*. When Demosthenes does not come forward to defend his policies, even though Aeschines disingenuously invites him to the *bēma*, Aeschines both imitates Demosthenes' metaphors, which he calls "marvels," and mocks his gestures, claiming that Demosthenes spun himself around on the *bēma* as though he were attacking Alexander while taking credit for inciting the revolts against the Macedonians in the Peloponnesus and in Northern Greece. Aeschines says:

καὶ πάλιν ὅτε κύκλῳ περιδινῶν σεαυτὸν ἐπὶ τοῦ βήματος ἔλεγες, ὡς ἀντιπράττων Ἀλεξάνδρῳ. (Aeschin. 3.167)

And again when you whirled yourself around in a circle on the *bēma* while you were speaking, as though you were moving against Alexander.

Aeschines' criticism of these gestures functions on two overlapping levels. First, he offers a straightforward ethical interpretation: like the solemn manner Demosthenes uses to conceal his bribe taking, his warlike motions hide his cowardly character. After describing the gestures and quoting Demosthenes' claims to have incited the revolts, Aeschines maintains that Demosthenes would never have led a village to revolt or even attacked a house if he knew there was danger inside. He is always on the lookout for money, but he never does "a man's work."[77] Jurors who accept Aeschines' depiction of Demosthenes' character, then, will find his gestures deceitful, indicative of Demosthenes' desire to conceal the truth from his audiences. Second, Aeschines also offers an implicit stylistic critique that reinforces his ethical interpretation. By placing his description of gestures immediately after his analysis of Demosthenes' metaphors, he is encouraging the jurors to interpret the gestures on a stylistic level. Just like the metaphors of vineyard work, butchery, and sewing that Aeschines mockingly quotes, spinning around and feigning military maneuvers are inappropriate for a speaker in the assembly. As Aeschines has already noted in his discussion of *aporrhēxai*, an "unpleasant" style correlates to an "unpleasant" character.

Furthermore, the movements Aeschines attributes to Demosthenes resemble the gestures of the vulgar *aulētai* whom Aristotle accuses of spinning themselves around and making violent motions.[78] Although Aeschines uses different verbs from Aristotle (*peridineō* instead of Aristotle's *kuliō*; *antiprattō* instead of Aristotle's *helkō*), the connotations of spinning and attacking are present in both descriptions. It is likely, therefore, that Aeschines is drawing on elite notions of gestural impropriety to attack Demosthenes. If Plutarch is correct that "the crowd considered Demosthenes' performances marvelous, but the men of taste, among whom was Demetrios of Phaleron, believed his artificial manner [*to plasma*] to be low, ignoble and effeminate," Aeschines would be exploiting a widespread prejudice against Demosthenes among the elite.[79] This conclusion is strengthened when we consider that Demosthenes characterizes the gestures that Aeschines likened to violent military motions as mere hand waves.[80] Clearly, something is at stake in the description of the gestures beyond an accurate description of what really happened. In Aeschines' telling, Demosthenes' gestures have become a symbolic representation of Demosthenes' tendency to act in an inappropriate manner. Like his "unpleasant" and "marvel"-like metaphors, Aeschines presents them as indicating flaws in Demosthenes' character. They also signal Demosthenes' lower social status to members of the audience sensitive to the social connotations of gesture and predisposed to agree with the opinion Plutarch ascribes to Demetrios. Recognizing that Aeschines' interpretation of his gestures poses a risk, Demosthenes tries to recover control of their meaning by insisting they were simple, natural motions of the hands and did not include spinning or attacking motions.

Whose account of Demosthenes' gestures is likely to be more correct? Probably not Demosthenes'. If his gestures were not known to be out of the ordinary, Aeschines could never have hoped to succeed in caricaturing them as he does. Significantly, he describes Demosthenes' awe-inspiring gestures as "usual," in *On the Dishonest Embassy*,[81] adding support to the conclusion that Demosthenes was known for gestures that other orators did not employ. Noteworthy gestures would also have had a life of their own after a performance had ended. First- and second-hand reports would have exaggerated the original gestures, and soon even witnesses would not have remembered exactly what they had seen. This would have created an atmosphere ripe for caricature and misrepresentation by future opponents. So, there is likely to be some truth at the heart of Aeschines' description of Demosthenes' gestures. Even if he did not really spin around and feign attacking motions, he must have done something more memorable than most speakers in the assembly. He probably adopted a pose and employed gestures that worked with his language to create an authoritative character qualified to advise the Athenians on military issues and to oppose Alexander, the same character he had adopted for himself since he first began to speak against Philip.

Aeschines himself implicitly acknowledges the role of Demosthenes' gestures in reinforcing this character. By accusing Demosthenes of hypocrisy for pairing warlike gestures with false claims of urging the Greeks to revolt against Alexander, he maintains that Demosthenes has designed his entire performance to mislead the Athenians. This criticism indicates the success of Demosthenes' strategy: Aeschines argues that Demosthenes' gestures and his language conceal his true nature, but he cannot claim that they are inconsistent with each other. For anyone who did not share Aeschines' belief in Demosthenes' secret cowardice and venality or maintain elite biases against certain movements, Demosthenes' gestures in the assembly would have seemed fully consistent with the man he claimed to be; they would have enhanced his performance, not undermined it.

In Aeschines' narrative, Demosthenes' gestures have ceased to be part of a consistent performance controlled by Demosthenes and have become a central element of a strategy to discredit him. Demosthenes responds to Aeschines' interpretation not by defending his gestures but by minimizing their importance.[82] In calling his gestures hand waves, Demosthenes may be recognizing that jurors could have been influenced by Aeschines' description if they were undecided about the wisdom of his policies but were inclined to vote against people who they believed had acted inappropriately or whom they considered inferior.

In addition to the jurors at the crown trial, there would also have been a large group of spectators[83] whose opinions would have been important to Demosthenes' and Aeschines' public standing after the trial. The desire to influence political opinion helps to explain why Aeschines published his speech after suffering a complete defeat. The opposing accounts of Demosthenes' gestures, then, are part of a contest for social status simultaneous with the dispute about Demosthenes' record as a politician. Each litigant tries to paint the other as socially inferior: Demosthenes exaggerates Aeschines' lower-class origins and menial jobs,[84] and Aeschines similarly attacks Demosthenes' profession as a speechwriter and his allegedly Skythian mother.[85] Aeschines describes Demosthenes' gestures for a similar end: audience members who recognized the ethical connotations of gesture would recognize the movements he describes as unsuitable for a socially elite Athenian.

Timarkhos' Gestures and the Decline of Oratory

Aeschines may have employed an ethical strategy in his description of Demosthenes' gestures because he had already succeeded in a similar strategy in his speech *Against Timarkhos* (Aeschines 1), where he accuses Timarkhos of having prostituted himself as a youth. Since Aeschines had no evidence that Timarkhos was ever actually a prostitute, he relied on rumors about Timarkhos' reputation and insinuations based on his physical appearance.[86] As part of this strategy, Aeschines describes Timarkhos' performance at a recent meeting of the assembly, and he contrasts his gestures with the staid poses of an earlier generation of orators. For Aeschines, Timarkhos' gestures are emblematic of the decline of Athenian politicians since the mid-fifth century.

Timarkhos' performance in the assembly, Aeschines implies, was a visual manifestation of his dissolute life and unfitness to act as an Athenian citizen. Contrasting him with earlier orators, he says:

ἐκεῖνοι μέν γε ἠσχύνοντο ἔξω τὴν χεῖρα ἔχοντες λέγειν, οὑτοσὶ δὲ οὐ πάλαι, ἀλλὰ πρώην ποτὲ ῥίψας θοἰμάτιον γυμνὸς ἐπαγκρατίαζεν ἐν τῇ ἐκκλησίᾳ, οὕτω κακῶς καὶ αἰσχρῶς διακείμενος τὸ σῶμα ὑπὸ μέθης καὶ βδελυρίας ὥστε τούς γε εὖ φρονοῦντας ἐγκαλύψασθαι, αἰσχυνθέντας ὑπὲρ τῆς πόλεως, εἰ τοιούτοις συμβούλοις χρώμεθα. (Aeschin. 1.26)

> Those men were ashamed [*eiskhunonto*] to hold their hand outside [their cloaks] when they were speaking, while this man here, not a long time ago but one day recently ripped off his cloak [*himation*] and fought a *pankration* naked in the assembly. His body was so wickedly and shamefully dissipated with drink and debauchery that right-thinking men veiled themselves, embarrassed [*aiskhunthentas*] on the city's behalf that we use counselors like him.

Although Timarkhos the naked *pankratistēs* must resemble the real Timarkhos, he is really the product of Aeschines' words acting upon the minds of the jurors, those who had seen Timarkhos' performance, those whom they told about it, and those who never heard about it before. Therefore, Aeschines' description of Timarkhos is not direct evidence for real Athenian gestures or their effects on the audience. Rather, it tells us how Aeschines equated his own version of the visual aspects of Timarkhos' performance with his dissolute life. He creates a Timarkhos whose wild, naked gesticulations contrast both with the modesty of traditional orators and with the modesty of right-thinking citizens. Aeschines frames his description of Timarkhos with two forms of the verb *aiskhunomai* ("feel shame or embarrassment")—*eiskhunonto* and *aiskhunthentas*—and so emphasizes that both groups feel the shame that Timarkhos ought to feel but does not.

Timarkhos' performance must have been memorable; otherwise, Aeschines' *pankration* metaphor would have been inappropriate. Perhaps his *himation* slipped, or, more likely, he flung it off in passion and delivered his appeal clad in only a tunic. In *On the Dishonest Embassy*, spoken at a trial three years after Timarkhos', Demosthenes even acknowledges Timarkhos' *propeteia*. The noun is from *propiptō*, which means "fall or throw oneself forward." Although *propeteia* ("a throwing of oneself forward") is usually used as a metaphor for abstract concepts such as rashness, it preserves a connotation of impetuous physical movement. It seems, therefore, to be Demosthenes' subtle admission that Timarkhos' gestures were unusually energetic.[87] Timarkhos must have calculated that these motions, whatever they were, were likely to hold the audience's attention and convince them to vote for his proposal.[88] Indeed, they may have succeeded. We know neither the content of Timarkhos' proposal nor the outcome of the vote,[89] but Aeschines steadfastly avoids alluding to Timarkhos' political views,[90] perhaps because they were generally popular.

Furthermore, by claiming that Timarkhos' strategy prompted the Athenians to pass a law against disorderly speakers, Aeschines seems tacitly to acknowledge that the gestures he caricatures may have been an effective strategy.[91] Aeschines even says that Timarkhos was one of several men who opposed this law "so they could keep speaking and living as they pleased."[92] The exact terms of the law are unknown, but it seems to have required the presiding tribe to punish speakers, and perhaps their supporters, for disorderly behavior.[93] Regardless of whether Aeschines' allegations are true, the law could plausibly be associated with Timarkhos' performance and Timarkhos could plausibly be said to have opposed it. Since Timarkhos was at least perceived as having an interest in keeping allegedly disorderly performances legal, some, if not all, Athenians must have believed that the performances benefited him. There is no real reason to doubt Aeschines when he says that the commotion caused by these performances stifled debate. This may, however, have been their point. From Timarkhos' perspective, a wild performance that caused such an uproar in the assembly that opposing voices were drowned out or ignored would have been a complete success. At any rate, the Athenians' concern over such performances suggests that the gestural techniques employed by orators like Timarkhos in the assembly would have been effective.

While he criticized Timarkhos' gestures, Aeschines seems to have complemented his words with an unconventional pose of his own. He tells us that he and his contemporaries are all accustomed to speak with their hand outside their *himatia*, while the fifth-century orators Perikles, Themistokles, and Aristeides showed more self-control and kept it tucked in. As proof of this claim, he adduces a statue of Solon on Salamis that shows the lawgiver with his hand inside his cloak.[94] According to Demosthenes, Aeschines imitated Solon's pose and perhaps even wore a felt cap like that of Solon during his speech.[95] Through this rigid, allegedly traditional pose, Aeschines makes himself a visual counterexample to the violent gestures he describes Timarkhos using.[96] Historical accuracy is not Aeschines' concern. Rather, he appeals to a belief common among at least some fourth-century Athenians that the supposed decline in the political leadership of Athens after the death of Perikles coincided with oratorical exuberance.[97]

The scholia to Aeschines call our attention to Kleon having "transgressed gestural custom" in his oratorical performances.[98] The scholia seem to be relying on the same information as the Aristotelian *Constitution of the Athenians*, which associates Kleon's performance style with his ability to corrupt the Athenians:

Περικλέους δὲ τελευτήσαντος τῶν μὲν ἐπιφανῶν προειστήκει Νικίας ὁ ἐν Σικελίᾳ τελευτήσας, τοῦ δὲ δήμου Κλέων ὁ Κλεαινέτου, ὃς δοκεῖ μάλιστα διαφθεῖραι τὸν δῆμον ταῖς ὁρμαῖς, καὶ πρῶτος ἐπὶ τοῦ βήματος ἀνέκραγε καὶ ἐλοιδορήσατο καὶ περιζωσάμενος ἐδημηγόρησε τῶν ἄλλων ἐν κόσμῳ λεγόντων. (*Constitution of the Athenians* 28.3)

After Perikles died, Nikias, who died in Sicily, was the leader of the noteworthy men, but Kleon the son of Kleainetos was the leader of the *dēmos*. It seems that he especially corrupted the *dēmos* by his impulsive movements, and he was the first one who screeched and shouted abuse upon the *bēma*. He rolled up his cloak while he spoke to the *dēmos*, even though other men used to speak in an orderly fashion.

The author of the *Constitution of the Athenians* shares the opinion of performance styles espoused by Aristotle himself in the *Poetics*. There, as we saw, Aristotle concludes that actors who use the gestures of inferior people indulge in an inferior form of mimesis. He associates this type of acting with the generation of actors who were prominent in the 420s and 410s, explicitly contrasting Kallippides with the older actor Mynniskos. Here, the author of the *Constitution* finds a similar decline in the quality of public speakers in the 420s, again exemplified by a change in performance style.

Aeschines does not grant Timarkhos Kleon's rhetorical power. Like Kleon, however, Timarkhos differs from the good advisers that Athens used to have; both Aeschines and the author of the *Constitution of the Athenians* pointedly mention Perikles. In this account, the principle distinction between orators like Kleon and Timarkhos and the orators of the past is not their policies but their performance styles. The criticism of Kleon's hitched-up cloak may reflect the same attitude that underlies Aeschines' criticism of Timarkhos' alleged nudity. Furthermore, Kleon's "impulsive movements" may refer to his gestures: the description of Kleon in Plutarch's *Life of Nikias*, which echoes the vocabulary of this passage, claims that he used to strike his thigh and run around while he spoke, as I have already noted.[99] For Aeschines, Timarkhos and, by extension, his *sunēgoros* Demosthenes are the culmination of the decline in oratory and in political leadership that began with Kleon. Through his own pose, Aeschines associates himself not only with Solon and Perikles' performance styles but also implicitly with their reputation as ideal citizens.[100]

Through this unusually restrained pose and lack of gestures, however, Aeschines opens himself up to the same kind of physiognomic attack that he brought against Timarkhos. Three years after Timarkhos' trial, Demosthenes rebutted Aeschines' analysis of Solon's statue in *On the Dishonest Embassy* (Demosthenes 19), a prosecution speech against Aeschines for taking bribes from Philip.[101] He maintains that the statue shows Solon reciting a poem, not a speech, and, more importantly, was sculpted nearly 200 years after Solon's death.[102] The excursus on the statue is not intended simply to make Aeschines look ignorant. Just as Aeschines used Timarkhos' gestures to reveal his dissolute character, Demosthenes uses Aeschines' covered hand to reveal his inner corruption. He seizes on the Solon story and Aeschines' pose primarily because of their relevance to the bribery charge: Aeschines urged orators to keep their hands inside their cloaks while his own hand was extended for bribes.[103]

The gestures of Aeschines and Timarkhos seem to have succeeded in impressing themselves on the memory of their audiences and entering into the common knowledge of the Athenians. Since both men were prominent politicians, this is not surprising. Ultimately, the gestures' very effectiveness made them a liability. As I have shown, however, we should not consider them only from the biased perspective of their opponents. What Aeschines terms Timarkhos' naked *pankration* may have been a calculated, and perhaps successful, way to persuade the assembly to approve a proposal. Another speaker who had no past history of alleged male prostitution and no reputation for dissolute living may have been able to make similar gestures without fear. Kleon's hitched-up cloak and forceful movements, for instance, may have been criticized by opponents but seem neither to have undermined his policies nor to have ended his career. Similarly, Aeschines' imitation of Solon may have been a successful way to convince at least some of the jurors to contrast his old-fashioned moderation and good sense with Timarkhos' lack of self-control. Anyone could have sailed to Salamis to verify Aeschines' interpretation of the statue, but Demosthenes' need to claim that he had done so three years later in *On the Dishonest Embassy* suggests that the imitation was a success that the Athenians were still talking about.

Since Aeschines won his trial against Timarkhos and was acquitted in the trial when Demosthenes discussed his imitation of Solon, albeit by a thirty-vote margin, the imitation cannot be said to have hurt him more than it helped him.[104]

CONCLUSIONS

In the *Orator*, Cicero writes, "The prudence of listeners has always been a check on the eloquence of speakers. For all who wish to win approval pay attention to what their audiences want, and they mold and fit themselves entirely to that and to their judgment and assent."[105] This principle would have guided most litigants' use of gestures in the Athenian courts, where the traditional gestures of formal speech would have irritated no one by their presence but would have excited remark by their absence. We have no way of knowing how often unorthodox gestures hurt litigants' cases, but, like allusions, word choice, and almost any rhetorical choice an orator makes, gestures have connotations and meanings that may lead the audience to the opposite of the intended conclusion.[106]

The effect of gestures is not limited to the people who actually see them being performed, since later audiences could hear them described and caricatured as parts of physiognomic arguments. Aeschines tried to present gestures that Demosthenes and Timarkhos may have used effectively in the assembly as signs of moral corruption in their trials, partly by taking advantage of elite notions of gestural propriety and concerns about the declining quality of Athenian politicians. Speakers, therefore, faced a difficult choice when deciding what gestures to use, since even effective gestures that were molded to the expectations of one audience could open a speaker to criticism before another audience.

The potentially harmful effects of unusual or inappropriate gestures should not lead us to conclude that all such gestures were risky. On the contrary, well-placed gestures could have helped make the difference between a successful performance and a failure, and well-prepared orators would know when to use the traditional gestures of formal speech and when to risk breaking out of appropriate and usual patterns to encourage their audience to accept their arguments or proposals. When we read Attic oratory today, we need to remember that arguments that seem facile or weak tell only part of the story.[107] Gestures would have been a fundamental, and sometimes contentious, aspect of persuasion.

PART TWO

THE LANGUAGE OF DEMONSTRATION AND VISIBILITY

THREE

SHOWING AND SEEING

The Procedural Terminology of Witnessing

In Athenian law, eyewitness testimony was the premier method of ascertaining facts. The Athenians and other Greeks used words referring to demonstration and visibility to characterize a range of procedures associated with securing the testimony of eyewitnesses. This semantic pattern is consistent among a variety of procedures, ranging from simple demonstrations of evidence, to revelations of contraband, to displays of legitimate children.[1]

INTRODUCTION: THE LANGUAGE OF WITNESSING IN AESCHYLUS' *LIBATION BEARERS*

After Orestes kills Aegisthus and Clytemnestra in Aeschylus' *Libation Bearers*, he displays their dead bodies to the chorus and to the audience. He twice commands them "Look!": first at the two corpses and second at the robe they used to trap Agamemnon before they killed him. He focuses on this robe, calling it a bond, a fetter, a hateful object, a lure, a shroud, a net, a snare, something to trip up the feet, a trick.[2] He pauses during his search for the right word, and he commands his servants to spread the robe out. Orestes says:

ἐκτείνατ' αὐτὸ καὶ κύκλῳ παραστάδον
στέγαστρον ἀνδρὸς δείξαθ', ὡς ἴδῃ πατήρ,
οὐχ οὑμός, ἀλλ' ὁ πάντ' ἐποπτεύων τάδε
Ἥλιος, ἄναγνα μητρὸς ἔργα τῆς ἐμῆς,[3]
ὡς ἂν παρῇ μοι μάρτυς ἐν δίκῃ ποτὲ
ὡς τόνδ' ἐγὼ μετῆλθον ἐνδίκως φόνον
τὸν μητρός. (983–989)

> Stretch out and display [*deixat(e)*] this covering for a man, standing nearby in a circle, so that my father, not my own, but Helios, the one who observes all these things from on high, may see [*idēi*] the unholy deeds of my mother, so that whenever my trial happens he may be present for me as a witness [*martus*] that I justly sought this murder of my mother.

The robe proves that Clytemnestra plotted to trap and kill Agamemnon in his bath, entangling him so that he could not resist. Still stained with Agamemnon's blood,[4] it is the best, and in fact the only, physical evidence that justifies Orestes' revenge. Realizing this, he calls it to the attention of Helios, hoping Helios can testify for him at his trial. Orestes prioritizes demonstration and sight. He orders his servants to "display" the robe so that Helios can "see" it. Merely hearing his words is insufficient; real knowledge comes with visual observation, and this is the kind of knowledge a witness needs in court. Indeed, the robe is visual evidence not just for Helios but also for the chorus and the audience. Orestes calls the chorus "hearers of these evils" right before he commands them to display the robe,[5] linking what they hear with the evidence they can see.

Helios sees everything, at least during the day, and his omniscience, like all the gods', should ensure that the just are rewarded and the unjust are punished without any prompting from Orestes. Orestes, however, speaks like an Athenian citizen worried about securing witnesses for his trial and not like someone willing to endure sufferings while he waits for the all-seeing gods to reward him. He is neither the first nor the last litigant to pin his hopes on witness testimony.

In one of the earliest accounts of a Greek trial, Hermes' parodic trial before Zeus for cattle rustling in the *Homeric Hymn to Hermes*, Apollo's argument depends on the witness who saw Hermes leading the cows away.[6] In fifth- and fourth-century Athens nearly every litigant seems to have called witnesses to support his version of events. Even the dog Labes in Aristophanes' *Wasps* relies on the cheese-grater to testify that he grated the cheese, which he is alleged to have stolen, for the soldiers.[7] Orestes' attempt to secure witnesses is unique, however, because it is the earliest literary example of the vocabulary of demonstrating in the language of witness testimony. There is a causal chain from Orestes' displaying the robe to Helios, to Helios' sight of it, and finally to Helios' status as a witness. Justice still depends on sight, but it is no longer the all-seeing sight of omnipotent gods. Rather it is the sight of witnesses who cooperate with litigants to prove that their actions are justifiable.

Although the usual Attic word for a witness, *martus*, is not related to words that mean "see,"[8] the semitechnical language of Athenian legal procedure strongly associates witness testimony with seeing and showing through what I call the vocabulary of demonstration and visibility. By the vocabulary of demonstration, I refer primarily to the verb *deiknumi* and its compounds *epideiknumi*, *apodeiknumi*, and *endeiknumi*. Although these words can have variations in meaning that I will address later, they share a core meaning of "demonstrate," "display," or "point out." Orestes employs this vocabulary of demonstration when he tells the chorus to "display" the robe, using *deixat(e)*, an aorist imperative of *deiknumi*. By the vocabulary of visibility, I refer primarily to the passive verb *phainomai* ("become visible," "be evident," or "appear"), the active verb *phainō* ("make visible, "make evident," or "illuminate"), and the adjective *phaneros* ("visible," "evident," or "apparent"). This vocabulary of demonstration and visibility is used in parallel ways in a broad assortment of legal contexts that involve witnesses. The active verbs refer to visual demonstrations before witnesses, and the adjective and passive verbs refer to things or people that have already been demonstrated and so are known to witnesses.

In this chapter and chapter 4, I will establish the legal connotations of the vocabulary of demonstration and visibility and then show how speakers in court employed the same vocabulary to present their speeches as authoritative sources of information parallel to actual visual demonstrations. Since no special knowledge would have been needed to understand these terms, they are not true legal jargon. Instead, they are semitechnical terms of legal procedure. The semantic pattern of demonstrating and appearing, of making visible and being visible, remains constant across a wide variety of scenarios that require witnesses, including cases in which witnesses are used to prove or disprove criminal conduct, the ownership of property, and the legitimacy of children. The language of demonstration and visibility forms a link among all of these procedures. When the Athenians needed to talk about anything that depended upon witness knowledge, they tended to do so in a uniform way.

To make this uniformity clear in English throughout this chapter and the next one, I render *deiknumi* and its compounds with "demonstrate" and *phaneros* and *phainomai* with "visible" and "become visible" whenever it results in idiomatic English translations. Since strict one-to-one correspondence could be awkward or misleading, however, I also use words such as "point out," "illuminate," and "reveal." Sometimes, I even use different English words to translate the same Greek word. For instance, depending on the context, I use "visible" and "evident" as translations of *phaneros* and "be visible" and "be evident" as translations of *phainomai*. In situations where *phainomai* and *phaneros* indicate manifest certainty rather than actual sight, I prefer "evident" to "visible."[9] To avoid confusion, I always provide transliterations of the key Greek terms in my translations, and I refer to the transliterated word in my discussion if a reference to the translation alone might be ambiguous. The variety of English equivalents for the words I discuss points to a central feature of my argument. The Athenians employed a small group of related words to refer to procedural actions that English distinguishes with a broader range of vocabulary.

WITNESSES AND TRUTH IN ATHENIAN LAW AND LEGAL DISCOURSE

Places, people, objects, and events that have been pointed out to witnesses and seen by them were the foundation of Athenian judicial knowledge. Indeed, Athenians relied on witnesses to establish the truth about what happened in the past. They took care to have witnesses for anything that might later be contested, including weddings, confrontations with opponents, summonses, challenges, statements before opponents, wills, paternity acknowledgements, and financial transactions.[10] When an Athenian was the victim of an unexpected assault, the first thing he did was call for support from witnesses who had observed it.[11] Into the late fourth century, witness testimony was more important even than written contracts.[12] It was particularly important in proving citizenship.[13]

Witness testimony was central in forensic arguments. Stephen Todd calculates that in the entire corpus of forensic oratory, there are 6.1 appeals to witnesses for every 100 paragraphs.[14] The frequency and type of witnesses vary among authors and types of speech.[15] Although individual speeches may lack witnesses, there does not seem to have been a type of speech that dispensed with them as a general rule. All scholars acknowledge the importance of witnesses in litigation, but there is still debate about what their purpose was. Sally Humphreys influentially argued that witnesses showed the jurors that a litigant enjoyed the support of prominent members of his social milieu, maintaining that who a witness was was much more important than what he said.[16] Until recently, this was taken to be the dominant model of witnessing in Athens. David Mirhady and Lene Rubinstein have shown, however, that witnesses' identities cannot be separated from their testimony; who they were seems to have depended on whether they knew information that would support the speakers.[17] Hence, disputes about family matters would require relatives to give testimony, not to show the approval of the family but because they knew the relevant information.[18]

No one, of course, would deny that witnesses were partisan. Speakers had to summon their own witnesses and convince them to testify for them. A witness' testimony was limited to a formulaic declaration either that a speaker's statement was true or that he had no knowledge of it. A witness would declare that he knew (*eidenai*) or was present at (*pareinai, paragenesthai*) whatever the speaker had declared to have occurred, but he would not recount it in his own words.[19] There was no cross-examination by the opponent.[20] The fundamental role of an Athenian witness, then, was to acknowledge facts rather than to present facts. There can be little doubt that a statement unsupported by witnesses was open to serious doubt. In *Clouds*, Strepsiades says that he would hang himself if he had no witnesses in a lawsuit. Similarly, Hippolytos fails to defend himself before Theseus because he has no witnesses.[21]

A speaker's statement was only as plausible as the witness who supported it. Both the author of the *Rhetoric for Alexander* and Aristotle suggest ways to bolster the credibility of supporting witnesses and to impugn the credibility of opposing witnesses.[22] False witnesses were enough of a problem that there was a special procedure, the *dikē pseudomarturiōn*, to prosecute them. Furthermore, even well-intentioned witnesses could be mistaken. As Thucydides recognizes, people who were present at the same event tend to describe it in different ways because of bias or selective memory.[23] Although Thucydides does not use the language of sight, his emphasis on presence recalls the language of forensic witness testimony. Similarly, a fragment of the rhetorical handbook attributed to Antiphon notes that the memory of witnesses can fail them.[24] Excessive reliance on witnesses, therefore, could lead to a false conclusion. As the *Oedipus Tyrannos* demonstrates, the Athenians were acutely aware of this.[25]

Despite all the potential pitfalls of relying on witnesses, litigants regularly assert that witness testimony makes a statement "true."[26] Antiphon's speech *On the Chorus Boy* (Antiphon 6) contains a particularly clear example:

καὶ εἰ μὲν πάνυ μὴ παρεγένοντο μάρτυρες, ἐγὼ δὲ παρειχόμην, ἢ
τοὺς παραγενομένους μὴ παρειχόμην, ἑτέρους δέ τινας, εἰκότως
ἂν οἱ τούτων λόγοι πιστότεροι ἦσαν τῶν ἐμῶν μαρτύρων· ὅπου
δὲ μάρτυράς τε ὁμολογοῦσι παραγενέσθαι, καὶ ἐγὼ τοὺς παραγενομένους παρέχομαι, <καὶ> εὐθὺς ἀπὸ τῆς πρώτης ἡμέρας
καὶ αὐτὸς ἐγὼ καὶ οἱ μάρτυρες ἅπαντες φανεροί ἐσμεν λέγοντες
ἅπερ νυνὶ πρὸς ὑμᾶς, πόθεν χρή, ὦ ἄνδρες, ἢ τἀληθῆ πιστὰ ἢ τὰ
μὴ ἀληθῆ ἄπιστα ποιεῖν ἄλλοθεν ἢ ἐκ τῶν τοιούτων; (Ant. 6.29)

If no witnesses at all had been present [*paregenonto*] and I were introducing them, or if I were not introducing the ones who had been present [*paragenomenous*] but some others, then it would be reasonable to
conclude that these men's words are more credible than my witnesses.
But since they agree that witnesses were present [*paragenesthai*], and
I am introducing those who were present [*paragenomenous*], and since
it's evident that from the very first day both I and all the witnesses
have been saying the same things we're saying to you now, how else,
gentlemen of the jury, if not from such things as these, can I make
true things trustworthy and false things untrustworthy?

The argument, of course, is polemical and probably misleading: the witness testimony could be true but nonetheless irrelevant. The passage,
however, shows the strong rhetorical connection between presence, witnesses, and truth. Things that are supported by the testimony of witnesses who were present are equated with things that are true, and they
are said to be the best basis for making just decisions. The emphasis on
witnesses being reliable because they were present extends throughout
the entire tradition of forensic oratory. In *Against Neaira* (Demosthenes
59), which postdates *On the Chorus Boy* by seventy or eighty years, Apollodoros calls witnesses to testify that Neaira got drunk and slept with
multiple men, including slaves, at a wild drinking party in honor of a
victory at the Pythian Games. He says, "And, to prove that I am speaking the truth, I will introduce to you witnesses who saw what happened
[*horōntas*] and who were present [*parontas*]."[27] Once again, we see the
strong rhetorical connection between witnesses and truth, as well as explicit references to the presence of witnesses who saw what happened.

It is not surprising that litigants would insist on the connection between witnesses and truth. One modern study has shown that jurors
tend to believe witnesses around eighty percent of the time, even when
those witnesses are wrong.[28] The American court system is only today

developing adequate safeguards against jurors' tendency to place excessive faith in witness testimony,[29] despite the attention that has been brought to the high frequency of false convictions based on misidentification by witnesses from at least the time of Sacco and Vanzetti.[30] In the Athenian courts, which lacked any real safeguards against jurors believing mistaken witnesses other than the threat of a *dikē pseudomarturiōn*, the number of witnesses and the consistency of their testimony must have directly correlated to the plausibility of a narrative, just as Antiphon's speaker says.

The significance of visual demonstration in Athenian legal discourse should not surprise us either. It is a commonplace of Greek thought that seeing is more trustworthy than hearing. Heraclitus is the first to say explicitly that "the eyes are more accurate witnesses than the ears," a statement echoed by Herodotus' Kandaules.[31] The misleading nature of speech is already explicit in Hesiod, whose Muses "know how to speak many false things as though they are true."[32] In Classical Athens, orators often paradoxically insist on the unreliability of language, or *logos*, their own special skill. The speakers in Thucydides, for instance, often say that it is foolish to listen to words instead of considering deeds,[33] and for Gorgias, *logos* is a great ruler and acts like a drug on its listeners, easily misleading them.[34] The Athenian courts raised this trust in eyewitnesses to the level of a rule, prohibiting hearsay evidence except in rare cases.[35]

The speaker of *On the Murder of Eratosthenes* (Lysias 1), who insists that his murder of his wife's lover was justifiable homicide, exploits the Athenian preference for witness testimony and distrust of hearsay evidence. He quotes the instructions he gave to his wife's servant when he was investigating the adultery, using the vocabulary of demonstration and visibility to contrast visual evidence with mere hearsay. The speaker claims to have said:

ἀξιῶ δέ σε ἐπ' αὐτοφώρῳ ταῦτά μοι ἐπιδεῖξαι· ἐγὼ γὰρ οὐδὲν δέομαι λόγων, ἀλλὰ τὸ ἔργον φανερὸν γενέσθαι, εἴπερ οὕτως ἔχει. (Lys. 1.21)

I demand that you demonstrate [*epideixai*] this affair to me manifestly.[36] I don't ask for words [*logōn*], but that the deed [*ergon*] be visible [*phaneron*], if it's really going on.

Quoting this command to the maid is a shrewd rhetorical ploy. The speaker presents himself as a typical Athenian who has no patience with rumors and trusts only what he can see with his own eyes. He later recounts how he found Eratosthenes in bed with his wife and declared, "I won't kill you, the law of the *polis* will."[37] The alleged reliance on visual evidence adds plausibility to the sensational claim that the speaker was merely a tool of the law and not a cold-blooded killer obsessed with revenge. The speaker's use of "demonstrate" (*epideixai*) and "visible" (*phaneron*) underscores the care he claims to have taken to secure his evidence.[38] The vocabulary and the narrative together portray the speaker of *On the Murder of Eratosthenes* as a responsible Athenian searching for and eventually acting in accord with visual evidence.

THE VOCABULARY OF DEMONSTRATION

As I have shown, the Athenians took care to secure witness support for anything that might be contested at a later time. The act of showing something to a witness, therefore, was a special kind of demonstration because it established a relationship between the witness and the event or object in question. The witness not only had seen it but was expected to attest it later on. To refer to these special demonstrations, the Athenians tended to use two verbs, *deiknumi* and its compound *epideiknumi*.

The speech *Against Euergos and Mnesiboulos* (Demosthenes 47), transmitted with the works of Demosthenes but probably written by Apollodoros, attests this use of *epideiknumi*. The speaker alleges that Euergos and his friend Theophemos mortally assaulted one of his servants while they were attempting to seize his property for payment of a debt. He explains that after he called a physician, he summoned two different sets of witnesses and showed them his dying servant. In both cases, the verb for the showing is *epideiknumi*. He says:

ἐγὼ αὐτὸς εἰσήγαγον ἰατρὸν ᾧ πολλὰ ἔτη ἐχρώμην, ὃς ἐθεράπευεν αὐτὴν ἀρρωστοῦσαν, καὶ ἐπέδειξα ὡς εἶχεν, εἰσαγαγὼν μάρτυρας. ἀκούσας δὲ τοῦ ἰατροῦ ὅτι οὐδὲν ἔτι εἴη ἡ ἄνθρωπος, πάλιν ἑτέρους μάρτυρας παραλαβὼν τήν τε ἄνθρωπον ἐπέδειξα ὡς εἶχεν, καὶ ἐπήγγειλα τούτοις θεραπεύειν. (Dem. 47.67)

I myself summoned a doctor whom I had used for many years, who cared for her while she was sick, and, summoning witnesses, I demonstrated [*epedeixa*] the condition she was in. Hearing from the doctor that the woman was still unresponsive, I again got hold of other witnesses and demonstrated [*epedeixa*] the condition she was in, and I charged my opponents to care for her.

Epideiknumi has the same function in *On the Estate of Philoktemon* (Isaeus 6), where the speaker tries to establish that his opponents concealed the death of his grandfather Euktemon from the rest of the family so that they could steal his furniture. The speaker explains that after his friends finally forced their way into the house they showed Euktemon's two-day old corpse and the empty rooms to witnesses. Once again, the verb for the demonstration is *epideiknumi*. "They immediately demonstrated [*epedeiknusan*] the conditions inside the house to the people who had followed them," he says.[39] Soon afterwards, the speakers of both speeches support their accounts by introducing the witness' depositions.

Like *epideiknumi*, the uncompounded verb *deiknumi* can also be used for a demonstration to witnesses. Orestes uses it in this way in the *Libation Bearers*, and so does the speaker of *Against Phainippos* (Demosthenes 42). He tells the jurors how he walked around Phainippos' property with witnesses to ascertain whether there were any stones recording mortgages on his estate. When they found none, he says, "I demonstrated [*edeixa*] that there was not a single mortgage stone upon his property, and I called them to witness this before Phainippos."[40] Then, he challenges Phainippos to demonstrate (*deixai*) any mortgage stones they may have overlooked to prevent debts from coming to light in the future.[41]

So far in this section, I have established that *epideiknumi* and, less frequently, *deiknumi*, are used to bring something to the attention of a witness so that he can attest to it in the future. Now, I turn to another example of the vocabulary of demonstration, *endeiknumi*, which means "point out" or "indicate" and which has a similar role in Athenian legal discourse. Individuals use it when they call witnesses' attention to people engaged in criminal activity, usually as part of the legal procedure known as an *endeixis*. *Endeixis* ("a pointing") is the noun equivalent of *endeiknumi*. Through this pointing procedure, an individual could denounce someone engaged in criminal activity to a magistrate.[42] Despite the visual connotation of the term, an *endeixis* could be a verbal or written denunciation brought against someone who was not present.[43] There is ample evidence, however, for the use of *endeiknumi* and its variant *endeiknuō* to point out someone who was visible.

Andocides' speech *On His Return* (Andocides 2) provides a good example. In this speech, Andocides describes his arrest by the Four Hundred for providing supplies to the democratic navy and the hearing that followed it before the *boulē*. He quotes the words Peisandros used when he pointed him out to the *boulē*: "*Bouleutai*, I point out [*endeiknuō*] to you this man [*touton*] who has imported grain and oars for our enemies."[44] There is no question that this was a visual demonstration, since Andocides notes that Peisandros was standing next to him and uses the deictic pronoun *touton*. In Aristophanes' *Knights*, the Paphlagonian brings a mock *endeixis* against the Sausage Seller and uses similar wording, complete with an emphatic deictic pronoun: "I point out [(*e*)*ndeiknumi*] this man here [*toutoni*]."[45] When the Sausage Seller retorts with an *endeixis* of his own, he says: "And, by Zeus, I this man [*touton*]."[46] The Sausage Seller's omission of the verb is characteristic of the syncopated syntax of stichomythia, but the deictic pronoun on its own is sufficient to show that the procedure involves a visual demonstration of the criminal.

Athenian legal terminology is notoriously fluid, and it is possible that procedural terms could be used in nontechnical ways without causing confusion. These examples of the visual use of *endeiknumi* may therefore not have been technical instances of the *endeixis* procedure, especially Andocides', which took place after his arrest and in front of the oligarchic *boulē*. Nonetheless, they demonstrate how the verb was used in actual situations; Andocides' credibility and Aristophanes' jokes rely on their audiences finding their use of *endeiknumi*/*endeiknuō* plausible. A visual demonstration was therefore a central feature in the Athenian quest for justice. By saying *endeiknumi*, the prosecutor demands that other people observe a criminal and so makes his status as a criminal a matter of public knowledge. The effect of saying *endeiknumi* was not unlike a modern mugshot. It was a way of broadcasting someone's status and therefore granting legitimacy to the prosecutor's allegation: in Athens, you were not really a criminal until other people saw you as a criminal.

This use of *endeiknumi* parallels the use of *epideiknumi* that I considered above, which is why I refer to them both as part of the vocabulary of demonstration. With *epideiknumi*, prospective litigants call witnesses' attention to something that they will have to testify to later. With *endeiknumi*, prospective prosecutors call magistrates' attention to a criminal. In both cases, the visual demonstration grants special legal significance to the person or thing that is seen. The beaten maid in *Against Euergos and Mnesiboulos* is no longer just a victim to be pitied and cared for but evidence to be remembered and testified to. Similarly, Andocides is no longer just a person, but a criminal to be punished.

For the Athenians, then, the vocabulary of demonstration was a prominent element of the procedural quest for justice. Although we are best informed about the Athenian legal system, we have reason to believe that similar uses of the vocabulary of demonstration were common throughout Greece. Cretan inscriptions, including the Law Code of Gortyn, use *deiknumi* and *apodeiknumi* to refer to a demonstration before witnesses.[47] Similarly, an inscription from the third century BCE found at Larisa uses *epideiknumi* for pointing out disputed land to arbitrators.[48] The central role played by *deiknumi* and its compounds in determining justice may even be reflected in the word for justice itself, since *dikē* also comes from the Proto-Indo-European root **deik-*.[49]

THE VOCABULARY OF VISIBILITY

In the passage from *On the Murder of Eratosthenes* discussed above, I translated the adjective *phaneron* as "visible" to stress the contrast with hearsay and to highlight its close connection to the visual demonstration referred to by *epideixai*. When *phaneros* is used as a semitechnical term in Athenian legal language, it often has this connotation, especially when it refers to events that happen in public and are seen by witnesses. Passages in Plato's *Laws* and in Antiphon's first tetralogy (Antiphon 2) clearly demonstrate this. In the section in the *Laws* on laws of sale, Plato's Athenian explains that anyone who has "become visible" (*phaneros genomenos*) selling counterfeit goods must be deprived of his merchandise and beaten. In this context, *phaneros* clearly means that the merchant's crime has been seen by witnesses, since those who are present and know what is going on are directed to convict him.[50]

The same phrase, "become visible," appears in Antiphon's first tetralogy. The defendant explains the thought process that would have kept him from assaulting and murdering his enemy, focusing on the negative consequences of the two possible outcomes: "For if I had become visible [*phaneros genomenos*] as a consequence of the deed itself, I was finished, and if I had escaped notice [*lathōn*] I clearly recognized that suspicion would be against me."[51] The two words *phaneros* and *lathōn* frame the options in visual terms: the defendant is either seen committing the crime or he escapes without anyone noticing him. The contrast with "escaping notice" also suggests that the phrase "become visible as a consequence of the deed itself" implies "caught in the act."[52] Similarly, when the speaker of *Against Theomnestos* (Lysias 10) uses a form of *phaneros* to gloss an archaic word in a law that seems to be about prostitutes parading themselves in public, he is relying on an audience that will understand *phaneros* to mean "visible."[53]

The speaker of *On the Chorus Boy* (Antiphon 6) takes advantage of this meaning of *phaneros* to argue that the homicide case against him is frivolous because his opponents had never tried to prevent him from acting as a member of the *boulē* and as one of its administrators, called a *prutanis*, for the period when his tribe was allotted this role, called a *prutaneia*. He maintains that they would never have let him perform such a prominent civic and religious function if they really suspected him of homicide. He says:

> οὗτοι δ' ἐπιστάμενοι μὲν τοὺς νόμους ἅπαντας, ὁρῶντες δ' ἐμὲ βουλεύοντα καὶ εἰσιόντ' εἰς τὸ βουλευτήριον—καὶ ἐν αὐτῷ τῷ βουλευτηρίῳ Διὸς Βουλαίου καὶ Ἀθηνᾶς Βουλαίας ἱερόν ἐστι, καὶ εἰσιόντες οἱ βουλευταὶ προσεύχονται, ὧν κἀγὼ εἷς ἦν, ὁ ταῦτα πράττων, καὶ εἰς τἆλλα ἱερὰ πάντα εἰσιὼν μετὰ τῆς βουλῆς, καὶ θύων καὶ εὐχόμενος ὑπὲρ τῆς πόλεως ταύτης, καὶ πρὸς τούτοις πρυτανεύσας τὴν πρώτην πρυτανείαν ἅπασαν πλὴν δυοῖν ἡμέραιν, καὶ ἱεροποιῶν καὶ θύων ὑπὲρ τῆς δημοκρατίας, καὶ ἐπιψηφίζων καὶ λέγων γνώμας περὶ τῶν μεγίστων καὶ πλείστου ἀξίων τῇ πόλει <u>φανερὸς</u> ἦν. (Ant. 6.45)

> These are the men who know all the laws and who have seen [*horōntes*] me acting as a *bouleutēs* and going into the *bouleutērion*—and in that very *bouleutērion* there is a shrine of Zeus of the *boulē* and of Athena of the *boulē*, and the *bouleutai* pray to it when they enter, and I was one of them, the one doing these things, and I was also going to all the other shrines with the *boulē*, both sacrificing and praying on behalf of this *polis*, and, in addition, I served as a *prutanis* for the entire first *prutaneia* except for two days, both overseeing the rites and sacrificing on behalf of the democracy, and also putting proposals to the vote and speaking my opinions about matters that were most significant and worthy of the most attention by the *polis*, and I was visible [*phaneros*] when I was doing all of this.

The speaker is emphatic about his opponents' knowledge of his activities, and so he not only catalogues all the things he did as a *bouleutēs*, he also refers pleonastically to his opponents' active seeing (*horōntes*) and his passive visibility (*phaneros*).⁵⁴ He maintains that all of his activity was public and known to witnesses, including his opponents, and they could have objected to it at any time.

In other speeches, speakers closely link the vocabulary of visibility to declarations of witness support, even if they do not refer to the act of seeing in the way Antiphon's speaker does. *For the Soldier* (Lysias 9) provides a clear example. The soldier who speaks has been accused of insulting a general, but he maintains that the supposedly insulting conversation occurred at Philios' bank and that the law is applicable only to insults made in the place where the general performs his official functions, called variously the *sunedrion* or *arkheion*. The soldier says, "I have produced witnesses [*marturas*] that I did not go to the *arkheion*, and, since I'm being fined unjustly I don't owe anything, and it's just for me not to pay it." Then he reinforces this reference to witness support with the vocabulary of visibility, saying, "For if I have evidently [*phaneros eimi*] not gone to the *sunedrion*, and the law declares that people who speak offensively inside of it have to pay the fine, then I have evidently [*phainomai*] committed nothing unjust and have been fined maliciously, without legal justification, and fraudulently."⁵⁵ Since witnesses testify that the speaker did not go to the *arkheion*, he can say that he has evidently (*phaneros*) not gone there. The combination of the reference to witnesses and the insistence on visibility is a similar kind of pleonasm to the combination of seeing and being visible in *On the Chorus Boy*. It underscores the amount of witness support that the speaker claims to have. Furthermore, the phrase, "then I have evidently [*phainomai*] committed nothing unjust" introduces a logical argument that develops from the premise stated in the preceding sentence. Since the conclusion is based on witness testimony, the speaker transfers the language of visual certainty to his own argument. The language reflects the importance of witnesses to his case, and it also subtly suggests to the jurors that his logical conclusion, as well as his absence from the *sunedrion*, is supported by visual evidence.

There is another good example of *phaneros* meaning "visible because seen by witnesses" in Gorgias' *Defense of Palamedes*.⁵⁶ The speech is a fictional defense speech written for the hero Palamedes, whom Odysseus is said to have charged with treason, framing him with a forged letter. The speech is compelling evidence for the link between witnesses and visibility, since it is a parody of a real forensic speech and exaggerates the vocabulary and conventions of the genre. Gorgias' Palamedes claims that he could not have planned to betray the Greeks at Troy because he could never have done it without being seen. His references to witnesses and visibility mutually reinforce each other.

First, claiming that he would not have risked employing an interpreter to help him talk with the Trojans, Palamedes says incredulously, "There was—do you really think?—a third witness [*martus*] of the things that had to be kept secret."[57] Later, he claims they could not have exchanged hostages as a sign of trust because, "The things that happened would have been visible [*phanera*] to all of you."[58] Still later, he argues that he could not have been paid to betray the Greeks, because all the people necessary to carry the money would have been witnesses. "If many men were carrying it," he says, "there would have been many witnesses [*martures*] of the plot, and if one man were carrying it, not much of it would have been carried."[59] Still later, he maintains that he could not have used the money anyway. He asks rhetorically, "If I used it, I would have become visible [*phaneros*], but if I didn't use it, how would I have been benefited by it?"[60] Finally, Palamedes argues that the process of opening the gates or erecting ladders or burrowing through the wall to let the Trojans into the Greek camp would have been impossible because of all the guards. He says:

> ἅπασιν ἄρα φανερὰ γένοιτο ἄν. ὑπαίθριος γὰρ ὁ βίος (στρατόπεδον γάρ) ἔστ' ἐν ὅπλοις, ἐν οἷς <πάντες> πάντα ὁρῶσι καὶ πάντες ὑπὸ πάντων ὁρῶνται. πάντως ἄρα καὶ πάντῃ πάντα πράττειν ἀδύνατον ἦν μοι. (Gorgias, *Palamedes* 12)

> It would, of course, have been visible [*phanera*] to all. For life is under the open sky (this is an army we're talking about) in a military camp, and everyone sees [*horōsi*] everything and everyone is seen [*horōntai*] by everyone else. Therefore, for me to do all these things was altogether and in all ways impossible.[61]

By the very nature of military life, Palamedes' actions would have been visible because the other soldiers would have seen him and become witnesses who could have testified to his crime. There is no comparable example of *martus* and *phaneros* used nearly synonymously across so many sentences in any surviving forensic speech. That Gorgias found the vocabulary worthy of parody, however, is good evidence that other orators used the terms in the same way, although without Gorgianic exuberance. Indeed, the Gorgianic usage complements the more understated use in Lysias' *For the Soldier*.

The examples from Lysias and Gorgias make clear that the vocabulary of visibility can be used in Attic forensic oratory to refer to the passive state of being seen by witnesses. In the same way, the active verb *phainō* ("show" or "illuminate") can refer to the process of showing evidence to witnesses by making it visible. The use of *phainō* in the procedure known as *phasis* provides a good example. Like *endeixis*, the *phasis* procedure enabled a concerned citizen to point out criminal activity to a magistrate.[62] Although *phasis* could entail a merely verbal denunciation,[63] *phainō* has a clearly visual sense in procedural contexts, as an example from Aristophanes' *Acharnians* will demonstrate. The sycophant Nikarkhos uses the verb for the visual demonstration of a Theban merchant's contraband lamp wicks for sale in Dikaiopolis' market. *Phainō* is a verb of illuminating rather than a verb of physical pointing, and so I translate it here as "shine a light on" or "illuminate." We use similar expressions in English when we refer to shedding light on obscure matters or, more relevant for this case, shadow economies and black markets. After the Theban merchant acknowledges that the wicks are his, Nikarkhos says, "I, the one here [*hodi*], illuminate [*phainō*] them as illegal imports."[64] Then, after the Theban protests, he goes on to say, "I'll shine a light on [*phanō*] you, too."[65] Finally, an incredulous Dikaiopolis asks, "You're really shining a light on [*phaineis*] him on account of a lamp wick?"[66] The use of *phainō* resembles the use of *endeiknumi* we considered above. Through this language of illuminating, Nikarkhos turns the bystanders into witnesses of the sale of illegally imported goods.[67] Once again, sight is the most important sense for gaining legally significant knowledge. Through *phasis*, some kind of criminal behavior is revealed to a bystander or a magistrate who sees it and therefore becomes a witness to it.

The Athenian distinction between property that is visible (*phanera* or, more rarely, *emphanēs*) and invisible (*aphanēs*) reflects the same link between visibility and witness support. Whether property was visible did not depend on the nature of the property but on the owner's relationship to it.[68] Property that the owner acknowledged as his own before witnesses was visible.[69] Without witnesses, the property remained invisible and anyone could claim title to it.[70] This concept of visible and invisible property underlies the central role of the vocabulary of demonstration and visibility in accounting terminology. Bookkeepers are said to make assets visible by presenting their books for examination. In the *First Speech against Aphobos* (Demosthenes 27), for instance, Demosthenes complains of his guardians' mismanagement of his property and refers specifically to their account books. He says:

λαβόντες δὲ καὶ τἄλλα αἰσχρῶς οὑτωσὶ πάντα, πλέον ἢ τὰ ἡμίσεα τῶν χρημάτων μηδὲ καταλειφθῆναι κοινῇ πάντες ἀμφισβητοῦσιν, ὡς πεντεταλάντου δὲ μόνον τῆς οὐσίας οὔσης ἐκ τοσαύτης τοὺς λόγους ἀπενηνόχασιν, οὐ πρόσοδον μὲν ἐξ αὐτῶν οὐκ <u>ἀποφαίνοντες</u>, τὰ δὲ κεφάλαια <u>φανερὰ</u> <u>ἀποδεικνύντες</u>, ἀλλὰ ταῦτα τὰ ἀρχαῖα οὕτως ἀναιδῶς ἀνηλῶσθαι φάσκοντες. καὶ οὐδ' αἰσχύνονται ταῦτα τολμῶντες. (Dem. 27.62)

And after they have taken all the rest of the estate in this so disgraceful manner, they all maintain by mutual consent that more than half the property was not left to me. As though the property were worth only five talents, they have handed over [*apenēnokhasin*] their accounts [*tous logous*] on the basis of such a valuation, neither <u>revealing</u> [*apophainontes*] a profit from them nor <u>demonstrating</u> [*apodeiknuntes*] the principle as <u>visible</u> [*phanera*], but saying in such a shameful way that this original amount has been spent. And, being bold enough to do this, they show no shame.

The verb "hand over" (*apenēnokhasin*) shows that Demosthenes is talking about physical ledgers that can be shown and examined, and the two participles "revealing" (*apophainontes*) and "demonstrating" (*apodeiknuntes*) refer to a visual demonstration of the ledgers' content.[71] The verb *apodeiknumi* is used similarly in *Against Diogeiton* (Lysias 32), when Diodotos' widow produces account books to show that Diogeiton lied about Diodotos' assets. The speaker explains how her children found a ledger and gave it to her, and that using this she "demonstrated [*apedeixen*] the written evidence of his assets."[72] One reason for the use of the language of demonstration and visibility in this context[73] is the ledgers' status as visible objects. A more important reason, however, is the concept of visible and invisible property. By presenting the contents of a ledger to witnesses, the assets and liabilities listed in it become "visible," as Demosthenes shows when he says his guardians were not "demonstrating [*apodeiknuntes*] the principle as visible [*phanera*]." The same set of terminology is used for assets in account books as for other types of property or, indeed, as for anything else that requires witnesses. A compound of *deiknumi* or *phainō* refers to the demonstration itself, and the adjective *phaneros* refers to the status of what has been demonstrated and so is now known.

Significantly, parallel terminology is used for the public acknowledgment of children, whether natural or adopted. Fathers acknowledged their newborns through a series of rituals, including carrying them around the hearth, giving them a name, and, for males, introducing them to their phratries.[74] The whole process, but especially the presentation before the phratry, was designed to guarantee the child's legitimacy in case of future challenges. It was a public demonstration of paternity, and authors often speak of it with the language of demonstration and visibility. The best examples come from Isaeus and use *phainō* and its compound *apophainō*, which in this context I translate as "reveal." In *On the Estate of Philoktemon* (Isaeus 6), the speaker recounts how Euktemon, who was angry at his son Philoktemon for refusing to allow him to recognize the son of his mistress as his own son, threatened to remarry, to "reveal [*apophanōn*] the children" born from his new wife, and to admit them into the family.[75] Pressured by his relatives, Philoktemon agrees to Euktemon's earlier demand, because he knew that even though his father was too old to have children with a new wife, the children "would be revealed [*phanēsointo*] in some other way."[76] The visual vocabulary equates legitimizing children with showing them to witnesses. The central role of witnesses is made particularly clear in *On the Estate of Pyrrhos* (Isaeus 3). The speaker maintains that the rival claimant for the estate is the husband of an illegitimate daughter of Pyrrhos and so has no testamentary right. He mocks the credibility of Pyrrhos' three uncles, who testified both that Pyrrhos married the girl's mother and that he acknowledged her as his daughter. The speaker says:

καὶ οἱ αὐτοὶ θεῖοι οὗτοι ἐν τῇ δεκάτῃ τῆς θυγατρὸς ἀποφανθείσης εἶναι ὑπὸ τοῦ ἀδελφιδοῦ κληθέντες μεμαρτυρήκασι παραγενέσθαι. (Isae. 3.30)

And these same uncles have testified as witnesses [*memarturēkasi*] that they were present [*paragenesthai*] on the tenth day when she was revealed [*apophantheisēs*] to be his daughter, since they were summoned by their nephew.

The speaker emphasizes the uncles' status as witnesses through the verb "testified as witnesses" (*memarturēkasi*) and by the reference to being present (*paragenesthai*). Significantly, his paraphrase of the uncles' testimony also uses a form of *apophainō*, "she was revealed" (*apophantheisēs*), showing that they testified to what they claimed to have seen.

William Wyse has suggested that *apophainō* has a negative connotation when it is used for the acknowledgement of children; the Isaean examples he cites all involve claims of legitimacy that are challenged by the speakers.⁷⁷ The word is more likely to be a neutral, semitechnical term, however, especially when we consider the parallel use of the vocabulary of demonstration in cases of adoption. In *On The Estate of Apollodoros* (Isaeus 7), the speaker, who is defending his own adoption, says that he would have thought adoptions above reproach where the adoptive father "had brought his adopted son to the sacred places, demonstrated [*apedeixe*] him to his relatives, and listed him in the public registers,"⁷⁸ as happened in his case. He even notes that this was a way for his father to make his wishes visible (*phaneras*)⁷⁹ and that it was all done in a visible manner (*phanerōs*).⁸⁰

The vocabulary of demonstration, revelation, and visibility, therefore, seems to have been regularly used for the presentation of children, whether infants or mature adoptees, and not to have carried a negative or positive connotation. The verbs were common enough that Herodotus even uses *apodeiknumi* as a synonym for "have a child," when he describes the Persian custom of honoring fathers who have many sons.⁸¹ We also find Aristotle using *apophainō* and *apodeiknumi* in the *Rhetoric* to describe mothers compelling fathers to acknowledge paternity: the mother of Mantias' child "made the revelation" (*apephēnen*), and, when Ismenias and Stilbon were quarreling over which of them was the father of the child of a woman from Dodona, the mother "demonstrated [*apedeixen*] the son of Ismenias." Both scenarios make sense only in the context of witnesses who were deciding the issue. Aristotle implies their presence when he says that "they recognized Ismenias' son Thettaliskos" because of the mother's declaration. Aristotle has no reason to choose words that carry a negative connotation, since he cites the two examples in support of the proposition that "women in every place distinguish the truth about their children" to illustrate how to make an enthymeme through induction.⁸²

THE LANGUAGE OF WITNESSING IN MEDICINE AND PHILOSOPHY

We have seen in this chapter that sight was the primary means of acquiring and verifying knowledge in the Athenian legal system and that words of demonstration and visibility had a correspondingly prominent place in the Athenian legal vocabulary. To demonstrate something was to legitimize its status by ensuring that witnesses knew about it and could testify to it. To say *epideiknumi* or *endeiknumi* was to ensure public knowledge that a crime had occurred or that someone was a criminal. Similarly, to say *apodeiknumi* or *apophainō* was to guarantee an asset or to acknowledge a child's legitimacy. The words embody the Athenian belief that showing and seeing are the most reliable means of sharing and gaining knowledge. As a result, the vocabulary of demonstration and visibility also has a strong connotation of legitimacy and truth. Indeed, to say that something was *phaneron*, or "visible," was akin to saying that something was "known" or even, in many cases, "true." When the speaker of *On the Murder of Eratosthenes* asks that his wife's adultery be "visible," he is speaking not just as a jealous husband but as a seeker for truth, and when the soldier in *For the Soldier* declares that "I have evidently not gone to the *sunedrion*," he means that he truly did not go there.

The primacy of sight as a means of acquiring knowledge is fundamental to Greek thought and not limited to judicial contexts. As I noted in the introduction, seeing and knowing are different tenses of the same verb: *eidon* ("see") is the aorist of the verb whose perfect is *oida* ("know," or more literally, "have seen"). Seeing is a common philosophical metaphor for knowing, even when the subject of inquiry cannot actually be seen. Both Hippocratic physicians and Pre-Socratic philosophers use the language of sight and visibility for their inquiries about invisible things. For Anaxagoras, the visible is a clue to the nature of the invisible. He says, "Visible things are the face of things which are unclear."[83] The author of the Hippocratic treatise *On the Art* similarly maintains that physicians can study invisible internal illnesses only through indications observable by the senses.[84] He even speaks of the "sight of the mind" as a means for understanding things that physical sight cannot comprehend.[85] For Plato, who is strongly influenced by the role of sight in mystery religions, seeing is the most common metaphor for knowing; it is the sense through which men gain knowledge of the forms of beauty.[86]

The uses of the vocabulary of visibility in legal, medical, and philosophical language probably influenced each other, since all three genres were concerned with a similar problem: how can we acquire reliable knowledge? Whether the knowledge would be used to convince jurors, treat an illness, or speculate on the nature of man and the universe, the problem was ultimately the same. Furthermore, there is no question that sophists and writers for the courts, especially in the late fifth century, were members of the same intellectual circles and sometimes were even the same people. In Aristophanes' *Clouds*, Socrates is a sophist who ponders the nature of the earth, the kosmos, and the gods, but Strepsiades and Pheidippides are more interested in his ability to teach them how to defeat their creditors in court. Gorgias wrote a treatise *On Not Being*, and he also wrote a mock forensic speech for Helen and the one for Palamedes discussed above. In Plato's *Republic*, Lysias is present when his father Kephalos hosts Socrates, Thrasymakhos, Glaukon, and other intellectuals. It is also likely that Antiphon the sophist is the same person as Antiphon the orator.[87] Finally, we know that sophists in general were intensely interested in techniques of persuasion, just like speech-writers and their clients. Within this intellectual milieu, interest in the relationship between sight and knowledge probably transcended generic boundaries.

Nonetheless, there is a scholarly tendency to underestimate the significance of legal language and legal thinking on philosophers and physicians. A fragment of Protagoras preserved in Didymus the Blind's *Commentary on the Psalms*,[88] however, directly links intellectual speculation on the nature of knowledge with the legal concept of witness-dependent knowledge. Protagoras uses not only the language of visibility but also the language of presence. The fragment states:

> φαίνομαι σοὶ τῷ παρόντι καθήμενος· τῷ δὲ ἀπόντι οὐ φαίνομαι καθήμενος· ἄδηλον εἰ κάθημαι ἢ οὐ κάθημαι.
>
> To you who are present, I am evidently [*phainomai*] sitting, but to someone who is absent, I am not evidently [*ou phainomai*] sitting. It is unclear whether I am sitting or not sitting.

Protagoras seems to maintain that we can know whether something exists only by direct observation. For those people who have not seen it themselves, the existence of something cannot be known. Protagoras couches this philosophical principle in the language of witness testimony. Presence, he states, is a necessary prerequisite for sensory experience of the external world and therefore for knowledge. As we have seen, presence is also the most fundamental element of witnesses' knowledge. When they affirm their testimony in court, they say either "I was present" or "I know." Furthermore, Protagoras speaks of knowledge in an explicitly visual formulation with the passive verb *phainomai*, which we have already observed in many legal situations that involve witness testimony.

Judicial knowledge requires something to be visible to someone who is present, so that he can vouch for it in the future. Protagoras, it seems, is not concerned about future testimony but about the nature of knowledge. Nonetheless, the fundamental principle of how we know is the same for Protagoras and for the courts, and so the fundamental vocabulary that associates knowing with sight is the same. In Didymus' discussion of the Protagoras fragment, he goes on to apply this doctrine to the moon:

οἷον ὁρῶ τὴν σελήνην, ἄλλος δὲ οὐκ ὁρᾷ· ἄδηλον εἰ ἔστιν ἢ οὐκ ἔστιν.

For example, I see [*horō*] the moon, but someone else does not see [*ouk horāi*] it. It is unclear whether it is or it is not.

Didymus may be quoting Protagoras in this sentence as well, but even if he is not, the parallel forms of *horaō* in the same position as the forms of *phainomai* in the sentence about sitting stress the visual force of Protagoras' language.

Protagoras may not be consciously imitating legal vocabulary, and there is probably not a direct line of descent from legal thinking about witnesses to his thinking about the nature of knowledge and existence. Protagoras' thought and language, which associate knowledge and existence with visibility, are, however, part of the same intellectual context as the legal thought and language that describe anything whose existence or truth is supported by witnesses, from crimes to property to legitimate children, as "visible" and "demonstrated." Furthermore, this legal terminology may have influenced philosophical language more than we usually suppose. Since all cases in Athens required hundreds of jurors, and trials seem to have happened at least half the days in the year, there can have been few Athenians who were untouched by the legal use of the vocabulary of demonstration and visibility. Protagoras himself was not an Athenian citizen, of course, and while he could have attended trials as a spectator, he would have lacked the habitual jurors' intimate familiarity with legal language. Nonetheless, he writes as part of a movement that included Athenian citizens and, more importantly, teachers of Athenian citizens and writers for Athenian trials. The visual idioms and terminology of the courts could have percolated through this group, acquiring new resonances and developing new connotations as different thinkers used them to express their own ideas. Acknowledging these connections does not take away from Protagoras' originality as a thinker or the speechwriters' originality as rhetorical strategists, but it helps us to place them more firmly in the intellectual and linguistic currents of the late fifth and fourth centuries.

CONCLUSIONS

The language of demonstration and visibility is a semantic link among a wide variety of legal contexts that refer to witnesses and witness testimony. Forms of *deiknumi*, *phainō*, their compounds, and the nouns and adjectives related to them point to the importance of sight as the most reliable source of legal knowledge. They also indicate that the Athenians were remarkably consistent in the way that they talked about securing evidence for anything that might be contested. The terms are not just metaphors. When litigants claim that something is "visible," they mean that witnesses have seen it: it was visible to them, and so, thanks to their testimony in court, the litigants can strongly associate it with the truth.

The same language of visibility appears in medical and philosophical texts, and a fragment of Protagoras actually uses it in a formulation that explicitly recalls not only the vocabulary but also the context of legal witnessing. This suggests that legal language and legal ideas could have influenced and been influenced by medical and philosophical thinking about the nature of knowledge.

In the next chapter, I will turn from the language of legal procedure to the language of persuasion. Litigants and speechwriters adopted the vocabulary of demonstration and visibility as a way to describe their verbal arguments. The rhetorical effectiveness of this strategy depended upon both the jurors' trust in witness evidence and their familiarity with the semitechnical meaning of this vocabulary in legal contexts.

FOUR

SAYING AS SHOWING, HEARING AS SEEING

In the courts, litigants often referred to their speeches as "demonstrations" and to their arguments as "visible" or "evident." Taking advantage of the semitechnical meanings of this vocabulary, they drew a parallel between jurors who were listening in the court and witnesses who had actually seen visual evidence. This chapter, therefore, studies the same set of terminology as chapter 3 but from a complementary and opposite perspective. Where chapter 3 examined how visual demonstrations are described by speech, this chapter examines how speech can be described as though it is a visual demonstration.

INTRODUCTION: ANTIPHON'S SECOND TETRALOGY AND THE JURORS' OBLIGATION TO SEE

We often think of Justice as a woman wearing a blindfold that protects her from bias.[1] No image could have been more foreign to the Greek conception of personified Justice (*Dikē*) than this blindfolded woman. As early as Hesiod, *Dikē* is associated with sight rather than blindness. She reports wrongdoers to her father, Zeus, who sees all things.[2] In Athenian tragedy, she becomes like her all-seeing father. *Dikē* "sees everything," says Euripides' Electra,[3] and her sight allows her to punish wrongdoers.[4] In the *First Speech against Aristogeiton* (Demosthenes 25), Demosthenes tells the jury that *Dikē* watches over the affairs of men and also looks at each individual juror as they cast their ballots.[5] Unlike Wealth (*Ploutos*) and Love (*Erōs*), *Dikē* is never called blind, nor, in the infrequent depictions of *Dikē*, is she ever shown with a blindfold or with her eyes closed.[6] The statue of the chief judge with his eyes closed in Egyptian Thebes is noteworthy to Diodorus and Plutarch precisely because it is unusual.[7]

—— THE LANGUAGE OF DEMONSTRATION AND VISIBILITY ——

Unlike *Dikē* herself, the Athenian jurors did not rely primarily on their sense of sight to recognize crimes and punish wrongdoers. Visual evidence was fundamental to the Athenian quest for justice, but seeing was the duty of witnesses. The jurors made their decisions by listening to arguments that sometimes included the testimony of witnesses, not by seeing the events in question themselves. Since the Athenian legal system put such an emphasis on visual knowledge, however, this created a challenge for both the jurors and the litigants: how can the jurors determine the truth about something they have not witnessed when their only information comes from two contradictory verbal accounts, and how can the litigants convince the jurors if they cannot show them what actually happened?[8]

Antiphon's second tetralogy (Antiphon 3), which contains more self-reflection on the process of legal argumentation than a real forensic speech would,[9] recognizes that the central problem of determining truth in the Athenian courts is that the jurors must rely on what the speakers tell them. Even though they can only listen to biased litigants and their supporters, Antiphon's defendant stresses the jurors' obligation to determine the truth. He speaks of this obligation in visual terms, saying:

τοῦτον μὲν εἰκὸς πρὸς τὴν ἑαυτοῦ κατηγορίαν προσέχοντα τὸν νοῦν μὴ μαθεῖν τὴν ἀπολογίαν μου, ὑμᾶς δὲ χρή, γιγνώσκοντας ὅτι ἡμεῖς μὲν οἱ ἀντίδικοι κατ' εὔνοιαν κρίνοντες τὸ πρᾶγμα εἰκότως δίκαια ἑκάτεροι αὐτοὺς οἰόμεθα λέγειν, ὑμᾶς δὲ ὁσίως ὁρᾶν προσήκει τὰ πραχθέντα· ἐκ τῶν λεγομένων γὰρ ἡ ἀλήθεια σκεπτέα αὐτῶν ἐστίν. (Ant. 3.4.1–2)

It is reasonable for my opponent, since he is focusing his attention on his own prosecution, not to understand my defense. You must understand it, however, since you know that although we, being litigants and therefore judging the affair according to our own biases, each reasonably believe we speak justly, it is fitting for you, in accordance with divine law, to see [*horan*] the things that have happened. For you have to look into [*skeptea*] the truth of the matter from the words that are spoken.

Since "look into" (*skopeō/skeptomai*) frequently occurs in forensic oratory to call the jurors' attention to an important point, its connotation of mental consideration is often stronger than its connotation of physical sight. In this passage, however, "see [*horan*] the things that have happened" and "you have to look into [*skeptea*] the truth of the matter" reinforce each other and indicate that the speaker is associating the jurors' responsibility to determine the truth with their sense of sight.[10] The jurors must become like witnesses, and like all-seeing *Dikē* herself, even though they can see only in a notional way that relies on what they hear from the speakers. Part of the challenge of making a good forensic speech, then, is encouraging the jury to associate themselves with witnesses so that they visualize the speaker's version of events and conclude that his arguments rest on visual evidence. One way that speakers do this is by using the vocabulary of demonstration and visibility to describe their speaking and the jurors' hearing.

JURORS AS WITNESSES

Many Athenian litigants describe their speeches with language appropriate for visual demonstrations.[11] Speakers speak with verbs of demonstrating, jurors hear and deliberate with verbs of seeing, and spoken claims are qualified with adjectives and adverbs of visual clarity. Litigants make claims such as, "As my speech goes on, the one who plotted against me with my opponent and who fraudulently arranged this very trial will be evident [*kataphanēs*] to you" or, conflating the senses of hearing and sight, "Anyone would see [*idoi*] your baseness for many reasons, but especially if he heard about the will."[12]

To a certain extent, visual language like this characterizes the Greek language in general, which is sensitive to a sensory overlap between seeing and hearing. Synaesthetic metaphors are common in Greek literature from the earliest periods.[13] In the *Odyssey*, for example, Demodokos "brought the song to light [*phaine*]."[14] Similarly, Solon chides his listeners because they "look at [*horate*] the tongue and the words of an unscrupulous man."[15] By the fourth century, however, the visual force of many words referring to sight or appearance had become weak or even nonexistent in many contexts. The Greek vocabulary of demonstration and visibility, like its English equivalents, could be used to refer to visual and verbal demonstrations without causing confusion. Sositheos, the speaker of Demosthenes' *Against Makartatos* (Demosthenes 43) shows this when he uses two forms of *epideiknumi* in the same paragraph to contrast a visual demonstration of his family tree with a verbal description of his family's history.[16]

In other contexts, especially ones that unambiguously emphasize the presence or absence of witness testimony, litigants and speechwriters take advantage of the visual, procedural connotations of words such as *epideiknumi* and *phaneros*.[17] They attempt to grant special authority to themselves as "demonstrators" and special value to their arguments as "demonstrated" and "evident." In the conceptual world that this language creates, the jurors are encouraged to consider their relationship with the speaking litigant parallel to the relationship witnesses have with the person who shows them visual evidence.

AUTHORITATIVE VERBAL ARGUMENTS

The Greek vocabulary of demonstration can designate statements as authoritative. The Proto-Indo-European root **deik-* refers to a special kind of showing, a "showing with authority," in Emile Benveniste's words.[18] In forensic contexts, *deiknumi* and its compounds can retain this fundamental meaning, preserving an authoritative connotation that simple verbs of saying such as *legō*, *phēmi*, and the aorist *eipon* lack. The Latin verb *dico*, which also developed from the **deik-* root, can similarly connote greater authority than the more pedestrian *loquor*.[19] In English, we often use "show" to distinguish authoritative speech from mere statements. There is a significant difference between "the defendant said he was home in bed at the time of the robbery" and "the defendant showed he was home in bed at the time of the robbery." "Showed" implies that the statement is based on evidence. While it falls short of the certainty that "the defendant proved he was home in bed at the time of the robbery" would imply, it suggests that listeners should consider this more than an unsubstantiated claim. Athenian litigants and speechwriters often use the vocabulary of demonstration in a similar way to this English use of "show."

In Athenian forensic oratory, the vocabulary of demonstration is closely associated with witnesses and visual evidence even when it does not refer to the actual visual demonstrations that I discussed in chapter 3. Speakers tend to use forms of *deiknumi*, *epideiknumi*, and *apodeiknumi* to describe arguments that are based wholly or partly on the testimony of witnesses,[20] and the formulaic phrase "to demonstrate [*epideiknunai/apodeiknunai*] with so many witnesses and proofs," appears with minor variations in Antiphon, Lysias, and Demosthenes.[21] In addition, the way that *apodeiknumi* and *epideiknumi* frequently introduce arguments supported by narrative accounts may reflect orators' tendency to insert witness testimonies into their narratives.[22] The speaker of Lysias'

Against Pankleon (Lysias 23), for instance, introduces a narrative supported by five different witness testimonies by saying, "That I have acted correctly in bringing this suit against Pankleon, the one here, for not being a Plataean, I will attempt to demonstrate [*apodeixai*] to you."[23] With *apodeiknumi* and *epideiknumi*, therefore, speakers can both point things out to witnesses and introduce verbal arguments in court based on witness testimony. Forensic oratory does not make the distinction common to other literary contexts in which *apodeiknumi* is limited to demonstrations or proofs based on (*apo-*) evidence and *epideiknumi* to demonstrations in front of (*epi-*) a public audience.[24]

Litigants use the same vocabulary of demonstration for verbal arguments based on laws. Aeschines says in *Against Ktesiphon* (Aeschines 3), "I will demonstrate [*epideixō*] to you from the laws themselves a great sign that I am speaking the truth,"[25] and the speaker of Demosthenes' *Against Nikostratos* (Demosthenes 53) says of his opponents, "There are many reasons why I think they are shamelessly claiming your property, but I will demonstrate [*epideixō*] them to you best from your own laws."[26] The vocabulary of demonstration, therefore, can mark an argument as especially authoritative because it is based on witnesses or laws.[27] The speaker of Isaeus' *On the Estate of Aristarkhos* (Isaeus 10) mentions them both when he says, "I think it has been sufficiently demonstrated [*apodedeikhthai*] from the things that have been said and witnessed and from the laws themselves."[28]

In phrases such as these, the vocabulary of demonstration draws a connection between what witnesses could actually see and what the jurors can only hear. This tactic is related to the common rhetorical strategy of attributing to the jurors special, authoritative knowledge. Whenever they can, litigants try to equate their jurors with witnesses,[29] even when it is unlikely that all the jurors, or even most of them, possess firsthand knowledge of their claims. In *Against the Grain Retailers* (Lysias 22), for instance, the speaker says to the jury, "I bring you forward as witnesses [*marturas*] that the defendants have been illegally changing the amount they charge for grain by as much as a drachma over the course of a single day."[30] Similarly, Theopompos in *On the Estate of Hagnias* (Isaeus 11) tries to prove that he did not inherit large fortunes from his brothers-in-law by telling the jurors, "You are all witnesses [*martures*] for me that my wife's brothers Khaireleos and Makartatos were not members of the liturgical class but of the class of men who possess meager wealth."[31] By suggesting in this way that the jurors all share common knowledge, the speakers encourage them to accept their arguments as reliable.[32]

THE LANGUAGE OF DEMONSTRATION AND VISIBILITY

In the *Rhetoric*, Aristotle describes the psychological effect of tactics that suggest the jurors know more than they actually do. He addresses the way that jurors respond to expressions "speechwriters employ to excess" such as "who does not know" or "everyone knows." "The listener," he writes, "agrees because he is ashamed, so that he may share in the knowledge that all other people also have."[33] Josiah Ober argues that speakers use this tactic to appeal to democratic ideology as well as to shame: since juries render their decisions on behalf of the entire *dēmos*, they ought to take into account whatever everyone knows.[34] Regardless of whether litigants play upon shame, democratic values, or a combination of both, they refer to common knowledge and to the jurors' status as witnesses to try to obscure the distinction between what the jurors know and what the jurors merely hear from them. Litigants create a scenario in which their authority as speakers derives from the alleged knowledge of the people judging them, a rhetorical construct that encourages the jurors to vote for a speaker because of what they know rather than what he has said.

The use of the vocabulary of demonstration is a variation on the same strategy. Instead of suggesting that jurors already know information that makes them witnesses in the speakers' favor, speakers imply that the jurors will come to know through their verbal demonstrations just as witnesses come to know through visual demonstrations. By using language to emphasize the parallel between witnesses who see and jurors who hear, speakers try to shape the way the jurors will respond to their arguments.

Litigants often take advantage of the authoritative connotation of the vocabulary of demonstration to contrast their speeches with their opponents'. In *Against Olympiodoros* (Demosthenes 48), the speaker Kallistratos claims that, while Olympiodoros can only speak (*legei*), he "will demonstrate in an evident manner" (*phanerōs epideixō*).[35] Similarly, in Lysias' *Against Philon* (Lysias 31), the speaker goes so far as to claim that he will make a demonstration (*apodeixō*) in a transparent way (*saphōs*) to prevent Philon from using lies to trick the *bouleutai* who were judging the *dokimasia*.[36] The contrast between unsupported speech and authoritative verbal claims based on visual evidence is an example of the familiar Greek opposition between "word" (*logos*) and "deed" (*ergon*), which is essentially a distinction between lies and facts.[37]

Speakers can also conceal the weaknesses of their argument through the vocabulary of demonstration and visibility by implying that it rests on visual evidence and disingenuously urging their jurors to "look into" the facts. *Against Nausimakhos and Xenopeithes* (Demosthenes 38) offers a good example. The speaker's father, Aristaikhmos, was the guardian of Nausimakhos and Xenopeithes, and they maintain that he had collected a debt owed to their father's estate by a certain Hermonax and failed to hand it over to them. Although the brothers had released Aristaikhmos from all liabilities, they claim that the debt in question was collected by Aristaikhmos after the release and so is not covered by it. In response, the speaker makes three arguments framed with the vocabulary of demonstration and visibility and other references to sight and witnesses.

First, he wants to demonstrate (*deixai*) that the debt cannot have been recovered after the release, because his father died too soon afterwards. Second, he will demonstrate (*epideixō*) that his own guardian Demaretos could not have recovered it either; Nausimakhos and Xenopeithes are themselves the best witnesses (*martures*) of this because "it will be evident [*phanēsontai*] that they never brought a suit against Demaretos while he was alive." Third, he says, "Anyone who examines [*skopōn*] and looks into [*theorōn*] this would see [*idoi*] not only that Demaretos didn't receive it, but also that it was impossible for him to receive it," because he never went to Bosporos, where Hermonax lived, and had no authority to collect it through an intermediary.[38] After some analysis of possible refutations to these points, he calls witnesses in support of them.

Some of the speaker's statements may well be true, but they support a very weak argument. He has failed to show that Demaretos did not send a collection agent to Bosporos or that Hermonax did not pay the debt on a visit to Athens;[39] someone who "examines and looks into" the matter carefully would be bound to realize this, since the only things his witnesses actually testify to is the time of Aristaikhmos' death, that no suit was brought against Demaretos, and that Demaretos never sailed to Bosporos. The speaker chooses visual language, however, to discourage the kind of consideration he ostensibly recommends. By emphasizing transparency and visual certainty, he attempts to conceal the way his argument merely denies possibilities without proving that they did not happen.

Similarly, litigants who pair the adverb *phanerōs* ("evidently," "in an evident manner," or "in a visible manner") with verbs of demonstrating[40] or with words that mean "prove" such as *elenkhō* or *exelenkhō*[41] are probably trying to imply that their arguments rely on more visual evidence than they really do. In *Against Spoudias* (Demosthenes 41), for instance, the speaker faults Spoudias for refusing to submit to the arbitration of friends "who were present at all these events and know what happened as well as we do" because he would have been "proven guilty by them in an evident manner" (*phanerōs . . . exelenkhomenōi*).⁴² With the language of visibility, the speaker encourages the jurors to accept Spoudias' guilt as an unambiguous fact.

THE VOCABULARY OF DEMONSTRATION AND VISIBILITY IN EPIDEICTIC CONTEXTS

Athenian forensic oratory had its own conventions, but it was at the same time part of a larger rhetorical culture that extended outside the courts and even beyond Athens. Forensic oratory shared some idioms and techniques of persuasion with other genres. The epideictic genre, which takes its name from *epideiknumi*, could also employ the vocabulary of demonstration and visibility to conflate the experiences of listening and looking. The connotations of these words and their effect on an audience would have depended on the context. Epideictic arguments were less dependent on witnesses and visual evidence than were forensic ones, and so epideictic speakers drew on a broader array of cultural associations when they used terms related to *epideiknumi* or *phainomai* in their speeches.⁴³

The Epideictic Connotations of Demonstrating

The modern concept of epideictic literature derives from Aristotle, who distinguishes the epideictic category (*epideiktikon genos*) of speeches from the forensic category (*dikanikon genos*) and the deliberative category (*sumbouleutikon genos*). Aristotle is sensitive to the visual force of *epideiktikon*, since he says that the hearers of speeches assigned to the epideictic category are spectators (*theōroi*) rather than judges (*kritai*). The jurors who hear forensic speeches and the assemblymen who hear deliberative speeches, on the other hand, Aristotle considers judges.⁴⁴ Despite Aristotle's emphasis on spectatorship, the language of demonstration often has little connection to witnesses or visual evidence in epideictic literature, even if we expand the category beyond Aristotle's definition of speeches that praise or blame, are concerned with the present, and seek to show that something is honorable or dishonorable.⁴⁵ In Plato, sophists often introduce presentations presented to the public or other intellectuals with the verb *epideiknumi*, and Alcidamas says that he uses writing to make sure his own demonstrations (*epideixeis*) can circulate among the masses.⁴⁶ In these contexts, the language of demonstration has a connotation of authoritative speech even when it lacks an unambiguously visual component because it is used for something that becomes a matter of public knowledge. Similarly, Herodotus' written *apodexis* (the Ionic version of *apodeixis*) ensures that the great deeds of men will not be forgotten, just as performances of epic or lyric poetry confer perpetual fame on their subjects.⁴⁷

The term *epideixis* can also have a negative connotation of "showing off" rather than a positive connotation of authority. In Thucydides' account of the Mytilene Debate, for instance, Diodotos paraphrases Kleon's charge that he accepted a bribe to give a demonstration (*epideixis*) during the Mytilene debate.⁴⁸ Diodotos is responding to the part of Kleon's speech where he accuses the Athenians of neglecting their responsibility as assemblymen by comparing them to "spectators of speeches."⁴⁹ Here, the vocabulary of spectatorship does not imply the authoritative viewing of witnesses but a passive observation devoid of consideration, and so *epideixis* means a display of ones' rhetorical talent regardless of whether one's argument is right or wrong. In *On the Crown* (Demosthenes 18), Demosthenes similarly accuses Aeschines of making an *epideixis* of eloquence and vocal dexterity rather than sincerely attempting to punish him.⁵⁰ The connotation of the vocabulary of demonstration, therefore, depends on the context. When it is not closely connected with witnesses and visual evidence, it can carry other, more negative senses associated with seeing.

Like forensic speakers, epideictic speakers can also exaggerate the validity of their arguments by presenting them with the vocabulary of demonstration and visibility. A passage in Plato's *Protagoras* illustrates this. Socrates doubts that excellence (*aretē*) can be taught, but he says to Protagoras, "If, therefore, you can demonstrate [*epideixai*] to us in a rather vivid manner [*enargesteron*] that *aretē* is something that can be taught, don't begrudge us but make the demonstration [*epideixon*]."⁵¹ Socrates uses the forms of *epideiknumi* for a type of speaking that proves a proposition. Nothing about either the proof or the proposition is visual, but Socrates qualifies the first *epideiknumi* with "in a rather vivid manner" (*enargesteron*). By describing a verbal proof with the vocabulary of demonstration and visibility, Socrates takes advantage of the primacy of sight as a way of gaining knowledge, just as speakers do in court when they strengthen forms of *epideiknumi* with adverbs like *phanerōs* ("evidently" or "in a visible manner") and *saphōs* ("clearly" or "in a transparent manner").

Socrates, of course, doubts that Protagoras can argue that *aretē* can be taught with sufficient authority to be convincing, and he uses the vocabulary of demonstration and visibility as a way to show what Protagoras' argument will lack. Other epideictic speakers, however, employ this language to strengthen their presentations.

Demonstration and Visibility in On the Art *and* On Breaths

Two anonymous works of Hippocratic medicine from the late fifth or early fourth century that Jacques Jouanna and Rosalind Thomas have associated with epideictic literature, *On the Art* and *On Breaths*,[52] describe their arguments with the vocabulary of demonstration and visibility even though they avowedly do not rely on visual evidence for their conclusions. By taking advantage of the words' positive connotations, they seek to convince their audiences that verbal demonstrations can hold equivalent authority to visual demonstrations and that logical arguments can hold equivalent authority to visual evidence.

At the end of *On the Art*, the author insists that his presentation, which he calls "the words being spoken now," proves the same things about the art, or *tekhnē*, of medicine as "the demonstrations [*epideixies*, Ionic plural of *epideixis*] of those who know the art, which they take greater pleasure in demonstrating [*epideiknuousin*] from deeds [*ergōn*] than from words [*logōn*], since they have not carefully studied speaking." For the author, the type of demonstration referred to by *epideiknumi* can be either verbal, through words, or visual, through deeds. In fact, the visual type is thought to be more effective, since "for most people, the more customary manner of believing is from whatever they see rather than from whatever they hear."[53] Although the author calls his treatise an *apodeixis*, he never calls it an *epideixis* nor refers to his own words with *epideiknumi*.[54] Nonetheless, he makes clear that he considers his own verbal demonstration a replacement for a visual demonstration by equating it with experts' *epideixies*.

In the very first sentence of *On the Art*, the author had criticized those who "make a demonstration [*epideixin*] of their own inquiry" by denying medicine's status as a *tekhnē* and denigrating medical discoveries and innovations.[55] Now, in the last sentence, he repeats *epideixis* for the only time in the entire treatise and reinforces it with *epideiknumi* to show that his work parallels the visual demonstrations of experts and not the self-serving displays of medicine's ignorant critics. Emphasizing the authoritative connotation of *epideixis* and *epideiknumi*, he claims to have proven medicine's claim to be a *tekhnē* with his words just as certainly as if he had used visual evidence. His verbal demonstration is as good as, if not better than, the visual demonstrations of physicians who have not been formally trained in speaking.

The ideal audience for *On the Art* will accept the author's arguments without needing to see anything. In the same way, medicine itself learns about internal diseases not through physical sight but through what the author calls "the sight of the mind" (*tēi tēs gnōmēs opsei*).[56] The author describes the doctor's recognition of these "invisible diseases" (*ta aphanea*)[57] primarily through visual language. When the patient's oral report on his symptoms is inadequate to create unerring clarity, his caregiver must look (*prosopteon*) to something else, namely, to reasonable inferences based on symptoms or tests.[58] The author calls the time it takes the doctor to determine the necessary course of treatment through such a process of reasoning the time "until the disease has been seen" (*es to ophthēnai*) and "while the disease is being seen" (*en hōi touto horatai*).[59] Some medical procedures yield visible clues, such as when certain foods encourage the emission of phlegm, whose appearance can then be examined as a sign of an internal illness. In this case, the author says that medicine "makes an inference based on what is seen [*ti ophthen*] concerning what cannot possibly be seen [*to ophthēnai*] by it."[60] Crucially, however, other symptoms, such as shortness of breath or the scent and texture of emitted fluids, are not visible but still provide indications of invisible diseases to the sight of the mind. The author of *On the Art*, then, has constructed a text whose audience learns in the same way as its subject matter. Medicine learns about invisible diseases through reason as though it is seeing them with the sight of the mind, and the listening or reading audience of *On the Art* learns about medicine as though they are seeing a doctor perform a visual demonstration.[61]

The metaphor of reason making invisible things visible also appears in *On Breaths*. The author claims that it is worthwhile to look at (*theēsasthai*) the power of air, which is exemplified by wind uprooting trees and swelling the sea into waves. Despite this visible evidence of signs of its power, air itself is "invisible [*aphanēs*] to sight but evident [*phaneros*] to reason."[62] He supports this argument with a series of examples introduced by the particle *gar* ("because") explaining why he makes this claim. The pattern of a form of *phaneros* followed by *gar* recurs throughout the speech. For instance, the author maintains it is evident (*phaneron*) that there is air in the sea because (*gar*) fish need it to live, and it is evident (*phaneron*) that air enters the body along with food or drink because (*gar*) people tend to belch after overeating because (*gar*) enclosed air rushes out.⁶³

Part of the rhetorical strategy of *On Breaths*, therefore, is to present the treatise as a demonstration that makes facts that the eyes cannot see evident through reason. The strength of the visual language varies throughout the work. When the author declares, "Moving on in this same treatise to the facts themselves, I will demonstrate [*epideixō*] that all diseases are offspring of this air,"⁶⁴ *epideixō* draws no overt visual connotation from its immediate context, although *On Breath*'s general concern with visibility and invisibility suggests that this use of the language of demonstration may reinforce the author's portrayal of his work as a verbal revelation of invisible information.

Some types of epideictic literature, therefore, can associate the vocabulary of demonstration and visibility with authoritative statements, just as forensic oratory can. Socrates suggests that a compelling argument needs to be "demonstrated" and "rather vivid." The author of *On the Art* insists that his verbal presentation about medicine is comparable to a doctor's visual demonstration. Moreover, the author of *On Breaths* describes logical deductions as evident, and in one case he even claims that sleep "bears witness" (*marturei*) to one of his claims.⁶⁵ Their concerns differ from the concerns of litigants, who try to reinforce their claims by linking them with real witness testimony through the vocabulary of demonstration and visibility. Since sophistic and medical speakers did not attempt to reconstruct the past in ways that were favorable to themselves, they were less dependent on witnesses than litigants were. Like litigants, however, they sought to convince audiences that closely associated knowing and seeing.

The context in which the vocabulary of demonstration and visibility appeared worked with the audience's expectations of the genre to determine how they would respond to it. The author of *On the Art* is careful to associate *epideiknumi* with a doctor's visual demonstration of his skill, while speakers in court are equally careful to associate it with eyewitnesses who saw visual evidence. As a result, jurors would not have responded to *epideiknumi* in the same way as the audience of *On the Art*. Their preconceived notions of what makes an argument convincing, developed from familiarity with legal procedure and legal argument, would have influenced the way they understood the word. Litigants and speechwriters took advantage of these expectations to suggest that their arguments were based on the secure testimony of witnesses, the kind of arguments that the jurors were predisposed to accept. The author of *On the Art*, on the other hand, stresses that his argument is parallel to the visual demonstration of a doctor, the kind of argument that he admits is likely to convince an audience doubtful about medicine's efficacy.

Demonstration in Funeral Oratory

Although speakers can adapt the vocabulary of demonstration and visibility to the needs of a wide variety of genres, these words were not appropriate for every rhetorical setting. The language of demonstration is very rare in one of the most characteristically Athenian oratorical genres, the funeral oration.[66] None of the six surviving funeral orations, including the certainly fictional ones that reflect the customs of the genre, calls itself a demonstration (*epideixis* or *apodeixis*), and only Aspasia, as quoted by Plato's Socrates, refers to her speaking with a verb of demonstrating. "Let us demonstrate [*epideixōmen*]," she says, "the way they did their deeds."[67] Since funeral orations are often considered the premier example of Athenian epideictic oratory, the rarity of this language is initially striking.

Speakers may, however, have considered it unnecessary to describe their speaking as a demonstration, since funeral orations neither make arguments based on witnesses nor compete with visual demonstrations. The language of demonstration may also have had a connotation of intellectualism or litigiousness that speakers chose to avoid. Furthermore, the men chosen to honor the war dead were emphatically not making displays of themselves, even if, in practice, funeral orations may have been opportunities to show off rhetorical talent. The most important demonstration was not being made by the speaker; it had already been made by the dead soldiers. The funeral orations of Demosthenes, Hyperides, Lysias, and Plato all use forms of *deiknumi*, *epideiknumi*, or *apodeiknumi* to describe how the dead soldiers or other people displayed their own or the city's virtue through their actions.[68] Since funeral orations honor the demonstrations of others, it would have been inappropriate for speakers to use the vocabulary of demonstration for themselves.

CONCLUSIONS

In forensic oratory and some types of epideictic oratory, speakers could take advantage of the central role of seeing in the Greek conception of knowledge by describing their presentations with the vocabulary of demonstration and visibility. The words played a specialized role in forensic speeches because of their status as semitechnical terms common to a range of Athenian procedures that involved witness testimony. Litigants and speechwriters used the vocabulary of demonstration and visibility to present themselves as authoritative sources of information that could help the jurors, in Antiphon's words, "see the things that have happened" and "look into the truth of the matter." They encouraged the jurors to reject their opponents' claims and to accept their arguments as though they were supported by witness testimony and visual evidence.

Parallels with epideictic rhetoric illustrate what is distinctive about forensic oratory. Since *On the Art* and *On Breaths* are concerned primarily with universal principles, the arguments they present are timeless. Whether medicine is an art or whether excess air causes illness are not questions tied to a particular occasion. The vocabulary of demonstration and visibility, therefore, reflects the general validity of the arguments and the replicable character of the presentations. In *On the Art*, the author maintains that his verbal demonstration teaches in a similar way to a hypothetical visual demonstration; in *On Breaths*, the author claims that logical arguments lead to evident conclusions about air and wind, even though air and wind are themselves invisible. Neither work, however, depends on particular visual evidence. Audience members may bring prejudice or prior knowledge to their encounter with *On the Art* or *On Breaths*, but the works seek to persuade on their own without supplementary proofs or evidence.

In the Athenian courts, litigants supported their speeches with a variety of ancillary material, including witness testimonies, laws, and documents. They also competed against opponents who called their own witnesses, cited their own laws, and presented their own evidence. Persuasion in the courts, therefore, was tied to its occasion in a way that epideictic persuasion was not. The use of the vocabulary of demonstration and visibility reflects this. Litigants do not present their arguments as demonstrations of timeless truths made visible to the eyes of the mind through reason but as demonstrations supported by particular witness testimonies and particular visual evidence. They encourage the jurors to think of themselves as witnesses who learn from an authoritative source within the context of a specific trial.

PART THREE

IMAGINARY SIGHT

─────── FIVE ───────

VISUALIZING CIVIC SUFFERING

Through techniques associated with *enargeia* ("vividness"), litigants encouraged jurors to imagine they were present at the events they hear described. Susceptible jurors would have experienced an imagined sense of presence and an emotional response corroborating the speakers' verbal claims. Especially for litigants with weak cases, the ability to manipulate imaginations could have been as important as actual proof.

INTRODUCTION: ANTISTHENES' *AJAX*

By likening verbal arguments to visual demonstrations, litigants and speechwriters may have convinced some jurors that they were relying on certain evidence, but their opponents were making unsubstantiated claims. Despite their best efforts to portray the jurors as witnesses, however, the jurors always remained listeners, trying to determine the truth from incomplete evidence and biased presentations. The Athenian legal system, like any system that relies on jury trials, trusted a group of people who have no personal knowledge of a dispute to resolve it in the most just way. The hundreds of jurors necessary for every Athenian trial guaranteed that even if some jurors were familiar with the details of the case and shared them with other jurors, insider knowledge would not carry particular weight in the final decision. This created fair trials, or at least the fairest trials possible, since people without firsthand knowledge of a case were less likely to have prejudices against either litigant. Fairness, therefore, trumps absolute certainty, leaving a paradox at the heart of the Athenian legal system. Eyewitness knowledge is subordinated to the collective judgment of the jurors, who must draw authoritative conclusions from whatever information the litigants choose to give them, regardless of whether it is complete or incomplete, truthful or deceptive.

Antisthenes' Ajax recognizes this paradox at the beginning of his speech arguing that he and not Odysseus should be awarded the arms of Achilles.[1] With the language of presence that characterizes the Athenian conception of witnessing, Ajax says:

> ἐβουλόμην ἂν τοὺς αὐτοὺς ἡμῖν δικάζειν οἵπερ καὶ ἐν τοῖς πράγμασι παρῆσαν· οἶδα γὰρ ὅτι ἐμὲ μὲν ἔδει σιωπᾶν, τούτῳ δ' οὐδὲν ἂν ἦν πλέον λέγοντι· νῦν δὲ οἱ μὲν παραγενόμενοι τοῖς ἔργοις αὐτοῖς ἄπεισιν, ὑμεῖς δὲ οἱ οὐδὲν εἰδότες δικάζετε. καίτοι ποία τις ἂν δίκη δικαστῶν μὴ εἰδότων γένοιτο, καὶ ταῦτα διὰ λόγων, τὸ δὲ πρᾶγμα ἐγίγνετο ἔργῳ; (Antisthenes, *Ajax* 1)

> I would have preferred the same men to be our judges who were also present at the events in question. For I know that all I would need to do was to keep silent, and there would be nothing more for my opponent to say. But as things are, those who were present for my actions [*ergois*] are absent, and you who don't know anything are judging. And yet, what kind of justice could there ever be when jurors do not know and their decision depends on words [*logōn*], while the event was happening by action [*ergōi*]?

The laconic and proud hero speaks of his jurors and of the adversarial process with more disdain than a real litigant would. Throughout the rest of the speech, Ajax continues to stress the importance of actions (*erga*) as a basis for judgment and to deny that language (*logos*) can ever lead to the truth.[2] Moreover, far from flattering the jurors, he later alludes a second time to their ignorance and even anticipates that they will be punished if they decide against him.[3] Through Ajax's voice, Antisthenes articulates the central epistemological challenge of the Athenian legal system: there is no way for the jurors to know what really happened.

Modern American courts accommodate this unavoidable gap in certainty by directing the jurors in criminal cases to convict only if the evidence places the defendant's guilt beyond a reasonable doubt. Although there was no reasonable-doubt rule in the Athenian courts, litigants routinely appeal to another kind of reasonableness, claiming that jurors should accept conclusions based on logical arguments as supplements to, and sometimes as replacements for, decisive evidence. Since these arguments tend to begin "it is probable [*eikos*] that . . . ," modern scholars call them "*eikos* arguments." In Ajax's opinion, any talk of probability would obscure the real issue: the jurors "are not judges of the things that are said but guessers [*doxastai*]."[4] Neither we nor the Classical Athenians would call a logical conclusion based on available evidence a guess. For Ajax, however, this is a difference in semantics and not in kind. He believes that any decision based on speech can never be more than a good guess, even if the reasoning leaves little room for serious doubt. Real knowledge of what happened is limited to the people who were present.

This simplistic position befits Ajax, whose opinions are notoriously free from nuance, but it places excessive emphasis on presence as a key to knowledge. Witnesses are not always sure of what they have seen, and sometimes people do things when no one is present who can testify to them later. Antisthenes' Odysseus, in his response to Ajax, even turns the presence of witnesses into a mark of vainglory rather than a measure of truth. Ajax's public displays of valor become simply a cheap way for an insecure man to show off, while Odysseus' choice to act in secret reflects true dedication to the Achaean cause.[5] In the end, Odysseus wins the debate.[6] Not only is he awarded Achilles' arms, but he proves the value of *logos* as a method of determining truth by using an *eikos* argument to predict Ajax's suicide.[7]

The relationship between presence and knowledge was a concern for real Athenian litigants and speechwriters as well as for Antisthenes' Ajax. But, rather than denying the jurors the possibility of knowing things they failed to witness, as Ajax does, they developed rhetorical strategies to exploit the jurors' lack of firsthand knowledge. In the method this chapter and chapter 6 will investigate, speakers use verbs of seeing to lead receptive jurors either to imagine they are present as spectators within the scenes they hear described or to identify with the emotions and reactions of spectators within the narratives. Through language and the power of suggestion, the speakers try to make the jurors visualize their version of events and accept it as true. If they succeed, the jurors become even more useful to them than real witnesses would be. Although not all jurors would have responded to speakers' prompting, susceptible jurors would have imagined they saw what a speaker wanted them to see and would have interpreted it in the way he wished.

IMAGINARY SIGHT

ENARGEIA AND FORENSIC ORATORY

Beginning in the era of the late Roman republic, rhetorical theorists say that verbal descriptions exhibit *enargeia* ("vividness") if they make an audience feel that they are seeing the events they are hearing or reading about.[8] Related to the adjective *enargēs*, which in Homeric poetry describes a god's visual presence in an epiphany[9] and in Aeschylus' *Persians* describes the dream Atossa "seemed to see,"[10] *enargeia* suggests something that suddenly, dazzlingly appears before the eyes. It is a common term in analyses of poetry and prose from the imperial era through late antiquity, often associated with descriptive passages called *ekphrases* (singular, *ekphrasis*). The first-century CE rhetorician Aelius Theon's pithy definition of *ekphrasis* shows how the two concepts are related: "An *ekphrasis* is a descriptive passage [*logos*] that brings vividly [*enargōs*] before the eyes [*hup(o) opsin*] whatever is being made clear [*to dēloumenon*]."[11] The phrase "bringing before the eyes" first characterizes the effects of language in Aristotle's *Rhetoric*,[12] and it later becomes standard terminology in both Greek and Latin.[13] Ancient rhetorical theorists recognized that narrative choices, such as an abundance of details, grammatical choices, such as the so-called historical present tense, and stylistic choices, such as metaphors, can all contribute to the "bringing before the eyes" characteristic of *enargeia*.[14] At heart, however, *enargeia* is as much a psychological process as a linguistic one, since it describes the effect of language on the mind.

Dionysius of Halicarnassus preserves an early definition of *enargeia* in his treatise on Lysias.[15] Although Dionysius analyzes Lysias' work from the perspective of a reader[16] rather than of a listener or a juror, his insights about *enargeia* illuminate why it would have been a persuasive tactic in the Athenian courts. His account of *enargeia* emphasizes the close relationship of visualization, presence, and persuasion. He writes:

ἔχει δὲ καὶ τὴν ἐνάργειαν πολλὴν ἡ Λυσίου λέξις. αὕτη δ' ἐστὶ δύναμίς τις ὑπὸ τὰς αἰσθήσεις ἄγουσα τὰ λεγόμενα, γίγνεται δ' ἐκ τῆς τῶν παρακολουθούντων λήψεως. ὁ δὴ προσέχων τὴν διάνοιαν τοῖς Λυσίου λόγοις οὐχ οὕτως ἔσται σκαιὸς ἢ δυσάρεστος ἢ βραδὺς τὸν νοῦν, ὃς οὐχ ὑπολήψεται γινόμενα τὰ δηλούμενα <u>ὁρᾶν καὶ ὥσπερ παροῦσιν</u> οἷς ἂν ὁ ῥήτωρ εἰσάγῃ προσώποις ὁμιλεῖν. ἐπιζητήσει τε οὐθέν, οἷον εἰκὸς τοὺς μὲν ἂν δρᾶσαι, τοὺς δὲ παθεῖν, τοὺς δὲ διανοηθῆναι, τοὺς δὲ εἰπεῖν. κράτιστος γὰρ δὴ πάντων ἐγένετο ῥητόρων φύσιν ἀνθρώπων κατοπτεῦσαι καὶ

τὰ προσήκοντα ἑκάστοις ἀποδοῦναι πάθη τε καὶ ἤθη καὶ ἔργα.
(Dionysius of Halicarnassus, *Lysias* 7)

Enargeia is a quality that the style of Lysias has in abundance. This consists in a certain ability to bring the things that are spoken before the senses [*hupo tas aistheseis*], and it arises out of his grasp of circumstantial details. Nobody who applies his mind [*dianoian*] to the speeches of Lysias will be so obtuse, insensitive, or slow-witted that he will not feel that he can see [*horan*] going on the things that are being made clear [*ta deloumena*] and that he interacts with the people whom the orator brings forth as though they are present [*hōsper parousin*]. And he will require no further evidence of what would be fitting [*eikos*] for them to do, suffer, plan, or say. For Lysias was the best of all orators at observing closely human nature and ascribing to each type of person the appropriate emotions, moral qualities, and actions.
(Adapted from Usher 1974)

Dionysius' "before the senses" (*hupo tas aistheseis*), "see" (*horan*), and "the things that are being made clear" (*ta deloumena*) resemble the language we have seen Aelius Theon using to define *ekphrasis*. They indicate that Dionysius is thinking of *enargeia* as causing an imagined shift from writing and reading to showing and seeing. Only an attentive reader who "applies his mind [*dianoian*]" will experience this shift and visualize the scene Lysias describes. The resulting sense of presence will be so great that he will accept Lysias' account without the *eikos* arguments so common in forensic speeches. Dionysius' emphasis on presence resembles Antisthenes' Ajax's insistence that jurors can have no real knowledge of the event they have to judge unless they were present for it. From his reading of Lysias, however, Dionysius realizes that imaginary presence can sometimes be an effective substitute for real presence. In other words, the imagined sense of presence produced by *enargeia* persuades by creating the illusion of knowledge in the jurors, who will require "no further evidence."

Dionysius lived more than three hundred years after Lysias' death. By placing the concept of *enargeia* squarely within the context of legal persuasion, however, he anchors his argument within a semantic tradition whose roots lie in Classical Athens. The Athenians of the fifth and fourth centuries used the adjective *enargēs* to describe crimes committed before witnesses. The best example is in *Against Meidias* (Demosthenes 21), where Demosthenes says that a verbal description of a crime can never replicate "the way *hubris* really and truly appears [*phainetai*] vivid [*enargēs*] to the victim and the people who see it [*tois horōsin*]."[17] Similarly, the guard in Sophocles' *Antigone* says that the person who buried Polyneikes is not *enargēs*, since no one saw the burial.[18] Passages such as these have led Kathy Eden to argue that *enargeia* originated as a legal notion.[19] In addition, *enargēs*, like *phaneros*, can describe verbal arguments as well as visible actions, implying that visual proof or witness testimony supports them. Also like *phaneros*, it sometimes appears in these contexts with other words that refer to sight or visual clarity.[20]

Regardless of the ultimate origin of the concept, it is clear that Dionysius understands *enargeia* to be a quality of language that encourages listeners or readers to imagine that what they hear or read is as vivid (*enargēs*) as Demosthenes says *hubris* is to the witnesses of an assault. Significantly, legal terms such as "witnesses" appear in discussions of *enargeia* even outside judicial contexts, suggesting that the legal connotations of the concept are never far below the surface. The bT scholion to *Iliad* 14.226–227, for instance, although it does not use the word *enargeia*, says that, through a detailed description of Hera's route from Olympos to Lemnos, Homer has prompted the mind (*dianoia*) of his audience to picture the places and has "made his account more plausible by bringing his readers in as witnesses [*marturas*]."[21]

Lawyers who talk about the role of visualization in contemporary legal argument also emphasize that it can prompt jurors to respond like witnesses. In terms that would be familiar to Dionysius, Leonard Decof, a personal injury lawyer and the author of the *Opening Statements* handbook in *The Art of Advocacy* series, writes that a good opening statement should tell a story "in such a way that the listener can visualize it." He presents this imagined visualization as a replacement for the jury's lack of first-hand, eyewitness knowledge. "Think of how easy it would be for a jury to decide your case," he writes, "if they had witnessed the accident, seen the plaintiff in the hospital, in surgery, in torturous rehabilitation, or in the plaintiff's routine at home, struggling to get through another day." Since they did not witness it, however, and cannot watch it on film, it is the lawyer's job "to make it happen all over again while the jury is watching, and make them a part of it."[22] Decof does not assign a name to this technique, but other legal rhetoricians call it a "word picture."[23] Through this method, according to law professor Steven Lubet, a speaker can transfer his mental image to the jurors and make them understand it in the way he or she wishes.[24] Similarly, James McElhaney, a law professor who wrote the "Litigation" column in the *American Bar*

Association Journal for twenty-five years, recommends that lawyers "practice thinking visually" in preparation for making word pictures for their jurors.[25]

This model of image transference from speaker to listener through language echoes Quintilian's and Pseudo-Longinus' discussions of *enargeia*. In their accounts, a skilled speaker first pictures a scene in his imagination and experiences the emotions he would have experienced had he seen it. Then, through language, he transfers the scene and its attendant emotional effects to his audience.[26] Some modern trial lawyers actively practice the preparation method recommended by Quintilian and Pseudo-Longinus. Through a technique called psychodrama, they stage dramatic reenactments of the events they intend to describe to the jurors, taking on the role of their own clients. Dana Cole, a law professor and advocate of psychodrama, maintains that it enables lawyers "to experience the facts rather than simply learn about them" and so equips them to recount to the jurors a story "rich with the emotional detail that can only be accessed by the experience."[27]

Even though the Athenians of the fifth and fourth centuries had not yet developed a formal theory of *enargeia*, litigants and speechwriters employed many of the techniques later theorists associate with it to influence their jurors' visual imaginations and to manipulate their emotions. Some of these techniques are subtle, like providing extra details and deictic markers to help a juror picture the scene of a crime in his mind. Details remain the most prominent element of *enargeia* throughout the ancient rhetorical tradition,[28] and psychology experiments conducted over the past thirty years have provided tentative support for the conclusion that highly detailed narratives influence jurors in their favor.[29] Nouns and verbs of seeing can complement detailed descriptions and encourage jurors to imagine they see what the speaker describes.[30] Aeschines is especially fond of such direct appeals to his jurors' visual imaginations. In *Against Ktesiphon* (Aeschines 3) alone, he asks the jurors three times to imagine they see something.[31]

MANIPULATING THE JURORS' IMAGINATIONS

Aeschines, Demosthenes, and Lycurgus offer three parallel examples of how litigants and speechwriters tried to guide the imaginations of their jurors by directly appealing to their senses of sight. Aeschines' *Against Ktesiphon*, Demosthenes' *On the Dishonest Embassy*, and Lycurgus'

Against Leokrates all include descriptions of suffering cities framed with the language of seeing. Aeschines describes the destruction of Thebes, and Demosthenes the ruins of Phokis. Although Lycurgus does not describe a ruined city, his account of the panic in Athens that followed the battle of Chaeronea shares core elements with the accounts in Aeschines and Demosthenes, especially the despair of women and the elderly. Roman-era and late-antique rhetorical handbooks identify sacked cities as a typical topic for *ekphrases*.[32] The fallen buildings and suffering inhabitants offer many opportunities for detailed description and emotional manipulation.[33] These three passages therefore form a unique set of case studies for studying appeals to the jurors' visual imaginations. The three orators make the chaos of the cities, in Decol's words, "happen all over again while the jury is watching, and make them a part of it." Furthermore, the scholia that accompany *On the Dishonest Embassy* contain a record of how ancient scholars understood the interaction of language, visualization, and emotional response.

Against Ktesiphon

Among the many ways Aeschines charges Demosthenes with having failed "consistently to speak and do the best things for the *dēmos*"[34] in *Against Ktesiphon* (Aeschines 3) is his blaming Demosthenes for Alexander's destruction of Thebes in 335.[35] He claims that Demosthenes could have used the money he received from the king of Persia either to bribe the Macedonian garrison to abandon Thebes without destroying it or to bribe the Arcadians to help save the Thebans.[36] It is unlikely, however, that Demosthenes could really have saved Thebes through bribery. Aeschines appears to have linked two unrelated events, Demosthenes' acceptance of Persian gold and the traumatic destruction of Thebes, to discredit him.[37] A central element of Aeschines' strategy is a direct appeal to the visual imagination of his jurors. He says to them:

> ἀλλ' ἐπειδὴ τοῖς σώμασιν οὐ παρεγένεσθε, ἀλλὰ ταῖς γε διανοίαις ἀποβλέψατ' αὐτῶν εἰς τὰς συμφοράς, καὶ νομίσαθ' ὁρᾶν ἁλισκομένην πόλιν, τειχῶν κατασκαφάς, ἐμπρήσεις οἰκιῶν, ἀγομένας γυναῖκας παῖδας εἰς δουλείαν, πρεσβύτας ἀνθρώπους, πρεσβύτιδας γυναῖκας ὀψὲ μεταμανθάνοντας τὴν ἐλευθερίαν, κλαίοντας, ἱκετεύοντας ὑμᾶς, ὀργιζομένους οὐ τοῖς τιμωρουμένοις, ἀλλὰ τοῖς τούτων αἰτίοις, ἐπισκήπτοντας μηδενὶ τρόπῳ τὸν τῆς Ἑλλάδος ἀλιτήριον στεφανοῦν, ἀλλὰ καὶ τὸν δαίμονα καὶ

τὴν τύχην τὴν συμπαρακολουθοῦσαν τῷ ἀνθρώπῳ φυλάξασθαι. οὔτε γὰρ πόλις οὔτ' ἀνὴρ ἰδιώτης οὐδεὶς πώποτε καλῶς ἀπήλλαξε Δημοσθένει συμβούλῳ χρησάμενος. (Aeschin. 3.157–158)

> But since you were not present [*paregenesthe*] in the flesh [*tois sōmasin*], look [*apoblepsat(e)*] with your minds [*tais ge dianoiais*] at their misfortunes, and suppose [*nomisat(e)*] that you see [*horan*] a city being captured, walls being razed, homes in flames, women and children being led to slavery, old men and old women unlearning late in the day what it means to be free, weeping, beseeching you, not angered at those punishing them but at those who caused these misfortunes, enjoining you in no way to crown the polluter of Hellas but to guard against the bad luck and the fate that follows close on the man's heels. For [*gar*] no city and no private individual that followed Demosthenes' advice has ever turned out well.

Aeschines begins by acknowledging that the jurors were not present at the destruction of Thebes, and he invites them to use their visual imaginations, twice urging them to "look" and to "see." *Tois sōmasin* ("in the flesh") and *tais dianoiais* ("with your minds") have the same position in the two clauses, underscoring through word order that imagined sight should replace bodily presence. With *ge*, an emphatic particle with no English equivalent, Aeschines calls particular attention to the words "with your minds," emphasizing that the jurors should participate actively in what he is about to say and not just listen to it.

By keeping his description as general as possible, Aeschines encourages the jurors to visualize what they think a conquered city and its inhabitants should look like. Jurors who have never seen Thebes need only picture "a city," "walls," "homes," "women and children," and "old men and old women," since neither adjectives nor definite articles specify these people and places as particular to Thebes. The jurors have to fill in the details for themselves, creating personalized images of Thebes and the Thebans. According to Demetrius' *On Style*, Theophrastus advised orators to give incomplete descriptions, making their audience supplement the gaps from their own experience. Through mental participation, Theophrastus says, each listener becomes a witness (*martus*) in the speaker's favor, and he feels well disposed to the speaker because he has been made to feel intelligent.[38]

Aeschines' strategy extends beyond flattery. Through a general description, he encourages the jurors to personalize their mental images of

Thebes with what they find most affecting or important. Some of them may actually have known exiled Thebans in Athens, but others would have drawn on their shared cultural knowledge of conquered cities.[39] Each juror, therefore, becomes a witness in Aeschines' favor primarily because, through Aeschines' influence, he himself has created the scene that he witnesses in his mind. Aeschines' words and the jurors' imaginations work together to develop individual images of the last moments of Thebes, each one of which is maximally affecting to the juror who creates it.

In the second half of this passage, Aeschines turns the jurors' visual imagination from the past to the present, from Thebes to Ktesiphon's trial. Thebes' elderly inhabitants, who in Aeschines' description have just lost their freedom to the Macedonians, now become his fellow prosecutors, or *sunēgoroi*, speaking to the jurors as jurors and not as spectators of Thebes' destruction. As the temporal and spatial settings of the jurors' imaginations shift, the indefinite nouns of Thebes' destruction also give way to definite nouns and an attributive participle referring to Demosthenes. In an indirect statement representing the voice of the old men and women, Aeschines calls Demosthenes "the polluter of Hellas" and urges the jurors "to guard against the bad luck and the fate that follows close on the man's heels." The jurors' unique mental pictures of the imagined past, therefore, have become the background for an unambiguous attack on Demosthenes in the present. As the passage ends, the distinction between the elderly Thebans and Aeschines himself blurs as the imagined scene gives way to the reality of the court. The last sentence, spoken in direct statement by Aeschines as himself, is the logical conclusion of the words attributed to the Thebans; as the *gar* shows, it explains the cause of their antipathy to Demosthenes.

Aeschines' account of the destruction of Thebes is focalized through the jurors rather than through the Thebans. He could have recounted the scene in terms of what the Thebans saw, describing them as witnesses who beheld their city in flames and watched one another being led into slavery. Instead, only the jurors are subjects of the verbs of seeing. Even removed in space and time, they are the primary witnesses of the Thebans' distress. Furthermore, although Aeschines is speaking, he conceals his authorial presence behind the second-person plural verbs that introduce the scene. He neither calls attention to himself with first-person verbs of speaking or demonstrating nor declares his own opinions about the scene he describes, compelling the jurors to draw their own conclusions about what they see in their imaginations. In Aeschines' presentation, the jurors' imagined presence, and not his words, becomes the ultimate source of authority for their knowledge of the destruction of Thebes.

On the Dishonest Embassy

Thirteen years before Aeschines and Demosthenes met in Ktesiphon's trial, Demosthenes prosecuted Aeschines for misconduct on the Athenian embassy to Philip in 346. In his speech *On the Dishonest Embassy* (Demosthenes 19), he describes the ruined cities of Phokis. His account is superficially similar to Aeschines' description of Thebes: like Aeschines, Demosthenes vaguely refers to ruined walls and homes and to women, children, and the elderly, trusting his listeners to fill in the details.[40] Unlike Aeschines, however, Demosthenes does not emphasize the jurors' imagined presence and conceal himself behind second-person verbs. Rather, he presents himself as both viewer and narrator, describing what he saw and encouraging the jurors to experience the devastation of Phokis through his eyes and to share in his emotional reactions.

The fate of the Phokians is a central element in Demosthenes' argument that Aeschines accepted bribes from Philip to prepare a peace treaty favorable to him and to promote his interests in Athens.[41] Lacking conclusive evidence of the bribery, Demosthenes relies heavily on a narrative that supports his argument. As Demosthenes tells it, Aeschines prevented the Athenians from voting to send military aid to Phokis by promising falsely that Philip's policy in central Greece would be favorable to the Athenians and Phokians.[42] Once they learned the Athenians had abandoned them, the Phokians surrendered to Philip, who then facilitated their punishment for impiety against Apollo at the hands of the Thebans and the other members of the Delphic Amphiktiony.[43] Although Aeschines denies that he made any promises about Phokis, Demosthenes constructs his narrative so that the destruction of the Phokian cities seems to confirm that Aeschines lied on Philip's behalf, which in turn seems to confirm that he accepted bribes.[44] Demosthenes presents the fall of Phokis as a sign of Athens' impotence against Philip, who arranged the Phokians' affairs as he wished without any regard for Athens.[45] He goes so far as to call it an *aiskhron*, a "mark of shame," that Athens, under Aeschines' influence, did nothing to save her allies, the Phokians, who had voted to prevent Athens' own destruction after the Peloponnesian War.[46]

The destruction of Phokis therefore has two main functions in Demosthenes' rhetorical strategy: as circumstantial evidence for Aeschines' guilt and as a sign of Philip's power and Athens' shame. He only briefly focuses on the Phokians' own suffering, recounting what he saw and how he felt when he traveled through the vanquished cities on his way to Delphi. Stressing the visual quality of his experience among the Phokians, Demosthenes says:

> ὃν μὲν τοίνυν τρόπον οἱ ταλαίπωροι Φωκεῖς ἀπολώλασιν, οὐ μόνον ἐκ τῶν δογμάτων τούτων ἔστιν ἰδεῖν, ἀλλὰ καὶ ἐκ τῶν ἔργων ἃ πέπρακται, θέαμα δεινόν, ὦ ἄνδρες Ἀθηναῖοι, καὶ ἐλεινόν· ὅτε γὰρ νῦν ἐπορευόμεθα εἰς Δελφούς, ἐξ ἀνάγκης ἦν ὁρᾶν ἡμῖν πάντα ταῦτα, οἰκίας κατεσκαμμένας, τείχη περιῃρημένα, χώραν ἔρημον τῶν ἐν ἡλικίᾳ, γύναια δὲ καὶ παιδάρια ὀλίγα καὶ πρεσβύτας ἀνθρώπους οἰκτρούς· οὐδ' ἂν εἷς δύναιτ' ἐφικέσθαι τῷ λόγῳ τῶν ἐκεῖ κακῶν νῦν ὄντων. (Dem. 19.64–65)

> One can see [*estin idein*] in what manner the wretched Phokians were destroyed not only from these decrees but also from the deeds [*ek tōn ergōn*] that have been done, a fearful spectacle [*theama*], Athenian gentlemen, and a pitiable one. For when we were traveling to Delphi just now, we had to see [*ex anankēs ēn horan hēmīn*] all these things, houses razed to the ground, walls stripped away, a country bereft of men in their prime, delicate women, a few small children, and sorry elderly people. No one would be able to approach the evils that are now there with speech [*tōi logōi*].

Demosthenes begins with an impersonal "one can see [*estin idein*]," with "see" meaning "know" or "learn." Through the impersonal construction, Demosthenes not only alerts the jurors to the possibility of knowing, he also invites them to follow his prompting and to know for themselves. The way that "one can see" is first from the documents that Demosthenes has just asked the clerk to read aloud, which record the Athenians' alliance with the Phokians, the Phokians' agreement to surrender their cities to Philip, and the Amphiktions' decision to destroy the Phokians' cities,[47] and second "from the deeds that have been done." As Demosthenes prepares to describe the outcome of the deeds, the seeing vocabulary acquires a stronger visual sense. "One can see" not only through the written record but also through what "we had to see" (*ex anankēs ēn horan hēmīn*), the visual testimony of Demosthenes himself. The two infinitives that mean "see," *idein* and *horan*, therefore, equate the activity of Demosthenes and his companions with the activity of the jurors.[48] Declaring that speech is inadequate to convey the horrors in Phokis, Demosthenes uses the parallel infinitive constructions to imply that the jurors are seeing the deeds through his eyes.

Although Demosthenes does not invoke the jurors' visual imaginations, the repeated references to seeing, the denigration of speech, and the insistence that the Phokians' destruction is a "spectacle" present his words as though they are visual evidence rather than straightforward verbal testimony. The word *theama* ("spectacle"), which appears only here in the surviving corpus of Attic forensic oratory, underscores the visual nature of Demosthenes' description. Furthermore, by separating the two adjectives that describe *theama* with the vocative "Athenian gentlemen" (*ō andres Athēnaioi*), Demosthenes represents verbally the effect of his rhetoric on his listeners. The word order places the jurors within the fearful and pitiable spectacle they are about to hear described.

By calling this spectacle fearful and pitiable, Demosthenes links his observation of the Phokians' sufferings to an emotional response. "Spectacle" is an appropriate word for Demosthenes' silent Phokis, where, unlike in Aeschines' Thebes, the characters neither cry nor implore. Aeschines never calls the destruction of Thebes a spectacle, and, more importantly, he could not describe what kind of emotions it excited in spectators, since his account has none. The old men and women show grief and anger, but they are participants rather than spectators. Aeschines' jurors had to determine for themselves how they would react to the image of Thebes they pictured in their minds. By identifying what he wants the jurors to consider the proper emotional reactions to the destruction of Phokis, however, Demosthenes provides a model for his jurors to follow as they see in their minds what he saw in person.

By visualizing the sufferings of the Phokians and condemning Aeschines for causing it, the jurors exercise the Athenians' customary role of supporting other Greeks who are suffering injustice. The sentence immediately preceding this passage describes this role in visual terms: it is Athens' ancestral custom, says Demosthenes, "to stand at the head of the Hellenes and not to overlook [*perihoran*] this kind of thing when it is going on."[49] The visual sense of "overlook" in Greek is often very weak, but the close proximity of "overlook," "one can see," and "we had to see" indicates that, when the jurors come to see through Demosthenes' language, they are recovering Athens' position as leader of the Greeks. Misled by Aeschines' machinations, they overlooked the Phokians' sufferings, but now Demosthenes is helping them to see.

The scholia to this section of *On the Dishonest Embassy* recognize the close connection between visualization and emotional response. They focus on the passage's visual quality, calling it an example of *diatupōsis* ("engraving" or "impression").[50] The term, nearly synonymous with *enargeia*, refers to a passage's ability to imprint itself on a listener's mind as a seal leaves its impression on wax or a stamp cuts an image into a coin.[51] Demosthenes is said to "bring the misfortunes under sight [*hup(o) opsin*] through his language [*logōi*] from the very form and manner of the *pathos*."[52] In the Demosthenic scholia, *pathos* can refer to the event that causes an emotional response or to the response itself. In this sentence, it seems to refer to an event, namely, the destruction of the Phokian cities, the "form and manner" of which Demosthenes describes.[53]

The next part of this scholion and the other scholia to this section explain how Demosthenes uses *diatupōsis* to lead the jurors to experience their own *pathos*, in the sense of an emotional response, while they hear his words. *Diatupōsis* "concerns itself with particulars,"[54] which in this case are the specific examples of the Phokians' misfortunes that Demosthenes says he saw. Furthermore, "particulars make the *logos* more alive [*empsukhoteron*], and *diatupōsis* delights in this."[55] One way that "particulars" give life to *logos* seems to be by affecting the emotions of the audience; another scholion says that *diatupōsis* is characterized by "saying something through *pathos*."[56] The scholia tell us that the reference to the ruined houses increases grief for the jurors, while the reference to the walls increases fear.[57] Similarly, calling the country "bereft of men in their prime" is said to cause pity and fear.[58]

The scholia explain that the audience experiences these emotions both because they are guided by Demosthenes' language and because they are compelled to participate intellectually in his description. A good example of the effect of language comes from a scholion analyzing the opening words of this passage. "He uses an opening," says the scholion, "that causes grief and lamenting in the audience because he mourns the Phokians' misfortune by calling them 'wretched.'"[59] Here, the scholion posits a direct link between the adjective Demosthenes chooses and the emotional response of his listeners.

The emotional effects the scholia ascribe to the "particulars" of the Phokians' suffering, however, require the audience to make mental inferences. For instance, as we have seen, one scholion distinguishes between the grief prompted by "houses razed to the ground" and the fear prompted by "walls stripped away." The preceding scholion describes the mental activity that "houses razed to the ground" generates in the listener. First, the listener must determine that "houses" is a metonym, since "the inhabitants also perished." Second, he must infer that the phrase "emphasizes the enemies' *hubris*, since razing to the ground is a terribly excessive form of misfortune."[60] The combination of these two insights—that people died when their homes were demolished and that the destruction was unnecessary—leads the audience to grieve on behalf of the Phokians. Fear, on the other hand, is always associated in the scholia to this passage with fear of future events rather than fear on behalf of the Phokians. So, when "walls stripped away" leads the listener to fear, he is fearing for himself and his *polis*. The scholia take for granted that the audience will always have the threat Philip poses to Athens and the rest of Greece in the front of their minds.[61] They infer, therefore, that when Demosthenes mentions the destruction of Phokis' walls, his audience will think of Philip's power rather than the Phokians' pain, and therefore will be frightened for Athens.

The scholia's judgment about which emotions are tied to which parts of the description may not accurately reflect the effect of Demosthenes' speech on all, or even any, of his original jurors. Nonetheless, it reflects the complex interaction between language, visualization, and emotion that underlies Demosthenes' strategy. As the scholia realize, Demosthenes' decision to characterize the destruction of Phokis as a fearful and pitiable spectacle affects how his audience interprets the "particulars" that he brings before their eyes. The urge to classify may have led the ancient commentators to draw an unconvincing distinction between the grief generated by the ruined houses and the fear generated by the ruined walls, but their focus on fear and grief, a close relative of pity, indicates they believe the audience shares in the emotions that Demosthenes associates with the spectacle.

Ruth Webb has compared this section of *On the Dishonest Embassy* to two imaginary speeches in the late-antique rhetorical theorist Sopatros' *Division of Questions* that exemplify the method of argument he calls *metastasis*, or "transfer of responsibility," where a speaker admits that he has committed a crime but argues that circumstances compelled him to do so.[62] In both passages, Sopatros' speakers justify their decisions by describing what they saw, and Webb argues that the references to seeing "transport the listeners into the scene" and "make them see the defendants' actions in a new light and to accept their arguments that they had no alternative but to do what they did."[63] The technique is similar to

Demosthenes' technique in his description of Phokis and the Phokians in *On the Dishonest Embassy*, although Demosthenes is not trying to justify his actions by an appeal to circumstances. Instead, he is trying to blacken Aeschines' character by portraying the pain his treachery caused Phokis and Athens. Nonetheless, in both Sopatros' invented speeches and Demosthenes' real speech, a description introduced with the vocabulary of seeing encourages the listeners to identify themselves with the viewing narrator and to share his reactions to what he sees. In *On the Dishonest Embassy*, Demosthenes leads the jurors to visualize the Phokians' sufferings, urges them to react to it with the emotions he describes, and, most importantly, directs their visualization against Aeschines, whom he accuses of making the Athenians overlook what he now makes visible.

Against Leokrates

In *Against Leokrates* (Lycurgus 1), Lycurgus uses a technique that resembles both Aeschines' technique in *Against Ktesiphon* and Demosthenes' in *On the Dishonest Embassy*. He has charged Leokrates with treason because he fled Athens after the battle of Chaeronea and lived as a metic for six years in Rhodes and Megara.[64] The trial seems to have taken place in 331, shortly before Aeschines' prosecution of Ktesiphon.[65] To stir up the jurors' patriotic anger against Leokrates' cowardice, Lycurgus describes the panicked conditions in Athens when news arrived of the defeat and the desperate citizens prepared to rely on elderly men for their defense. Emphasizing the sense of sight, he says:

> ὁρᾶν δ' ἦν ἐπὶ μὲν τῶν θυρῶν γυναῖκας ἐλευθέρας, περιφόβους κατεπτηχυίας καὶ πυνθανομένας εἰ ζῶσι, τὰς μὲν ὑπὲρ ἀνδρός, τὰς δ' ὑπὲρ πατρός, τὰς δ' ὑπὲρ ἀδελφῶν, ἀναξίως αὑτῶν καὶ τῆς πόλεως ὁρωμένας, τῶν δ' ἀνδρῶν τοὺς τοῖς σώμασιν ἀπειρηκότας καὶ ταῖς ἡλικίαις πρεσβυτέρους καὶ ὑπὸ τῶν νόμων τοῦ στρατεύεσθαι ἀφειμένους ἰδεῖν ἦν καθ' ὅλην τὴν πόλιν τότ' ἐπὶ γήρως ὁδῷ περιφθειρομένους, διπλᾶ τὰ ἱμάτια ἐμπεπορπημένους. πολλῶν δὲ καὶ δεινῶν κατὰ τὴν πόλιν γιγνομένων, καὶ πάντων τῶν πολιτῶν τὰ μέγιστα ἠτυχηκότων, μάλιστ' ἄν τις ἤλγησε καὶ ἐδάκρυσεν ἐπὶ ταῖς τῆς πόλεως συμφοραῖς, ἡνίχ' ὁρᾶν ἦν τὸν δῆμον ψηφισάμενον τοὺς μὲν δούλους ἐλευθέρους, τοὺς δὲ ξένους Ἀθηναίους, τοὺς δ' ἀτίμους ἐπιτίμους· ὃς πρότερον ἐπὶ τῷ αὐτόχθων εἶναι καὶ ἐλεύθερος ἐσεμνύνετο. (Lycurgus 1.40–41)

One could see [*horan ēn*] free [*eleutheras*] women at their doors, cowering in great fear and asking if they were still alive, some out of concern for their husband, others their father, others their sons. They were being seen [*horōmenas*] in a manner unworthy of themselves and of their *polis*. And one could also spot [*idein ēn*] some of the men, renounced by their bodies, older than the age of conscription, and excused by the laws from serving in the military, wandering destitute throughout the entire *polis* on the threshold of old age, with their cloaks fastened double in a soldierly manner. And while many terrible things were happening throughout the *polis* and all the citizens had suffered the greatest ill luck, nearly anyone [*tis*] would have mourned and wept over the misfortunes of the *polis*, when one could see [*horan ēn*] the *dēmos* voting to make slaves into free men and foreigners [*xenoi*] into Athenians and to return the franchise to the disenfranchised. Before, the *dēmos* used to boast that it was autochthonous and free [*eleutheros*].

Like Aeschines, Lycurgus avoids drawing attention to himself as the narrator, using no first-person verbs or pronouns. Instead of focalizing the scene through the jurors' imaginations, as Aeschines does, or emphasizing an emotional transfer from a viewing narrator to a listening audience, as Demosthenes does, however, Lycurgus uses the impersonal third-person imperfect form of the verb "to be" with an infinitive of seeing three times. The impersonal constructions alert the audience to what it was possible to see: not a continuous story but a series of representative images. They invite the jurors to visualize the scenes on the doorsteps of Athenian houses, in the streets, and in the assembly. Some of the jurors would have experienced the confusion in the city, and their memories would work with Lycurgus' words to sharpen and personalize their mental pictures of the general scenes Lycurgus sketches.

Lycurgus uses more definite articles and adjectives than Aeschines does in his description of Thebes or Demosthenes in his description of Phokis, but his Athenian matrons and old men remain generic, allowing his jurors to picture these desperate figures as their own mothers, sisters, fathers, and grandfathers. The word *polis*, however, always appears with a definite article. Unlike Aeschines and Demosthenes, who were happy for their jurors to picture Thebes and Phokis as any destroyed cities, Lycurgus emphasizes that his scene happened in "the *polis*," in Athens. While each juror may be picturing his own friends and family, his own house and his own streets, they are all sharing in visualizing Athens shaken to its core by news of the defeat. Furthermore, the generalized descriptions of the women and men lead up to the specific references to "all the citizens" suffering ill luck and "the *dēmos*," the collective which includes all the jurors, voting away its freedom. Lycurgus' three appeals to the jurors' visual imaginations, therefore, move from the general to the specific; throughout his account of what "one could see," however, he stresses that all of this took place in a specific place, the *polis* of the Athenians.

The sight Lycurgus describes is particularly offensive to the jurors as Athenian citizens not only because of the sufferings of women and the elderly but also because of the change from Athens' customarily superior position. Immediately after this section, Lycurgus goes on to say that the *polis* "experienced such a change" that it was no longer a military leader but forced to beg for help from people it once protected.[66] Everything that Lycurgus says "one could see" reflects this unexpected—and unthinkable—change: free women cower in fear and ask after their missing relatives, elderly men drill haphazardly in the streets, the *dēmos* votes to expand citizenship to non-Athenians.

Throughout Lycurgus' description, he emphasizes that the images he conjures up are unworthy of a free people. The passage is framed by two uses of the adjective *eleutheros* ("free"): once to describe the Athenian matrons crouching at their doors and once to describe the entire *dēmos*. The repetition calls attention to the women as a microcosm of the *polis*. Their visual display before an audience, implicit in the participle *horōmenas* ("they were being seen"), is unworthy of themselves and of Athens as a whole.[67] Significantly, Lycurgus classifies the sight of the women not as a cause of pity or grief but as a violation of societal norms. Being seen in a position of weakness is unworthy for the women as Athenians. The *dēmos*' decision to vote on a proposal to expand citizenship, which Lycurgus also presents as a visual spectacle, is similarly unworthy of the *polis*. In both cases, Lycurgus presents the things that "one could see" as harmful to the Athenians' corporate identity.

Like Demosthenes in *On the Dishonest Embassy*, Lycurgus links sight with a specific emotional response. He says, "Nearly anyone [*tis*] would have mourned and wept over the misfortunes of the city, when one could see [*horan ēn*] the *dēmos* voting to make slaves into free men and foreigners into Athenians and to return the franchise to the disenfranchised." In *Against Ktesiphon*, the grief of the elderly Thebans is part of the scene that Aeschines asks the jurors to visualize. Here, as in *On the Dishonest Embassy*, the grieving is not part of the scene Lycurgus describes, but is an emotional response experienced by someone who is observing it. With *tis* ("anyone"), Lycurgus creates a model spectator for the jurors to follow as they picture in their minds the images that "one could see." The emotions Lycurgus attributes to this "anyone" are all oriented towards the *polis*. He connects the mourning and tears over the misfortunes of the city directly to the spectacle of the *dēmos* voting to expand citizenship.[68] The grief is for public misfortunes and for Athens' change from greatness to desperation. When the jurors picture to themselves the scenes that Lycurgus describes, they should react in this way, outraged on behalf of the *polis* that was forced to sink so low by the dire initial reports from Chaeronea.

For Lycurgus to win the trial, he needed to convince the jurors of Leokrates' lack of loyalty to Athens. It was not enough for them to pity the sufferings of individual Athenians; they needed to grieve over the misfortunes of "all the citizens." This is why Lycurgus is so careful to direct the emotional response to the spectacle he describes towards the *polis* as a whole. Later, he will tell the jurors that "no one in the *polis* was idle" except Leokrates while the Athenians were preparing defenses.[69] With his visual description, Lycurgus tries to instill in the jurors the kind of patriotism that inspired a renewed dedication to Athens among the people who experienced it. They should share in the emotional response of the "one" who could see, the "anyone" mourning for Athens' lost greatness and motivated to help save the *polis* and the *dēmos*. Filled with these emotions, they will be more likely to agree with Lycurgus' characterization of Leokrates as not merely a coward but a traitor as well.

CONCLUSIONS

Although Antisthenes' *Ajax* lamented that his jurors could not render a just decision because they were not present at the event they were obliged to judge, Athenian litigants and speechwriters tried to turn the jurors' absence to their advantage. Through techniques associated with *enargeia*, speakers manipulated their jurors' imaginations and encouraged them, in Dionysius of Halicarnassus' words, to feel they could "see" the events in question unfolding "before the senses" as though they were "present." Ajax would perhaps be reassured to learn that this imagined sense of presence was not, on its own, always sufficient to influence a jury's decision. Like Aeschines in his case against Ktesiphon and Demosthenes in his case against Aeschines, Lycurgus failed against Leokrates, losing by a single vote.[70]

While this should not lead us to conclude that appeals to the jurors' visual imaginations were all doomed to failure, it should make us think about these particular passages and their roles in a losing cause. Appeals to the imagination, like all rhetorical techniques, are double-edged swords. They can strengthen already strong cases, but they can also conceal the problems in weak ones. Since Aeschines, Demosthenes, and Lycurgus delivered each of these speeches as prosecutors in trials motivated by politics as much as by concern for the laws, they may have been particularly interested in guiding the jurors' imaginations and manipulating their emotions to distract them from weaker parts of their cases.

No matter how effectively the jurors were led to visualize Thebes or Phokis or Athens, visualization is just one of many factors that would have affected their final decisions. Even successful appeals to the jurors' imaginations are not panaceas for weak cases or silver bullets against strong opponents. The story preserved in the *Lives of the Ten Orators* attributed to Plutarch about the Rhodians' reaction to *Against Ktesiphon* illustrates that no matter how much listeners may like the first speech they hear, they can always prefer the next one: "Aeschines read his speech *Against Ktesiphon* to the Rhodians, making a display of it. When everyone was marveling that he had been defeated despite making this speech, he said, 'You wouldn't marvel, Rhodians, if you had heard Demosthenes speaking in response.'"[71]

SIX

SHARED SPECTATORSHIP

*Bridging the Gap between
Past and Present and Here and There*

Another way that litigants and speechwriters try to manipulate the jurors' imaginations is by describing scenes in their speeches that resemble the situation in the courtroom. For instance, a speaker can give a speech about people listening to a speech or about people looking at a victim or a defendant, just as the jurors are doing in court. By emphasizing these parallels, speakers encourage the jurors to imitate the reactions of the lookers and listeners they hear about. Through a related technique, speakers can also influence how the jurors react to what they see in court by comparing it to what the jurors may have seen in the past.

INTRODUCTION: AN INTERNAL AUDIENCE IN DEMOSTHENES, *AGAINST ANDROTION*

In *Against Androtion* (Demosthenes 22), Demosthenes' client Diodoros accuses Androtion of excessive zeal in collecting debts owed to the *polis*. Diodoros describes him bursting into the home of an anonymous Athenian citizen and driving him to desperate measures to escape arrest. He draws the jurors' attention to the citizen's wife, saying:

καίτοι, ὦ ἄνδρες Ἀθηναῖοι, τί οἴεσθε ὁπότ' ἄνθρωπος πένης (ἢ καὶ πλούσιος, πολλὰ δ' ἀνηλωκὼς καί τιν' ἴσως τρόπον εἰκότως οὐκ εὐπορῶν ἀργυρίου), ἢ τέγος ὡς τοὺς γείτονας ὑπερβαίνοι, ἢ ὑποδύοιτο ὑπὸ κλίνην ὑπὲρ τοῦ μὴ τὸ σῶμα ἁλοὺς εἰς τὸ δεσμωτήριον ἕλκεσθαι, ἢ ἄλλα ἀσχημονοίη ἃ δούλων, οὐκ ἐλευθέρων ἐστὶν ἔργα, καὶ ταῦθ' ὑπὸ τῆς ἑαυτοῦ γυναικὸς ὁρῷτο ποιῶν, ἣν ὡς ἐλεύθερος ἠγγυήσατο καὶ τῆς πόλεως πολίτης, ὁ δὲ τούτων

αἴτιος Ἀνδροτίων εἴη, ὃν οὐδ' ὑπὲρ αὑτοῦ δίκην λαμβάνειν ἐᾷ
τὰ πεπραγμένα καὶ βεβιωμένα, μή τί γε ὑπὲρ τῆς πόλεως; (Dem.
22.53)

> And yet, Athenians, what do you think whenever a poor man (or even
> a rich one, whose expenditures have been many and who is perhaps
> likely in some way to be short of money), either walks over his roof to
> his neighbors or gets down under his bed so that he may not be seized
> bodily and dragged to prison? Or whenever he disgraces himself in
> other actions that are characteristic of slaves, not free men, and he is
> seen doing them by his wife, whom he married as a free man and a
> citizen of the *polis*? And whenever the one responsible for these things
> is Androtion, who because of what he has done and the way he has
> lived is not permitted to introduce a lawsuit on his own behalf, never
> mind one on behalf of the *polis*?

Diodoros employs the detailed description that ancient scholars often associate with *enargeia*, and he also adds the reference to the wife's sight, underscoring the visual nature of his account and providing an audience for the man's shameful change of status. Because the wife observes her husband as a character inside Diodoros' story, I call the wife an "internal audience."[1] The jurors, on the other hand, are an "external audience" because they listen to the story and are not characters in it. As an external audience, the jurors hear about the wife watching her husband attempting to escape Androtion, and so they interpret the story not only from their own perspective as jurors but also from the internal perspective of the wife.

A scholion imagines that the wife reacts to what she sees by comparing her husband to a slave and saying, "You tricked me with your words. You were wed as a free man, but now you are revealed as a slave. I thought I had a citizen, and I used to call my husband an Athenian, but it seems I didn't realize my own misfortune with a slave for a husband."[2] The scholion perceptively calls our attention to what Diodoros does not say. Since he does not describe the wife's reaction, the jurors listening to the speech must infer it from their knowledge of Athenian marriage and of the distinction between citizens and slaves. For only a minute, they must see through the eyes of a woman, perhaps imagining how their own wives would react if they were themselves hounded by Androtion. Like this scholion, some of the jurors who put themselves in the woman's place may have imagined her responding with anger and self-pity, but others may have drawn on their knowledge of women and marriage to imagine her experiencing grief, sympathy, or other emotions.

At the same time that the phrase "and he is seen doing them by his wife" operates on this imaginative emotional level, another scholion theorizes that the presence of a witness adds verisimilitude to Diodoros' story. It reads: "So that no one may say, 'But no one saw him doing these things, and it wasn't so terrible,' look how he provides the witness for himself from the house, discovering the keenest proof from the wife."[3] The scholia, therefore, recognize the complex rhetorical effect of Demosthenes' reference to the wife's observation of her husband's shame. Her role as a witness may have led some jurors to trust Diodoros' account more readily, and her unstated reaction may have prompted other jurors to imagine her reaction and to sympathize with it. The two responses are not mutually exclusive: some jurors may both have considered her a witness and imagined what it would be like to see through her eyes. Internal audiences are not uncommon in Athenian forensic oratory, and, like this wife, they can play multiple rhetorical roles at the same time. This chapter focuses on one particular role: the internal audience as a model for the jurors to identify with and imitate. Just as Diodoros' jurors must imagine seeing through the eyes of the citizen's wife and imagine her reactions, jurors in other trials are encouraged to identify themselves with internal audiences and react the way they react. In the passage of *On the Dishonest Embassy* I discussed in chapter 5, Demosthenes resembles an internal audience, since he observes the destruction of Phokis and encourages the jurors to experience the emotions he describes. Since Demosthenes is the speaker, however, he is not an internal audience in the sense I am using the term in this chapter. Here, I consider how speakers create characters other than themselves who look or listen within their narratives. They encourage the jurors, who are looking and listening in court, to imagine sharing the experience of these internal audiences and to imitate their emotions and reactions. A speaker who employs this technique tries to make the jurors consider themselves witnesses who support his case. Susceptible jurors will both visualize what the speaker wants and, even more importantly, react to it in a way that makes them sympathetic to him and his arguments.

IMAGINARY SIGHT

INTERNAL AUDIENCES IN THUCYDIDES' HISTORY AND THE LYSIANIC FUNERAL ORATION

Forensic oratory was not the only Athenian genre to encourage external audiences to imitate the reactions and emotions of internal audiences by emphasizing the senses of seeing or hearing. Plutarch considers this technique characteristic of *enargeia* in historiography. His analysis of Thucydides' description of the battle in Syracuse harbor reveals how Thucydides designed his narrative to elicit specific emotions in his readers by describing how an internal audience reacts to what they see. Although orators employ internal audiences differently from Thucydides, Plutarch's discussion is the earliest attempt to explain the technique, and his insights, as we will see, are relevant for oratory as well as for historiography. Orators, and particularly forensic orators, adapt the basic features that Plutarch recognizes to their unique circumstances.

Thucydides' Account of the Battle in Syracuse Harbor

In *Whether the Athenians Were More Famous when It Came to War or when It Came to Wisdom*, Plutarch states that a transfer of emotions from the internal audience of spectators within the text to the external audience of readers is characteristic of the *enargeia* he attributes to Thucydides' style. Plutarch writes:

> ὁ γοῦν Θουκυδίδης ἀεὶ τῷ λόγῳ πρὸς ταύτην ἁμιλλᾶται τὴν ἐνάργειαν, οἷον θεατὴν ποιῆσαι τὸν ἀκροατὴν καὶ τὰ γινόμενα περὶ τοὺς ὁρῶντας ἐκπληκτικὰ καὶ ταρακτικὰ πάθη τοῖς ἀναγινώσκουσιν ἐνεργάσασθαι λιχνευόμενος. (3 347a)

> Thucydides, for example, always strives in his writing for this vividness [*enargeian*], desiring eagerly to make the reader [*akroatēn*][4] a spectator [*theatēn*], so to speak, and to produce for those reading the startling and disturbing emotions that happened in the people who could see [*tous horōntas*].

As one example of Thucydidean *enargeia*, Plutarch cites the battle in the harbor of Syracuse in book 7, where the narrator describes the spectators onshore experiencing shifts in emotion during the course of the battle.[5] In this section, Thucydides' reader learns about the battle not primarily from the narrator's perspective or the participants' perspectives, but from the perspective of these passive observers. I call them passive because they do not affect the outcome of the battle. Instead, they watch it, and what they see affects them. Andrew Walker therefore calls the battle scene a type of *mise en abyme*. Literally "placed in the abyss," *mise en abyme* refers to the mirror effect created by certain works of art. Examples are a painting of someone looking at a painting or a movie about someone watching a movie. In this case, people who did not participate in the battle read about people who did not participate in the battle. The internal audience of spectators onshore mirrors the external audience of readers.

The language of sight in Thucydides' text links the external and internal audiences, encouraging readers who exercise their visual imaginations to observe the Athenians' defeat at the same time as the spectators onshore are watching it. Throughout the battle account, Thucydides connects the emotions of the Athenians onshore to what they see.[6] The battle was a spectacle (*tēs theās*), and they had an uneven view (*epopsin*) of it. The engagement was so close to them that they could not all look (*skopountōn*) at the same place. Some of them could see (*idoien*) the Athenians winning and were encouraged, but others saw (*blepsantes*) them being defeated and lamented, and the sight (*tēs opseōs*) affected their judgment even more than the battle affected the participants themselves. Still others were looking (*apidontes*) at a part of the battle where the two sides were evenly matched, and they acted out their mental uncertainty by swaying their bodies from side to side.[7] By describing the battle in the harbor as a spectacle, recounting it from the perspective of its spectators and emphasizing what Walker calls the "link between vision and the emotions," Thucydides urges his readers to adopt the spectators' viewpoint and to share in their responses.[8]

Although Walker does not emphasize it, the spectators in Thucydides' narrative are influenced by what they hear as well as by what they see. While the battle was evenly matched, they could "hear [*akousai*] everything at the same time," both doleful wailing and victorious shouts.[9] Thucydides does not directly link these contradictory sounds with the spectators' emotions, but there is no question that he associates them with their alternation between hope and despair. First, by describing the sounds immediately after recounting the emotional turmoil and corresponding physical motion caused by watching the uncertain engagements, he implies that they reinforce the spectators' emotions. Second, he follows his description of the sailors' shouts with the statement that they "suffered nearly the same things" as the men on the shore,[10] placing the account of sounds securely within the discussion of emotions that initially focused on sight. Third, Thucydides describes the Syracusan victory—the culmination of this entire passage—through sound rather than sight. The Syracusans, he writes, "made a great uproar and cheered" as they put the Athenians to flight.[11] Thucydides then continues to devote most of his attention to the witnesses on land rather than the sailors, and he recounts how they all despaired with laments and groans. Since Thucydides attributes this emotional reaction to an experience he describes as aural rather than visual, it is unlikely that he is drawing a firm distinction between sight and sound as emotional catalysts.

The scene in Syracuse's harbor, therefore, is even more of a *mise en abyme* than a focus on spectatorship alone suggests. The external audience of readers not only observes from the perspective of the spectators onshore but also hears while they are hearing. Hearing is a particularly strong link between the two groups, since Thucydides' original readers would probably have heard the text read aloud.[12] As a result, there are two senses through which emotions can be conveyed from the internal audience, from whose perspective Thucydides narrates the battle, to the external audience. Although Thucydides initially emphasizes the link between vision and the emotions, the shared experience of hearing continues to encourage the external audience to identify themselves with the internal audience and to experience the same emotions they do.

The Lysianic Funeral Oration

The speaker of the Lysianic funeral oration (Lysias 2) employs a similar technique to Thucydides in his account of the battle of Salamis, chapters 34–43. Although this funeral oration may never have been delivered, it reflects the conventions of the genre and is contemporary evidence for the techniques employed in actual performances of funeral orations.[13] When I refer here to speaker and listeners, I am referring to the hypothetical speaker and listeners that the Lysianic funeral oration presupposes by virtue of its genre and intended occasion.

As a funeral oration rather than a historical narrative, the speech more frequently acknowledges its listeners than Thucydides' text does. Throughout this section, for instance, the speaker uses rhetorical questions to ask them to consider actively the implications of the scene he describes.[14] Like Thucydides,[15] he also encourages them to share in the emotional reactions of an internal audience, namely, the Athenians who witnessed the battle, by recounting their mental turmoil and emphasizing their senses of sight and hearing.

The speaker begins to describe the battle by asking rhetorically, "Who [*tis*] would not have been afraid if he saw [*idōn*]" the land army and the fleet of the Persians.[16] Like the indefinite "one can see" in Demosthenes' *On the Dishonest Embassy* or Lycurgus' *Against Leokrates*, this "who" (*tis*) invites the listeners to imagine what it was like to look at the arriving forces in 480.[17] By engaging their imaginations, Lysias' speaker adds a new feature to Thucydides' technique. While Thucydides implicitly stressed the parallels between the internal audience and the external audience through the senses of seeing and hearing, Lysias' speaker uses a rhetorical question to encourage his listeners to put themselves in the position of the Athenians watching the Persians approach and to experience their fear. He then explores the psychological response of this internal audience by describing what they see and hear.

Lysias' speaker first focuses on the Athenians onshore, asking, "What thought did they have, those who gazed on [*hoi theōmenoi*] the men in those ships, with their own salvation in doubt and danger coming on?"[18] He then shifts to the men in the ships, also asking what they were thinking. They would, he suggests, have worried more about what the survivors would suffer if the Persians won than about their own deaths. Distress leads them to extend their hands to one another and to weep for themselves.[19] The speaker qualifies these emotional actions with causal participial phrases, including "knowing their own ships were few and seeing [*horōntes*] the enemy's many ships"[20] and "hearing [*akouontes*] at the same time the singing of the Greeks and barbarians mixed together, the exhortations of both sides and the cries of the men being killed."[21] As in Thucydides' account of the battle in the harbor of Syracuse, the general confusion of Salamis leaves the Athenians uncertain about whether they are winning or losing. Furthermore, "through the presence of fear, they actually believed they saw [*idein*] many things they did not see [*eidon*], and heard [*akousai*] many things they did not hear [*ēkousan*]."[22] Fear is the Athenians' predominant emotion, and it is closely connected to seeing and hearing, first arising from what they see and hear and then prompting them to see and hear things in their imaginations. By focusing on fear, Lysias' speaker can convey the extent of the danger the Athenians faced, and so emphasize the significance of their victory.

The use of the vocabulary of seeing and hearing acts as a bridge between the emotions of the participants in the battle and the imaginations of the audience of the funeral oration. The speaker first invites the external audience to imagine what emotions arise from seeing, and then he attempts to guide their emotional reactions by continuing to emphasize the link between the senses and the participants' emotions. The technique is fundamentally the same as in Thucydides' account of the battle in the harbor of Syracuse, although the conventions of the funeral oration, such as rhetorical questions, more directly encourage the external audience to exercise their imaginations than Thucydides' narrative does. The performance context of the funeral oration may also have encouraged them to identify themselves with the looking and listening Athenians at the battle of Salamis. The annual burial ceremony for the Athenians who died in war seems to have been a visual spectacle as much as an opportunity to hear the ritual speech. The Athenians who attended would have seen a procession and games, and the monument to the dead was decorated with sculpture and inscriptions. Even the speech itself, which featured a single orator standing before an enormous crowd, must have been a visually captivating event as well as an aural experience.

In both Lysias' funeral oration and Thucydides' account of the sea battle, imagination plays a central role in the transfer of emotions from the internal audiences to the external audiences. The external audiences cannot actually watch the battle of Salamis or the battle in Syracuse's harbor, and so they only become what Plutarch calls "like spectators" through a conscious or unconscious act of mental identification with the internal audiences. Only a listener or reader with an impressionable imagination, therefore, will experience the *enargeia* that Plutarch describes.

INTERNAL AUDIENCES IN FORENSIC ORATORY

The performance conventions of the Athenian courts allowed the jurors to share more closely in the experiences of internal audiences than the readers and hearers of Thucydides' history or the Lysianic funeral oration could. Litigants were not, in most circumstances, narrating events of the distant past but relatively recent events involving people present in the court and visible to the jurors. As a result, they could describe internal audiences observing the same people the jurors were observing in court. The jurors and the internal audiences, therefore, share in a visual experience that is partly real, since they see the same people, and partly imaginary, since they see them in different places at different times. Within the narrative created by a litigant and speechwriter, for instance, the internal audience may see a defendant committing a crime, while, in the court, the jurors see him sitting on a bench or standing on the *bēma*. By stressing the similarities between the court setting and the past events they describe, litigants and speechwriters can blur these temporal and spatial distinctions and bring reality and imagination closer together.

There are other ways that litigants and speechwriters try to blur these distinctions. M. P. de Bakker, for instance, has recently explored Demosthenes' "ability to draw links between the space outside the law courts and the Assembly and the space of those venues themselves where the speeches were delivered," which he calls, "the performance space." De Bakker focuses on spaces and the objects within them, both in the court and within the speech itself, and he especially considers how the objects in the court and the places and objects inside narratives can contribute to characterization. Like me, de Bakker is interested in ways that speakers can help jurors "visualize the events that had happened elsewhere against the backdrop of the performative space itself," although he does not consider the role of internal audiences in creating this effect.[23] By examining internal audiences in forensic oratory, therefore, I illustrate another way of creating the phenomenon de Bakker analyzes in Demosthenes and further develop his insight that blurring the distinction between past and present and here and there was a central aspect of persuasion in forensic performances.

As jurors identify themselves with an internal audience, their physical sight complements their mental sight. They are encouraged not only to interpret the narrated events from the perspective of the internal audience but also to develop mental images of the past populated by the people they actually see in the court. Litigants can further increase the jurors' impression of a shared sensory experience by quoting or paraphrasing past speeches, so that the jurors hear them at the same time as the listeners within the narrative. The internal audiences, since their experience mirrors the experience of the jurors, serve as a model for what the jurors should think and how they should react. If the jurors follow the speaker's lead and experience what Plutarch calls "the startling and disturbing emotions that happened in the people who could see," they will respond to the disputed events in the way the speaker wants. Lysias' *Against Diogeiton* and *Against Teisis* exemplify two different methods of leading jurors to identify with an internal audience and to have a sense of being present at an event that happened in the past but is being orally recreated in the court.

Against Diogeiton

Against Diogeiton (Lysias 32) is a prosecution speech against Diogeiton for maladministration of his wards' property. It dates to around 400.[24] The wards were the two male children of Diogeiton's daughter and his brother Diodotos, who died during Thrasyllos' Ephesus campaign in 409.[25] They allege that Diogeiton systematically embezzled their inheritance throughout his guardianship.[26] The speaker is the husband of their sister.[27] The case against Diogeiton seems strong, but we cannot discount the possibility that the wards have fabricated the charge of embezzlement in an attempt to recover assets lost in the last years of the Peloponnesian War and under the Thirty.[28]

Within his speech, the speaker quotes another speech that the mother of the defendants gave at a family meeting accusing her father Diogeiton of embezzlement and lying.[29] Through a combination of direct and indirect speech, Diogeiton's daughter is presented as speaking to an internal audience of family members in the past. She is also speaking, through her son-in-law, to the jurors in the present. The jurors and the internal audience, therefore, seem to share the auditory experience at the same time. For Lysias and the speaker at the trial, the jurors are the more important audience, since the purpose of the quoted speech is to persuade them to convict Diogeiton.[30] Gagarin has shown that the daughter of Diogeiton "delivers a forensic speech in appropriate forensic language and style." She presents the entire case against Diogeiton in an abbreviated form, and she uses "parallelism, repetition, anaphora, asyndeton, and direct address of the accused." The speech follows the structure of a forensic speech with an introduction, a narrative, documentary evidence, and a peroration. It even begins with the forensic commonplaces that the speaker is inexperienced, is compelled to speak by the circumstances, and will reveal everything.[31] Lysias, then, creates a forensic speech within a forensic speech, with an internal audience that mirrors the external audience of jurors.

To have a chance of convincing the jurors, Diogeiton's daughter's speech needs to be plausible. If a speech given by a woman to her male relatives about accounting and inheritance was unimaginable, the jurors would have ignored or mocked it.[32] Therefore, although it is possible that the family meeting never happened and that Lysias composed Diogeiton's daughter's speech as an example of the kind of speech that the jurors could have imagined being given at a meeting like this, it is not necessarily a complete fabrication.[33] We may have a speech like the speeches in Thucydides, which adhere as closely as possible to the general content of the speeches that were actually spoken, although they are presented in Thucydides' own words.[34] If this is true, the forensic structure and style of Diogeiton's daughter's speech make it likely that Lysias has reworked it to emphasize the parallels between the family meeting and the trial. Regardless of whether the speech is a revision or an invention, however, the speaker takes advantage of these parallels to encourage the jurors to imitate the emotions and opinions of the family members.

Immediately after Diogeiton's daughter ends her speech, Lysias' speaker emphasizes the reaction of the internal audience of family members in a long, elaborate sentence. The placement of this sentence at the conclusion of the narrative, immediately before the speaker calls his witnesses, points to its rhetorical significance. He says:

> τότε μὲν οὖν, ὦ ἄνδρες δικασταί, πολλῶν καὶ δεινῶν ὑπὸ τῆς γυναικὸς ῥηθέντων οὕτω διετέθημεν πάντες οἱ παρόντες ὑπὸ τῶν τούτῳ πεπραγμένων καὶ τῶν λόγων τῶν ἐκείνης, ὁρῶντες μὲν τοὺς παῖδας, οἷα ἦσαν πεπονθότες, ἀναμιμνησκόμενοι δὲ τοῦ ἀποθανόντος, ὡς ἀνάξιον τῆς οὐσίας τὸν ἐπίτροπον κατέλιπεν, ἐνθυμούμενοι δὲ ὡς χαλεπὸν ἐξευρεῖν ὅτῳ χρὴ περὶ τῶν ἑαυτοῦ πιστεῦσαι, ὥστε, ὦ ἄνδρες δικασταί, μηδένα τῶν παρόντων δύνασθαι φθέγξασθαι, ἀλλὰ καὶ δακρύοντας μὴ ἧττον τῶν πεπονθότων ἀπιόντας οἴχεσθαι σιωπῇ. (Lys. 32.18)

> At that time [*tote men oun*], gentlemen of the jury [*ō andres dikastai*], since many awful things had been spoken by the woman, all of us who were present were so affected [*dietethēmen*] by the things the defendant [*toutōi*] had done and by her words, seeing [*horōntes*] the boys, how much they had suffered, remembering the dead man, how he left behind him an unworthy administrator of his property, and reflecting on the difficulty of finding the kind of person you can trust in personal matters, that, gentlemen of the jury [*ō andres dikastai*], none of us who were present was able to utter a single word. But rather, weeping no less than the sufferers themselves, we left, departing in silence.

The language marks a shift from the direct speech of the family meeting to the here and now of the court. "At that time" (*tote men oun*) shows that the speaker is no longer speaking as his mother-in-law in the past but as himself in the present.³⁵ The aorist tense of the main verb, "were affected" (*dietethēmen*), also places the speaking in the present and the action of the meeting in the past. Finally, as the two vocatives, "gentlemen of the jury," demonstrate, the speaker is now directly addressing the jurors. With two vocatives in the same sentence, the speaker is clearly calling the jurors' attention to the internal audience's reaction.

Can we reasonably conclude that Lysias designed this sentence to present that reaction as a model for the jurors? We can, for two reasons. First, with the genitive absolute "since many awful things had been spoken by the woman" and the genitive of means "by her words," the speaker stresses the effect of the words of Diogeiton's daughter. These words are what the jurors, like the internal audience, have just heard. Second, the participial tricolon, "seeing [*horōntes*] the boys, how much they had suffered, remembering the dead man, how he left behind him an unworthy administrator of his property, and reflecting on the difficulty of finding the kind of person you can trust in personal matters," begins with a marked reference to sight. On the level of the narrative, the participle "seeing" refers to the members of the family meeting. On the level of the performance, however, it also calls attention to the jurors' sight of the two brothers in the court. Furthermore, the deictic pronoun *toutōi* points to Diogeiton, the defendant who is present in the court. The sentence, therefore, takes advantage of the resemblance of the situation in the court to that in the narrative. Like the family members, the jurors have heard the speech of Diogeiton's daughter and can see both the wards and Diogeiton himself. The emotional response of the family members is presented as the natural and inevitable response to a situation very much like the one the jurors themselves are experiencing. This is not to say that the speaker expects the jurors to start weeping and to depart in silence. Nevertheless, his performance is designed to manipulate their emotions against Diogeiton by subtly stressing the auditory and visual parallels between the situation in his narrative and their experience in the court. The tears may also have a slight forensic connotation, recalling the tearful supplication of children whom litigants parade before jurors.

Against Teisis

Another Lysianic speech, *Against Teisis* (Lysias, fr. 278–279 Carey),³⁶ emphasizes a shared viewing experience rather than a shared listening experience as the primary mechanism for encouraging the jurors to identify with an internal audience. The speaker of *Against Teisis*, which survives in two fragments, elides the distinction between what the jurors see in the court and what he tries to make them see in their imaginations.

The longer fragment (fr. 279 Carey), preserved by Dionysius of Halicarnassus, contains a narrative account of what seems to be a particularly wanton crime.[37] Two young men, Teisis and Arkhippos, get into an argument at the wrestling ground. Teisis tells his guardian and lover, Pytheas,[38] about the dispute, and Pytheas advises him to make a pretense of reconciliation and to bide his time until he can deal with Arkhippos alone. So, Teisis pretends to be friends with Arkhippos and invites him to his house on the night of the horserace at the festival of the Anakeia.[39] When Arkhippos arrives, Teisis' slaves tie him to a pillar, and Teisis whips him repeatedly. Then he locks Arkhippos in a room overnight, and the slaves whip him more in the morning. The speaker is Arkhippos' friend, who accompanied him to Teisis' house but was thrown out before Teisis started whipping Arkhippos.[40]

The speaker concludes his narrative of the crime with a visual episode that takes place before an internal audience. Arkhippos is so injured after the two whippings that his brothers have to carry him on a couch out of Teisis' house and into the samples market in Peiraieus called the *deigma*.[41] The speaker says:

> οὐ δυναμένου δὲ βαδίζειν, ἐκόμισαν αὐτὸν εἰς τὸ δεῖγμα ἐν κλίνῃ καὶ ἐπέδειξαν πολλοῖς μὲν Ἀθηναίων πολλοῖς δὲ καὶ τῶν ἄλλων ξένων οὕτως διακείμενον, ὥστε τοὺς ἰδόντας μὴ μόνον τοῖς ποιήσασιν ὀργίζεσθαι ἀλλὰ καὶ τῆς πόλεως κατηγορεῖν, ὅτι οὐ δημοσίᾳ οὐδὲ παραχρῆμα τοὺς τὰ τοιαῦτα ἐξαμαρτάνοντας τιμωρεῖται. (Lys. fr. 279 Carey 6)

> And since he couldn't walk, they bore him to the *deigma* on a couch, and they pointed him out [*epedeixan*] to many Athenians as well as to the rest of the people present, many foreigners. He was so affected that the people who saw him [*tous idontas*] not only got angry at the perpetrators but also denounced the *polis*, because it was not publicly and on the spot seeking vengeance from the people who had committed crimes like this.

The speaker presents the procession as a kind of spectacle by emphasizing the seeing and showing of Arkhippos' bruised body. The word for "they pointed out" is *epedeixan* (an aorist form of *epideiknumi*), and the related term *deigma* literally means "a showing" or "a demonstration." The two words come from the same root, and so the public display of Arkhippos' injuries is underscored not only by the word used for the showing but also by the place where the showing occurs. Furthermore, the speaker makes clear that there is an internal audience who see the display, referring explicitly to "the people who saw him."

The sight of Arkhippos wounded and lying on a cot incites this internal audience to anger against both the criminals and the *polis*. These may well have been the natural emotional responses to such a display, but their role in the speech is rhetorical rather than documentary. Lysias' speaker wants the external audience of jurors to respond to his spoken narrative in the same way as the internal audience responds to the display of Arkhippos. He even goes so far as to attribute to the internal audience an opinion about the *polis*' sluggish enforcement of malefactors that makes more sense within the context of the trial than it does on the day of the crime. The speaker wants the jurors to channel their anger into preventing Teisis from getting away with beating Arkhippos. He may also want them to feel that the anger against the *polis* may be directed towards them if they fail to convict; that an acquittal will anger victims or encourage future criminals are common Lysianic arguments.[42]

It is likely that the jurors would identify with the internal audience. Through deictic pronouns, the speaker of *Against Teisis* consistently emphasizes that the main characters in his narrative are also present in the courtroom and visible to the jurors. The narrative begins:

> Ἄρχιππος γὰρ οὑτοσί, ὦ Ἀθηναῖοι, ἀπεδύσατο μὲν εἰς τὴν αὐτὴν παλαίστραν, οὗπερ καὶ Τεῖσις ὁ φεύγων τὴν δίκην. (Lys. fr. 279 Carey 1)

> Arkhippos, this man here [*houtosi*], Athenians, undressed for exercise at the same wrestling ground where Teisis, the defendant, was also.

The deictic iota in *houtosi* and the qualifier "the defendant" (*ho pheugōn tēn dikēn*) directly link the narrative and the courtroom setting. As the jurors hear about the argument at the wrestling ground and its aftermath, they also see the participants before them. This was true, of course, in nearly every Classical Athenian trial. The speaker of *Against Teisis*, however, calls particular attention to it with *houtosi*. Significantly, *houtosi* also appears in the first sentence of *Against Teisis*, which refers to the court situation and not to the past time of the narrative. The author known as the "Anonymous Seguerianus" preserves this sentence in his handbook as an example of how to begin a speech "whenever you are speaking on behalf of someone else."[43] The speech begins:

ἐπιτήδειός μοί ἐστιν Ἄρχιππος ούτοσί, ὦ <ἄνδρες> δικασταί.
(Lys. fr. 278 Carey = Anonymous Seguerianus 7)

Arkhippos, this man here [*houtosi*], is a good friend of mine, gentlemen of the jury.

Both the narrative within the speech and the speech itself begin by calling the jurors' visual attention to Arkhippos. *Houtosi*, therefore, acts as a bridge between the here and now of the court and the past time of the narrative.

In addition, the speaker uses *toutoni*, the accusative singular of *houtosi*, at the moment of the first whipping. He says:

ἐπειδὴ δὲ ἔνδον ἐγενόμεθα, ἐμὲ μὲν ἐκβάλλουσιν ἐκ τῆς οἰκίας, τουτονὶ δὲ συναρπάσαντες ἔδησαν πρὸς τὸν κίονα, καὶ λαβὼν μάστιγα Τεῖσις, ἐντείνας πολλὰς πληγάς, εἰς οἴκημα αὐτὸν καθεῖρξε. (Lys. fr. 279 Carey 4)

After we were inside, they threw me [*eme*] out of the house, but this man here [*toutoni*] they seized and tied to the pillar. Picking up a whip, Teisis left no slack in it and struck many blows. Then, he shut him up in a room.

The three characters in this sentence are all present in the court: "me" (*eme*), "this man here" (*toutoni*), and Teisis.[44] The emphatic placement of *eme* and *toutoni* at the beginning of their clauses, which I have not preserved in my translation, indicates that the speaker is calling special attention to the participants: they are not just characters in the narrative, but figures the jurors can see before them. Furthermore, the iota at the end of *toutoni* once again links the here and now with the narrative time. The speaker could have called Arkhippos by name or used a less-marked pronoun like *auton*, which he used for Arkhippos in the preceding sentences and would therefore have caused no ambiguity. Nonetheless, he chose to use the strongly visual deictic word. The visual orientation of the narrative towards the here and now of the court would encourage the jurors to associate the wounded Arkhippos they hear about with the Arkhippos they see before them and so, a few sentences later, to identify with the internal audience that sees Arkhippos being carried through the *deigma*.

One reason for the narrative's emphasis on seeing and showing could be that Arkhippos' wounds have healed in the time between the whipping and the trial. In chapter 1, I discussed visual displays of wounds during trials as proofs that a victim had suffered an attack.[45] The narrative showing of wounds in *Against Teisis* may be replacing such a visual demonstration. Since the jurors would not be able to see the wounds for themselves and so achieve first-hand visual knowledge of Arkhippos' suffering, the speaker encourages them to identify with people who, he claims, did have visual knowledge.

The deictic pronouns are as important to the persuasive *enargeia* of *Against Teisis* as the language of seeing and showing. Through *houtosi* and *toutoni*, the narrative orients itself in terms of what the jurors can see as well as what they hear about and are encouraged to imagine. A more precise way to say this is that *houtosi* and *toutoni* in the narrative of *Against Teisis* point to people within the discourse and outside the discourse at the same time.[46] They blend what Karl Bühler calls anaphora, *demonstratio ad oculos* ("ocular deixis"), and *Deixis am Phantasma* ("imagination-oriented deixis").[47]

Anaphora describes the function of deictic language to point to things within a text. Texts use anaphora when they say things such as "see above" or when they refer to someone or something already mentioned as "this" or "that." Greek deictic pronouns often have at least a slight anaphoric sense when they take the place of someone or something already mentioned by name. As I have already noted, however, anaphora on its own is an inadequate explanation for the use of *toutoni* in *Against Teisis*, since Lysias could just as easily have replaced Arkhippos' name with a word like *auton* that has a sufficiently anaphoric sense to have prevented ambiguity. *Demonstratio ad oculos*, on the other hand, describes the function of deictic language to point out something that is visible. It refers directly to the performance context.[48] The first line of *Against Teisis*, "Arkhippos, this man here [*houtosi*], is a good friend of mine, gentlemen of the jury," is a clear example of *demonstratio ad oculos*. With *houtosi* and perhaps an accompanying gesture, the speaker brings the jurors' visual attention to Arkhippos. This type of deixis, which presumes an audience who can see as well as hear, is common in forensic speeches.[49]

Finally, *Deixis am Phantasma* describes the function of deictic language to point out something that is not present within the performance context and is therefore visible only to the sight of the mind. According to Bühler, one effect of *Deixis am Phantasma* is to "displace" the hearer in his imagination to the scene of a narrative. Therefore, the speaker can describe a narrated scene with deictic words as though the hearer is actually physically present within it.[50] The effect of *Deixis am Phantasma* is the same as the effect of *enargeia*: it turns the listener into a spectator of something that he can only see with his mind's eye.[51]

Deixis am Phantasma is a well-known feature of Greek poetry.[52] It may also operate in some prose speech genres with extended narratives of past events that can activate the imagination of the audience. It is highly unlikely, however, that there was any long-lasting mental displacement for the audience of forensic speeches. The jurors need to use both memory and imagination to process forensic narratives cognitively, but speakers are careful to keep their narratives anchored to the here and now of the court, frequently interrupting their accounts to comment or analyze or to address the jurors directly.

Deixis am Phantasma, therefore, is by itself an inadequate model for understanding deictic pronouns in *Against Teisis* or in other forensic narratives. While forms of *houtosi* and other deictic clues do help the jurors to visualize the narrative account in their minds, they at the same time also point to people who are present in the court. Hence, the jurors' imaginations are always tempered by the here and now of the performance context, and their sight is never just with their minds' eyes. *Deixis am Phantasma*, therefore, never exists apart from *demonstratio ad oculos*. Even when the jurors hear about a past crime like Teisis' assault on Arkhippos, they are constantly reminded that the participants are also visible to them in the court. This visibility in the here and now encourages the jurors to identify with the internal audience at the end of the narrative and to respond to Teisis' treatment of Arkhippos in the same way they did.

MEMORY AND RITUAL IN THE TRIAL OF ANDOCIDES

In cases like Diogeiton's or Teisis', litigants and speechwriters can exploit parallels between the jurors and the internal audiences within their narratives to bridge the gap between the here and now of the court and the location of a past event they describe. As jurors mentally associate themselves with an internal audience, speakers encourage the jurors to empathize with their cases. Not all cases lend themselves to this tactic, however. Sometimes, there may be no way for a speechwriter plausibly to insert an internal audience into a description of the past. Other times, this type of imagined identification may not be consistent with a speech's overall strategy. A prosecution speech from the trial of Andocides illustrates how one litigant took advantage of the unique circumstances of his case and tried to bridge the gap between past and present without using an internal audience by appealing to the jurors' own memories.

Against Andocides

In 415, shortly before the Athenian fleet sailed for Sicily, two overlapping groups of Athenian aristocrats committed two acts of impiety: mutilating the divine images known as herms and profaning the Eleusinian Mysteries by performing them in private homes in the presence of the uninitiated. The panicked Athenians considered the two acts of impiety signs of an antidemocratic conspiracy.[53] Andocides admitted some degree of guilt in one or both affairs and went into exile. Returning to Athens after the end of the Peloponnesian War, he faced trial in 400 or 399 for exercising the rights of a citizen despite having admitted impiety. *Against Andocides* (Lysias 6), a speech transmitted under Lysias' name but perhaps composed by someone else, is one of the prosecution speeches from this trial.[54]

Because of the secret and sacred nature of the Mysteries, anyone who witnessed the profanation would have been guilty of impiety. As a result, there was no way for the author of *Against Andocides* to create an internal audience of witnesses for the jurors to identify with without implicating them in the profanation. Instead, the speaker relies on the combined effect of Andocides' physical presence in the court and the jurors' memory of a shared ritual experience to bridge the gap between past and present, enabling the jurors to "see" in their minds Andocides profaning the Mysteries. Because all the jurors were initiates, they would have been familiar with what went on at the Mysteries.[55]

Near the end of *Against Andocides*, the speaker describes Andocides' alleged profanation of the Mysteries, prefacing it with an appeal to the jurors' visual imaginations. He conflates the profanation with the mutilation of the herms, in which Andocides seems to have been more clearly implicated.[56] The speaker says:

ἀλλὰ προσέχετε τὸν νοῦν, δοκείτω δ' ὑμῖν ἡ γνώμη ὁρᾶν ἃ οὗτος ἐποίει, καὶ διαγνώσεσθε ἄμεινον. οὗτος γὰρ ἐνδὺς στολὴν μιμούμενος τὰ ἱερὰ ἐπεδείκνυ τοῖς ἀμυήτοις καὶ εἶπε τῇ φωνῇ τὰ ἀπόρρητα, τῶν δὲ θεῶν, οὓς ἡμεῖς νομίζομεν καὶ θεραπεύοντες καὶ ἁγνεύοντες θύομεν καὶ προσευχόμεθα, τούτους περιέκοψε. καὶ ἐπὶ τούτοις ἱέρειαι καὶ ἱερεῖς στάντες κατηράσαντο πρὸς ἑσπέραν καὶ φοινικίδας ἀνέσεισαν, κατὰ τὸ νόμιμον τὸ παλαιὸν καὶ ἀρχαῖον. ὡμολόγησε δὲ οὗτος ποιῆσαι. (Lys. 6.50–51)

But hold your mind intent. Let your judgmental capacity [*gnōmē*] seem to see [*horan*] what this man [*houtos*] was doing, and decide the case [*diagnōsesthe*] better. For after this man [*houtos*] put on a robe, he imitated [*mimoumenos*] the sacred things [*ta hiera*] and pointed them out [*epedeiknu*] to the uninitiated, and he spoke with his own voice the things that cannot be spoken. And the gods whom we honor and to whom we sacrifice and pray, offering them service and purifying ourselves, he mutilated. Because of this, priestesses and priests cursed him as they stood facing west, and they shook out their purple garments, in accordance with our ancient and long-standing custom. This man [*houtos*] admitted he did these things.

In an elaborate periphrasis, the speaker asks that the jurors' "judgmental capacity [*gnōmē*] seem to see [*horan*]." *Gnōmē* is not the subject of "see" (*horaō* or *eidon*) anywhere else in Classical Greek literature,[57] and Lysias seems to have chosen it for its judicial connotations, since every juror swore to employ "the most just *gnōmē*."[58] To capture this judicial sense, I have translated *gnōmē* here as "judgmental capacity." By making the jurors' collective judgmental capacity the instrument of visualization, the speaker directly links their decision in the court with what they picture in their minds. The imperative "decide the case" (*diagnōsesthe*) may also contribute to the judicial overtones of this sentence, since Mirhady has shown that *gnōmē* and *diagignōskō* are often used in contexts that describe judging without bias based on questions of fact.[59]

What the speaker encourages the jurors to visualize through their judgmental capacity is already partially familiar to them. As initiates, they have all attended the Mysteries and witnessed the secret ritual. Now, the speaker wants the jurors to have an image of this ritual in the front of their minds, an image set in the large hall at Eleusis known as the *telestērion*. While the jurors are remembering their own initiations, the speaker describes Andocides performing the same ritual in a private house, in front of the uninitiated. The motivation for the jurors' visualization, therefore, is twofold. It is based on the jurors' individual memories of their initiations and on the speaker's description of Andocides' impious actions. Because of the unique circumstances of the trial, there is no need for the speaker to encourage the jurors to identify with the emotions and opinions of an internal audience. Through memory and visualization, the jurors themselves can picture Andocides' profanation against the background of mental images conjured up by the speaker's words combining with their own memories.

In encouraging the jurors to let their "judgmental capacity [*gnōmē*] seem to see [*horan*]," therefore, the speaker recognizes that the jurors' specialized ritual knowledge can be made to influence their juridical duty. He may also attempt to blend together their physical sight and their mental sight with the double use of *houtos* in the seven words that follow *horan*, first as the subject of the relative clause and then as the subject and first word of the sentence that describes the profanation. The repetition calls emphatic attention to it being Andocides who profaned the Mysteries, Andocides, who is present before the jurors at that very moment. *Houtos*, therefore, is not merely a neutral anaphoric pronoun repeated for emphasis. Although it lacks the emphatic deictic iota, it is also a true deictic pointer designating the defendant in physical space as well as in the verbal narrative. Perhaps, the speaker even points him out as he utters the second *houtos*, and the jurors' physical eyes turn to Andocides while their mental eyes see him mocking their initiations. Underscoring the parallels between the past and present, he concludes this section by using *houtos* to refer to Andocides in the here-and-now of the court, saying, "This man [*houtos*] admitted he did these things."

The invocation of sight is more than a clever way to bridge the temporal and spatial gap between the court and the profanations of 415. The jurors, as initiates themselves, would know that sight is the primary means by which initiates experience the Mysteries.[60] Hearing the speaker's *horan*, the jurors would not only remember the ritual they had seen but would also remember the benefits conferred on them by that seeing. The mention of sight exemplifies the seriousness of the profanation: it undermines both the ritual itself and the jurors' status as initiates who are blessed because they have seen.

The relationship among seeing, showing, and blessedness is already present in the account of Demeter's foundation of the Mysteries near the end of the *Homeric Hymn to Demeter*.[61]

ἡ δὲ κιοῦσα θεμιστοπόλοις βασιλεῦσι
δεῖξε, Τριπτολέμῳ τε Διοκλεῖ τε πληξίππῳ,
Εὐμόλπου τε βίῃ Κελεῷ θ' ἡγήτορι λαῶν,
δρησμοσύνην θ' ἱερῶν καὶ ἐπέφραδεν ὄργια πᾶσι,
σεμνά, τά γ' οὔ πως ἔστι παρεξίμεν οὔτε πυθέσθαι,
οὔτ' ἀχέειν· μέγα γάρ τι θεῶν σέβας ἰσχάνει αὐδήν.
ὄλβιος ὅς τάδ' ὄπωπεν ἐπιχθονίων ἀνθρώπων·
ὃς δ' ἀτελὴς ἱερῶν, ὅς τ' ἄμμορος, οὔ ποθ' ὁμοίων
αἶσαν ἔχει φθίμενός περ ὑπὸ ζόφῳ εὐρώεντι. (473–482)[62]

> Going to the ones who look after the laws, the kings Triptolemos and Diokles who spurs on horses and the strength of Eumolpos and Keleos leader of armies, she pointed out [*deixe*] the performance of the sacred rites and showed [*epephraden*] to all of them the holy rituals [*orgia semna*], which no one may transgress or ask questions about or mention. For some great reverence for the gods keeps the voice in check. Of men who dwell on earth, blessed [*olbios*] is he who has seen [*opōpen*] these things. But he who is uninitiated in the sacred rites and he who has no share of them never has a portion of similar blessings when he is dead, down below in the mouldy gloom.

When she is instituting the Mysteries, Demeter shows them to the Eleusinian kings: *deixe* and *epephraden* refer specifically to a visual demonstration.[63] Furthermore, the contrast between "he who has seen" and "he who is uninitiated" equates initiation with the sight of Demeter's "holy rituals." It is through this sight that one becomes "blessed" and avoids the unhappy afterlife that awaits the uninitiated.[64] It is not permitted for anyone to speak about the "holy rituals" after he has seen them since "great reverence for the gods" prevents him. The importance of unspeakable knowledge in the context of the Mysteries appears again in Isocrates' *Panegyrikos*.[65]

A fragment of Sophocles and a fragment of Pindar that are generally believed to refer to initiation into the Mysteries also emphasize the blessings after death that come from sight.[66] Similarly, in Euripides' *Herakles*, Herakles tells Amphitryon that he defeated Kerberos in a fight, but he qualifies this by noting, "I was lucky [*eutukhēs(a)*], since I had seen [*idōn*] the rituals of the Mysteries."[67] The pattern established in the *Hymn* is continued here: due to the sight of Demeter's rites, a person becomes blessed and enjoys happiness in the underworld. *Eutukhēs(a)*, "I was lucky," here is functionally equivalent to the *Hymn*'s "blessed" (*olbios*). Herakles, of course, is a unique initiate because he is able to return from the underworld; it is significant, however, that his sight enables him to return.

Even the titles of the participants make clear the prominence of seeing and showing in the Mysteries. The official called the *hierophantēs*, or "hierophant," is the one who shows (*-phantēs* < *phainō*) the sacred things (*ta hiera*).[68] The terms for the two levels of initiates, the *mustai* (singular, *mustēs*) and the *epoptai* (singular, *epoptēs*),[69] also reflect the role of sight. *Mustēs* comes from the verb *muō*, which means "close the eyes";[70] the *mustēs* is blind, either literally or figuratively, until he or she has completed the stage of initiation called the *muēsis*.[71] *Epoptēs* comes from *ephoraō*, literally "observe," or "look upon," and so the *epoptai* are those who see, or as Kevin Clinton translates, the "viewers."[72] Sight was not limited to those initiates who had completed the *epopteia*, the second stage of initiation. Walter Burkert states, "The *Epopteia* repeats, renews, and deepens that which had been laid as a foundation in the *muēsis*. Already the *mustai* were permitted to see the blissful 'sight.' The *epoptai* may simply have seen more or, more importantly, differently."[73]

This survey of fifth- and fourth-century literature and of titles associated with the ritual demonstrates that the most important moment of the Eleusinian Mysteries came when the hierophant showed something to the initiates. Later literary and epigraphic sources confirm this.[74] We have some idea of what this moment was like: the *telestērion* is lit by flickering torches, there is a gong, there is a big fire, the hierophant emerges from the small room called the *anaktoron*,[75] there is perhaps a proclamation: "Potnia gave birth to a sacred boy, Brimo to Brimon."[76] We do not know, however, what the hierophant showed and the initiates saw.[77] The most likely option is a cut blade of wheat,[78] because of the connection between the Mysteries and agriculture as Demeter's two gifts to the Athenians.[79] Other possibilities are a cult statue or cult objects[80] or even sacred movements.[81] The solution is probably beyond recovery, but, for our purposes, what was seen matters much less than that the seeing occurred and guaranteed the blessedness promised by Demeter to initiates.[82]

Andocides' jurors physically see Andocides in court, but, in their minds, they picture this moment. Andocides is adopting the role of the hierophant,[83] imitating his movements (*mimoumenos*),[84] showing (*epedeiknu*) the sacred things (*ta hiera*), and speaking the secret words to the uninitiated. This description involves all the important details of the Mysteries that I adduced above: there is movement of some sort by the hierophant, there are the secret ritual words that are implied in the *Hymn to Demeter* and in Isocrates' *Panegyrikos*, and, most importantly, there is the visual demonstration. When the jurors saw the real hierophant doing these same things in the *telestērion* at Eleusis, they became *olbioi* ("blessed"). Now, they visualize Andocides not merely mocking the hierophant but profaning this entire reciprocal relationship of showing and seeing.[85] Through the use of *horan*, the speaker of *Against Andocides* brings this profanation to vivid life for the jurors. He wants them to remember that this was not just a novel way for sympiosiasts to vary the tedium of too many nights of drinking games and flute-girls. This was an attack on Demeter's gift to the jurors, an attack on the blessedness that they had received because they had seen.

We may reasonably wonder whether the shock value of the profane Mysteries had worn off after fifteen years between the profanation and the trial. In 415, it clearly was great enough that Alkibiades was afraid to return to Athens and face trial, and the speaker of *Against Andocides* evidently hopes to rekindle some of that horror in the jurors' imaginations by appealing to their visual experience as initiates. He had enough confidence in his appeal to the jurors' sight to allude to it again at the very end of his speech, when he states: "You have seen [*eidete*], you have heard his crimes."[86] Part of his decision to use these words here may have been stylistic,[87] but in a speech that has made use of seeing vocabulary to stress the jury's status as initiates, it seems reasonable to conclude that this "you have seen" recalls, at least in part, the profanation that the jury has just "seen" in chapters 50–51. The combination of seeing and hearing may also have prompted some of the jurors to remember the secret words they heard during their initiations, the secret words that Andocides is said to have disclosed to the uninitiated.

On the Mysteries

In his defense speech, which survives under the title *On the Mysteries*, Andocides himself also recognizes the persuasive power of invoking the visual experience of the jurors' initiations. After he finishes defending himself against the charges of profanation, he twice alludes to the jurors' status as initiates who have seen, warning them that they will be guilty of impiety if they punish him, since he is innocent.[88] As in *Against Andocides*, the mention of seeing highlights the jurors' responsibility as initiates. It reminds them that, because they saw and became blessed, they have a responsibility both to Demeter and to the other initiates to protect the Mysteries from impiety. Although it is impossible to know what weight the jurors placed on these arguments, it is clear that the litigants expected them to be taken seriously. We may infer that Andocides' were more convincing than his opponents', since, even aside from his eventual acquittal, he ends his rebuttal of the Mysteries charges with a direct address to the audience, requesting their applause.[89]

Andocides also seems to have perceived the persuasive power of mental images that bridge the gap between what the jurors see in court and what they picture in their minds. At the end of his speech, he attempts to instill in the jurors' minds a new image to replace the one his opponent created of him profaning the Mysteries. The care Andocides takes with this new image and its emphatic placement at the very end of his long speech suggests that he considered his opponent's attempt to manipulate the jurors' imaginations a potent threat. Unlike the speaker of *Against Andocides*, Andocides does not try to blend together what the jurors see in the court with the past events they hear him describe. In his own way, however, he also attempts to bridge the gap between reality and imagination. He urges the jurors to imagine that they see his ancestors interceding for him and to join in their support.

This image relies not on the memory of a shared ritual experience but on the jurors' admiration for Athens' past and reverence for the dead. It exploits the reciprocal relationship of vision and memory. First, Andocides notes that no one passing by his family's house has ever remembered being poorly treated by one of his dead relatives. Although the account lacks an explicit reference to sight, he clearly considers the physical house a visible spur to mental reflections on the virtues of its inhabitants.[90] Later, he reverses the cause and effect, making memory prompt an imaginary vision. After vaguely summarizing his family's services to Athens,[91] Andocides says:

> μὴ τοίνυν, εἰ αὐτοὶ τεθνᾶσι, καὶ περὶ τῶν πεπραγμένων αὐτοῖς ἐπιλάθησθε, ἀλλ' ἀναμνησθέντες τῶν ἔργων νομίσατε τὰ σώματα αὐτῶν ὁρᾶν αἰτουμένων ἐμὲ παρ' ὑμῶν σῶσαι. (Andoc. 1.148)

> Do not, therefore, because my relatives have died, also forget the things they have done. Instead, remember their deeds and think that you're seeing [*nomisate . . . horan*] them in the flesh, asking you to save me.

Andocides tells the jurors to picture his ancestors "in the flesh," not merely to imagine their voices or their angry reaction to his condemnation. Some of the jurors would have known what some of Andocides' recently deceased ancestors looked like, but this is primarily an attempt to appeal to the jurors' idealized image of Athenians from the noble past of the *polis*. If Andocides' strategy works, his jurors will picture people who look like members of what Andocides terms "the oldest household of all and always the most open-handed to anyone in need."[92] The visualization, therefore, is based not so much on the jurors' individual memories of physical appearance but on a collective, idealized memory of Athenian values. This imagined group of dead relatives takes the place of the parents, wives, and children who customarily plead for litigants, since Andocides is the only living member of his household.

If Andocides has his way, his ancestors will not be the only people pleading for him. Since he has no living relatives, he tells the jurors, "Take the place of my father, of my brothers, of my children."[93] Then, echoing the language he used to describe the pleading of the dead, he says, "Ask yourselves to save me, and save me yourselves" (ὑμεῖς με παρ' ὑμῶν αὐτῶν αἰτησάμενοι σώσατε).[94] As the similar wording makes clear (αἰτουμένων ἐμὲ παρ' ὑμῶν σῶσαι and με παρ' ὑμῶν αὐτῶν αἰτησάμενοι σώσατε), Andocides expects the jurors themselves to plead on his behalf in the same way as the dead ancestors he has just conjured up. The living and dead Athenians, therefore, will cooperate in saving Andocides, one of "the citizens everyone agrees on, who are fit and willingly able to be good men."[95]

As everyone in the jury would have known from popular tradition and from the painting in the Stoa Poikile, the living and the dead cooperated at one of the most important moments in the history of democratic Athens: the defeat of the Persian invaders in the battle of Marathon.[96] Andocides of course is not making a comparison to Marathon, although it may be in the back of his and the jurors' minds.[97] Nonetheless, he is drawing on a tradition that recognizes that living and dead Athenians can act together at moments of crisis in the service of high democratic ideals. Moreover, at the end of a speech defending himself against accusations of complicity in one of the greatest antidemocratic scandals in Athenian history, and delivered in 400 or 399, soon after the overthrow of the Thirty in 404–403, Andocides wants to leave his jurors convinced that saving him would be the height of democratic action. To ensure that this is the final message the jurors will take from his defense,

Andocides calls supporters to the *bēma* "who have already given proof of the greatest excellence towards your majority."[98] So, at the culmination of Andocides' performance, he constructs a scenario in which a mental image of his idealized ancestors joins with the jurors and with the democratic politicians such as Anytos and Kephalos who are supporting him to plead for his life.

With his appeal to his jurors' visual imaginations, therefore, Andocides aligns himself with his ancestors who were loyal to the Athenian *dēmos*. The emphasis on picturing the dead also has a darker subtext. By the late fifth century, the power of the dead to affect the living and of the living to invoke their aid against enemies seems to have become an accepted aspect of Athenian religion.[99] The dead's threatening power played a prominent role in Athenian litigation, even if it is rarely invoked in formal arguments. In Antiphon's third tetralogy (Antiphon 4), the defendant claims that he will turn the murdered man's vengeance against the jurors if they wrongfully convict him.[100] The dead also played a prominent role in litigants' curses against their opponents, their witnesses, and sometimes even the jurors.[101] Plato's *Laws* states as a general rule, "It is natural for the souls of the dead to care especially for their own descendants and to honor those who treat them well and punish those who treat them badly."[102] Andocides' insistence that the jurors picture his relatives "in the flesh" needs to be interpreted against this background. Some of his jurors would surely have thought of the dangers they would face from disregarding the wishes of Andocides' relatives, brought bodily back from the underworld by a combination of language and imagination. Yet even those jurors impervious to the horrors of infernal threats may have been swayed by the thought of this visualized household being destroyed "by its roots" and left with no one to perform the customary rites for the dead.[103]

Andocides' attempt to guide his jurors' visual imaginations, therefore, counterbalances his opponent's. Where the speaker of *Against Andocides* appealed to their reverence for the Mysteries and their status as blessed initiates, Andocides subtly appeals to another side of Athenian religion, the power of the dead. This is not to say that the jurors had to assess the relative danger to themselves of incurring Demeter's wrath by acquitting Andocides or incurring Andocides' ancestors' wrath by convicting him. For most of the jurors, the visual images would not have posed such a stark choice. Nonetheless, both Andocides and the speaker of *Against Andocides* seek to manipulate the jurors' imaginations and subconscious or semiconscious religious fear in their own favor. The speaker of *Against Andocides* exploits the jurors' status as initiates and encourages them mentally to transfer Andocides from the court into a scene of profanation based on their own transformative visual experience. Andocides himself plays on their sense of civic virtue and their fear of the vengeful dead to conjure up his dead ancestors before their eyes and to encourage them to become the dead's allies on his behalf. For both speakers, the court becomes the background for the jurors to visualize people and events favorable to themselves.

CONCLUSIONS

All of the speeches I have examined in this chapter take advantage of the double nature of visuality: real sight and imaginary sight. By creating internal audiences who see and hear similar things to what the jurors see and hear, the speakers of *Against Diogeiton* and *Against Teisis* blur the distinctions between the court and the location of earlier events. The jurors join the internal audiences in an act of shared spectatorship that is partly real and partly imaginary, and the speakers encourage them to identify with the internal audiences and to adopt their emotions and judgments as their own. While the speaker of *Against Andocides* does not employ an internal audience, he exploits the unique circumstances of Andocides' trial to urge the jurors to visualize Andocides profaning the Mysteries at the same time that they see him in court. By appealing to the jurors' memories of a shared ritual experience, the speaker tries to bridge the gap not only between past and present but also between reality and insinuation. Andocides himself then tries to offset the power of this recreated profanation by conjuring up a mental image of his dead ancestors pleading on his behalf, something his living supporters are also preparing to do.

Although forensic orators often employ standardized strategies and formulaic language, every case and every speaker is different. Thus, while manipulation of the jurors' imaginations is a frequent tactic, all litigants and speechwriters approach it in a slightly different way. As my analysis in this chapter and chapter 5 has shown, there was no single way to create *enargeia* in the Athenian courts. The individual strategies I have discussed are all variations on the same theme, however. Whether a litigant uses an internal audience or a direct appeal to his jurors' imaginary sight, he still recognizes the persuasive effect of making his jurors consider themselves witnesses on his behalf. The prevalence of this tactic also gives us insight into the nature of the Athenians' imaginations. In a world without constant visual stimuli from photographs, photocopies, books, movies, computer screens, and television, audiences had to accustom themselves to visualize in their minds what today, more often than not, we can see before our eyes. When jurors exercised their imaginations to see what litigants described for them, they were using the same capacity they did in the theater, where they followed the promptings of messengers and pictured deaths, meetings, and battles that happened off-stage. Therefore, while litigants and speechwriters exploit their jurors' visual imaginations for their own specifically legal ends, they also reveal their place in a culture that prized imagination in many contexts.

CONCLUSION

I began this book by arguing that the rhetoric of seeing is one of the few performance features of Attic forensic oratory that we can study from the texts that survive. These texts reveal three main ways that speakers appealed to their jurors as both lookers and listeners. First, seeking to exploit the jurors' gaze in their favor, speakers urged the jurors to interpret what they could see in ways favorable to themselves and unfavorable to their opponents. Second, taking advantage of the central role of visual evidence in Athenian law and legal procedure, speakers presented their verbal arguments as though they were especially authoritative by describing them with the same vocabulary that characterizes visual demonstrations to witnesses. Third, attempting to influence their jurors' imaginations, speakers urged them to create mental pictures of the episodes they heard about, which sometimes paralleled the scene in the court.

Although I have analyzed these three aspects of the rhetoric of seeing through individual examples, they are not discrete phenomena. They are all parts of a single rhetorical strategy that emphasizes the sense of sight. Within a single speech, individual instances can reinforce each other and encourage the jury to associate the speaker and his case with visibility. In Demosthenes' *On the Crown* (Demosthenes 18), for example, Demosthenes uses the vocabulary of demonstration and visibility to support his claim that Philip did not defeat him in planning or in preparations but only by good luck. "What are the demonstrations [*apodeixeis*] of my claims?" he says, "They are vivid [*enargeis*] and evident [*phanerai*]. Just look into [*skopeite*] them."[1] This language gains extra potency because Demosthenes has associated himself with vividness and visibility throughout the speech.

In the famous account of the emergency session of the assembly after Elateia fell to Philip, for instance, Demosthenes recreates the meeting for the jurors and describes his own role in visual, almost epiphanic terms. He prepares to quote his own speech by saying, "If someone did not understand these things and had not examined them carefully from the very beginning, even if he were patriotic and even if he were rich, he would have had no chance of knowing what needed to be done or of being able to advise you. But then on that day, I myself, the one here [*houtos*], appeared [*ephanēn*], and coming forward I spoke to you."[2] After quoting his speech, Demosthenes contrasts himself with Aeschines, using his own derogatory nickname, Battalos ("stammerer" or, less likely, "anus"), and referring to Aeschines as Oinomaos, the mythical king of Olympia Aeschines had once played during what Demosthenes claims was an insignificant acting career. Demosthenes repeats the same word, *ephanēn*, this time with a different connotation. "Then, on that occasion, I, Battalos of Paiania, was evidently [*ephanēn*] worth more to my country than you, Oinomaos of Kothokidai."[3] Paiania was Demosthenes' deme, and Kothokidai was Aeschines'. By framing his speech in the assembly with the vocabulary of visibility, Demosthenes emphasizes that his status as Athens' loyal defender and adviser should be evident to the jurors. When he uses similar language later on to describe the evidence for Philip's failure to defeat him, it is part of the same strategy of associating himself and his actions with evidence and visibility.

Along the same lines, physical sight, imaginary sight, and the language of demonstration and visibility can reinforce each other within a single speech. Near the end of *Against Ktesiphon* (Aeschines 3), the counterpart to *On the Crown*, Aeschines combines an appeal to physical sight with an appeal to imaginary sight. He asks the jurors to look around the court and see the disgraceful type of people who support Demosthenes, and a few minutes later he urges them to picture Solon and Aristeides standing on the *bēma* as examples of real service to Athens.[4] Similarly, the speaker of Lysias' *Against Philon* (Lysias 31) combines physical sight with the vocabulary of demonstration, claiming that his words, which he describes with a form of *apodeiknumi*, work together with what the jurors see to prove his point.[5]

Persuasion is a process, and the effect of the rhetoric of seeing is cumulative. It depends on multiple elements of individual speeches working together and reinforcing each other from the beginning of a performance until its end. Just as importantly, the rhetoric of seeing can also complement other rhetorical and stylistic techniques. It is just one tool that contributes to persuasion, and we should not exaggerate its significance at the expense of other techniques that speechwriters and litigants use.

At heart, the rhetoric of seeing takes advantage of the ancient Greek tendency to trust visual evidence and witnesses who have seen what they are testifying about. This link between seeing and believing extended beyond legal contexts. Homer's Eumaios is a trustworthy source of information about the suitors' return from ambush because he saw their ship with his own eyes, the nurse in Sophocles' *Women of Trachis* is a trustworthy source of information about Deianeira's suicide because she was standing close to her and saw it, and the author of the Hippocratic *On Fleshes* is a trustworthy source of information that children can be born at seven months because he has seen it happen.[6] It would be surprising if forensic oratory were the only genre to take advantage of this pervasive faith in witnesses and visual evidence through the rhetoric of seeing, and I have explored its links with medicine, philosophy, historiography, and other rhetorical genres.

The fact that forensic oratory employs persuasive tactics that resemble the techniques of other genres should not lead us to understate the distinctions between what went on in the courts and what went on outside them. Forensic oratory is unique among ancient genres for two fundamental reasons that transcend any superficial similarities: the speeches were always followed by the jurors' votes, and the speeches had to be consistent with written laws and legal procedures. Ultimately, these two characteristics of forensic oratory govern every rhetorical tactic that litigants and speechwriters employ, including the rhetoric of seeing.

Influencing the jurors' vote was the ultimate goal of every Athenian forensic speech. Many of them even end by commanding the jurors to cast their votes for the speaker with an imperative form of *psēphizomai* ("vote"). For a defendant, a successful speech could mean the difference between exile and freedom, poverty and prosperity, death and life. For a prosecutor or plaintiff, a successful speech could secure the recovery of lost assets, take vengeance for an injured victim, or settle a score with a political enemy. Other Greek genres, even competitive performance genres such as deliberative oratory in the assembly or dramatic contests in the theater, would not have affected performers' own lives in such significant and immediate ways, at least under normal conditions. When Thucydides encourages his readers to identify with an internal viewing audience, or when the author of *On Breaths* uses the vocabulary of demonstration to present his claims about air as authoritative, or when musi-

CONCLUSION

cians in the theater complement their songs with forceful gestures, they are not trying to convince an audience that is about to exercise direct power over their fate. They can succeed in ways that litigants cannot.

The speaker of Lysias' *Against Teisis* (Lysias frs. 278–279 Carey), on the other hand, would have failed even if he successfully led his jurors to imagine Teisis' wounds, to identify themselves with the viewers in the *deigma*, and to feel anger at Teisis, unless they also voted to convict him. For this reason, Lysias is careful to anchor the rhetoric of seeing to the context of the trial, emphasizing that Teisis and Arkhippos are not characters in a story but people present in the court. Other speakers also link the rhetoric of seeing with the trial and the courtroom: Timarkhos in court is the same Timarkhos who Aeschines claims made obscene gestures in the assembly, Meidias in court is the same Meidias whom Demosthenes holds responsible for Straton's silence, and Demosthenes in court is the same Demosthenes whom Aeschines' Thebans blame for their suffering. It is not enough to persuade your jurors by appealing to their sense of sight unless you can also convince them that what they see, imagine they see, or associate with visual evidence should affect their vote in the trial.

As well as anchoring the rhetoric of seeing to the context of the trial, litigants and their speechwriters must also tailor it to the specific question that the jurors are asked to address and to the laws and procedures governing that question. In *For the Disabled Man* (Lysias 24), the speaker draws attention to his disability not simply to attract the jurors' pity but to refute the charge that he is sufficiently able to earn his own living without state support. Similarly, the speakers of *For Polystratos* (Lysias 20) ask the jurors to look at Polystratos' appearance only because they know that his old age will seem incompatible with the lead role he is charged with taking in the extreme revolutionary government of the Four Hundred. Lycurgus guides the jurors' imaginations through the panic in Athens after the battle of Chaeronea in *Against Leokrates* (Lycurgus 1) because the scenes they picture will support his charge that Leokrates treasonously abandoned the city in its hour of need. Finally, all speakers who employ the vocabulary of demonstration and visibility in cases that rely on the presence or absence of witnesses and visual evidence claim particular authority for themselves because of the special role of this same vocabulary in the procedural language of witnessing. In other contexts, the effect of the words might not be as powerful. The rhetoric of seeing may not always have succeeded, but speakers al-

CONCLUSION

ways employed it strategically in a way that reflected the particular circumstances of their trials.

Alastair Blanshard has recently called Attic oratory the "most intertextual of genres."[7] In attempting to convince their jurors, litigants and speechwriters can sometimes refer to familiar and unfamiliar myths, poems, historical episodes, or works of art. By introducing such central elements of Athenian culture, forensic oratory places its arguments within a cultural context that jurors can interpret in favorable ways. When litigants and speechwriters employ the rhetoric of seeing, they similarly situate their arguments within a set of cultural values and concepts that prioritize sight and visibility. Through tactics such as the ones I have explored in this book, they turn the jurors' gaze to their own advantage.

APPENDIX OF SPEECHES

In this appendix, I provide a brief summary of each speech that is significant for my argument and assign it to one of three broad categories: physical sight (chapters 1–2), the language of demonstration and visibility (chapters 3–4), and imaginary sight (chapters 5–6). In the case of the language of demonstration and visibility, I also note whether it exemplifies the semitechnical terminology of witnessing (chapter 3). I also include the speeches that I discuss within the context of these categories, even if they do not fit into one of them. The summaries are intended to provide basic context and background. More detailed discussions of the speeches and their dates can be found in standard handbooks such as MacDowell 2009 or Usher 1999, as well as in the University of Texas Press series *The Oratory of Classical Greece*.

Aeschines 1: *Against Timarkhos* (346/345)
Prosecution speech in a "scrutiny of public speakers." In a "scrutiny of public speakers," a jury determined whether someone had committed one of the actions that rendered him ineligible to speak in the assembly. Aeschines maintains that his political enemy Timarkhos has lost this right because he had been a prostitute as a young man and had wasted his inheritance.
  Physical sight (chapter 2)

Aeschines 2: *On the Dishonest Embassy* (343)
Defense speech against Demosthenes' charge that Aeschines had accepted bribes to promote a peace treaty that favored Philip of Macedon's interests rather than the interests of Athens (see Demosthenes 19). Aeschines defends his actions during the peace negotiations with Macedon

———————— APPENDIX OF SPEECHES ————————

in 346, and he describes Demosthenes as an incompetent and untrustworthy politician.
Physical sight (introduction and chapter 2)

Aeschines 3: *Against Ktesiphon* (330)
Prosecution speech for proposing an illegal decree. In 336, Ktesiphon proposed that the Athenians award Demosthenes a crown in gratitude for his work rebuilding the city walls and because of his lifetime of service to Athens. Aeschines maintained that the proposal was illegal because of procedural irregularities and, more importantly, because Ktesiphon had lied about Demosthenes' record of service. The case did not come to trial until 330. Demosthenes' response is Demosthenes 18.
Physical sight (chapter 2), the language of demonstration and visibility (chapter 4), imaginary sight (chapter 5)

Andocides 1: *On the Mysteries* (400 or 399)
Defense speech. Andocides argues that he is entitled to exercise the rights of an Athenian citizen, countering the charge that he had forfeited his rights by participating in two notorious acts of impiety in 415, the profanation of the Eleusinian Mysteries and the mutilation of the herms.
Imaginary sight (chapter 6)

Andocides 2: *On His Return* (between 410 and 405)
A speech delivered to the assembly. The exiled Andocides has returned to Athens and argues that he should be allowed to stay. During the speech, he discusses his arrest by the Four Hundred in 411 during an earlier attempt to return to Athens.
The language of demonstration and visibility: the semitechnical language of witnessing (chapter 3)

Antiphon 2: *First Tetralogy* (before 411, but probably from the 430s or earlier)
Four model speeches from a fictional homicide trial. A slave died after identifying the defendant as the murderer. Since there are no living witnesses, both the plaintiff and the defendant argue based on probability rather than evidence.

APPENDIX OF SPEECHES

The language of demonstration and visibility: the semitechnical language of witnessing (chapter 3)

Antiphon 3: *Second Tetralogy* (before 411, but probably from the 430s or earlier)
Four model speeches from a fictional homicide trial. A boy died after he was struck by a javelin. The plaintiff argues that the javelin-thrower is guilty of unintentional homicide, but the javelin-thrower's father maintains that the victim is responsible for his own death, since he ran in the path of the javelin.
The language of demonstration and visibility (chapter 4)

Antiphon 4: *Third Tetralogy* (before 411, but probably from the 430s or earlier)
Four model speeches from a fictional homicide trial. The victim died after a drunken fight with the defendant. Both sides address the defendant's intent and the possibility that the victim died because of inadequate medical care. The defendant is imagined to go into exile rather than give a final speech, perhaps signaling the weakness of his case.
Discussed in the sections on physical sight (chapter 1) and imaginary sight (chapter 6)

Antiphon 6: *On the Chorus Boy* (419)
Defense speech from a homicide trial. A boy training for a chorus in the defendant's home died after drinking a drug. The defendant argues that he had nothing to do with the death and that the charge is politically motivated.
The language of demonstration and visibility: the semitechnical language of witnessing (chapter 3)

Antisthenes: *Ajax* (late 5th–mid 4th century)
Speech composed for the hero Ajax for the mythical trial between him and Odysseus to determine which of them would be awarded the arms of the dead Achilles. Ajax emphasizes his martial prowess.
Discussed in the section on imaginary sight (chapter 5)

APPENDIX OF SPEECHES

Demosthenes 18: *On the Crown* (330)
Defense speech on behalf of Ktesiphon, who had proposed in 336 that Demosthenes be honored with a crown because of his contributions to Athens. Aeschines maintained that Demosthenes was not a benefactor of Athens, and so Ktesiphon's decree was illegal (Aeschines 3). In this speech, Demosthenes defends his record and justifies his actions.
  Discussed in the section on the vocabulary of demonstration and visibility (chapter 4)

Demosthenes 19: *On the Dishonest Embassy* (343/342)
Prosecution speech against Aeschines for accepting bribes to promote a peace treaty that favored Philip of Macedon's interests rather than the interests of Athens (see Aeschines 2). Demosthenes recounts the events preceding and following the second embassy to Macedon in 346 in a way that seems to confirm his charge.
  Physical sight (chapter 2), imaginary sight (chapter 5)

Demosthenes 21: *Against Meidias* (346)
Prosecution speech for assault. Demosthenes charges Meidias, with whom he has a long-standing quarrel, with punching him at the Dionysia of 348 while he was performing the official function of *khorēgos*. A *khorēgos* was the financial sponsor of a chorus that performed in honor of Dionysus.
  Physical sight (chapters 1, 2), discussed in the section on imaginary sight (chapter 5)

Demosthenes 22: *Against Androtion* (355/354)
Prosecution speech for proposing an illegal decree. The politician Androtion has proposed a decree that the assembly grant special honors to the *boulē* of 356/355, of which Androtion was a member. In response, Androtion's enemy Euktemon prosecutes him, claiming that the decree was illegal for a number of procedural reasons, including that Androtion has no right to propose decrees at all because he had been a prostitute and is in debt to the Athenian treasury. This speech was spoken by Euktemon's supporter Diodoros.
  Imaginary sight (chapter 6), discussed in the section on physical sight (chapter 2)

APPENDIX OF SPEECHES

Demosthenes 25: *Against Aristogeiton* (probably 325 or 324)
Prosecution speech spoken by Demosthenes against Aristogeiton for exercising rights to which he is not entitled. Demosthenes was second speaker in a prosecution team led by Lycurgus that charged Aristogeiton with illegally making speeches in the assembly and the court even though he owed money to the Athenian treasury. The speech focuses on the flaws in Aristogeiton's character.
  Physical sight (chapter 1), discussed in the section on the language of demonstration and visibility (chapter 4)

Demosthenes 27: *First Speech against Aphobos* (364/363)
Prosecution speech for maladministration of a ward's property. Demosthenes has charged his guardians with incompetently managing and stealing from his father's estate while they were supposed to be maintaining it for him. This is the prosecution speech against one of his guardians, Aphobos.
  The language of demonstration and visibility: the semitechnical language of witnessing (chapter 3)

Demosthenes 36: *For Phormion* (350/349)
Prosecution speech for bringing an illegal suit. When the Athenian banker Pasion died, he made his former slave Phormion the guardian of his younger son Pasikles and the interim manager of his property, including his bank. Now, Pasion's adult son, Apollodoros, has accused Phormion of failing to pay back to the estate a loan he had taken to finance the bank's operation. Phormion has preemptively countersued Apollodoros, claiming that Apollodoros' suit is illegal because he had granted Phormion a formal release from all obligations associated with the bank. A supporter of Phormion, perhaps Demosthenes himself, delivers the speech.
  Physical sight (chapter 1)

Demosthenes 37: *Against Pantainetos* (347/346)
Prosecution speech for bringing an illegal suit. Pantainetos managed a silver refinery that he rented from Demosthenes' client Nikoboulos and Nikoboulos' friend Euergos. While Nikoboulos was away from Athens, Euergos evicted Pantainetos from the refinery for failing to pay the

rent. The two men then sold the refinery, and Pantainetos brought separate suits against each of them for causing him financial harm. In the case against Nikoboulos, Pantainetos accused Nikoboulos of sending a slave named Antigenes to seize money from one of Pantainetos' slaves and to repossess the refinery. Before the case came to trial, Nikoboulos countersued Pantainetos, claiming that Pantainetos' suit against him was inadmissible on various procedural grounds.
    Physical sight (chapter 1)

Demosthenes 38: *Against Nausimakhos and Xenopeithes* (ca. 346, but the evidence is inconclusive)
Prosecution speech for bringing an illegal suit. Nausimakhos and Xenopeithes have charged the four sons of their deceased guardian with holding money owed to the estate of their father. One of the sons has preemptively countersued them, and Demosthenes has written this speech for him. The son maintains that Nausimakhos and Xenopeithes' suit is illegal because they had given his father a formal release from all obligations connected with the guardianship and because the time in which wards may sue guardians has passed.
    The language of demonstration and visibility (chapter 4)

Demosthenes 41: *Against Spoudias* (no evidence for the date, but it is thought to come from early in Demosthenes' career, perhaps the late 360s or 350s)
Inheritance speech. The speaker and Spoudias are married to the daughters of Polyeuktos, who has died. The speaker claims that Spoudias owes money to the estate of Polyeuktos and has sued him to recover it.
    The language of demonstration and visibility (chapter 4)

Demosthenes 42: *Against Phainippos* (after the late 340s and perhaps 328/327)
Speech from a trial to determine which litigant is wealthier and so has to contribute money to a liturgy. The speaker argues that Phainippos is wealthier than he is. He accuses Phainippos of concealing his wealth by not submitting an accurate list of his property and, among other things, falsely claiming that his land is encumbered by mortgages.

The language of demonstration and visibility: the semitechnical language of witnessing (chapter 3)

Demosthenes 43: *Against Makartatos* (probably the late 340s)
Inheritance speech. The speaker Sositheos argues that his son has a stronger claim to the estate of Hagnias than Makartatos. Makartatos has inherited the estate from his father Theopompos, who had been awarded it in an earlier court proceeding and possessed it until his death (see Isaeus 11). Sositheos argues that his son is Hagnias' first cousin once removed, through a posthumous adoption by Hagnias' deceased first cousin, and is thus a closer relative to Hagnias than Makartatos' father Theopompos, who was only a second cousin.
The language of demonstration and visibility (chapter 4)

Demosthenes 45: *First Speech against Stephanos* (350/349 or soon afterwards)
Prosecution speech for false witnessing. The speech is attributed to Apollodoros and delivered by him. Stephanos was a witness against Apollodoros in an earlier suit involving Phormion's bank (Demosthenes 36). In this speech, Apollodoros prosecutes him for lying in that case. He also attacks the characters of Stephanos, Phormion, and his own brother Pasikles.
Discussed in the section on physical sight (chapter 2)

Demosthenes 47: *Against Euergos and Mnesiboulos* (probably 356/355 or 354/353)
Prosecution speech for false witnessing. The speaker accuses Euergos and Mnesiboulos of lying about a challenge to torture a slave when they acted as witnesses in an earlier suit that a certain Theophemos had brought against him for assault.
Physical sight (chapter 1), the language of demonstration and visibility: the semitechnical language of witnessing (chapter 3)

Demosthenes 48: *Against Olympiodoros* (ca. 342)
Inheritance Speech. The speaker Kallistratos claims that he and Olympiodoros had devised a plan to split the estate of their dead relative Ko-

mon. When Olympiodoros defeated all the other potential claimants in court, he inherited the property and refused to give half to Kallistratos. Kallistratos is suing him for failing to satisfy their agreement.

The language of demonstration and visibility (chapter 4)

Demosthenes 53: *Against Nikostratos* (after 368/367)
Prosecution speech against a public debtor. The speech is attributed to Apollodoros and delivered by him. Apollodoros has charged Nikostratos with pretending that two slaves belong to him and not to his brother Arethousios, who owes money to the Athenian treasury. If the slaves really belong to Arethousios, then they should be sold and the proceeds used to pay down the debt.

The language of demonstration and visibility (chapter 4)

Demosthenes 59: *Against Neaira* (343–339)
Two speeches, both attributed to Apollodoros. The second and longer one is delivered by him. Neaira is living with Apollodoros' enemy Stephanos (see Demosthenes 45), and they have children together. Apollodoros charges that Neaira is not an Athenian, and so this arrangement is not a marriage and their children are not Athenian citizens. The speech includes a long section of allegations about Neaira's career as a prostitute.

The language of demonstration and visibility: the semitechnical language of witnessing (chapter 3)

Dinarchus 3: *Against Philokles* (323)
Prosecution speech for disobeying the assembly and accepting bribes. Dinarchus accuses the general Philokles of admitting Harpalos into Athens against the direct orders of the assembly and of accepting bribes from him. Harpalos was a former official of Alexander the Great who hoped to foment a rebellion against Alexander.

Discussed in the section on physical sight (chapter 1)

Gorgias: *Defense of Palamedes* (plausibly assigned to the 5th century)
Defense speech composed for the imaginary trial of the hero Palamedes, whom Odysseus charged with accepting a bribe to conspire with the

Trojans against the Greeks. Palamedes' speech relies heavily on probability arguments.
The language of demonstration and visibility: the semitechnical language of witnessing (chapter 3)

Hyperides 1: *In Defense of Lykophron* (333)
Defense speech against a charge of adultery. Lycurgus and Ariston have charged that Lykophron was having an affair with the sister of Dioxippos during her first marriage and has attempted to continue the relationship now that she has remarried. Lykophron argues that the prosecution's story is implausible, attacks his opponent Ariston, and describes his own record of good citizenship.
Discussed in the section on physical sight (chapter 1)

Isaeus 3: *On the Estate of Pyrrhos* (380s–340s)
Prosecution speech for false witnessing. When Pyrrhos died, his adopted son Endios, the son of his sister, inherited his property. More than twenty years later, Endios died childless. A certain Xenokles claimed the estate, saying that his wife Phile was Pyrrhos' legitimate daughter. Endios' mother also claimed the estate, maintaining that Phile's mother had never married Pyrrhos and that, as his sister, she was his closest living relative. The speaker, Endios' younger brother, is prosecuting Nikodemos, the brother of Phile's mother, for falsely testifying that Phile's mother had married Pyrrhos.
The language of demonstration and visibility: the semitechnical language of witnessing (chapter 3)

Isaeus 5: *On the Estate of Dikaiogenes* (ca. 389)
Prosecution speech against Leokhares, who had acted as surety for a financial agreement. The case involves two men named Dikaiogenes, whom I designate Dikaiogenes II and Dikaiogenes III, to distinguish them from Dikaiogenes I, their mutual ancestor who appears in the speech but not in this summary. Dikaiogenes II had adopted his first cousin Dikaiogenes III and divided his estate between him and his own sisters. This arrangement gave rise to litigation between Dikaiogenes III and the husbands and sons of Dikaiogenes II's sisters. Twenty-two years after Dikaiogenes II had died, Dikaiogenes III agreed to give two-thirds

APPENDIX OF SPEECHES

of the estate to the sons of Dikaiogenes II's sisters, led by Menexenos. At this point, however, the estate had declined in value and was encumbered by mortgages. Menexenos, therefore, prosecutes Dikaiogenes III's friend Leokhares, who had acted as surety for the agreement. He claims that Dikaiogenes III had agreed to surrender two-thirds of the estate free from all liabilities, even though, according to Leokhares, this was not stated explicitly in the written agreement. The speech is a sustained character attack on Dikaiogenes III.

Discussed in the section on physical sight (chapter 1)

Isaeus 6: *On the Estate of Philoktemon* (365/364 or 364/363)
Prosecution speech for false witnessing. The speaker argues that his friend Khairestratos is entitled to the estate of Euktemon because he had been adopted by Euktemon's son Philoktemon, who had predeceased his father. He claims further that Euktemon has no legitimate living sons or grandsons with a stronger claim to the estate than Khairestratos'. In this speech, he charges the rival claimant Androkles with falsely testifying that Euktemon has two legitimate living sons.

The language of demonstration and visibility: the semitechnical language of witnessing (chapter 3)

Isaeus 7: *On the Estate of Apollodoros* (after 357/356 and probably 354)
Inheritance speech. The speaker Thrasyllos argues that he is entitled to the estate of Apollodoros (a different Apollodoros from the one whose works survive in the Demosthenic corpus), even though Apollodoros had died before completing all the procedural steps necessary to adopt Thrasyllos. The rival claimant is Apollodoros' first cousin, the daughter of his uncle Eupolis. Thrasyllos describes Apollodoros' long-standing quarrel with Eupolis' family and close relationship with his family.

The language of demonstration and visibility: the semitechnical language of witnessing (chapter 3)

Isaeus 10: *On the Estate of Aristarkhos* (probably either 378–371 or ca. 355, but the evidence is inconclusive)
Inheritance speech. The speaker maintains that he is entitled to the estate of his first cousin Aristarkhos (II), who had inherited the estate of their grandfather, also named Aristarkhos (I), through posthumous

adoption. The rival claimant is Aristarkhos II's brother, to whom Aristarkhos II has left the estate. The speaker argues that the posthumous adoption of Aristarkhos II by Aristarkhos I was a fraudulent way to cut his mother, Aristarkhos I's daughter, out of the inheritance.

> The language of demonstration and visibility (chapter 4)

Isaeus 11: *On the Estate of Hagnias* (probably the early 350s)
Defense speech against the charge of mistreating an orphan. The speaker Theopompos defends himself on the charge of depriving the son of his deceased brother Stratokles of a share of Hagnias' estate, which Theopompos had been awarded by the courts. He argues that Stratokles' son is not entitled to inherit, because as Hagnias' second cousin once removed, he is too distant a relative. Theopompos himself, however, is a second cousin (as was Stratokles), and so, he argues, is closely enough related to inherit. Demosthenes 43 is from a later trial about the same estate.

> Discussed in the section on the language of demonstration and visibility (chapter 4)

Isocrates 18: *Against Kallimakhos* (sometime soon after 404/403, probably 402)
Prosecution speech for bringing an illegal suit. Kallimakhos has charged the speaker with failing to pay a debt owed to him. The speaker has preemptively prosecuted Kallimakhos, claiming that this charge was illegal because it ran counter to the terms of the amnesty that followed the civil strife of 404/403. During the speech, he discusses Kallimakhos' involvement in an earlier attempt to frame someone for murder.

> Physical sight (chapter 1), the language of demonstration and visibility (chapter 4)

Lycurgus 1: *Against Leokrates* (331)
Prosecution for treason. Lycurgus argues that Leokrates committed treason because he left Athens after the defeat at Chaeronaea in 338 and lived in Rhodes and Megara. In the speech, Lycurgus contrasts Leokrates' cowardice with the heroism of the contemporary Athenians and their ancestors.

> Imaginary sight (chapter 5)

APPENDIX OF SPEECHES

Lysias 1: *On the Murder of Eratosthenes* (403–ca. 380)
A defense speech from a homicide trial. The speaker Euphiletos argues that he was justified in killing his wife's lover Eratosthenes after he caught them in bed together.
  The language of demonstration and visibility: the semitechnical language of witnessing (chapter 3)

Lysias 2: *Funeral Oration* (probably ca. 390)
Every year the Athenians chose someone to deliver a speech as part of the funeral ceremony in honor of the soldiers who had died that year. This funeral oration honors the Athenians who died fighting with their Corinthian allies sometime in the late 390s or early 380s. As a metic, Lysias may never have actually delivered it.
  Imaginary sight (chapter 6)

Lysias 3: *Against Simon* (a few years after 394)
Defense speech for assault. The speaker and his opponent were involved in a long-running and sometimes violent quarrel over a youth named Theodotos. The speaker maintains that he is not guilty of assaulting Simon, and he describes a series of violent altercations that he claims Simon caused.
  Discussed in the section on physical sight (chapter 1)

Lysias 6: *Against Andocides* (400 or 399)
Prosecution speech against Andocides for illegally exercising the rights of an Athenian citizen despite having taken part in the profanation of the Eleusinian Mysteries and the mutilation of the herms in 415. Andocides' defense survives as Andocides 1. This is a supporting speech, not the speech of the main prosecutor.
  Imaginary sight (chapter 6)

Lysias 9: *For the Soldier* (probably from the first quarter of the 4th century)
Defense speech. The speaker, a soldier named Polyainos, maintains that he is not liable to pay a fine for slandering a general because he made the

insulting remarks in a bank and not in the *sunedrion*, the place where the generals perform their official duties.

The language of demonstration and visibility: the semitechnical language of witnessing (chapter 3)

Lysias 10: *Against Theomnestos* (384/383)
Prosecution speech from a trial for defamation. The speaker argues that Theomnestos is guilty of defamation because he called him a father-killer in an earlier trial, even if the word Theomnestos used is not specifically mentioned in the law against defamation.

Physical sight (chapter 1), the language of demonstration and visibility: the semitechnical language of witnessing (chapter 3)

Lysias 12: *Against Eratosthenes* (ca. 403/402)
Prosecution speech probably delivered at the accounting (*euthunai*) of Eratosthenes, a former member of the Thirty, the oligarchic regime that briefly ruled Athens in 404/403. Lysias accuses Eratosthenes of complicity in the murder of his brother Polemarkhos. If Lysias' status as a metic prevented him from speaking in court, he may have circulated this speech as a pamphlet.

Discussed in the section on the relationship of seeing to power and knowledge (introduction)

Lysias 16: *For Mantitheos* (394–ca. 389)
Defense speech from a scrutiny (*dokimasia*) before the *boulē*. Mantitheos' opponent has argued that Mantitheos should not be permitted to serve on the *boulē* because he was a cavalryman under the Thirty. Mantitheos maintains that his good character is more significant than this charge, which he denies.

Physical sight (chapter 1)

Lysias 20: *For Polystratos* (probably soon after 411)
Two defense speeches delivered by Polystratos' son and a supporter on behalf of Polystratos, who is charged with participating in the oligarchy of the Four Hundred. The speakers seek to minimize Polystratos'

part in the Four Hundred's government and to describe his sons' loyalty to Athens.
    Physical sight (chapter 1)

Lysias 22: *Against the Grain Retailers* (probably early in 386)
Prosecution speech accusing the grain retailers of manipulating the price of grain in their favor during a food shortage in Athens.
    Discussed in the section on the language of demonstration and visibility (chapter 4)

Lysias 23: *Against Pankleon* (403–ca. 380)
Defense speech. At an earlier date, the speaker had brought a charge against Pankleon. Pankleon then preemptively countersued him, claiming that the suit was procedurally invalid because it had been brought to the archon who deals with metics rather than Athenian citizens. Pankleon maintains that he is a Plataian and therefore an Athenian. (The citizens of Plataia were offered Athenian citizenship after Plataia was destroyed in 427 because of Plataia's historically close ties to Athens.) In this speech, the speaker argues that Pankleon is not only not a Plataian but is also a slave.
    The language of demonstration and visibility (chapter 4)

Lysias 24: *For the Disabled Man* (403–ca. 380)
Defense speech from a scrutiny (*dokimasia*) before the *boulē*. The speaker argues that he is entitled to receive a disability pension, even though his opponent has accused him of being able-bodied.
    Physical sight (chapter 1)

Lysias 31: *Against Philon* (within a few years after 403/402)
Prosecution speech from a scrutiny (*dokimasia*) before the *boulē*. The speaker argues that Philon is not qualified to join the *boulē* because he supported neither the democrats nor the oligarchs in the civil strife of 404/403.
    Physical sight (chapter 1), the language of demonstration and visibility (chapter 4)

APPENDIX OF SPEECHES

Lysias 32: *Against Diogeiton* (ca. 401/400)
Prosecution speech for maladministration of a ward's property. The speaker accuses Diogeiton of embezzling the estate of his brother Diodotos while he was supposed to be maintaining it for his nephews. The nephews were also Diogeiton's grandchildren, since his daughter had married his brother. The speaker is the nephews' brother-in-law.

The language of demonstration and visibility: the semitechnical language of witnessing (chapter 3), imaginary sight (chapter 6)

Lysias, frs. 278–279 Carey: *Against Teisis* (= fr. 2 in the University of Texas series) (403–ca. 380)
Prosecution speech for assault. The speaker accuses Teisis of luring Arkhippos to his house under pretense of friendship so that he could tie him to a column and whip him until he was close to death.

Imaginary sight (chapter 6)

NOTES

INTRODUCTION

1. Athenaeus 13.590d–f. Cf. Pseudo-Plutarch, *Lives of the Ten Orators* 849e; Quintilian, *Orator's Education* 2.15.9; Sextus Empiricus, *Against the Professors* 2.4. C. Cooper 1995; O'Connell 2013.
2. Isoc. 18.52–54; Dem. 25.62.
3. Cicero, *Orator* 55–56.
4. *Rhetoric for Herennius* 3.19–27; Cicero, *On the Orator* 3.213–227; *Orator* 55–60; Quintilian, *Orator's Education* 11.3. Fantham 1982; 2004, 292–298; Gunderson 2000, 59–86.
5. *Rhetoric for Herennius* 3.19.
6. Arist. *Rhet.* 3.1.5 1403b35–1404a8.
7. Theophrastus, frs. 666.24, 712, 713 Fortenbaugh. On this work see Fortenbaugh 1985; 2005, 145–150, 397–415.
8. Philodemus, *Rhetoric* 4 col. 18.18–19.16, pp. 1.200–201 Sudhaus: "But some people have recently spoken a lot of nonsense about instruction in delivery, even though many of the heroes and those who came after them were delivering their speeches in an admirable manner, as it is possible to learn from the poets, from the historians, and from the writings which they have left behind themselves. The handbook writers have made public knowledge of something that really does exist, even though statesmen have kept it hidden, namely that they make their deliveries through a method that enables them to seem reverent and noble and, most importantly, enables them to deceive their hearers and also to exaggerate. No practitioner of another skill needs any of these things, especially not the philosophers." (ἀλλὰ δὴ τὰ μὲν περὶ τῆς ὑποκρίσεως παραγγέλματα πρώην τισὶν ἐφλυαρήθη, θαυμαστῶς δὲ καὶ τῶν ἡρώων καὶ τῶν μετ' αὐτοὺς ὑπεκρεί[ν]οντο πολλοί, καθάπερ ἔστιν λαβεῖν τὰ μὲν παρὰ ποιητῶν, τὰ δὲ καὶ παρ' ἱστορικῶν, κἀξ ὧν αὐτοὶ γραπτῶν καταλελοίπασιν. οἱ δὲ τεχνογράφοι καὶ φανερὸν καθιστᾶσιν τὸ κατ' ἀλήθειαν μὲν ὑπάρχον, ἐπικρυπτόμενον δ' ὑπὸ τῶν πολειτικῶν, ὅτι τοῦ φανῆναι σεμνοὶ καὶ καλοὶ κἀγαθοί, μάλιστα δ[ὲ τ]οῦ πλ[α]νῆσαι τοὺς

ἀκού[οντας], ἔτι δὲ τοῦ δεινῶσαι μεθοδεύουσι τὰς ὑποκρίσεις, ὧν οὐδενὸς ὁ τῶν ἄλλων τεχνείτης, οὐχ ὅτι τῶν κατὰ φιλοσοφίαν προσδεῖται.)

9. E. Hall 2006, 353–392. See also Easterling 1999; Duncan 2006, 58–89; Fredal 2006; Worman 2008, 213–274. Cf. Thomas 2003 on other genres of prose performance.

10. See the brief overview of performance studies in Goldhill 1999, 10–20. Schechner 2003 and Reynolds 2014 are general introductions to the field. On words and actions "doing" things, see Searle 1969; Austin 1975; J. Butler 1988. On performance and anthropology, see, e.g., Turner 1969, 1982, 1986, 1990; Bauman 1977.

11. Goldhill 1999, 1–10.

12. Austin 1975, 12.

13. Dover 1968, 148–174; Usher 1976; Schloemann 2002, 135–137. Some Athenian jurors may not have approved of litigants who memorized speeches written by someone else (Pseudo-Arist. *Rhetoric for Alexander* 36.37–42 1444a16–1444b7; cf. *POxy* 410 col. 4.114–123).

14. Ober and Strauss 1990, especially 255–258; E. Hall 2006, 353–392. On the fundamental distinction between Athenian drama and oratory, see especially Bers 1994; 2009, 30–43. Edward M. Harris kindly shared with me his work in progress on "How to 'Act' in an Athenian Court: Emotions and Forensic Performance." This essay will show how litigants talk about their emotions differently from tragic characters.

15. Alcidamas, *On the Sophists* is a polemic in favor of extemporaneous oratory. On amateur speakers, see Bers 2009, 7–24.

16. On Homeric poetry as composition in performance, see Lord 2000, 99–123, 151–152, with Nagy 1996a, 30–63, and 1996b, 7–38. For the suggestion that the *Iliad* is intended to be performed in three sections, see Taplin 1992, 1–45. On the ritual performance and re-performance of what we now term choral lyric poetry, see Nagy 1990, 345–349; Calame 2001, 89–206.

17. Nervegna 2007, 15–18.

18. There are exceptions. Speeches delivered in the assembly were less ephemeral than forensic speeches, since the *polis* preserved summaries of some of them in inscribed decrees. Some epideictic speeches would have been performed multiple times.

19. Cf. Dover 1968, 170–171, and Worthington 1996, 172–177, for slightly different lists.

20. We may compare the account in Pseudo-Plutarch, *Lives of the Ten Orators* 840d–e where Aeschines re-performs his speech *Against Ktesiphon* for the Rhodians. While probably untrue, it testifies to the use of Attic forensic orations as epideictic showpieces.

21. Plutarch, *On Talkativeness* 5 504c: Λυσίας τινὶ δίκην ἔχοντι λόγον συγγράψας ἔδωκεν· ὁ δὲ πολλάκις ἀναγνοὺς ἧκε πρὸς τὸν Λυσίαν ἀθυμῶν καὶ λέγων τὸ μὲν πρῶτον αὑτῷ διεξιόντι θαυμαστὸν φανῆναι τὸν λόγον, αὖθις δὲ καὶ τρίτον ἀναλαμβάνοντι παντελῶς ἀμβλὺν καὶ ἄπρακτον· ὁ δὲ Λυσίας γελάσας 'τί οὖν;' εἶπεν 'οὐχ ἅπαξ μέλλεις λέγειν αὐτὸν ἐπὶ τῶν δικαστῶν;'

22. Steel 2009.
23. Cf. Vasaly 1993, 3–6; John Henderson 2009, 287–289.
24. Cf. E. Hall 2006, 357–358.
25. On performance as "that which occurs *between* actors and spectators," see Fischer-Lichte 2010, 29–31.
26. On the ephemeral nature of performance and the problems associated with performance archives, with specific reference to ancient drama, see Fischer-Lichte 2010 and Michelakis 2010.
27. Arist. *Rhet.* 3.12.2 1413b19–21: οἷον τά τε ἀσύνδετα καὶ τὸ πολλάκις τὸ αὐτὸ εἰπεῖν ἐν τῇ γραφικῇ ὀρθῶς ἀποδοκιμάζεται, ἐν δὲ ἀγωνιστικῇ οὔ, καὶ οἱ ῥήτορες χρῶνται· ἔστι γὰρ ὑποκριτικά. Throughout *Rhet.* 3.12, *en agōnistikēi* is contrasted with *hē graphikē*, which suggests that Aristotle understood it to mean a spoken rather than a written style. Since *agōn* is the technical term for trial, he probably meant it to refer specifically to forensic performances. Cf. Aquila Romanus (*de figuris* 30, p. 31 ll. 23–26 Halm = p. 45 ll. 5–8 Elice), who paraphrases *en agōnistikēi* as "legal delivery and debate" (*actioni . . . et certamini*).
28. Alcidamas, *On the Sophists* 16.
29. Alcidamas, *On the Sophists* 13 with Mariss 2002, 186–191. Cf. POxy 410 col. 1.1–12 = p. 231 D.I.1–4 Radermacher. C. Cooper (2004, 149–151) and E. Hall (2006, 356–357) discuss speechwriters imitating certain extemporaneous techniques to give the impression that the speeches were not prepared in advance. On written and spoken styles, see also O'Sullivan 1992, 42–62.
30. Gagarin 1999, 168; Thomas 2003, 180.
31. Cf. Gagarin 1999, 163 n. 8; E. Hall 2006, 358. Worthington (1991 and 1992, 36–39) argues for extensive posttrial revision because of the elaborate ring compositions he detects in some speeches.
32. Dionysius of Halicarnassus, *Isocrates* 18 = Arist. fr. 128 Gigon. Dover 1968, 25–26.
33. Goldhill 1996, 18–21; 1998, 106–109; 1999, 1–10 (quote at 5); 2000, 165–175. Cf. Farenga 2006, 4–8.
34. On the link between shame and being seen, see Dover 1974, 226–229, 236–238; Williams 1993, 75–102, especially 78–82, and 220. More generally on shame in the Greek world, see Dodds 1951, 1–63; Konstan 2003.
35. Arist. *Rhet.* 2.6.18 1384a34–38: καὶ τὰ ἐν ὀφθαλμοῖς καὶ τὰ ἐν φανερῷ μᾶλλον· ὅθεν καὶ ἡ παροιμία, τὸ ἐν ὀφθαλμοῖς εἶναι αἰδῶ. διὰ τοῦτο τοὺς ἀεὶ παρεσομένους μᾶλλον αἰσχύνονται καὶ τοὺς προσέχοντας αὐτοῖς, διὰ τὸ ἐν ὀφθαλμοῖς ἀμφότερα.
36. Agathon (39), fr. 22 *TrGF*; Sophocles, *Ajax* 462–465 with Williams 1993, 85, 198 n. 37. Williams (78–79 with 194–195 nn. 10, 11, and 83 with 196 n. 22) also cites and discusses a number of Homeric passages that show a connection between shame and being seen.
37. Sartre 2003, 276–305 (quote at 285) with Catalano 1974, 159–168, and Jay 1993, 276–298.

38. Sutton 1992, 9–12; Frontisi-Ducroux 1996, 83–85. On the role of the "male gaze" in film theory, see especially Mulvey 2009, 14–27.

39. Love: A. C. Pearson 1909, 256–257; Halperin 1986, 63–64 n. 5; Bartsch 2000, 91 n. 45. Glory: Segal 1995, 187–191. Moderation: Ludwig 2002, 261–318. Contact with the divine: Cioffi 2014, 3–7.

40. Konstan 2003, 1045, notes that being seen by others is not "fundamental" to the Greek sense of shame but rather "an aggravating factor."

41. Skinner 2014, 107, cites Alcman 3 for the power of the gaze and Sappho 31 for the power of the one who is seen.

42. Pl. *Phaedrus* 251c; *Cratylus* 420b with Skinner 2014, 107; *Timaeus* 45b–d. Cf. Bartsch 2000, 74–78, on Platonic sight as a middle ground between the doctrines of intromission and extramission.

43. Arist. *On Dreams* 459b.

44. Herodotus 1.8–12.

45. Pl. *Republic* 4 439a–441c, 10 603c–d.

46. Aeschin. 2.179: ταυτὶ τὰ μικρὰ μὲν παιδία καὶ τοὺς κινδύνους οὔπω συνιέντα. For children brought before jurors, see also Andoc. 1.148–149; Lys. 20.34, 21.25; Isoc. 15.321; Dem. 19.281, 310; 21.99, 182, 186–188; Aeschin. 2.152; Hyp. 2.9; 4.41; Pl. *Apology* 34c. Cf. Aristophanes, *Wasps* 975–978. For discussion of this tactic, see S. Johnstone 1999, 115 with 172 nn. 37, 38, 39; Naiden 2006, 99–100; Lateiner 2009, 118–119.

47. Aeschylus, *Suppliants* 197–199: φθογγῇ δ' ἑπέσθω πρῶτα μὲν τὸ μὴ θρασύ, / τὸ μὴ μάταιον δ' ἐκ †μετώπω σωφρονῶν† / ἴτω προσώπων ὄμματος παρ' ἡσύχου. I translate Dindorf's conjecture σεσωφρονισμένων for μετώπω σωφρονῶν, but the sense is clear even in the transmitted text. E. Hall 2006, 360.

48. Arist. *Metaphysics* 1 980a21–27.

49. Cf. Goldhill 2000, 165–173. For a criticism of Goldhill's model in light of the difference between the roles of *theōros* and *theatēs*, see Nightingale 2004, 49–52.

50. Lys. 12.100: παύσομαι κατηγορῶν. ἀκηκόατε, ἑοράκατε, πεπόνθατε, ἔχετε· δικάζετε.

51. Lanni 1997.

52. Pseudo-Arist. *Constitution of the Athenians* 53.3 and 68.1 with Rhodes 1981, 728–729.

53. We hear of very large juries—6,000, 1,500, 2,000, 700, 500 jurors—from the late fifth and early fourth centuries (Andoc. 1.17; Plutarch, *Perikles* 32.4; Lys. 13.35; Isoc. 18.54; Isae. 5.20), but we have no evidence of how many jurors were required for normal trials.

54. In the fifth century, there were 6,000, and the number was probably similar in the fourth. Aristophanes, *Wasps* 662; Pseudo-Arist. *Constitution of the Athenians* 24.3. On the oath, see Mirhady 2007.

55. Pseudo-Arist. *Constitution of the Athenians* 63.3.

56. Hansen 1991b, 186. Hansen 1979 proposes slightly lower numbers (150–200

days a year) using a similar calculation. Aristophanes, *Assemblywomen* 681–686 is the earliest unambiguous reference to multiple courts sitting on the same day.

57. On the three different processes of sortition used by the Athenians, see MacDowell 1978, 35–40; Boegehold 1995, 21–42. On how many jurors had to volunteer for service on any given day in order for the system to work, see Mirhady and Schwarz 2011.

58. Aristophanes, *Knights* 797–800; Schol. to Aristophanes, *Wasps* 88a, 300b. Rhodes 1981, 338.

59. Cf. Aristophanes, *Lysistrata* 624–625 with Jeffrey Henderson 1987, 152–153.

60. The demographics of Athenian juries are controversial. The model I propose here is most similar to those of Crichton 1991–1993, 62–67, and Jones 2008, 59–60. Other scholars (Markle 1990; Todd 2007b) have argued that the majority of jurors were farmers. Roy 1995 suggests that Lys. 29.12 may imply that more jurors came from the city of Athens proper (the *astu*) than from Peiraieus.

61. Pseudo-Arist. *Constitution of the Athenians* 63–69 with Boegehold 1995, 36–41.

62. Boegehold 1995, 3–16; Blanshard 2014, 246–255.

63. Aristophanes, *Wasps* 89–90 with the additional evidence cited at Boegehold and Crosby 1995, 205–206. Wooden benches were also set up in the Delian courts. See *IG* XI, 2 287 A 81 (250 BCE) and *IG* XI, 2 145.37–38 (302 BCE) with the supplements of Tréheux 1984, 334–335 n. 33 and the discussion at Csapo 2007, 105. For "inward-facing circles," see Ober 2008, 199–205.

64. Boegehold and Crosby 1995, 201–205.

65. Cf. Hansen 1989, 232.

66. For a tentative discussion of acoustics in Athenian performance spaces, see C. L. Johnstone 1996, 2001.

67. MacDowell 1963, 1–7. On pollution from killing, see Parker 1983, 104–143, especially 116–119.

68. Ant. 5.11. Cf. Pseudo-Arist. *Constitution of the Athenians* 57.4. I use "sanctuary" as a general term encompassing temples, sacred enclosures, and hero shrines.

69. Dem. 23.63–78 and Pseudo-Arist. *Constitution of the Athenians* 57.3. Arist. *Politics* 4 1300b24–30 is generally thought to refer to Athenian practice.

70. Travlos 1971, 83–90 with figs. 106–114.

71. Lipsius 1905–1915, 1.132–133; MacDowell 1963, 71; Sealey 1983, 278–279.

72. The standard account of the homicide courts and their procedures remains MacDowell 1963. For testimonia, see Boegehold and Crosby 1995, 121–150. On the oaths, see also the discussion in Faraone 1999, 104–111.

73. On the court *en Phreattoi*, see Carawan 1990; Boegehold 1995, 49–50. Dem. 23.78 seems unsure of where it even was, and Arist. *Politics* 4 1300b29–30 says that cases under its jurisdiction are rare. On the procedure at the Prytaneion, see Sealey 2006.

74. Wallace 1989, 94–97 with 251–252, nn. 1, 22–23; Hansen and Pedersen 1990.

75. This was at least the official sentiment in Athens. MacDowell 1963, 42–43. See Lanni 2006, 78–114, on differences in procedure and legalism between the homicide courts and the regular courts.

76. *IG* I³ 104.18–19, 24–25. Due to a lacuna in Pseudo-Arist. *Constitution of the Athenians* 57.4, we have no way of knowing whether the *ephetai* continued to judge into the late fifth century. For a history of scholarship on this question, see Carawan 1991; Kapparis 1999, 187–189; Lanni 2006, 84–86 with nn. 51–56.

77. See Henrichs 1994, 39–46, on the cult of the Semnai Theai and its relationship to the homicide court. Blanshard 2014, 262–263, considers the effects of the ritual atmosphere of the Delphinion and the Areopagos on litigants.

78. Cf. Rhodes 1981, 717.

79. For an overview, see Peters 2008.

80. Balkin and Levinson 1999; Balkin 2011, 91–94.

81. Ramshaw 2010.

82. The role of written laws and legal precedent in Athenian legal decisions is beyond the scope of this introduction. For discussion, see Lanni 2006, 41–74 (quote at 42), which argues that the Athenian courts "emphasized discretionary and equitable assessments rather than the regular and predictable application of abstract, standardized rules," and E. M. Harris 2013, 246–273 (quote at 273), which argues that "the Athenians were concerned about consistency and had the oral and written resources to enable them to pursue this aim. The attempt to judge cases according to consistent rules is one of the hallmarks of the rule of law." On Athenian jurors "participating in law writing as a performance tradition," see Farenga 2006, 310–329 (quote at 315).

83. Almog and Aharonson 2004.

84. Cf. Todorov 1977, 80–84.

85. On whether, and why, these animations are persuasive, see Dunn, Salovey, and Feigenson 2006.

86. Hibbitts 1994. On legal metaphors in general, see M. R. Smith 2008, 197–248, and the articles collected in *Symposium: Using Metaphor in Legal Analysis and Communication* 2007. On the "understanding as seeing metaphor," see Lakoff and Johnson 1980, 103–104.

87. Amsterdam and Hertz 1992, especially 95–96, from which the quotes are taken.

88. Amsterdam and Bruner 2000, 143–164, 293–307.

89. Amsterdam and Bruner 2000, 152.

CHAPTER 1

1. On the Sweet trial, see Hays 1937, 195–233; Boyle 2004; Vine 2004. The quotation from Hays' opening statement is from Hays, 1937, 217.

2. Hays 1937, 232.

3. On deictic pronouns used primarily but not exclusively to point out people present in the court, see de Bakker 2012, 396. For a general overview of deixis in Greek, see Bakker 2010. There is a more detailed discussion of deictic pronouns later in this chapter (p. 34) and in chapter 6 (pp. 154–157).

4. E. Hall 2006, 353–392. The discussion of isomorphism is on 354.

5. On the ability of metics and *xenoi* to participate in the Athenian legal system, see Todd 1993, 194–199, 316–340, and, with specific reference to metics, Whitehead 1977, 89–97; Patterson 2000; Kamen 2013, 47–49. Whitehead (1977, 111) uses earlier interpretations of grave inscriptions to estimate that anywhere from 1 in 5 to 1 in 9 metics was of non-Greek origin in the fourth century. In the fifth century, however, non-Greek metics seem to have been considerably rarer (Németh 2001).

6. Isae. 5.7–8. On the status of Melas, see Ghiggia 2002, 148 with n. 115. It is clear from fr. adesp. 161 *TrGF* that the Athenians thought of the Egyptians as darker skinned than themselves. Cf. Aeschylus, *Suppliants* 496–498.

7. Hyp. 3.3 with Whitehead 2000, 287–288. For more examples of anti-Egyptian sentiment, see Whitehead 1977, 112; Isaac 2004, 353–355.

8. The Classical Athenians were not free of prejudices that we might consider racist, but appearance was not the determining factor. See Isaac 2004, 109–133; Lape 2010, especially 31–41 for an explanation of why "race" is a useful category for analyzing ancient Athenian ideas about belonging, even if skin color was not of primary importance; McCoskey 2012, 9–10; Poddighe 2012.

9. Pseudo-Xenophon, *Constitution of the Athenians* 1.10. Cf. Lape 2010, 187.

10. Osborne 2011, 133–138.

11. E.g., Aeschin. 3.171–173. On these kinds of insults in forensic oratory and Old Comedy and their relationship to democratic ideology, see Lape 2010, 61–94.

12. Pl. *Republic* 495e. Socrates presents the coppersmith in terms of what he looks like, asking if people who have turned to philosophy even though they are unsuited for it "are different to see [*idein*]" than this coppersmith.

13. Theophrastus, *Characters* 26.4 with Diggle 2004, 469–473.

14. Athenaeus 12.552d = p. 57 Jensen = p. 103 fr. 15b Colin. E. Hall 2006, 378. Philippides' thinness seems to have been notorious. See the list of comic quotations at Olson 2008, 43 n. 53.

15. Dem. 37.55–56. E. Hall 2006, 381.

16. Lys. 16.19: ὥστε οὐκ ἄξιον ἀπ' ὄψεως, ὦ βουλή, οὔτε φιλεῖν οὔτε μισεῖν οὐδένα, ἀλλ' ἐκ τῶν ἔργων σκοπεῖν.

17. There is a long and unnecessary tradition of emending the text so that it refers more specifically to Mantitheos' appearance. Hamaker's (1843, 62–63) influential emendation of εἴ τις τολμᾷ (if someone is bold) to εἴ τις κομᾷ (if someone wears his hair long) in paragraph 18 has been accepted by Carey and all twentieth-century editions of Lysias that I have consulted. On the significance of hair see, besides Hamaker's own comments, Blass 1887–1898, 1.520–521 n. 6; E. Hall 2006, 380. As Craik 1999 points out, however, the transmitted text's reference to boldness is consistent with the rest of the speech, and there is no reason to emend it. Along

the same lines, Dobree's (1831, 233) proposed emendation of κοσμίως ἀπερχόμενοι, "those who conduct themselves in an orderly manner when they depart," to κοσμίως ἀμπεχόμενοι, "those who dress in an orderly manner" in paragraph 19, also accepted almost universally, is unnecessary. Dobree himself qualifies it with *mox*. There is no need for the text to refer to visual characteristics that would have been evident to the jurors.

18. Lys. 10.29: καὶ μὲν δή, ὦ ἄνδρες δικασταί, ὅσῳ μείζους εἰσὶ καὶ νεανίαι τὰς ὄψεις, τοσούτῳ μᾶλλον ὀργῆς ἄξιοί εἰσι. δῆλον γὰρ ὅτι τοῖς μὲν σώμασι δύνανται, τὰς δὲ ψυχὰς οὐκ <εὖ> ἔχουσιν.

19. Pseudo-Arist. *Rhetoric for Alexander* 36.11 1442b4–5: οἷς ἂν νομίζῃς τοὺς κριτὰς ἐπιπλήξειν, προκαταλάμβανε αὐτοὺς καὶ ἐπίπληττε. My translation follows Chiron's (2002, 98).

20. Pseudo-Arist. *Rhetoric for Alexander* 36.7 1442a23–24.

21. Arist. *Rhet.* 1.12.5 1372a21–23. The next clause (1372a23–26) does refer specifically to vision, since it maintains that people who commit crimes "in an excessively open [ἐν φανερῷ] way that is also before people's eyes [ἐν ὀφθαλμοῖς]" will get away with them because no one would have thought it necessary to prepare for crimes in such a setting. This is not an argument based on appearance, however. Throughout this book, I follow Kassel's (1976) text of the *Rhetoric*.

22. Pseudo-Arist. *Rhetoric for Alexander* 36.7–15 1442a20–1442b28.

23. Arist. *Rhet.* 2.8.14 1386a28–1386b1, quotation at 1386a33–34. S. Smith (1999, 67–68) associates this passage with Aristotle's definition of pity (2.8.2 1385b13–16), which also emphasizes the importance of sight in arousing pity by repeating forms of *phainomai*. Smith writes, "Aristotle defines pity as 'a certain pain at seeing [*phainomenōi*] a destructive or painful evil happening to one who does not deserve it and which a person might expect himself or one of his own to suffer, and this when it is seen [*phainetai*] close at hand.'"

24. On the connotations of "before the eyes" in Aristotle, see further chapter 2, p. 59, and chapter 5, p. 124.

25. Arist. *Rhet.* 2.8.15 1386b2–8. Munteanu (2014, 92–93) identifies the reference to clothing here as a way to arouse pity by imitating or impersonating those who are worthy of pity.

26. Arist. *Rhet.* 2.8.14 1386a32–33: "Those people who help the effect with gestures, sounds, display of feeling (αἰσθήσει), and acting in general are necessarily more pitiable." Spengel (1867, 2.237) proposed ἐσθῆσι (clothing), as an emendation for this unique use of αἴσθησις, which Ross (1959, 93) and Rapp (2002, 1.92, 2.657) both accept. Kassel (1976, 97) rejects it. If Spengel is correct, we have further evidence that Aristotle is thinking here primarily of the visual effects of a performance.

27. Arist. *Rhet.* 3.15.5 1416a21–24.

28. Arist. *Rhet.* 2.4.15 1381b1–2.

29. Arist. *Rhet.* 3.7.6 1408a25–30. Kennedy 2007, 210.

30. Worman 2002, 3.

31. Bourdieu 1977, 72–95. For an overview of Bourdieu's theory, see Worman 2002, 3–4.
32. Arist. *Rhet.* 3.7.7 1408a31–32.
33. Boyle 2004, 293–294. Cf. Hays 1937, 229.
34. Arist. *Rhet.* 2.24.2 1400b37–1401a12 with Kennedy 2007, 185 n. 188. Cf. Isoc. 9.65–69.
35. The oligarchy known as the Four Hundred overthrew the Athenian democracy in 411 and briefly ruled Athens. On the date and authorship of *For Polystratos*, see Gomme, Andrewes, and Dover 1981, 202–203; Usher and Najock 1982, 103–104. Storey (2012, 313) proposes that the sentiments expressed in *For Polystratos* recall Aristophanes, *Frogs* 686–692, where the chorus seems to sympathize with Athenian citizens caught up in what Storey (311) calls the "witch hunt" that followed the overthrow of the Four Hundred.
36. Wilamowitz-Moellendorff 1893, 2.363–364. Cf. Gomme, Andrewes, and Dover 1981, 201; Rubinstein 2000, 148 n. 70.
37. The shift from third-person to first-person pronouns is the primary indicator that we have two speeches. Additionally, in 1–10, words are frequently repeated in different forms in adjoining sentences (Lys. 20.2, 4, 8–9), a phenomenon common to another early Attic prose work, the *Constitution of the Athenians* of Pseudo-Xenophon (the "Old Oligarch"). Marr and Rhodes (2008, 173–175 appendix 6) list examples. Paragraphs 11–36 lack this repetition technique.
38. Hyp. 1.10; Cf. Hyp. 4.11–13.
39. Euxenippos' prosecutors seem to have done this, prompting Hyperides' defense of the practice in Hyp. 4.11–13. On hostility to the practice of *sunēgoria* in public cases, see Rubinstein 2000, 163–168, 218–231.
40. Lys. 20.1, 2. Cf. Dover 1997, 63–64; Boegehold 1999, 85.
41. Lys. 20.6, 8, 14 (2x, once following a καί), 16, 22.
42. Arist. *Rhet.* 2.13.13–14 1390a11–19.
43. Ant. 4.3.2.
44. Lys. 3.4. On the embarrassment associated with age-inappropriate homosexual behavior, see W. V. Harris 1997, 364–365; Todd 2007a, 277–278, 310.
45. Cf. Carey 1989, 89–92, for the close relationship between character, narrative, and proof in Lys. 3.
46. Lys. 20.34. On such visual display, see p. 11.
47. On verbal ring composition in oratory, see Worthington 1991; 1992, 27–39. The examples he discusses are considerably more elaborate than this one.
48. Dinarchus 1.111 with MacDowell 2009, 109.
49. Dem. 36.2 (2x), 8, 9, 11, 12, 14, 15, 22, 31, 32, 47, 53, 56 (2x), 61.
50. Dem. 36.36, 53–54, 61.
51. Dem. 36.55–57.
52. Dem. 36.56.
53. Dem. 36.57. Cf. Dem. 36.2, where he also uses forms of *houtosi* for both Apollodoros and Phormion.

54. Dem. 36.61.
55. Lysias is now generally thought to be the author, but there are no grounds for certainty. Usher and Najock 1982, 103–104; Weißenberger 1987, 149–152; Carey 1989, 183–184.
56. On bouleutic *dokimasiai*, see Feyel 2009, 160–171.
57. Carey 1989, 179.
58. Lys. 31.5–14. Carey 1989, 180–182; Whitehead 2006, 137–141. On Lysias' depiction of Philon as more like a metic than a citizen, see Bakewell 1999, 15–17.
59. For witness testimony to Philon's wealth and refusal to contribute to the arming of the Acharnians, see Lys. 31.14, 16.
60. Lys. 31.17–19.
61. Lys. 31.32.
62. We may compare Lys. 30.33 ("you see [*horate*] my opponents eagerly saving their friends") where, despite the reference to what the jury can see, sight is not the primary element of the argument. It is likely that the metaphor of "seeing the preparation" of one's opponents in Lys. fr. 118 Carey and Aeschin. 3.1 grows out of this use of the vocabulary of sight.
63. Lys. 31.32.
64. Aeschin. 3.52.
65. For the background to the speech and issues of composition and delivery, see MacDowell 1990, 1–37; E. M. Harris 2008, 75–87. E. M. Harris 1989 argues that Aeschines is lying about the settlement.
66. Dem. 21.83–92. As E. M. Harris points out, Meidias' case against Straton may not have been as baseless as Demosthenes makes it seem, since a court had upheld the disenfranchisement. See E. M. Harris 2008, 78, 119 n. 147, which refers to MacDowell 1990, 314.
67. For examples of κάλει with witnesses in *Against Meidias*, see 82, 93, 107, 121, and 174.
68. Dem. 21.87.
69. MacDowell 1990, 35–36, 318–319.
70. Schol. to Dem. 21.95 (321, 323, 324 Dilts). Usher (1999, 227 n. 197) compares Straton to the mute Ajax in *Odyssey* 11.563.
71. Schol. to Dem. 21.95 (323 Dilts): "For what relative will not pity a relative, if he looks at [*theasamenos*] him? And what citizen a citizen, and what old man an old man, and what member of the common people someone who has attended the assembly with him?" (τίς μὲν γὰρ συγγενὴς θεασάμενος οὐκ ἐλεήσει τὸν συγγενῆ; τίς δὲ πολίτης τὸν πολίτην; τίς δὲ πρεσβύτης τὸν πρεσβύτην; τίς δὲ δημότης τὸν συνεκκλησιάσαντα;)
72. Schol. to Dem. 21.95 (324 Dilts): "For it's clear that the poor people will pity the poor man." (δῆλον γὰρ ὅτι οἱ πένητες τὸν πένητα ἐλεήσουσιν.) Schol. to Dem. 21.96 (333 Dilts): "He stirs up envy against him by mentioning his wealth. For the common people hate people like him because of their poverty." (φθόνον αὐτῷ

συνάγει διὰ τῆς ὑπομνήσεως τοῦ πλούτου· μισοῦσι γὰρ τοὺς τοιούτους οἱ δημόται διὰ τὴν πενίαν.)

73. MacDowell 1990, 31–32; Ober 1996, 86–106; Fredal 2001, 259–265; Hendren 2015.

74. Menander Rhetor 443.16–18.

75. The case is complicated, and the word "rent" only approximates the financial relationship. There is a brief overview in the appendix.

76. Carey and Reid 1985, 150; E. Hall 2006, 377.

77. Dem. 37.39.

78. Dem. 37.48: τῷ τ' ἀκαθάρτῳ καὶ μιαρῷ Προκλεῖ, τῷ μεγάλῳ τούτῳ, καὶ Στρατοκλεῖ τῷ πιθανωτάτῳ πάντων ἀνθρώπων καὶ πονηροτάτῳ.

79. Dem. 37.23–24.

80. Dem. 37.15. L. Pearson 1976, 99–102.

81. Isoc. 18.53–54. E. Hall 2006, 361–362. On the procedure, see MacDowell 1963, 53–54; Carawan 1991, 3–5. There is a similar scene in Chariton, *Khaireas and Kallirhoe* 5.7.10–5.8.3.

82. Dem. 25.62. See E. Hall 2006, 377. The speech's Demosthenic authorship has been doubted since antiquity. For a defense, see MacDowell 2009, 311–312.

83. Dem. 47.41.

84. Xenophon, *Memorabilia* 3.4.1.

85. Aeschin. 2.93; 3.51, 212; Dem. 40.32. E. Hall 2006, 380; Phillips 2007, 78–79, 91.

86. Dem. 40.33.

87. The authenticity of the speech has been doubted, but it is now generally believed to have been written by Lysias for actual courtroom delivery. Dillon 1995, 37–39, is the most recent summary of arguments in favor of its authenticity. On how the speaker could have afforded to hire a speechwriter, see Todd 2000, 253–254.

88. On the pension and the procedure, see Pseudo-Arist. *Constitution of the Athenians* 49.4 with Rhodes 1981, 570–571; Dillon 1995, 52; Feyel 2009, 81–85.

89. "Disabled" carries modern connotations that may be inappropriate or misleading for Classical Athens (Rose 2003, 95–100). Nonetheless, it is convenient and more specific to the circumstances of the dispute than the vague "who lacks ability."

90. Lys. 24.4–5.

91. Garland (1995, 37) suggests that witnesses would have been of little use, since disabilities were easy to fake. Safeguards against false testimony would not, however, have been any weaker in cases involving disabilities than in cases about other issues that lent themselves to misrepresentation.

92. Lys. 24.6, 10–12, 19–20.

93. See Edwards and Usher 1985, 267: "The defendant no doubt made gestures and movements at this point in order to exaggerate his disability." Cf. E. Hall 2006, 380.

94. Rose 2003, 98.

95. Mocking responses to his opponent include his horsemanship is a result of his disability (Lys. 24.10–12); if he is able-bodied, he must be eligible to be an archon (Lys. 24.13); the dispute is more appropriate for an heiress' inheritance than a state pension for an invalid (Lys. 24.14). The speaker's statement that he is not responsible for the character of his customers (Lys. 24.19–20) is the only attempt to ridicule his opponent that is not based on his disability. Significantly, none of the humor is self-mockery, despite the Greek tendency to laugh at the disabled, on which see Garland 1995, 73–86.

96. Lys. 24.2, 7.

97. Edwards and Usher 1985, 263–264. On the other hand, Rose (2003, 97) states, "Throughout the speech, the defendant never solicits pity for his impairment, even though an appeal to one's misfortunes was an acceptable courtroom tactic." There is a similar sentiment at Garland 1995, 37. Tearful supplication, however, is not the only way to stir a jury's pity.

98. Lys. 24.22–23.

99. Carey 1990.

100. Dinarchus 3.3.

101. See Todd 2007a, 640 with nn. 57–60. The epitome is ancient: POxy 2537.6–15 = Lys. fr. 208 Carey (late second or early third century CE) refers to both speeches.

102. Lys. 11.10–11 paraphrases Lys. 10.28–30 but omits the reference to appearance; Lys. 11 begins after omitting the reference to seeing the jurors in Lys. 10.1.

CHAPTER 2

1. The story is preserved in two versions in Rabe's *Prolegomenon Sylloge*, no. 4, 24–27, (= 1.26–29 Patillon *CR*) and no. 17, 269–273. My description and translations all come from no. 17, the longer version. Cf. Aelian, *Historical Miscellany* 14.22. Farenga 1979; Gera 2003, 197; T. Cole 2007, 37–38 with n. 1.

2. Goldin-Meadow 2007.

3. Kendon 2004, especially 108–157; McNeill 2005; Enfield 2009.

4. On the *dilēmmaton skhēma*, see Hermogenes, *On Invention* 4.6 (3.1.109–111 Patillon *CR* = 192–194 Rabe). Cf. Hermogenes, *On Issues* 5.20–21 (2.51–52 Patillon *CR* = 68–69 Rabe); Arist. *Rhet.* 2.23.15 1399a17–28.

5. On who Korax was and what he taught, see T. Cole 2007.

6. Aristophanes, *Clouds* 1399–1439.

7. Pl. *Laws* 7.816a: ὅλως δὲ φθεγγόμενος, εἴτ᾽ ἐν ᾠδαῖς εἴτ᾽ ἐν λόγοις, ἡσυχίαν οὐ πάνυ δυνατὸς τῷ σώματι παρέχεσθαι πᾶς.

8. Diogenes Laertius 1.70: λέγοντα μὴ κινεῖν τὴν χεῖρα· μανικὸν γάρ.

9. *Iliad* 3.218–219: σκῆπτρον δ᾽ οὔτ᾽ ὀπίσω οὔτε προπρηνὲς ἐνώμα, / ἀλλ᾽ ἀστεμφὲς ἔχεσκεν, ἀιδρεῖ φωτὶ ἐοικώς. Cf. Eustathius, *Commentary on the Iliad*

4.235.1–6 van der Valk; Schol. to *Iliad* 18.506b. Sittl 1890, 207; R. P. Martin 1989, 95–96.

10. *Iliad* 1.245–246.

11. Handrich 2011.

12. Ball 2003, 7–11; Crawford and Morris 2011, 30, 33–36; Haydock and Sonsteng 2011, 292, 654–655; Fontham and Vitiello 2013, 221–222. Cf. Cicero, *Orator* 59–60, which emphasizes moderation (*moderatio; nihil ut supersit*) in gesturing, and Quintilian, *Orator's Education* 11.3.180–184, which emphasizes that delivery (*actio*) should come from one's own nature (*ex natura sua*), that moderateness (*modum*) should rule, and that even when exuberant gestures are acceptable they still ought to be tempered (*temperanda*). On the importance of appropriateness in Quintilian's account of gestures, see Fögen 2009, 28–29.

13. Cicero, *Brutus* 141: *gestus erat non verba exprimens, sed cum sententiis congruens—manus umeri latera supplosio pedis status incessus omnisque motus cum verbis sententiisque consentiens.*

14. Cicero, *On the Orator* 3.220. J. Hall 2004, 144–147. Cf. Quintilian, *Orator's Education* 11.3.88–91.

15. Quintilian, *Orator's Education* 11.3.65.

16. Corbeill 2004, 3.

17. On these so-called five canons of rhetoric (*Rhetoric for Herennius* 3.1; Cicero, *On the Orator* 1.142, *On Invention* 1.9) and their place in an "eclectic" theory of rhetoric that arose sometime after the mid-second century BCE, see Gaines 2007, 166–168.

18. Cicero, *On the Orator* 1.142.

19. See, for example, Ant. 1.1, 5.1–7; Lys. 17.1, 19.1; Isae. 1.1–2; Dem. 27.2, 41.2, 48.1.

20. Boegehold 1999, 78–79. Quintilian (*Orator's Education* 11.3.67) uses the trivial example of shaking the head "no" while affirming something to make the important point that incongruent gestures can threaten credibility. Cf. Clason 2010, 62, which suggests that modern litigators should use "natural hand gestures" to establish that they are "not so different from the jurors."

21. Arist. *Rhet.* 3.2.3 1404b14–15: ἐπεὶ καὶ ἐνταῦθα, εἰ δοῦλος καλλιεπεῖτο ἢ λίαν νέος, ἀπρεπέστερον, ἢ περὶ λίαν μικρῶν.

22. Arist. *Rhet.* 3.2.4 1404b18–21: διὸ δεῖ λανθάνειν ποιοῦντας, καὶ μὴ δοκεῖν λέγειν πεπλασμένως ἀλλὰ πεφυκότως (τοῦτο γὰρ πιθανόν, ἐκεῖνο δὲ τοὐναντίον· ὡς γὰρ πρὸς ἐπιβουλεύοντα διαβάλλονται, καθάπερ πρὸς τοὺς οἴνους τοὺς μεμιγμένους). Artificial naturalness needs to be avoided as well, since, as Bers (2013, 32–34) argues, audiences could perceive the artificiality of "too perfect a copy" of natural speech.

23. Quintilian, *Orator's Education* 11.3.65–184. Fantham 1982; Maier-Eichhorn 1989; Gunderson 2000, 59–86; J. Hall 2004.

24. Katsouris 1989, 141–199; Hughes 2012, 149–157. Cf. Green 2002, 105–121.

25. Boegehold 1999, 78–93, on oratory. Edwards (2013, 23–25) is skeptical of many of Boegehold's specific examples.

26. Aristophanes, *Knights* 345–350; Euripides, *Electra* 909–910; Pl. *Phaedrus* 228a–c.

27. Dionysius of Halicarnassus, *Demosthenes* 53–54.

28. Arist. *Rhet.* 2.8.14 1386a32–33: ἀνάγκη τοὺς συναπεργαζομένους σχήμασι καὶ φωναῖς καὶ αἰσθήσει καὶ ὅλως ἐν ὑποκρίσει ἐλεεινοτέρους εἶναι. See chapter 1, p. 31 with n. 26.

29. Arist. *Rhet.* 2.8.15 1386b2–8. See chapter 1, pp. 30–31 and chapter 5, p. 124.

30. C. L. Johnstone 1996, 122–126 with fig. 4; 2001, 127–131; H. A. Thompson 1996, vi. Cf. Bers 2013, 38–40.

31. Plutarch, *Nikias* 8.6.

32. Bers 2013, 39–40.

33. Aeschin. 3.167. The text is quoted on p. 71.

34. Aeschin. 2.49: καὶ τερατευσάμενος, ὥσπερ εἴωθε, τῷ σχήματι καὶ τρίψας τὴν κεφαλήν, ὁρῶν ἐπισημαινόμενον τὸν δῆμον καὶ ἀποδεχόμενον τοὺς παρ' ἐμοῦ λόγους. Cf. Demades, fr. 75 de Falco = Tzetzes, *Chiliades* 6.121–139. This describes Demosthenes scratching his head, coughing, and drawing his eyebrows together, but it is almost certainly a late pastiche of passages from Aeschines and Demosthenes himself. To the parallels cited by de Falco, add Dem. 19.314 for the drawn eyebrows.

35. Aeschin. 1.26. The text is quoted on pp. 74–75.

36. Catoni 2008, 96–99, 213–240. Cf. Goldhill 1999, 4–5. P. Zanker 1995, 22–31, links the composed appearance of Anakreon as a symposiast in the bronze statue erected on the acropolis in ca. 440 BCE with what the Athenians called *kalokagathia*, literally, "beauty and goodness," a concept encompassing civic virtue, moral goodness, and, at least when it is used by aristocratic Athenians, elite social status.

37. Pl. *Republic* 392c.

38. Pl. *Republic* 395b–c. The extent to which mimesis in *Republic* 3 requires the performer to assimilate himself fully to the person he imitates or simply to adopt his habits of speaking and acting is beyond the scope of this discussion. For the argument that mimesis requires psychological identification, see Ferrari 1989, 115–116; Murray 1996, 170–171; Halliwell 2002, 72–85. For the argument that Socrates instead conceives of mimesis as creating an appearance without any psychological identification, see Lear 2012, especially 205–209.

39. Pl. *Republic* 393c. Cf. Burnyeat 1999, 269. On the union of *skhēma* and *phōnē* representing mimesis through poetry or acting, while the union of *skhēma* and *khrōma* represents mimesis through painting or sculpting, see Catoni 2008, 251–256.

40. Murray 1996, 170. Emlyn-Jones and Preddy's (2013, 1.251) "appearance," however, is too limited.

41. Pl. *Republic* 395c.

42. Pl. *Republic* 395d.

43. Pl. *Republic* 395d–396a. Murray 1996, 177, specifically associates imitation of the workmen with imitation of their bodily movements.

44. Pl. *Republic* 396d.

45. Pl. *Republic* 397a. Socrates does permit the guardians to imitate inferior people "for the sake of play" (396e), on which see Ferrari 1989, 119.

46. Pl. *Republic* 397a.

47. Pl. *Republic* 397b. Power 2010, 139–140, argues that Socrates is describing musicians who add mimetic bodily movements to their performances.

48. Murray 1996, 180, here translates *skhēmasin* "gesture." Emlyn-Jones and Preddy 2013, 1.265 translate it "gestures."

49. Pl. *Republic* 398a–b.

50. On the meaning of *lexis* extending beyond speaking style in the context of mimesis, see Murray 1996, 4.

51. Pl. *Republic* 396c.

52. Lear (2012, 214–215) argues that exposure to "unbridled mimesis" will teach the children of Socrates' ideal city to find pleasure in a variety of things and therefore flit from activity to activity and not focus on doing their proper task well.

53. Green 2002, 105–106, with reference to Pl. *Republic* 1.327b2–4 and the "Choregos Vase" of the early fourth century (once J. Paul Getty Museum 96.AE.29, now Naples, Museo Archeologico Nazionale 248778). For discussion of the vase, see also Taplin 1993, 55–63. There is a black-and-white image at Green 2002, 96 fig. 14 and a color image at Denoyelle 2010, 107 fig. 3.3. Cf. Hughes 2012, 152.

54. On mimesis in Plato and Aristotle, see Woodruff 1992. On this passage of Aristotle, see Catoni 2008, 158.

55. On the role of the *aulētai* in choral performances, see P. Wilson 2000, 68–70; 2002, 60–61. Barker 2004, 203–204, suggests that "Skylla" is a play, and Power 2010, 142–143, that it is a dithyramb.

56. On gestures associated with the New Music, with specific reference to this passage, see Power 2010, 142–143 with n. 344.

57. Arist. *Poetics* 26 1461b34–35. I translate λίαν γὰρ ὑπερβάλλοντα as "because he was overdoing it so much." Mynniskos won victories at the Dionysia in 450/449 (*IG* II² 2325.24) and 423/422 (*IG* II² 2318.119) and perhaps at the Lenaia in 419/418 (*IG* II² 2325.251). The *Life of Aeschylus* mentions him as Aeschylus' second actor (test. 1.15 *TrGF*). Kallippides, five times victorious at the Lenaia by 419/418 (*IG* II² 2319.82–83, 2325.252), was his younger contemporary. See Csapo 2002, 127.

58. Arist. *Poetics* 26 1462a1–6. The words I translate as "gestural signals" are τοῖς σημείοις, which in context are clearly referring to gestures. Halliwell 1995, 137, translates them as "visual signals."

59. Arist. *Poetics* 17 1455a22–32. Cf. Sifakis 2002, 162–164; Catoni 2008, 159–160. On the necessity of gestures and performance to Aristotle's understanding of tragic poetry, see Scott 1999, especially 35–38 with reference to *Poetics* 26 1462a8–11.

60. Csapo 2002, 127–131. Cf. Roselli 2011, 184.

61. Dickey 2007, 51. For a discussion of the later sources of the Demosthenic scholia, see Heath, 2004, 132–213.

62. Dem. 22.53.

63. Schol. to Dem. 22.53 (143 Dilts): ἢ ἄλλα ἀσχημονοίη] νόει πάντα ἃ ποιοῦσιν οἱ φωραθῆναι φοβούμενοι, γυναικῶν ὑποκρινόμενοι φωνήν τε καὶ σχῆμα, θεράποντες εἶναι δοκοῦντες, τὰ τῶν δούλων μεταχειριζόμενοι καὶ τὰ ἄλλα ἁπλῶς. For further discussion of this section of *Against Androtion*, see chapter 6, pp. 141–143.

64. Hesk 1999, 220–226.

65. Dem. 45.68–69. Hesk 1999, 220–226.

66. Dem. 21.195. This is one of the places where *skhēma* probably refers to a range of visible features. Fredal 2001, 259–265.

67. Worman 2008, 213–274, emphasizes how "Demosthenes and Aeschines treat the mouth as a denigrating metonymy for the visible performances of their enemies."

68. E.g., Theophrastus, *Characters* 4.4, 5.6 with Diggle 2004, 210–211, 232–235.

69. Arist. *Rhet*. 3.16 1417a 36–38: ἔτι ἐκ τῶν παθητικῶν λέγε, διηγούμενος καὶ τὰ ἑπόμενα καὶ ἃ ἴσασι, καὶ τὰ ἰδίᾳ ἢ ἑαυτῷ ἢ ἐκείνῳ προσόντα.

70. Arist. *Rhet*. 3.16 1417a38–1417b3 = Aeschines the Socratic, fr. 92 Giannantoni. Fredal 2001, 253–254.

71. Aeschin. 3.97, 149, 159. On the role of an *eirēnophulax*, see Ryder 1976.

72. Aeschin. 3.72.

73. On Aeschines' objections to Demosthenes' choice of words, see Lossau 1964, 10–13.

74. Aeschin. 3.59.

75. Dem. 18.232. Cf. Dionysius of Halicarnassus, *Demosthenes* 57.

76. We may compare Aeschines' interpretation of Homeric poetry in *Against Timarkhos*, where he encourages the jurors to accept as authoritative his claim that Homer made Achilles and Patroklos lovers by, as Ford (1999, 253) puts it, "equating being a sound citizen with being among those 'in the know' about poetry."

77. Aeschin. 3.167.

78. It should come as no surprise that Aeschines criticizes Demosthenes in the same way that Aristotle criticizes bad actors, since both Aeschines and Demosthenes regularly mock each other's acting ability and theatrical behavior. See Duncan 2006, 58–89; Easterling 1999.

79. Plutarch, *Demosthenes* 11.3: τοῖς μὲν οὖν πολλοῖς ὑποκρινόμενος ἤρεσκε θαυμαστῶς, οἱ δὲ χαρίεντες ταπεινὸν ἡγοῦντο καὶ ἀγεννὲς αὐτοῦ τὸ πλάσμα καὶ μαλακόν, ὧν καὶ Δημήτριος ὁ Φαληρεύς ἐστιν.

80. Dem. 18.232.

81. Aeschin. 2.49. See n. 34 above.

82. Catoni 2008, 248–249, notes that Demosthenes tries to sever the connection Aeschines has drawn between gestures and character, asking the jurors to judge him based on what he did rather than the gestures he made.

83. Aeschin. 3.56. Lanni 1997.
84. Dem. 18.258–262.
85. Aeschin. 3.171–173.
86. On the trial, Timarkhos' life, Aeschines' strategy, and Athenian sexual mores, see N. Fisher 2001, 1–67; Lape 2006; Worman 2008, 241–247; Wohl 2010a, 43–50.
87. Dem. 19.251. MacDowell 2000, 309; N. Fisher 2001, 153. Cf. Isoc. 5.90 and Letter 2.8, both of which use *propeteia* to refer to Cyrus' decision to rush out into the enemy ahead of his own soldiers at the battle of Cunaxa.
88. Fredal 2006, 168.
89. N. Fisher 2001, 153, suggests that it was the proposal to execute Athenians who sold arms to Philip mentioned in Dem. 19.286.
90. N. Fisher 2001, 53–56.
91. Aeschin. 1.33–35 with N. Fisher 2001, 163–164.
92. Aeschin. 1.34.
93. Besides the references at N. Fisher 2001, 163–164, see also Roisman 2004, 267–268.
94. Aeschin. 1.25.
95. Dem. 19.252, 255. On the *pilidion*, or felt cap, see Plutarch, *Solon* 8.1 with MacDowell 2000, 311, and Yunis 2005, 190 n. 228. Fredal 1998, 222–223, suggests that the *touto* in Aeschin. 1.25 ("This [*touto*], Athenians, is a reminder and an imitation of Solon's gesture. In this manner, he used to speak to the *dēmos* of the Athenians.") could refer to Aeschines' own pose.
96. Cf. Sissa 1999, 160, which stresses that Aeschines contrasts Solon's body, which the audience could not see because it was wrapped in a cloak, with Timarkhos' body, which was visible because it was naked.
97. Cf. Ford 1999, 247–248.
98. Schol. to Aeschin. 1.25 (62 Dilts): "Kleon the demagogue is said to have transgressed gestural custom and to have hitched up his cloak when he addressed the *dēmos*." (λέγεται δὲ Κλέων ὁ δημαγωγὸς παραβὰς τὸ ἐξ ἔθους σχῆμα περιζωσάμενος δημηγορῆσαι) Kleon rose to prominence in the 420s. Popular in the assembly and successful as a general until he died in battle in 422, Kleon was intensely disliked by Aristophanes and Thucydides, who are our main sources for his life and policies.
99. Plutarch, *Nikias* 8.6. See p. 60.
100. Cf. P. Zanker 1995, 48–49.
101. There is a more detailed discussion of *On the Dishonest Embassy* in chapter 5 (pp. 131–136).
102. Dem. 19.251–255. Cf. Schol. to Aeschin. 1.25 (62 Dilts). N. Fisher 2001, 151–152; Farenga 2006, 334–336; Catoni 2008, 245–248. Whether Demosthenes is actually telling the truth about the statue is a separate question.
103. Dem. 19.255.
104. Plutarch, *Demosthenes* 15.5; Pseudo-Plutarch, *Lives of the Ten Orators* 840c.

105. Cicero, *Orator* 24.
106. Wohl 2010a, 2010b.
107. Cf. Valerius Maximus 8.10. ext. 1.

CHAPTER 3

1. In O'Connell 2016, I present a briefer version of the argument in this chapter and consider *On the Murder of Herodes* (Antiphon 5) as a case study.
2. Aeschylus, *Libation Bearers* 973–1006.
3. I print the transmitted text, on which see Garvie 1986, 321–322. West (1990, 262–263) argues that this line is interpolated, but this and other textual issues are immaterial to my argument about the language of demonstration.
4. Aeschylus, *Libation Bearers* 1012–1013.
5. Aeschylus, *Libation Bearers* 980: τῶνδ᾽ ἐπήκοοι κακῶν.
6. *Homeric Hymn to Hermes* 190–211, 354–355.
7. Aristophanes, *Wasps* 962–966.
8. Boeotian, on the other hand, preserves another word for witness, *histōr*, which is derived from the same root as *eidon*, the aorist verb that means "see" or "know" (Nagy 1990, 250–251). There is also a rare word *optēr*, related to the verb *horaō* ("see"), which means "one who sees" and is used in Attic oratory once (Ant. 5.27) to mean witness.
9. When used with a supplementary participle rather than an infinitive, *phainomai* implies that something is "manifest" or "plainly true" rather than simply an apparent possibility (LSJ *phainō* B.II; G. L. Cooper 1998, 1.812–813 §56.4.5; Rijksbaron 2006, 121 n. 6). While this construction does not always mean that something is verifiable because it can actually be seen, it is sometimes linked directly with visual evidence. In Thucydides 6.55, for instance, Thucydides contrasts a conclusion based on an inscription that is visible on a stone (φαίνονται + participle) with his own logical conclusions (εἰκός, δοκεῖ μοι). Cf. Bers 2011, 677. *Phainomai* appears far more often with participles than with infinitives in Attic forensic oratory, perhaps reflecting the concern of litigants and speechwriters with visual evidence.
10. Mirhady (2002, 262–264 with nn. 37–47) collects the abundant ancient evidence.
11. Aristophanes, *Acharnians* 926, *Birds* 1031, *Clouds* 494–496, 1222–1223, 1297, *Frogs* 528, *Peace* 1119, *Wasps* 1435–1440, *Wealth* 932; Menander, *Perikeiromene* 384–385; Dem. 47.36, 38, 60; 53.16; Isae. 3.19. This list is compiled from the citations at Rea 1975, 129; Bain 1982; and Mirhady 2002, 264 n. 48. Cf. Lys. 3.14, 20 and Lys. fr. 194 Carey.
12. Thomas 1989, 41–42; Rydberg-Cox 2003, 662–663. Cf. Arist. *Rhet.* 1.15.21 1376b2–5; Isae. 9.7–13.
13. Scafuro 1994, 158–170, especially 164 on the preference for witnesses over documents.

14. Todd 1990, 39. Rubinstein 2005, 115–119, is a list of types of witnesses called in forensic speeches.

15. Todd 1990, 31–32, 39; Rubinstein 2005.

16. Humphreys 2007, especially 144–145, 158–159, 202. Cohen (1995, 107–110) goes beyond Humphreys' argument and maintains that the primary role of witnesses was to support the speaker, even if that required lying. Cf. Todd 1990, 30–31.

17. Mirhady 2002, 262–264 with n. 31; Rubinstein 2005, 103–105. Cf. Carey 1994, 183–184.

18. Scafuro 1994, 158–170; Mirhady 2002, 269. Cf. Lys. frs. 194 and A3a col. 4.9–12 Carey.

19. Dem. 46.6. Thür 2005, 152–155.

20. What seem to be interrogations of witnesses are more likely to be cases in which the witnesses simply assent to testimony read by the speaker. See Andoc. 1.14; Aristophanes, *Wasps* 962–966 with Thür 2005, 159 n. 39. Interrogation of opposing litigants (*erōtēsis*) is well attested (Carawan 1983).

21. Aristophanes, *Clouds* 776–782; Euripides, *Hippolytos* 1022–1024. Mirhady 2004, 28–29.

22. Pseudo-Arist. *Rhetoric for Alexander* 15.1–6 1431b20–1432a3 with Mirhady 2002, 268. Arist. *Rhet.* 1.15.19 1376a29–33 suggests that the reader can learn how to talk about witnesses, including whether they have good or bad reputations, by consulting the topics about enthymemes.

23. Thucydides 1.22.3.

24. Ant. fr. 71 Thalheim = 6.1 Gernet.

25. For the witness testimony that Laios was murdered by multiple robbers, see Sophocles, *Oedipus Tyrannos* 122–123. That the eyewitness is wrong about the number of murderers is characteristic of the play, where the blind Teiresias knows the truth (302–303) and Oedipus blinds himself after he discovers it.

26. Mirhady 2002, 266. For variations on the sentence "I will produce witnesses of these things to show that I am speaking the truth" (ὡς οὖν ἀληθῆ λέγω, μάρτυρας τούτων παρέξομαι), see Ant. 5.83, 84; Andoc. 1.18, 112, 123; Lys. 3.20; 13.42, 66, 68, 81; 19.23, 27; 23.8, 14; 31.14, 23; Dem. 18.135, 137; 19.146, 213; 21.82, 93, 107, 121, 174; 29.26, 53; 37.8, 31; 39.24; 40.7; 47.24, 27; 49.18; 52.21, 31; 53.18, 20, 21, 25; 54.9; 55.12; 57.27; 59.25, 32, 34, 40, 48, 53, 61, 70, 84. Cf. Lys. 10.5; 21.10; Dem. 21.167 for the claim that the jurors already know the truth, but the speaker will call witnesses anyway.

27. Dem. 59.34: καὶ ὅτι ταῦτ' ἀληθῆ λέγω, τοὺς ὁρῶντας ὑμῖν καὶ παρόντας μάρτυρας παρέξομαι.

28. Loftus 1996, 18–19, with reference to Wells, Lindsay, and Ferguson 1979. Cf. Cutler and Penrod 1995, 181–196; Loftus, Doyle, and Dysart 2013, 119–130.

29. See especially *State v. Henderson*, 27 A.3d 872 (N.J. 2011) with the unsigned discussion in "Recent Cases," *Harvard Law Review* 2012, 125: 1514–1521; Trenary 2013; National Academy of Sciences 2014. On American jurors' mistaken beliefs about the reliability of eyewitness identifications, see Lampinen, Neuschatz, and Cling 2014, 242–244. Whether eyewitnesses provide reliable testimony depends to

a large extent on the techniques used to interview them. The method known as cognitive interviewing, for instance, has been shown to elicit correct information from eyewitnesses more effectively than traditional police questioning (R. P. Fisher, Ross, and Cahill 2010).

30. Misidentification by eyewitnesses has contributed to more than 70% of the wrongful convictions in the United States that have been overturned based on DNA evidence and have been catalogued by the Innocence Project. For further information, see "The Causes" at http://www.innocenceproject.org. Regardless of whether the Italian-born anarchists Nicola Sacco and Bartolomeo Vanzetti were innocent of murder, Felix Frankfurter's critique of the case against them, originally published in the *Atlantic Monthly*, brought the problems of eyewitness identifications to the attention of the American public (1927, 30–34).

31. Heraclitus, fr. 34 [F21] Graham = B101a Diels-Kranz: ὀφθαλμοὶ τῶν ὤτων ἀκριβέστεροι μάρτυρες. Herodotus 1.8: ὦτα γὰρ τυγχάνει ἀνθρώποισι ἐόντα ἀπιστότερα ὀφθαλμῶν.

32. Hesiod, *Theogony* 27: ἴδμεν ψεύδεα πολλὰ λέγειν ἐτύμοισιν ὁμοῖα.

33. The most prominent example is in Kleon's speech during the Mytilene Debate (Thucydides 3.37–40, especially 38).

34. Gorgias, *Helen* 8–14. Cf. Euripides, *Hecuba* 814–819.

35. Dem. 46.7, 57.4. Todd 1990, 28–29.

36. I follow E. M. Harris (2006, 373–390) in translating *ep(i) autophōrōi* as "manifestly" rather than "in the act."

37. Lys. 1.26: οὐκ ἐγώ σε ἀποκτενῶ, ἀλλ' ὁ τῆς πόλεως νόμος.

38. See p. 93 below on why I translate *phaneron* here as "visible."

39. Isae. 6.41: οὗτοι δὲ τοῖς ἀκολουθήσασι παραχρῆμα ἐπεδείκνυσαν τὰ ἔνδον ὡς εἶχε. There is another example in a document preserved in *Against Makartatos* (Dem. 43.70), probably a later forgery since it is not included in the manuscript stichometry (Canevaro 2013, 12–13). The forger seems to have been sensitive to Athenian legal language, however, since he includes not only *epideiknumi* as the verb for the demonstration to witnesses but also *parakaleō*, the technical verb for summoning witnesses (Cf. Lys. 14.28, Dem. 34.29) in preparation for the demonstration.

40. Dem. 42.5: ἔδειξα καὶ διεμαρτυράμην ἐναντίον Φαινίππου, ὅτι οὐδεὶς ὅρος ἔπεστιν ἐπὶ τῇ ἐσχατιᾷ.

41. Dem. 42.5: "If he claimed [there were any additional mortgage stones], I ordered him to say so right away and to demonstrate [*deixai*] them, so any debt that existed then would not be revealed later on." (εἰ δέ φησιν, εἰπεῖν ἐκέλευον αὐτὸν ἤδη καὶ δεῖξαι, ὅπως μὴ ὕστερον ἐνταῦθα χρέως γενόμενον ἀναφανήσεται.) Cf. the similar language and construction at 42.28.

42. The formation of *endeiknumi* in fact corresponds exactly to the German "anzeigen," which means "report to the police." The only people subject to *endeixis* seem to have been those who exercised citizens' rights after losing them, exiles who

returned to Athens without reprieves, the class of criminals known as *kakourgoi*, and, perhaps, violators of certain import and export regulations. Hansen 1976, 18.

43. MacDowell 1978, 75; Hansen 1991a, 199. Cf. Pollux 8.49.

44. Andoc. 2.14: βουλευταί, ἐγὼ τὸν ἄνδρα τοῦτον ἐνδεικνύω ὑμῖν σῖτόν τε εἰς τοὺς πολεμίους εἰσαγαγόντα καὶ κωπέας. On the Four Hundred, see the discussion in chapter 1, p. 33 with n. 35.

45. Aristophanes, *Knights* 278: τουτονὶ τὸν ἄνδρ᾽ ἐγὼ ᾽νδείκνυμι.

46. Aristophanes, *Knights* 280: ναὶ μὰ Δία κἄγωγε τοῦτον.

47. *IC* IV 47.21–22: "If he [a slave who was given as security for a debt] dies, let him [the creditor] make a demonstration before two witnesses" (αἰ δέ κ᾽ ἀποθάνηι, δεικσάτō | ἀντὶ μαιτύρōν δυōν). Cf. lines 24 and 32 in the same inscription. *IC* IV 72 col. 1 39–46: "If the slave on whose account a man has been defeated takes refuge in a temple, let him [the man who has been defeated] summon [the man who was successful] in the presence of two free adult witnesses and make a demonstration at the temple where he has taken refuge, either himself or another for him; and if he does not summon or make a demonstration, let him pay what is written" (αἰ δέ | κα ναεύēι ὁ δōλος ὁ̄ κα νικαθε̄ι, καλίον ἀντὶ μαιτύρōν δυōν δ|ρομέōν ἐλευθέρōν ἀποδεικσάτō|ō ἐπὶ τōι ναōι ὄπē κα ναεύēι ē̄ αὐτὸς ē̄ ἄλος πρὸ τούτō· αἰ δέ | κα μē̄ καλε̄ι ē̄ μē̄ δείκσει, κατισ|[τάτ]ō τὰ ἐγ[ρα]μένα). The translation of the second passage is adapted from Willetts 1967.

48. *IG* IX, 2 521.5–18, especially 12–13: "which the Kondaians also pointed out [*epedeiknuon*] to the judges" (ἧς καὶ Κον[δαι]|εῖς ἐπεδείκ[ν]υον τοῖς κριταῖς). Cf. Nagy 1990, 318–319.

49. Cf. Palmer 1950, 157–168; Benveniste 1973, 385–388.

50. Pl. *Laws* 11 917d–e: ὁ δὲ δὴ φανερὸς γενόμενός τι πωλῶν τοιοῦτον, πρὸς τῷ στερηθῆναι τοῦ κιβδηλευθέντος, ὁπόσης ἂν τιμῆς ἀξιώσῃ τὸ πωλούμενον, κατὰ δραχμὴν ἑκάστην τῇ μάστιγι τυπτέσθω πληγὰς ὑπὸ κήρυκος ἐν τῇ ἀγορᾷ κηρύξαντος ὧν ἕνεκα μέλλει τύπτεσθαι.

51. Ant. 2.2.3: ἔκ τε γὰρ αὐτοῦ τοῦ ἔργου φανερὸς γενόμενος ἀπωλλύμην, λαθών τε σαφῶς ἤδη τήνδε τὴν ὑποψίαν εἰς ἐμὲ οὖσαν. Reiske proposed ἰοῦσαν for οὖσαν, which makes the sentence easier (". . . I knew clearly that this suspicion would come to me"). For the argument in favor of the transmitted text, see Gagarin 1997, 131.

52. Cf. Maidment 1941, 60 n. a; Gagarin 1997, 131. When the Athenians wanted to contrast behavior done openly and in secret, they regularly used *phaneros* to refer to the open actions. See e.g., Lys. 8.5–6. Note also the use of *phaneros* to describe the irregular public voting of the *boulē* under the Thirty at Lys. 13.37. For the phrase *en tōi phanerōi* meaning "in public" or "in the open," see Isoc. 2.30; Pl. *Laws* 5 745a; Xenophon, *Hellenica* 2.3.43, 5.3.16, 6.4.16, *Memorabilia* 1.1.10, *Cyropaedia* 7.5.55, 8.1.31 (cf. Pl. *Republic* 2.3 360a–d), *Cavalry Commander* 5.7; Dem. 18.235; Arist. *Poetics* 11 1452b12, *History of Animals* 3.1 510a9, 4.8 533a4; Aeneas Tacticus 11.7, 29.12. The phrase becomes increasingly common in later Greek.

53. Lys. 10.19. Todd 2007a, 683–684.

54. This reciprocal use of "seeing" (*horaō/eidon* or *opsis*) and "being visible" (*phaneros/phainomai*) is common in Greek literature. It is most familiar in descriptions of epiphanies, where the seeing and reciprocal visibility are often followed by a verb of recognition (*gignōskō*, less often *noeō*; e.g., *Iliad* 1.194–200; *Odyssey* 16.155–163 with Cioffi 2014, 3–7), but it appears in a wide variety of situations that refer to seeing, including Xenophon, *Agesilaus* 7.2 (the public lawfulness of Agesilaus); Arist. *History of Animals* 8.48 631a15–20 (dolphins taking care of a dead dolphin); Theophrastus, *History of Plants* 7.4.3 (turnip seeds); Autolycus, *Risings and Settings* 2.1 (the zodiac).

55. Lys. 9.9–10: ἐγὼ δ᾽ ὅτι μὲν οὐκ εἰσῆλθον εἰς τὸ ἀρχεῖον, μάρτυρας παρεσχόμην, ἀδίκως δὲ ζημιωθεὶς οὔτ᾽ ὀφείλω οὔτ᾽ ἐκτεῖσαι δίκαιός εἰμι. εἰ γὰρ <u>φανερός εἰμι</u> μὴ ἐλθὼν εἰς τὸ συνέδριον, ὁ δὲ νόμος τοὺς ἐντὸς πλημμελοῦντας ἀγορεύει τὴν ζημίαν ὀφείλειν, ἠδικηκὼς μὲν οὐδὲν <u>φαίνομαι</u>, ἔχθρᾳ δὲ ἄνευ τούτου παραλόγως ζημιωθείς.

56. The *Palamedes* is often dated to before 411, on the assumption that it influenced Antiphon, but this is far from conclusive. Buchheim 1989, 173–174.

57. Gorgias, *Palamedes* 7: τρίτος ἄρα <u>μάρτυς</u> γίνεται τῶν κρύπτεσθαι δεομένων.

58. Gorgias, *Palamedes* 8: ταῦτα δὲ γινόμενα πᾶσιν ὑμῖν ἂν ἦν <u>φανερά</u>.

59. Gorgias, *Palamedes* 9: πολλῶν γὰρ κομιζόντων πολλοὶ ἂν ἦσαν <u>μάρτυρες</u> τῆς ἐπιβουλῆς, ἑνὸς δὲ κομίζοντος οὐκ ἂν πολύ τι τὸ φερόμενον ἦν.

60. Gorgias, *Palamedes* 10: χρώμενος δ᾽ ἂν <u>φανερὸς</u> ἐγενόμην, μὴ χρώμενος δὲ τί ἂν ὠφελούμην ἀπ᾽ αὐτῶν.

61. I provide a similar translation in O'Connell 2016, 6.

62. Some evidence suggests that a *phasis* involved pointing out property that was either illegally possessed or somehow implicated in a crime, while an *endeixis* involved pointing out an actual criminal (MacDowell 1991; Hansen 1991a with the supplements in Wallace 2003, 167 n. 1). It is likely the terms could be used in overlapping ways without causing procedural confusion (Wallace 2003, 180–181).

63. This seems to have been the case in *phaseis* concerning mining regulations, orphans' estates, and impiety. MacDowell 1991, 195–198. Since *phēmi* ("speak") and *phainō* ("illuminate") may both come from the PIE root *b^heh_2– (Beekes 2010, 2.1567), it is unsurprising that *phasis* can refer to both visual showing and verbal denunication.

64. Aristophanes, *Acharnians* 911–912: ἐγὼ τοίνυν ὁδὶ / <u>φαίνω</u> πολέμια ταῦτα.

65. Aristophanes, *Acharnians* 914: καὶ σέ γε <u>φανῶ</u> πρὸς τοῖσδε.

66. Aristophanes, *Acharnians* 917: ἔπειτα <u>φαίνεις</u> δῆτα διὰ θρυαλλίδα.

67. MacDowell 1991, 188: "Since the passages are from a comedy, we cannot assume that they necessarily follow the legal procedure of real life in every detail; Aristophanes, in order to avoid boring his audience, may have omitted some formalities which in real life would have been necessary. But the main point must be true to life since otherwise the joke would be ineffective; and so we can safely infer

that in real life a *phasis* was initiated by the prosecutor saying φαίνω or φανῶ and pointing to the goods as well as to the defendant. He reveals now to the bystanders (φαίνω) and will reveal to a magistrate or official (φανῶ) the goods which ought not to be there."

68. Gabrielsen 1986, 101 with n. 7. Visible property generally refers to land, and invisible property to money and other movables (Harpocration ἀφανὴς οὐσία καὶ φανερά = Lys. fr. 172 Carey with Ferrucci 2005, 149–152), but land can be invisible property (Lys. 32.23; Dem. 28.7. Gabrielsen 1986, 105–108), and movables can be visible property (Isae. 8.35, 11.43. Cf. Ferrucci 2005, 150).

69. Gabrielsen 1986, 103–104; S. Johnstone 2005, 250–255.

70. In Isoc. 17.7–9 the speaker has no way of proving that money belongs to him, since he had publicly denied having it. Cf. Lys. fr. 287 Carey. See the discussions at Gabrielsen 1986, 103; Ferrucci 2005, 162–163. S. Johnstone (2005, 255–257, 262–267) stresses the need for trust in monetary transactions that did not involve witnesses.

71. Cf. the use of *apophainō* for "revealing" debts made visible by mortgage stones in Dem 42.5 (quoted at n. 41 above).

72. Lys. 32.14: καὶ τούτων τὰ γράμματα ἀπέδειξεν. Cf. Lys. 32.22.

73. For other examples, see Lys. 32.6, 20, 25, 27; Dem. 27.19, 53.28.

74. Pomeroy 1997, 67–82.

75. Isae. 6.22: ἐπειδὴ δὲ οὔθ᾽ ὁ υὸς αὐτῷ Φιλοκτήμων συνεχώρει οὔθ᾽ οἱ φράτερες εἰσεδέξαντο, ἀλλ᾽ ἀπηνέχθη τὸ κούρειον, ὀργιζόμενος ὁ Εὐκτήμων τῷ υἱεῖ καὶ ἐπηρεάζειν βουλόμενος ἐγγυᾶται γυναῖκα Δημοκράτους τοῦ Ἀφιδναίου ἀδελφήν, ὡς ἐκ ταύτης παῖδας ἀποφανῶν καὶ εἰσποιήσων εἰς τὸν οἶκον, εἰ μὴ συγχωροίη τοῦτον ἐᾶν εἰσαχθῆναι.

76. Isae. 6.23: φανήσοιντο δ᾽ ἄλλῳ τινὶ τρόπῳ.

77. Wyse 1904, 510.

78. Isae. 7.1: εἴ τις αὐτὸς ζῶν καὶ εὖ φρονῶν ἐποιήσατο καὶ ἐπὶ τὰ ἱερὰ ἀγαγὼν εἰς τοὺς συγγενεῖς ἀπέδειξε καὶ εἰς τὰ κοινὰ γραμματεῖα ἐνέγραψεν.

79. Isae. 7.2: ἐκεῖνον μὲν γὰρ τὸν τρόπον ποιησάμενος φανερὰς κατέστησε τὰς αὐτοῦ βουλήσεις.

80. Isae. 7.2: καὶ γὰρ οὕτως αὐτῶν φανερῶς πεπραγμένων ὅμως ὑπὲρ τῆς θυγατρὸς τῆς Εὐπόλιδος ἥκουσι περὶ τῶν Ἀπολλοδώρου χρημάτων πρὸς ἐμὲ ἀμφισβητήσοντες.

81. Herodotus 1.136: ἀνδραγαθίη δὲ αὕτη ἀποδέδεκται, μετὰ τὸ μάχεσθαι εἶναι ἀγαθόν, ὃς ἂν πολλοὺς ἀποδέξῃ παῖδας· τῷ δὲ τοὺς πλείστους ἀποδεικνύντι δῶρα ἐκπέμπει βασιλεὺς ἀνὰ πᾶν ἔτος.

82. Arist. *Rhet*. 2.23.11 1398a32-b5: ἄλλος ἐξ ἐπαγωγῆς, οἷον ἐκ τῆς Πεπαρηθίας, ὅτι περὶ τῶν τέκνων αἱ γυναῖκες πανταχοῦ διορίζουσι τἀληθές· τοῦτο μὲν γὰρ Ἀθήνησι Μαντίᾳ τῷ ῥήτορι ἀμφισβητοῦντι πρὸς τὸν υἱὸν ἀπέφηνεν ἡ μήτηρ, τοῦτο δὲ Θήβησιν Ἰσμηνίου καὶ Στίλβωνος ἀμφισβητούντων ἡ Δωδωνὶς ἀπέδειξεν Ἰσμηνίου τὸν υἱόν, καὶ διὰ τοῦτο Θετταλίσκον Ἰσμηνίου ἐνόμιζον.

83. Anaxagoras, fr. 63 [F23] Graham = B21a Diels-Kranz = Sextus Empiricus,

Against the Professors 7.140a: ὄψις γὰρ τῶν ἀδήλων τὰ φαινόμενα. Graham 2004, 13–15, is a recent discussion of the fragment.

84. Hippocrates, *On the Art* 9–12. O'Connell 2015 discusses the language of demonstration, seeing, and knowledge in *On the Art*. There is a further discussion of the language of visibility in *On the Art* at chapter 4, pp. 114–115.

85. Hippocrates, *On the Art* 11.2: "As many things as flee from the sight of the eyes, the sight of the mind has apprehended." (ὅσα γὰρ τὴν τῶν ὀμμάτων ὄψιν ἐκφεύγει, ταῦτα τῇ τῆς γνώμης ὄψει κεκράτηται.) On the word *gnōmē*, see chapter 6, p. 159.

86. Pl. *Phaedrus* 250b–c. Cf. the language of sight in the allegory of the cave, *Republic* 7 514a–517c. Riedweg 1987, 1–69.

87. Gagarin 2002a, 37–52. For the separatist position, see Pendrick 2002, 1–26.

88. Protagoras, fr. 21 [F2] Graham. See Gagarin 2002b, which refers to earlier scholarship.

CHAPTER 4

1. An alternate interpretation, that the blindfold blinds Justice to the truth, has been known since the fifteenth century. Resnik and Curtis 2011, 62–133.

2. Hesiod, *Works and Days* 256–273. West 1978, 221, 223–224.

3. Euripides, *Electra* 771.

4. Sophocles, fr. 12 *TrGF*; Euripides, frs. 223.86–87; 255 *TrGF*; Dionysius (76), fr. 5 *TrGF*; fr. adesp. 421 *TrGF*; Cf. Aeschylus, *Libation Bearers* 61–65; *Orphic Hymn* 62.1–5; Proclus, *Hymn* 1.38; *Palatine Anthology* 7.357.

5. Dem. 25.11 = Orphic fr. 33 Bernabé. G. Martin 2009, 190–199; Bernabé and Jiménez San Cristóbal 2011, 86–87. On the authenticity of the speech, see MacDowell 2009, 310–312; G. Martin 2009, 200–202.

6. Shapiro 1993, 39–44. Wealth (*Ploutos*) is blind as early as Hipponax, fr. 36 West, and his blindness is a central theme of Aristophanes, *Wealth*. The blind Love (*Erōs*) is rarer, but see Theocritus 10.19–20; Orphic fr. 144 Bernabé = Proclus, *Commentary on Plato's Timaeus* 33c (2.85.26–27 Diehl).

7. Plutarch, *Isis and Osiris* 10 355a; Diodorus Siculus 1.48.6.

8. Cf. Isoc. 15.53: "If I were being tried like a person who had acted wrongly in regard to certain activities, I wouldn't be able to present them to you to see, but you would have to conjecture based on what was said and make your decision about what was done as well as you could." (εἰ μὲν τοίνυν ἠγωνιζόμην ὡς περὶ πράξεις τινὰς ἡμαρτηκώς, οὐκ ἂν οἷός τ᾽ ἦν ἰδεῖν ὑμῖν αὐτὰς παρασχεῖν, ἀλλ᾽ ἀναγκαίως εἶχεν εἰκάζοντας ὑμᾶς ἐκ τῶν εἰρημένων διαγιγνώσκειν ὅπως ἐτύχετε περὶ τῶν πεπραγμένων.)

9. For a defense of Antiphon's authorship and a discussion of the purpose and audience of the tetralogies, see Gagarin 2002a, 52–62, 103–109.

10. Lys. fr. 425 Carey also stresses the jurors' obligation to listen to both the prosecution and the defense to make a just decision, but it refers to hearing rather than to seeing.

11. Despite the widespread appearance of the language of demonstration in forensic oratory, the use of these words was a matter of personal preference and not an inevitable feature of the genre. Neither Hyperides nor Dinarchus, for instance, ever describes his own or the speaker's verbal demonstration with *apodeiknumi*, *epideiknumi*, or *deiknumi* in their surviving forensic speeches and fragments.

12. Dem. 33.3: ὁ μὲν οὖν μετὰ τούτου μοι ἐπιβεβουλευκὼς καὶ τὸν ἀγῶνα τουτονὶ κατεσκευακὼς προϊόντος τοῦ λόγου καταφανὴς ὑμῖν ἔσται. Dem. 29.42: πολλαχόθεν μὲν οὖν ἄν τις ἴδοι τὴν σὴν πονηρίαν, μάλιστα δ' εἰ περὶ τῆς διαθήκης ἀκούσειεν.

13. See Stanford 1936, 46–62; Tarrant 1960; Segal 1977; Catrein 2003, 14–17; the essays collected in S. Butler and Purves 2013, especially Dozier 2013 on visual metaphors in Quintilian's analysis of oratory. For an overview of the literature related to synaesthesia, see Stevens 2008, 162, n. 3.

14. *Odyssey* 8.499: φαῖνε δ' ἀοιδήν. For a discussion of the semantics of *phainō* in this passage in light of the use of *deiknumi* in archaic choral poetry, see Nikolaev 2012, 563–564.

15. Fr. 11.7 West: ἐς γὰρ γλῶσσαν ὁρᾶτε καὶ εἰς ἔπη αἱμύλου ἀνδρός.

16. Dem. 43.18: "First, gentlemen of the jury, I planned to write on a board all Hagnias' relatives and so make a demonstration [*epideiknuein*] of them to you one by one. Since, however, I realized that not all the jurors would have an equal chance to see, but that those sitting at a distance would be left out, it is necessary to instruct you equitably through speech. For this is common to everyone. We will even try to make our demonstration [*epideixai*] about Hagnias' family through the fewest words as we can." (τὸ μὲν οὖν πρῶτον διενοήθην, ὦ ἄνδρες δικασταί, γράψας ἐν πίνακι ἅπαντας τοὺς συγγενεῖς τοὺς Ἁγνίου, οὕτως ἐπιδεικνύειν ὑμῖν καθ' ἕκαστον· ἐπειδὴ δ' ἐδόκει οὐκ <ἂν> εἶναι ἐξ ἴσου ἡ θεωρία ἅπασι τοῖς δικασταῖς, ἀλλ' οἱ πόρρω καθήμενοι ἀπολείπεσθαι, ἀναγκαῖον ἴσως ἐστὶν τῷ λόγῳ διδάσκειν ὑμᾶς· τοῦτο γὰρ ἅπασι κοινόν ἐστι. πειρασόμεθα δὲ καὶ ἡμεῖς ὡς ἂν μάλιστα δυνώμεθα διὰ βραχυτάτων ἐπιδεῖξαι περὶ τοῦ γένους τοῦ Ἁγνίου.)

17. Along the same lines, Hibbitts (1994, 242–245) argues that legal discourse in the United States favored visual vocabulary at least up to the late 1980s in part because of the importance of visual evidence and witness testimony in American law.

18. Benveniste 1973, 386.

19. Cf. the discussion of *dico* and *loquor* at Habinek 2005, 70–74.

20. E.g. Ant. 6.15–16, 32, 41; Lys. 7.42; 20.26, 28; 31.16; fr. 114 Carey; Isae. 2.17; 3.6–7, 55; 6.5–7, 10, 12, 62, 64, 65; 8.6, 28; 9.35; 10.15; 12.7; Dem. 27.18; 29.33; 30.14–17, 25; 37.2, 17; 40.19; 44.15; 45.8; 47.31–32; 48.46; 50.29; 57.17, 46; 59.62. Cf. Herodotus 5.45.1–2 and *IG* XII, 6.1 155.11–13 with Nagy 1990, 316–319.

21. Ant. 5.81; Lys. 4.12; Dem. 27.47, 40.60.

22. De Bakker 2012, 395.
23. Lys. 23.1: ὡς δὲ ὀρθῶς τὴν δίκην ἔλαχον τουτῳὶ Παγκλέωνι οὐκ ὄντι Πλαταιεῖ, τοῦτο ὑμῖν πειράσομαι <u>ἀποδεῖξαι</u>.
24. Cassin 1995, 195–202; Lloyd 1996, 56–57; Thomas 2000, 221–222.
25. Aeschin. 3.46: ὅτι δ᾽ ἀληθῆ λέγω, μέγα σημεῖον ὑμῖν τούτου ἐξ αὐτῶν τῶν νόμων <u>ἐπιδείξω</u>.
26. Dem. 53.26: κατὰ πολλὰ μὲν οὖν ἔμοιγε δοκοῦσιν εἶναι ἀναίσχυντοι ἀμφισβητοῦντες τῶν ὑμετέρων, οὐχ ἥκιστα δὲ ὑμῖν αὐτοὺς <u>ἐπιδείξω</u> ἐκ τῶν νόμων τῶν ὑμετέρων.
27. Similarly, speakers in the assembly can use the vocabulary of demonstration for presentations based on written documents other than laws. See Dinarchus 1.1: "The council of the Areopagos spoke just and true demonstrations [*apodeixeis*] about this specific written report [*apophaseōs*]." (περὶ μὲν αὐτῆς τῆς ἀποφάσεως τῆς ἐξ Ἀρείου πάγου βουλῆς δικαίας καὶ ἀληθεῖς ἀποδείξεις εἰρηκυίας.) *Apophasis* (genitive, *apophaseōs*) here refers to the written document compiled by the Areopagos in the wake of the Harpalos affair. Hyp. 5.6 uses forms of *graphō* ("write") and *prosgraphō* ("write as an appendix") to describe its production. On the *apophasis* procedure, see Wallace 1989, 113–119, and on the Harpalos affair and Demosthenes' trial, see most recently Worthington 2013, 310–325, which refers to earlier scholarship. *Epideiknumi* seems to have been the regular verb for presenting written documents in the assembly. See *IG* I³ 78a = *IE* 28a ll. 59–60; *IG* I³ 35 ll. 16–18 (a likely supplement). Cf. Thucydides 5.77.8.
28. Isae. 10.15: ἔκ τε τῶν εἰρημένων καὶ μεμαρτυρημένων καὶ ἐξ αὐτῶν τῶν νόμων ἱκανῶς ἡγοῦμαι ἀποδεδεῖχθαι.
29. E.g., Andoc. 1.37; Lys. 7.25, 10.1, 12.74; Isae. 3.40; Dem. 21.18, 217; 23.168; Aeschin. 1.89, 2.122; Dinarchus 1.95. Cf. Gorgias, *Palamedes* 15. For discussion of this trope, see Todd 2007a, 661–662. See also the analysis of the tactic at Schol. to Dem. 20.75 (175 Dilts).
30. Lys. 22.12: καὶ τούτων ὑμᾶς μάρτυρας παρέχομαι.
31. Isae. 11.48: ἐμοὶ δὲ μάρτυρές ἐστε πάντες ὅτι οἱ τῆς ἐμῆς γυναικὸς ἀδελφοί, Χαιρέλεως καὶ Μακάρτατος, οὐ τῶν λῃτουργούντων ἦσαν ἀλλὰ τῶν βραχεῖαν κεκτημένων οὐσίαν.
32. On common knowledge in the courts, see Allen 2000a, 169; Ober 2008, 160–210.
33. Arist. *Rhet.* 3.7.7 1408a32–36: πάσχουσι δέ τι οἱ ἀκροαταὶ καὶ ᾧ κατακόρως χρῶνται οἱ λογογράφοι, "τίς δ᾽ οὐκ οἶδεν;" "ἅπαντες ἴσασιν·" ὁμολογεῖ γὰρ ὁ ἀκούων αἰσχυνόμενος, ὅπως μετέχῃ οὗπερ καὶ οἱ ἄλλοι πάντες. For parallels in oratory, mostly from Isocrates, see Spengel 1867, 2.381–382. Cf. W. E. Thompson 1976, 57, on Isae. 11.48.
34. Ober 1989, 149–151.
35. Dem. 48.39: "The things which this man <u>says</u>, gentlemen of the jury, are false insinuations, unjust allegations and cowardly <u>tricks</u> for depriving me of what

he owes me. But what I will say to you, namely that this man is a liar, will not be an insinuation at all. I will demonstrate in an evident manner, by speaking proofs which are true and known to everyone and introducing witnesses about everything." (ἃ μὲν οὖν, ὦ ἄνδρες δικασταί, οὗτος λέγει, ὑπόνοιαι πλασταί εἰσι καὶ προφάσεις ἄδικοι καὶ πονηρίαι ἐπὶ τῷ ἀποστερῆσαι ἃ προσήκει αὐτὸν ἀποδοῦναι ἐμοί. ἃ δὲ ἐγὼ ἐρῶ πρὸς ὑμᾶς, ὅτι οὗτος ψεύδεται, ταῦτα δὲ ὑπόνοια οὐδεμία ἔσται, φανερῶς δὲ ἐπιδείξω τὴν τούτου ἀναισχυντίαν, τεκμήρια λέγων ἀληθινὰ καὶ πᾶσι γνώριμα, καὶ μάρτυρας παρεχόμενος περὶ ἁπάντων.) Cf. Dem. 33.35–36, 40.38–39, 52.20, 55.12, 57.62.

36. Lys. 31.16: "So that he cannot trick you by lying, I will now make a demonstration to you in a transparent way about these things as well, since I won't be able to disprove him if I go through them later." (ἵνα οὖν μὴ ἐγγένηται αὐτῷ ψευσαμένῳ ἐξαπατῆσαι, καὶ περὶ τούτων ἤδη σαφῶς ὑμῖν ἀποδείξω, ἐπειδὴ ὕστερον οὐκ ἐξέσται μοι παρελθόντι ἐνθάδ' ἐλέγχειν αὐτόν.)

37. E.g. Ant. 3.3.3; Lys. 7.30; Isoc. 18.65; Isae. 2.38; Dem. 41.20. Parry 1981, 47–51, calls this the "popular distinction" between *logos* and *ergon*, where *logos* is associated with falsehood and *ergon* with truth. For the more elaborate use of the antithesis, especially in Thucydides, see, besides Parry, Ober 1998, especially 53–63.

38. Dem. 38.9–11: ὅτι δ' ὕστερον οὐκ ἔνι τὴν κομιδὴν γεγενῆσθαι τούτων τῶν χρημάτων (τοῦτο γὰρ πλάττουσιν οὗτοι καὶ παράγουσιν), τοῦτο βούλομαι δεῖξαι. τὸν μὲν γὰρ πατέρ' οὐδ' ἂν αἰτιάσαιντο λαβεῖν (τέτταρσι γὰρ ἢ τρισὶ μησὶν ὕστερον ἢ διελύσατο πρὸς τούτους ἐτελεύτησεν). ὡς δ' οὐδὲ Δημάρετον τὸν καταλειφθέντα ἡμῶν ἐπίτροπον λαβεῖν οἷόν τε (καὶ γὰρ τοῦτον ἔγραψαν εἰς τὸ ἔγκλημα), καὶ τοῦτο ἐπιδείξω. μέγιστοι μὲν οὖν ἡμῖν εἰσιν οὗτοι μάρτυρες (οὐδαμοῦ γὰρ φανήσονται δίκην εἰληχότες ζῶντι τῷ Δημαρέτῳ)· οὐ μὴν ἀλλὰ καὶ τὸ πρᾶγμα ἄν τις αὐτὸ σκοπῶν καὶ θεωρῶν ἴδοι οὐ μόνον οὐχὶ λαβόντα, ἀλλ' οὐδ' ἐνὸν αὐτῷ λαβεῖν.

39. MacDowell 2009, 82.

40. Lys. 12.56, 25.14; Isoc. 17.54, 18.56, 20.4; Isae. 8.9; Dem. 18.131, 26.1, 38.22, 48.39, 54.30, 59.111; Aeschin. 2.111. Cf. Alcidamas, *Odysseus* 22; Isoc. 15.102; Dem. Letter 2.1. For examples in nonforensic contexts, see Dem. 6.2, 7.36, 12.18; Isoc. 4.145, 8.104, 9.65, 10.4; Pl. *Hippias maior* 304d.

41. Ant. 2.3.9, 4.3.6, 4.4.9; Lys. 7.11, 8.12, 19.4, 30.8, 32.2; Isae. 11.4; Dem. 18.136; 19.176; 23.206; 28.9; 29.3, 5 (the noun *elenkhos*); 30.5 (the noun *elenkhos*); 41.13, 15; 42.29; 55.2, 14; 58.54; Aeschin. 3.40, 125, 221; Dinarchus 1.1.

42. Dem. 41.14–15: "And yet, who could have proven the lack of substance in my opponent's charges or my own better than the people who were present at all these events and know what happened as well as we do, the shared acquaintances and friends of us both? But it is clear that it wouldn't have benefitted him to reach a settlement after he had been proven guilty by them in an evident manner." (καίτοι τίνες ἂν ἄμεινον καὶ τῶν τούτου καὶ τῶν ἐμῶν ἐγκλημάτων τὰ μηδὲν ὄντα ἐξήλεγξαν τῶν παραγεγενημένων ἅπασι τούτοις, τῶν εἰδότων οὐδὲν ἧττον ἡμῶν

τὰ γενόμενα, τῶν κοινῶν ἀμφοτέροις καὶ φίλων ὄντων; ἀλλὰ δῆλον ὅτι τούτῳ ταῦτ' οὐκ ἐλυσιτέλει, <u>φανερῶς ὑπ' αὐτῶν ἐξελεγχομένῳ</u> τοῦτον τὸν τρόπον λαβεῖν διάλυσιν.)

43. On the overlap between forensic and epideictic oratory, see Thomas 2003, 173–174. As the notes to the rest of this chapter show, my understanding of *epideixis* is especially indebted to Thomas' work.

44. Arist. *Rhet.* 1.3.2 1358b2–8.

45. Cf. Thomas 2003, 173–175.

46. Alcidamas, *On the Sophists* 31. Muir (2001, 64) suggests that Alcidamas could be referring to "handouts" distributed at his performances or to souvenir texts sold afterwards. On oral and written *epideixeis*, see Demont 1993, especially 192–201; Thomas 2003.

47. Herodotus, Proem. On the semantics of *apodexis* here, see Nagy 1990, 217–227; Thomas 2000, 260–269.

48. Thucydides 3.42.3: "Most dangerous are those who even charge their opponents with accepting bribes to make some kind of demonstration [*epideixin*]." (χαλεπώτατοι δὲ καὶ οἱ ἐπὶ χρήμασι προσκατηγοροῦντες ἐπίδειξίν τινα.)

49. Thucydides 3.38.4: "You are yourselves at fault, since you have organized these contests negligently. You are the kind of people who are used to being spectators of speeches and hearers of deeds." (αἴτιοι δ' ὑμεῖς κακῶς ἀγωνοθετοῦντες, οἵτινες εἰώθατε θεαταὶ μὲν τῶν λόγων γίγνεσθαι, ἀκροαταὶ δὲ τῶν ἔργων.)

50. Dem. 18.280: "Indeed, Aeschines, I think that you've undertaken this trial because you wanted to make some kind of demonstration [*epideixin*] from those words and to exercise your voice, not because you wanted vengeance for any crime." (καί μοι δοκεῖς ἐκ τούτων, Αἰσχίνη, λόγων ἐπίδειξίν τινα καὶ φωνασκίας βουλόμενος ποιήσασθαι τοῦτον προελέσθαι τὸν ἀγῶνα, οὐκ ἀδικήματος οὐδενὸς λαβεῖν τιμωρίαν.)

51. Pl. *Protagoras* 320b–c: εἰ οὖν ἔχεις ἐναργέστερον ἡμῖν <u>ἐπιδεῖξαι</u> ὡς διδακτόν ἐστιν ἡ ἀρετή, μὴ φθονήσῃς ἀλλ' <u>ἐπίδειξον</u>. In chapters 5 and 6 I explore the concept of *enargeia* ("vividness"), the nominal form of Plato's adjective *enargesteron* ("in a rather vivid manner").

52. Thomas 2000, 251; Jouanna, 2012. On the problem of Hippocratic authorship, see Lloyd 1991, 194–223; Jouanna 1999, 56–71.

53. Hippocrates, *On the Art* 13.1.

54. On this issue, see Thomas 2000, 251–252, 261–263; Mann 2012, 230–231.

55. Hippocrates, *On the Art* 1.1.

56. There is further discussion of this phrase in chapter 3, p. 101.

57. Hippocrates, *On the Art* 11.4: τὰ ἀφανέα. On the relationship of the visible and the invisible in medical texts and Greek thought of this period, see Thomas 2000, 200–211.

58. Hippocrates, *On the Art* 11.4.

59. Hippocrates, *On the Art* 11.5.

60. Hippocrates, *On the Art* 12.4. On the interpretation of this difficult passage, see Mann 2012, 221–223.
61. Cf. Demont 1993, 193.
62. Hippocrates, *On Breaths* 3.2–3. Thomas 2000, 205. The author of *On Breaths* uses a variety of terms for air, including *aēr*, *pneuma*, and *phusai*. Because of the brevity of my discussion, I do not attempt to distinguish the nuances of these words.
63. Hippocrates, *On Breaths* 3.3, 7.2. Cf. 9.1.
64. Hippocrates, *On Breaths* 5.2.
65. Hippocrates, *On Breaths* 14.2.
66. The standard account of funeral orations and their role in Athenian self-identity remains Loraux 1986.
67. Pl. *Menexenos* 237b: τὴν τῶν ἔργων πρᾶξιν ἐπιδείξωμεν.
68. Dem. 60.12, 18; Hyp. 6.16, 24, 29; Lys. 2.8, 10, 41, 43, 55, 56, 58, 63, 64, 67, 69; Pl. *Menexenos* 241a, 242d, e.

CHAPTER 5

1. The *Ajax* is fr. 53 Giannantoni, and its counterpart the *Odysseus* is fr. 54 Giannantoni. I punctuate the section I quote slightly differently from Giannantoni.
2. Antisthenes, *Ajax* 1, 7, 8. On the role of *logos* and knowledge in Ajax's and Odysseus' speeches, see Eucken 1997, 252–259. Antisthenes himself is supposed to have said that "*logos* is that which makes clear [*dēlon*] that which was or is" (fr. 151 Giannantoni = Diogenes Laertius 6.3: λόγος ἐστὶν ὁ τὸ τί ἦν ἢ ἔστι δηλῶν). For Antisthenes' views about *logos*, see, besides Eucken, Denyer 1991, 27–33; Prince 2006, 80–82.
3. Antisthenes, *Ajax* 4, 8.
4. Antisthenes, *Ajax* 8: οὐ κριταὶ τῶν λεγομένων ἀλλὰ δοξασταὶ κάθησθε.
5. Antisthenes, *Odysseus* 6, 9. For language of display and secrecy in the *Ajax*, see 3, 5, 8. Cf. Worman 2002, 186–187.
6. Of course, we know this only in hindsight, since he is awarded Achilles' weapons. Scholars continue to debate if Antisthenes' debate actually has a winner. For ethical interpretations of the arguments and characters of Ajax and Odysseus, see Eucken 1997; Prince 2006, 82–86.
7. Antisthenes, *Odysseus* 5: "But if we ought to make a conjecture based on probability [*ek tōn eikotōn*], I believe that you will do some evil to yourself because of your evil anger." (ἀλλ' εἴπερ ἐκ τῶν εἰκότων τι χρὴ τεκμαίρεσθαι, ὑπὸ τῆς κακῆς ὀργῆς οἴομαί σε κακόν τι σαυτὸν ἐργάσεσθαι.) Cf. Eucken 1997, 262–263.
8. On *enargeia* as a feature of literary style, see G. Zanker 1981; Meijering 1987, 14–53; Calame 1991; Vasaly 1993, 89–104; Bakker 2005, 157–160; Nünlist 2009, 194–198; Otto 2009; Webb 2009, especially 87–130; Berardi 2012; Bussels 2012, 57–80; Plett 2012; Lombardo 2013; Squire 2013; Sheppard 2014, 19–46. On the use of *enar-*

geia in philosophical contexts, see Allen 2010, 26, 58–63; Ierodiakonou 2011; Bussels 2012, 66–71.

9. *Iliad* 20.131; *Odyssey* 3.420, 4.841, 7.201, 16.161. Cf. Hesiod, *Catalogue of Women* fr. 165.5 Merkelbach-West; Aeschylus, *Seven against Thebes* 136; Lys. 6.3; Isoc. 10.61.

10. Aeschylus, *Persians* 179–180: ἀλλ' οὔτι πω τοιόνδ' <u>ἐναργὲς εἰδόμην</u> / ὡς τῆς πάροιθεν εὐφρόνης; 188: ὡς ἐγὼ 'δόκουν ὁρᾶν.

11. Aelius Theon 2.118.7–8 Spengel = 66 Patillon: ἔκφρασίς ἐστι λόγος περιηγηματικὸς ἐναργῶς ὑπ' ὄψιν ἄγων τὸ δηλούμενον. Cf. Aelius Theon 2.119.31–32 Spengel = 66 Patillon. Similar definitions appear in Pseudo-Hermogenes, *Progymnasmata* 10.1 (1.202 Patillon CR = 22 Rabe) and Anonymous Seguerianus 96, 111.

12. Arist. *Rhet.* 3.10–11 1410b6–1413b2. Although Aristotle does not use the word *enargeia*, he does speak of *energeia*, a sense of "movement" or "actuality" created by language that contributes to a "bringing before the eyes." On this expression in another context of the *Rhetoric*, see chapter 1, pp. 30–31, and chapter 2, p. 59. Cf. Epicharmus, fr. 214 *PCG* = B 12 Diels-Kranz: "The mind sees and the mind hears; everything else is mute and blind." (νοῦς ὁρῇ καὶ νοῦς ἀκούει· τἆλλα κωφὰ καὶ τυφλά.)

13. E.g. Dionysius of Halicarnassus, *Lysias* 7 (ὑπὸ τὰς αἰσθήσεις, properly, "before the senses"); *Rhetoric for Herennius* 4.68–69 (*ante oculos*); Cicero, *On Invention* 1.104 (*ante oculos*), 2.78 (*ante oculos*); *On the Orator* 3.202 (*sub aspectum*); *Divisions of Oratory* 20 (*ante oculos*). For discussion of the passages from Cicero, see Innocenti 1994, 356–359.

14. The most convenient list of stylistic features associated with *enargeia* is in Lausberg 1998, 359–366 §810–819. Also see the discussions in Meijering 1987, 39–44; Nünlist 2009, 194–198; Bussels 2012, 77–80.

15. For a discussion of Dionysius' understanding of *enargeia*, see Berardi 2010, 180–185.

16. On Dionysius' tendency to describe reading as visual perception, see Wiater 2011, 81–83.

17. Dem. 21.72: οὐδεὶς ἄν, ὦ ἄνδρες Ἀθηναῖοι, ταῦτ' ἀπαγγέλλων δύναιτο τὸ δεινὸν παραστῆσαι τοῖς ἀκούουσιν οὕτως <u>ὡς ἐπὶ τῆς ἀληθείας καὶ τοῦ πράγματος τῷ πάσχοντι καὶ τοῖς ὁρῶσιν ἐναργὴς ἡ ὕβρις φαίνεται</u>.

18. Sophocles, *Antigone* 263. Cf. Sophocles, *Oedipus Tyrannos* 535, *Electra* 877–878.

19. Eden 1986, 72–73; Webb 2009, 89–90. See Meijering 1987, 52–53 for the argument that the concept originates in poetics rather than in rhetoric.

20. Dem. 6.19 (used with *idein*); 14.4; 17.20 (used with *horaō*); 18.300 (used with *skopeō*); 19.115 (used with *skopeō*, 263 (used with *horaō*); 21.115; 61.20; Isoc. 8.73 (used with *dēloō*), 11.37, 12.238, 15.243. Cf. Hesiod, *Melampodia* fr. 273 Merkelbach-West.

21. τῇ γὰρ ὀνομασίᾳ τῶν τόπων συμπαραθέουσα <u>ἡ διάνοια τῶν ἐντυγχανόντων ἐν φαντασίᾳ καὶ ὄψει τῶν τόπων γίνεται</u>. ἅμα οὖν τὸ ἀργὸν περιέφυγεν, οὐκ εὐθὺς ἀγαγὼν αὐτὴν ἐπὶ τὰ προκείμενα χωρία· μάρτυρας γοῦν ἐπαγόμενος τοὺς ἀκούοντας πιθανωτάτην καθίστησι τὴν διήγησιν. See Nünlist

2009, 185–193, for a discussion of "authentication" in the Homeric scholia with particular attention to this passage. Nünlist translates the phrase of the scholion that clearly refers to *enargeia*, ἐν φαντασίᾳ καὶ ὄψει τῶν τόπων γίνεται, as "enters into an imaginative and visual perception of the places."

22. Decof 2014, §1.09.6a. Cf. Burns 1999, 50–52; Hamlin 2008, 342–343.

23. Fontham 2013, 89–90.

24. Lubet 2006, 295–297.

25. McElhaney 1995, 74.

26. Quintilian, *Orator's Education* 6.2.26–36; Pseudo-Longinus, *On the Sublime* 15. Webb 2009, 93–100. Cf. Meijering 1987, 14–21; Lausberg 1998, 361 §811.

27. D. K. Cole 2001, 34.

28. E.g. Quintilian, *Orator's Education* 8.3.63–72; Demetrius, *On Style* 217. Meijering 1987, 39–42; Webb 2009, 90–93.

29. Nisbett and Ross 1980, 41–62; Reyes, Thompson, and Bower 1980; Bell and Loftus 1985, 1988, 1989; Shedler and Manis 1986, 26–31; M. G. Wilson, Northcraft, and Neale 1989; Bensi, Nori, Strazzari, and Giusberti 2003; Guadagno, Rhoads, and Sagarin 2011; Sevier 2011–2012, 317–337.

30. On the importance of verbs of sight in encouraging visualization in modern readers, see Esrock 1994, 183.

31. Aeschin. 3.153, 157, 244. In 186, Aeschines appeals to the imagination without using a verb of sight when he tells his jurors to "go in your mind to the Stoa Poikile" (προέλθετε δὴ τῇ διανοίᾳ καὶ εἰς τὴν στοὰν τὴν ποικίλην). On Aeschines' manipulation of his jurors' visual imaginations in *Against Ktesiphon*, see Hobden 2007. In *On Imitation* (epitome 5.5 = 39.23–25 Aujac), Dionysius of Halicarnassus even calls Aeschines "vivid" (*enargēs*).

32. *Rhetoric for Herennius* 4.51. Pseudo-Herodian, *De figuris* 47 Hajdú (= 8.603 Walz), says of Aeschin. 3.157 that Aeschines "made an ekphrasis of the passage" (ἐξέφρασε τὸν λόγον) by omitting conjunctions. On the sacked city as a literary motif, see Paul 1982. There is a stylistic analysis of fourth- and third-century BCE accounts of sacked cities in Agatharcides' *On the Erythraean Sea* (second century BCE). According to Photius' summary, Agatharchides believes the Attic orators offer better examples than the third-century Magnesian orator Hegesias of "how to lead the emotional experience [*pathos*] under the eyes [*hup(o) tēn opsin*] through *enargeia*" (πῶς τὸ πάθος ὑπὸ τὴν ὄψιν ἀγάγοι διὰ τῆς ἐναργείας). Agatharchides, fr. 21 *GGM* = Photius, *Bibliotheca* 445b38–447b5, quotation at 446b18–19.

33. Quintilian, *Orator's Education* 8.3.67–70.

34. Aeschin. 3.49: ὅτι διατελεῖ λέγων καὶ πράττων τὰ ἄριστα τῷ δήμῳ.

35. On Thebes' destruction, see Diodorus Siculus 17.8.3–14; Arrian, *Anabasis* 1.7–8; Plutarch, *Alexander* 11.9–12, *Demosthenes* 23.1–2; Justin 11.3.6–4.8. Worthington 2004, 42–47.

36. Aeschin. 3.156, 239–240. Cf. Dinarchus 1.18–21.

37. Worthington 2010.

38. Theophrastus, fr. 696 Fortenbaugh = Demetrius, *On Style* 222 with Fortenbaugh 2005, 310–316.

39. Descriptions and depictions of conquered cities and their inhabitants would have been familiar to an Athenian audience from an array of artistic media. The fall of Troy, for instance, was a favorite topic of vase paintings (e.g., Boston, Museum of Fine Arts 59.178) and tragedies (e.g., Euripides, *Andromache*, especially 103–116, and *Trojan Women*, especially 474–499), as well as a prominent part of the Epic Cycle (*Ilioupersis*, especially paragraphs 2–4 of Proclus' summary). There are detailed images of the vase available at the MFA website, and a black and white image accompanies a discussion of the Kassandra scene at Connelly 1993, 111 fig. 45. On the jurors' individual contributions to their mental images, see Webb's analysis of Quintilian, *Orator's Education* 8.3.64–65 (2009, 107–110).

40. Cf. Webb 2009, 152–153. Aelius Theon (2.62.21–63.15 Spengel = 5–6 Patillon) even implies (probably wrongly) that Aeschines used Demosthenes as a model. Cf. Pseudo-Hermogenes, *On the Method of Forceful Speaking* 33 (5.85–86 Patillon CR = 450–451 Rabe). Webb 2009, 114–115.

41. Dem. 19.8, 30. On this so-called "Peace of Philokrates," see E. M. Harris 1995, 63–77; MacDowell 2000, 1–14; Efstathiou 2004.

42. Dem. 19.19–24, 34–63. For Aeschines' account of these promises, see Aeschin. 2.119–120.

43. Dem. 19.53–54, 59–61, 325. On Philip's role in the end of the Third Sacred War, see Buckler 1989, 137–142; Worthington 2008, 99–103.

44. Dem. 19.27–28. See L. Pearson 1976, 158–163, for an overview of Demosthenes' narrative, and Frazier 1994 on the relationship between the arrangement of the speech and Demosthenes' argument. The scholia to Hermogenes, *On Issues* (7.374.9–29 Walz) states that the argument is an example of the *sunkataskeuazomenos stokhasmos*, "co-confirmatory conjecture," since the false promises leading to the destruction of Phokis seem to confirm Aeschines' bribe-taking and since Aeschines' bribe-taking seems to confirm that he made false promises about Phokis. See Heath 1995, 99–100.

45. Dem. 19.64.

46. Dem. 19.66. For shame (*anaiskhuntia*) as a characteristic of Aeschines, see Dem. 19.72 with L. Pearson 1976, 163.

47. Dem. 19.61–64. Diodorus Siculus 16.60.1–3 seems to preserve the decree of the Amphiktions.

48. The different aspects of *idein* and *horan*, which I have not attempted to capture in my translation, reflect that Demosthenes' sight of the Phokians' sufferings was an ongoing process of perception, lasting throughout his time in Phokis, while the jurors' come to know in a single act of realization through Demosthenes' argument.

49. Dem. 19.64: ἢ προεστάναι τῶν Ἑλλήνων πάτριον καὶ μηδὲν τοιοῦτον περιορᾶν γιγνόμενον.

50. Schol. to Dem. 19.64, 65 (156b, 157c, 160 Dilts). On *diatupōsis* in Demos-

thenes, see Blass 1887–1898, 3.180. Cf. also the analysis of Dem. 21.72 in Pseudo-Longinus, *On the Sublime* 20.1.

51. Webb 1997, 115–116; 2009, 51–52 with n. 51. The term is related to Aristotle's concept of memory as images left as imprints (*tupoi*) on the mind (*On Memory* 450a30–32).

52. Schol. to Dem. 19.64 (156b Dilts): ἐξ αὐτοῦ <δὲ> τοῦ εἴδους καὶ τοῦ τρόπου τοῦ πάθους ὑπ᾽ ὄψιν ἄγει τῷ λόγῳ τὰς συμφοράς. Cf. Schol. to Dem. 19.65 (157c Dilts): "The rhetorical figure *diatupōsis*: whenever you are like someone making a replica and bringing the events to sight through words." (διατύπωσις τὸ σχῆμα, ὅταν ὥσπερ διατυποῖ καὶ εἰς ὄψιν ἄγῃ τὰ πράγματα διὰ τῶν λόγων.)

53. Cf. Schol. to Dem. 19.65 (160 Dilts), which glosses the phrase "houses razed to the ground" by noting that, "he has turned to the forms [*ta eidē*]" (μεταβέβηκεν ἐπὶ τὰ εἴδη).

54. Schol. to Dem. 19.64 (156b Dilts): βούλεται δὲ ἡ διατύπωσις τὰ καθ᾽ ἕκαστον περιεργάζεσθαι.

55. Schol. to Dem. 19.65 (160 Dilts): τὰ γὰρ καθ᾽ ἕκαστον ἐμψυχότερον τὸν λόγον ἐργάζεται καὶ χαίρει τούτῳ ἡ διατύπωσις.

56. Schol. to Dem. 19.65 (157c Dilts): "*Diatupōsis* differs from *ekphrasis* in that *diatupōsis* says something through *pathos* while *ekphrasis* is just like a narrative." (διαφέρει δὲ ἡ διατύπωσις τῆς ἐκφράσεως τῷ τὴν μὲν διατύπωσιν διὰ πάθος τι λέγεσθαι, τὴν δὲ ἔκφρασιν ὥσπερ διήγημά τι εἶναι.)

57. Schol. to Dem. 19.65 (161 Dilts): "'walls stripped away': Through the houses he has increased grief, and through the walls he has increased fear." (τείχη περιῃρημένα] διὰ μὲν τῶν οἰκιῶν τὸν γόον ηὔξησε, διὰ δὲ τῶν τειχῶν τὸν φόβον.)

58. Schol. to Dem. 19.65 (162 Dilts): "'A country bereft of men in their prime': The *pathos* is twofold. For here there are both fear and pity together. 'Who were taken away?' 'The men who were in their prime.' He turns the *pathos* away from inanimate things towards animate things." (χώραν ἔρημον τῶν ἐν ἡλικίᾳ] διπλοῦν τὸ πάθος· ἐνταῦθα γὰρ ὁμοῦ καὶ φόβος καὶ ἔλεος. 'τίνες γὰρ οἱ ἀνῃρημένοι;' 'οἱ ἄνδρες οἱ ἐπὶ τῆς ἡλικίας.' ἀπὸ δὲ τῶν ἀψύχων μεθίστησι τὸ πάθος ἐπὶ τὰ ἔμψυχα.)

59. Schol. to Dem. 19.64 (156b Dilts): προοιμίῳ κέχρηται γόον καὶ θρῆνον ἐμποιοῦντι τοῖς ἀκούουσι· ταλαιπώρους γὰρ ὀνομάσας τὴν τύχην ὠδύρατο.

60. Schol. to Dem. 19.65 (160 Dilts): τῶν οἰκιῶν, φησί, κατεσκαμμένων ἀπολώλασι καὶ οἱ ἔνοικοι. ἔχει δὲ καὶ τῆς ὕβρεως τῶν πολεμίων ἔμφασιν· ἡ γὰρ κατασκαφὴ περιεργότερον εἶδος τῆς συμφορᾶς.

61. Schol. to Dem. 19.64 (153a Dilts): "So that he may not give a speech that lacks armor, and also so that the *polis*' danger—once it is added on—may make the *pathos* more serious, he exaggerates just like someone in a tragedy, mixing in the fear consequent upon the things that are going on." (ἵνα δὲ μὴ ψιλὸν ποιήσηται τὸν λόγον, ὥσπερ ἐν τραγῳδίᾳ δεινολογούμενος παραμίγνυσι καὶ τὸν ἐκ τῶν πραγμάτων παρεπόμενον φόβον, ἵνα καὶ ὁ τῆς πόλεως κίνδυνος προστεθεὶς

χαλεπώτερον τὸ πάθος ἐργάσηται.) Schol. to Dem. 19.65 (157a Dilts): "He begins from fears, so that what has happened already may be an image and an example of what is going to happen and so that they may not only mourn the Phokians but may also be afraid on behalf of the other Greeks." (ἀπὸ τῶν φόβων δὲ ἄρχεται, ἵνα εἰκὼν καὶ παράδειγμα γένηται τὸ γεγονὸς τοῦ μέλλοντος καὶ μὴ μόνον ὀδύρωνται Φωκέας, ἀλλὰ καὶ ὑπὲρ τῶν ἄλλων Ἑλλήνων δεδίωσι.)

62. Webb 2009, 146–154. For an introduction to Sopatros and his work, see Maggiorini 2012, 9–62, and, more briefly, Kennedy 1983, 104–109.

63. Webb 2009, 148.

64. Lycurgus 1.14–19, 21–27, 58. On the speech and Lycurgus' rhetorical strategy, see Allen 2000b. On the Battle of Chaeronea, see Ma 2008, 73–76, which refers to earlier scholarship.

65. E. M. Harris 2001, 159 n. 1.

66. Lycurgus 1.42: τοσαύτῃ δ᾽ ἡ πόλις ἐκέχρητο μεταβολῇ.

67. Although the frequent assertions in Athenian literature that respectable women should never leave their homes nor be seen by males (e.g., Euripides, *Trojan Women* 647–650; Lys. 3.6) are exaggerations (Cohen 1989, 7–9; 1991, 150–154, 164–166), they nonetheless reflect an idealized view of women's place in society. For the prostitute and ritual participant as unique among women in Classical Athens because they are "visible in the public sphere," see Gilhuly 2009, 1–2 with n. 2.

68. Lape 2010, 274–277, argues that Lycurgus considers this proposal the "real tragedy" of Chaeronea.

69. Lycurgus 1.44: οὐδεὶς δ᾽ ἦν ἀργὸς τῶν ἐν τῇ πόλει.

70. Aeschin. 3.252. For Demosthenes' defeat in the embassy trial and Aeschines' defeat in the crown trial, see Plutarch, *Demosthenes* 15.5, 24.2–3; Pseudo-Plutarch, *Lives of the Ten Orators* 840c.

71. Pseudo-Plutarch, *Lives of the Ten Orators* 840d–e.

CHAPTER 6

1. I borrow the term from D. S. Levene's (1997, 140) work on Tacitus. Despite its ultimate derivation from *audio* ("to hear"), "audience" can refer both to spectators and to listeners (*Oxford English Dictionary*, "audience" II.7-5). I prefer it to "internal observer," although that would be a suitable description of the woman in this passage, because later in this chapter I discuss internal audiences who listen as well as look.

2. Schol. to Dem. 22.53 (145 Dilts): 'ἀπὸ τῶν ῥημάτων ἐξηπάτησάς με,' φήσειεν ἂν ἡ γυνή, 'ὡς ἐλεύθερος συνήφθης, νῦν δὲ ἀπεδείχθης ἀνδράποδον· πολίτην ᾤμην ἔχειν καὶ Ἀθηναῖον ἐκάλουν τὸν ἄνδρα, ἐλάνθανον δέ, ὡς ἔοικεν, οἰκέτην δυστυχήσασα σύνοικον.'

3. Schol. to Dem. 22.53 (144 Dilts): ἵνα γὰρ μή τις εἴπῃ, 'ἀλλ᾽ οὐδεὶς ἑώρα

ταῦτα ποιοῦντα, καὶ τὸ δεινὸν ἔλαττον ἦν,' ὅρα πῶς οἴκοθεν αὐτῷ προσπορίζει τὸν μάρτυρα, πικρότατον ἔλεγχον ἀπὸ τῆς γυναικὸς ἐξευρών.

4. *Akroatēs* in Plutarch generally means "reader" and not "hearer." See the entry in LSJ. On *akouō* meaning "read," see Schenkeveld 1992.

5. Plutarch, *Whether the Athenians Were More Famous when It Came to War or when It Came to Wisdom* 3 347b. The text is corrupt, but it is clear that Plutarch is quoting and paraphrasing Thucydides 7.71.1–3.

6. On sight in Thucydides, see, besides Walker 1993, Greenwood 2006, 19–41, especially 38–40, on the Sicilian expedition and the battle in the Syracuse harbor. Hornblower 2004, 342–346, argues that Thucydides uses spectatorship at athletic competitions as his model for spectatorship at the sea battle.

7. Thucydides 7.71.2–3.

8. Walker 1993, 360–363, 369–370 (quote at 360). Gribble (2006, 454) argues that the "'individual's-eye view' of human events is a crucial element of that empathetic 'understanding' of human events which Thucydides' work aims to provide." On Tacitus' use of an "internal audience" to Vitellius' downfall whose viewpoint the reader comes to share, see Levene 1997, 140.

9. Thucydides 7.71.4: πάντα ὁμοῦ ἀκοῦσαι.

10. Thucydides 7.71.5: παραπλήσια δὲ καὶ οἱ ἐπὶ τῶν νεῶν αὐτοῖς ἔπασχον.

11. Thucydides 7.71.5: πολλῇ κραυγῇ καὶ διακελευσμῷ χρώμενοι.

12. There is secure evidence for public readings of historiography in the Hellenistic and imperial periods, but not for fifth- and fourth-century Athens (Momigliano 1980, 362–368). For arguments in favor of oral readings of Thucydides' text to small groups of people (not necessarily by Thucydides himself), see Thomas 1992, 103–104; 2003, 163; Morrison 2007, 220–221. Cf. Kelly 1996. Even someone studying the text alone is likely to have read it aloud. See Greenwood 2006, 16.

13. On the date and authenticity of the Lysianic funeral oration, see Todd 2007a, 157–164.

14. Lys. 2.34, 39, 40, 42.

15. Thucydides 7.71 is probably the model for this part of Lys. 2. Todd 2007a, 242–243 with nn. 49 and 50.

16. Lys. 2.34: τὸ ναυτικὸν τὸ τῶν βαρβάρων, ὃ τίς οὐκ ἂν ἰδὼν ἐφοβήθη.

17. Levene (1997, 142) notes that "the reader is implicitly included" among the observers of Vitellius' attempted abdication in Tacitus 3.68.1 through a similar combination of an indefinite pronoun and reference to sight: *nec quisquam adeo rerum humanarum immemor quem non commoveret illa facies* ("No one could be so thoughtless of human affairs that that appearance would not move him"). Tacitus goes on to say of the spectators, *nihil tale viderant, nihil audierant* ("They had never seen such a thing, nor had they heard it").

18. Lys. 2.35: ποίαν δὲ γνώμην εἶχον ἢ οἱ θεώμενοι τοὺς ἐν ταῖς ναυσὶν ἐκείναις, οὔσης καὶ τῆς αὐτῶν σωτηρίας ἀπίστου καὶ τοσούτου προσιόντος κινδύνου.

19. Lys. 2.35–37.
20. Lys. 2.37: εἰδότες μὲν τὰς σφετέρας ναῦς ὀλίγας οὔσας, ὁρῶντες δὲ πολλὰς τὰς τῶν πολεμίων.
21. Lys. 2.38: ἀκούοντες δ᾽ ἐν ταὐτῷ συμμεμειγμένου Ἑλληνικοῦ καὶ βαρβαρικοῦ παιῶνος, παρακελευσμοῦ δ᾽ ἀμφοτέρων καὶ κραυγῆς τῶν διαφθειρομένων.
22. Lys. 2.39: ἦ που διὰ τὸν παρόντα φόβον πολλὰ μὲν ᾠήθησαν ἰδεῖν ὧν οὐκ εἶδον, πολλὰ δ᾽ ἀκοῦσαι ὧν οὐκ ἤκουσαν. This is presumably a reference to the supernatural events that Herodotus (8.84.2, 94.2–3) reports about the battle of Salamis. Todd 2007a, 243 with n. 51.
23. De Bakker 2012, quotes at 395 and 411.
24. What survives of the speech is quoted by Dionysius of Halicarnassus, *Lysias* 23–27 as an example of Lysias' virtues as a forensic orator. On its date and authenticity, see Carey 1989, 204–208.
25. Lys. 32.4–7; Dionysius of Halicarnassus, *Lysias* 21. On Thrasyllos' campaign in Ephesus, see Xenophon, *Hellenica* 1.2.6–13.
26. The suit was probably a *dikē epitropēs* (Rubinstein 2000, 28), on which see Harrison 1968–1971, 1.119–121; Becker 1968.
27. Lys. 32.2. On possible reasons why the brothers asked their brother-in-law to serve as their *sunēgoros*, see Rubinstein 2000, 68; Todd 1993, 205. On narrative technique in this speech, see Edwards 2007.
28. Cf. Davies 1971, 153, with Carey 1989, 206.
29. Lys. 32.12–17. For a discussion of the technical aspects of direct speech in Lysias, see Bers 1997, 182–186.
30. Cf. Gagarin 2001, 167: "Lysias has given her a forensic voice, because she is, in fact, speaking not to her son-in-law but to the jurors."
31. Gagarin 2001, 165–167. Cf. the detailed analysis of Diogeiton's daughter's speech at Buis 2005, 199–207.
32. Buis 2005, 208–210. Walters 1993, 198–200, proposes that Diogeiton's daughter is actually the guiding force behind the attempt to recover money from her father.
33. Gagarin 2001, 165–167, and Foxhall 1996, 149, consider the speech a fabrication.
34. Thucydides 1.22.1 with Rusten 1989, 11–14. Cf. Buis 2005, 210.
35. Bers 1997, 186 with n. 107.
36. Fr. 2 in Todd 2000.
37. Dionysius of Halicarnassus, *Demosthenes* 11. The speech cannot be dated. For general discussion see Cohen 1995, 137–138; Todd 2000, 347–351.
38. Spatharas (2006, 49–51) theorizes that the original quarrel involved Arkhippos insulting Teisis for being the willing love slave of his own guardian. Cf. N. Fisher 2001, 197.
39. On the festival, see Parker 2005, 457.
40. Lys. fr. 279 Carey 1–4.

41. The term *deigma* regularly means "sample" in mercantile contexts (Casanova 1995, 29–30), and in Athens the term was extended to the place where the samples were shown (Pollux, *Onomasticon* 9.34; Schol. to Aristophanes, *Knights* 979). There are other Classical references to the *deigma* in Xenophon, *Hellenica* 5.1.21 and Dem. 35.29, 50.24.

42. Cf., e.g., Lys. 28.17, 30.23–24.

43. Lys. fr. 278 Carey = Anonymous Seguerianus 7. There is no doubt that this is the first sentence of the speech, since Anonymous Seguerianus cites the first words of Dem. 54, 21, 51 and Isoc. 14 in the same paragraph as examples of other ways to begin speeches.

44. The manuscripts have τίς rather than Τεῖσις, which is almost certainly a scribal error. See Carey's apparatus. Even if *tis* is correct, *eme* and *toutoni* are sufficient to keep the jurors' attention focused on the people in the court while they hear about the events in Teisis' house.

45. See p. 47.

46. I base this terminology on Bakker 2005, 156.

47. Bühler 1990, 94–95.

48. Fillmore (1997, 62) calls this gestural deixis. "By the *gestural* use of a deictic expression, I mean that use by which it can be properly interpreted only by somebody who is monitoring some physical aspect of the communication situation."

49. For an extreme example of the ambiguity of deictic pronouns outside their performance context, see *Accusation against the Members of a Society for Defamation* (Lys. 8) with the attempt at an explication in Todd 2007a, 544–545.

50. Bühler 1990, 137–157. Cf. Fillmore 1997, 62–63, on "symbolic" deixis.

51. Bühler 1990, 152–154. Virgil, *Aeneid* 2.29–30, which Lausberg (1998, 365 §815) adduces as an example of "adverbs of place (and pronominal stems) which express presence," is a good example of *Deixis am Phantasma*. The deictic adverbs allow Aeneas' audience and the readers of the poem to picture for themselves the deserted places of the Greek camp as though Aeneas is really pointing them out. Cf. Nünlist 2009, 196, on the role of deictic pronouns in achieving *enargeia*.

52. See, for instance, Latacz 1985; Vamvouri Ruffy 2004; the essays collected in Felson 2004; Bakker 2005, 154–176; De Jong 2012. Bonifazi 2014 and Felson and Klein 2014 are encyclopedia articles with bibliographies that cite literature through 2014.

53. The fullest contemporary account is Thucydides 6.27–29, 53, 60. Besides the references cited in the following notes, see the detailed discussion in Gomme, Andrewes, and Dover 1970, 264–288.

54. See Todd 2007a, 403–408, esp. 403–404 n. 19 for a discussion of authorship and authenticity, with references.

55. Andoc. 1.29, 31, 32.

56. Although MacDowell 1962, 167–180, argues that Andocides admitted involvement in the affair of the Mysteries and not the affair of the herms, and that he cleverly conceals this in his speech, most modern scholars have concluded that An-

docides' own version is substantially true (Marr 1971; Hansen 1975, 81 nn. 16 and 21; Furley 1996, 52–57; Todd 2004, 90). Pelling 2000, 34–37, explains the dangers inherent in attempting reconstructions of what Andocides actually did in the affairs of the herms and Mysteries.

57. But note the phrase "sight [*opsei*] of the *gnōmē*" (τῇ τῆς γνώμης ὄψει) in Hippocrates, *On the Art* 11.2 with Mann 2012, 195–196.

58. Dem. 20.118, 23.96, 39.40–41, 57.63; Arist. *Politics* 3.1287a26. See Mirhady 2007 for a discussion of the oath, with special reference to this phrase. Mirhady translates the relevant section of the oath as, "I will vote . . . concerning matters about which there are no laws by the most just understanding" (*gnomei tei dikaiotatei*). Whether Mirhady is right that "concerning matters about which there are no laws" was not part of the oath is immaterial to my argument.

59. Mirhady 2007, 53–59. A good example is Dem. 52.2.

60. The terminology of experiencing is from Arist. fr. 963 Gigon. See Burkert 1987, 69.

61. Scholars continue to debate the relationship of the myth of the *Hymn* to the ritual of the Mysteries. Sourvinou-Inwood (2003, 30), maintains that the myth forms the basis for a sacred drama performed during the Mysteries, whereas Clinton (1992, 35–36), argues that "the core episodes of the *Hymn to Demeter* do not reflect the cult myth of the Mysteries but are *aitia* of the Thesmophoria and similar festivals of women." Parker (1991, 4–17), argues that the *Hymn*, although it tells a Panhellenic myth, is closely related to the Mysteries ritual. Even Clinton (1992, 36–37), acknowledges that the end of the *Hymn* is clearly about the Mysteries.

62. For textual issues, see Richardson 1974, whose text I print.

63. Cf. Richardson 1974, 302.

64. Cf. Burkert 1987, 21.

65. Isoc. 4.28.

66. Sophocles, fr. 837 *TrGF*; Pindar, fr. 137 Snell-Maehler.

67. Euripides, *Herakles* 613: τὰ μυστῶν δ' ὄργι' εὐτύχησ' ἰδών.

68. Cf. Hesykhios, *hierophantēs*: ὁ τὰ μυστήρια δεικνύων.

69. See Clinton 2003, 57, 60, for a discussion of the tense and aspect of the verbs used to describe the stages of initiation.

70. Chantraine 1999, 728–729: *muō*. But cf. Burkert 1987, 136–137 n. 36: "The connection with *myo*, 'to shut one's eyes or lips,' may be just popular etymology."

71. Clinton 2003, 50, notes that "evidence from other mystery cults shows that it was the practice for an initiate to be blinded."

72. Clinton 2003, 50, 60.

73. Burkert 1983, 275 with n. 3.

74. Cf. *Palatine Anthology* 11.42; *IG* II² 3661 = *IE* 641; Orphic testimonium 713 T 4 Bernabé = *P. Mil. Vogl.* I 20.18–32.

75. The key references are Apollodoros (244), fr. 110b *FGrH*; Plutarch, *On Progress in Virtue* 81e; *IG* II² 3764.3–4 (ca. 217/218 CE); *IG* II² 3811.1–2 (after 250 CE). Cf. Burkert 1983, 276 with n. 8, 286–287 with n. 57; Parker 2005, 351–352.

76. Hippolytus, *Refutation of all Heresies* 5.8.40.

77. Parker 2005, 351–352, is instructive on the issue of how many people could have seen the central revelation and whether this mattered.

78. Hippolytus, *Refutation of All Heresies* 5.8.39. Cf. Burkert 1983, 290–291 with n. 77; 1987, 80–81; Parker 2005, 357–360; Sourvinou-Inwood 2003, 35–37.

79. *Homeric Hymn to Demeter* 470–482; Isoc. 4.28.

80. Richardson (1974, 302–303) and Mylonas (1961, 273–274) believe there were cult objects. Burkert (1983, 287 with n. 63, following Kerényi 1967, 111) denies the existence of a statue because one is not mentioned in the texts relating to the profanation, but surely Alkibiades and the other participants could have used something in its place. Cf. Parker 2005, 353 n. 112.

81. At one extreme, dance steps are attested in multiple literary and iconographic sources: Burkert 1983, 288 with nn. 65 and 66; Parker 2005, 353 with n. 113. At the other extreme, an apparent sacred marriage between the hierophant and the "priestess" appears in Asterios, *Homily* 10.9.1: Burkert 1983, 284–286; Parker 2005, 356–357.

82. Cf. Burkert 1987, 93 with 163 n. 18.

83. For a discussion of the *stolē* that Andocides is said to be wearing, see Clinton 1974, 32–35.

84. See Burkert 1983, 287 n. 63.

85. The seriousness of seeing by the uninitiated is also evident in Andromakhos' charges in Andoc. 1.12.

86. Lys. 6.55: εἴδετε, ἠκούσατε τὰ τούτου ἁμαρτήματα.

87. In the last two Oxford pages of the speech, the speaker uses the combination of *horaō/eidon* and *akouō* three times (Lys. 6.50, 54, 55); *horaō/eidon* and *akouō* are combined, with or without *kai*, only one other time in the Lysianic corpus, at the end of *Against Eratosthenes* (Lys. 12), on which see introduction p. 12. As well as emphasizing the ritual implications of seeing, the speaker may also have been exploiting the two concepts as a polar expression (Kemmer 1903, 245–246) using the faculties of sight and hearing to emphasize that the audience knows about Andocides' crimes in every possible way.

88. Andoc. 1.31 (ἑοράκατε τοῖν θεοῖν τὰ ἱερά), 32 (ὑπέρ τε τῶν ἱερῶν ἃ εἴδετε).

89. Andoc. 1.33 with MacDowell 1962, 86.

90. Andoc. 1.146–147.

91. Andoc. 1.147. On the politics of Andocides and his ancestors, see MacDowell, 1962, 1–2; Missiou 1992, 15–54.

92. Andoc. 1.147: οἰκία δὲ πασῶν ἀρχαιοτάτη καὶ κοινοτάτη ἀεὶ τῷ δεομένῳ.

93. Andoc. 1.149: ὑμεῖς τοίνυν καὶ ἀντὶ πατρὸς ἐμοὶ καὶ ἀντὶ ἀδελφῶν καὶ ἀντὶ παίδων γένεσθε.

94. Andoc. 1.149.

95. Andoc. 1.149: τοὺς δὲ ὄντας πολίτας ὁμολογουμένως, οἷς προσήκει ἀνδράσιν ἀγαθοῖς εἶναι καὶ βουλόμενοι δυνήσονται.

96. Plutarch, *Theseus* 35.5; Pausanias 1.15.3, 32.5.
97. Cf. Andoc. 1.142, which describes the Athenians who fought in the Persian Wars as the source of freedom for all Greece.
98. Andoc. 1.150: οἵτινες ὑμῖν ἀρετῆς ἤδη τῆς μεγίστης εἰς τὸ πλῆθος τὸ ὑμέτερον ἔλεγχον ἔδοσαν.
99. Johnston 1999, 28–29.
100. Ant. 4.2.8 with Gagarin 1997, 167: "The idea that the defendant can direct the dead man's revenge is novel."
101. For an overview of the social and ritual context of Attic curse tablets and their relationship to the courts, see Riess 2012, 164–234.
102. Pl. *Laws* 11 927b: τὰς τῶν κεκμηκότων ψυχάς, αἷς ἐστιν ἐν τῇ φύσει τῶν αὑτῶν ἐκγόνων κήδεσθαι διαφερόντως καὶ τιμῶσίν τε αὐτοὺς εὐμενεῖς εἶναι καὶ ἀτιμάζουσιν δυσμενεῖς.
103. Andoc. 1.146. MacDowell 1962, 163; Edwards 1995, 188.

CONCLUSION

1. Dem. 18.300: τίνες αἱ τούτων ἀποδείξεις; ἐναργεῖς καὶ φανεραί. σκοπεῖτε δέ.
2. Dem. 18.172–173: ὁ γὰρ μὴ ταῦτ᾽ εἰδὼς μηδ᾽ ἐξητακὼς πόρρωθεν ἐπιμελῶς, οὔτ᾽ εἰ εὔνους ἦν οὔτ᾽ εἰ πλούσιος, οὐδὲν μᾶλλον ἤμελλεν ὅ τι χρὴ ποιεῖν εἴσεσθαι οὐδ᾽ ὑμῖν ἕξειν συμβουλεύειν. ἐφάνην τοίνυν οὗτος ἐν ἐκείνῃ τῇ ἡμέρᾳ ἐγὼ καὶ παρελθὼν εἶπον εἰς ὑμᾶς. On the epiphanic language in this section, see Slater 1988.
3. Dem. 18.180: τότε τοίνυν κατ᾽ ἐκεῖνον τὸν καιρὸν ὁ Παιανιεὺς ἐγὼ Βάτταλος Οἰνομάου τοῦ Κοθωκίδου σοῦ πλείονος ἄξιος ὢν ἐφάνην τῇ πατρίδι. On the meaning of "Battalos" and the joke behind calling Aeschines the "Oinomaos of Kothokidai" ("pairing the heroic with the ordinary"), see Yunis 2001, 211–212.
4. Aeschin. 3.255–258.
5. Lys. 31.12. See chapter 1, pp. 38–39.
6. *Odyssey* 16.470; Sophocles, *Women of Trachis* 889; Hippocrates, *Fleshes* 614.
7. Blanshard 2014, 268.

BIBLIOGRAPHY

Allen, D. S. 2000a. *The World of Prometheus: The Politics of Punishing in Democratic Athens*. Princeton: Princeton University Press.

Allen, D. S. 2000b. "Changing the Authoritative Voice: Lycurgus' *Against Leocrates*." *Classical Antiquity* 19: 5–33.

Allen, D. S. 2010. *Why Plato Wrote*. Malden, MA: Wiley-Blackwell.

Almog, S., and E. Aharonson. 2004. "Law as Film: Representing Justice in the Age of Moving Images." *Canadian Journal of Law and Technology* 3: 1–18.

Amsterdam, A. G., and J. Bruner. 2000. *Minding the Law*. Cambridge, MA: Harvard University Press.

Amsterdam, A. G., and R. Hertz. 1992. "An Analysis of Closing Arguments to a Jury." *New York Law School Law Review* 37: 55–122.

Austin, J. L. 1975. *How to Do Things with Words*. 2nd edition. Edited by J. O. Urmson and M. Sbisà. Cambridge, MA: Harvard University Press.

Bain, D. 1982. "Another Menandrean Summoning of Witnesses." *Zeitschrift für Papyrologie und Epigraphik* 49: 42.

Bakewell, G. 1999. "Lysias 12 and Lysias 31: Metics and Athenian Citizenship in the Aftermath of the Thirty." *Greek, Roman, and Byzantine Studies* 40: 5–22.

Bakker, E. J. 2005. *Pointing at the Past: From Formula to Performance in Homeric Poetics*. Washington, DC: Center for Hellenic Studies.

Bakker, E. J. 2010. "Pragmatics: Speech and Text." In *A Companion to the Ancient Greek Language*, edited by E. J. Bakker, 151–167. Malden, MA: Wiley-Blackwell.

Balkin, J. M. 2011. *Constitutional Redemption: Political Faith in an Unjust World*. Cambridge, MA: Harvard University Press.

Balkin, J. M., and S. Levinson. 1999. "Interpreting Law and Music: Performance Notes on 'The Banjo Serenader' and 'The Lying Crowd of Jews.'" *Cardozo Law Review* 20: 1513–1572.

Ball, D. 2003. *Theater Tips and Strategies for Jury Trials*. 3rd edition. Louisville, CO: National Institute for Trial Advocacy.

Barker, A. 2004. "Transforming the Nightingale: Aspects of Athenian Musical Discourse in the Late Fifth Century." In *Music and the Muses: The Culture of*

'Mousikē' in the Classical Athenian City, edited by P. Murray and P. Wilson, 185–204. Oxford: Oxford University Press.

Bartsch, S. 2000. "The Philosopher as Narcissus: Vision, Sexuality, and Self-knowledge in Classical Antiquity." In *Visuality Before and Beyond the Renaissance: Seeing as Others Saw*, edited by R. S. Nelson, 70–97. Cambridge: Cambridge University Press.

Bauman, R. 1977. *Verbal Art as Performance*. Rowley, MA: Newbury House Publishers.

Becker, D. 1968. "Die attische δίκη ἐπιτροπῆς." *Zeitschrift der Savigny-Stiftung Für Rechtsgeschichte—Romanistische Abteilung* 98: 30–93.

Beekes, R. 2010. *Etymological Dictionary of Greek*. With the assistance of L. van Beek. 2 volumes continuously paginated. Leiden: E. J. Brill.

Bell, B. E., and E. F. Loftus. 1985. "Vivid Persuasion in the Courtroom." *Journal of Personality Assessment* 49: 659–664.

Bell, B. E., and E. F. Loftus. 1988. "Degree of Detail of Eyewitness Testimony and Mock Juror Judgments." *Journal of Applied Social Psychology* 18: 1171–1192.

Bell, B. E., and E. F. Loftus. 1989. "Trivial Persuasion in the Courtroom: The Power of (a Few) Minor Details." *Journal of Personality and Social Psychology* 56: 669–679.

Bensi, L., R. Nori, E. Strazzari, and F. Giusberti. 2003. "Vividness in Judgements of Guilt." *Perceptual and Motor Skills* 97: 1133–1136.

Benveniste, E. 1973. *Indo-European Language and Society*. Translated by E. Palmer. Coral Gables, FL: University of Miami Press.

Berardi, F. 2010. "La teoria dello stile in Dionigi di Alicarnasso: Il caso dell' *enargeia*." In *Les noms du style dans l'antiquité gréco-latine*, edited by P. Chiron and C. Lévy, 179–200. Louvain: Éditions Peeters.

Berardi, F. 2012. *La dottrina dell' evidenza nella tradizione retorica greca e latina*. Perugia: Editrice "Pliniana."

Bernabé, A., and A. I. Jiménez San Cristóbal. 2011. "Are the 'Orphic' Gold Leaves Orphic?" In *The "Orphic" Gold Tablets and Greek Religion: Further Along the Path*, edited by R. G. Edmunds III, 68–101. Cambridge: Cambridge University Press.

Bers, V. 1994. "Tragedy and Rhetoric." In *Persuasion: Greek Rhetoric in Action*, edited by I. Worthington, 176–195. London: Routledge.

Bers, V. 1997. *Speech in Speech: Studies in Incorporated* Oratio Recta *in Attic Drama and Oratory*. Lanham, MD: Rowman & Littlefield.

Bers, V. 2009. *Genos Dikanikon: Amateur and Professional Speech in the Courtrooms of Classical Athens*. Washington, DC: Center for Hellenic Studies.

Bers, V. 2011. Review of *The Greeks and Their Past: Poetry, Oratory, and History in the Fifth Century BCE*, by J. Grethlein, Cambridge: Cambridge University Press, 2010. *American Journal of Philology* 132: 674–677.

Bers, V. 2013. "Performing the Speech in Athenian Courts and Assembly: Adjusting the Act to Fit the *Bēma*?" In *Profession and Performance: Aspects of Oratory in the Greco-Roman World*, edited by C. Kremmydas, J. Powell, and L. Rubinstein, 27–40. London: Institute of Classical Studies.

Blanshard, A. 2014. "The Permeable Space of the Athenian Law-court." In *Space, Place, and Landscape in Ancient Greek Literature and Culture*, edited by K. Gilhuly and N. Worman, 240–275. Cambridge: Cambridge University Press.

Blass, F. 1887–1898. *Die attische Beredsamkeit*. 3rd edition. 3 volumes. Leipzig: B. G. Teubner.

Boegehold, A. L. 1995. *The Lawcourts at Athens: Sites, Buildings, Equipment, Procedure, and Testimonia*. Princeton: The American School of Classical Studies at Athens.

Boegehold, A. L. 1999. *When a Gesture Was Expected: A Selection of Examples from Archaic and Classical Greek Literature*. Princeton: Princeton University Press.

Boegehold, A. L., and M. Crosby. 1995. "Testimonia." In *The Lawcourts at Athens: Sites, Buildings, Equipment, Procedure, and Testimonia*, by A. L. Boegehold, 117–241. Princeton: The American School of Classical Studies at Athens.

Bonifazi, A. 2014. "Deixis (Including 1st and 2nd Person)." In *Encyclopedia of Ancient Greek Language and Linguistics*, edited by G. K. Giannakis, volume 1, 422–429. Leiden: E. J. Brill.

Bourdieu, P. 1977. *Outline of a Theory of Practice*. Translated by R. Nice. Cambridge: Cambridge University Press.

Boyle, K. 2004. *Arc of Justice: A Saga of Race, Civil Rights, and Murder in the Jazz Age*. New York: Henry Holt and Company.

Buchheim, T. 1989. *Gorgias von Leontinoi: Reden, Fragmente und Testimonien*. Hamburg: Felix Meiner.

Buckler, J. 1989. *Philip II and the Sacred War*. Leiden: E. J. Brill.

Bühler, K. 1990. *Theory of Language*. Translated by D. F. Goodwin. Amsterdam: John Benjamins.

Buis, E. J. 2005. "El caso de la viuda de Diódoto, o una poética de la ausencia: Retórica judicial y enunciación femenina en Lys., 32.12–17." *Les Études Classiques* 73: 193–215.

Burkert, W. 1983. *Homo Necans: The Anthropology of Ancient Greek Sacrificial Ritual and Myth*. Translated by P. Bing. Berkeley: University of California Press.

Burkert, W. 1987. *Ancient Mystery Cults*. Cambridge, MA: Harvard University Press.

Burns, R. P. 1999. *A Theory of the Trial*. Princeton: Princeton University Press.

Burnyeat, M. F. 1999. "Culture and Society in Plato's Republic." *The Tanner Lectures on Human Values* 20: 217–324.

Bussels, S. 2012. *The Animated Image: Roman Theory on Naturalism, Vividness, and Divine Power*. Berlin: Akademie Verlag.

Butler, J. 1988. "Performative Acts and Gender Constitution: An Essay in Phenomenology and Feminist Theory." *Theatre Journal* 40: 519–531.

Butler, S., and A. Purves, eds. 2013. *Synaesthesia and the Ancient Senses*. Durham: Acumen.

Calame, C. 1991. "Quand dire c'est faire voir: L'évidence dans la rhétorique antique." *Études de Lettres* 4: 3–22.

Calame, C. 2001. *Choruses of Young Women in Ancient Greece: Their Morphology, Religious Role, and Social Functions*. New and revised edition. Translated by D. Collins and J. Orion. Lanham, MD: Rowman and Littlefield.

Canevaro, M. 2013. *The Documents in the Attic Orators: Laws and Decrees in the Public Speeches of the Demosthenic Corpus*. Oxford: Oxford University Press.

Carawan, E. 1983. "*Erotesis*: Interrogation in the Courts of Fourth-Century Athens." *Greek, Roman, and Byzantine Studies* 24: 209–226.

Carawan, E. 1990. "Trial of Exiled Homicides and the Court at Phreatto." *Revue internationale des droits de l'antiquité*. 37: 47–67.

Carawan, E. 1991. "ΕΦΕΤΑΙ and Athenian Courts for Homicide in the Age of the Orators." *Classical Philology* 86: 1–16.

Carey, C. 1989. *Lysias: Selected Speeches*. Cambridge: Cambridge University Press.

Carey, C. 1990. "Structure and Strategy in Lysias XXIV." *Greece & Rome* 37: 44–51.

Carey, C. 1994. "Legal Space in Classical Athens." *Greece & Rome* 41: 172–186.

Carey, C., and R. A. Reid. 1985. *Demosthenes: Selected Private Speeches*. Cambridge: Cambridge University Press.

Casanova, G. 1995. "ΔΕΙΓΜΑ: Testimonianze del vocabolo, con un papiro inedito." *Aegyptus* 75: 27–36.

Cassin, B. 1995. *L'effet sophistique*. Paris: Gallimard.

Catalano, J. S. 1974. *A Commentary on Jean-Paul Sartre's* Being and Nothingness. New York: Harper & Row.

Catoni, M. L. 2008. *La communicazione non verbale nella Grecia antica: Gli* schemata *nella danza, nell'arte, nella vita*. 2nd edition. Torino: Bollati Boringhieri.

Catrein, C. 2003. *Vertauschte Sinne: Untersuchungen zur Synästhesie in der römischen Dichtung*. Munich: K. G. Saur.

Chantraine, P. 1999. *Dictionnaire étymologique de la langue grecque: Histoire des mots*. New edition with a supplement by A. Blanc, C. de Lamberterie, and J.-L. Perpillou. Paris: Klincksieck.

Chiron, P. 2002. *Pseudo-Aristote: Rhétorique à Alexandre*. Paris: Les Belles Lettres.

Cioffi, R. L. 2014. "Seeing Gods: Epiphany and Narrative in the Greek Novels." *Ancient Narrative* 11: 1–42.

Clason, S. S. 2010. *Forensic Rhetoric: The Force of Closing Arguments*. El Paso: LFB Scholarly Publishing.

Clinton, K. 1974. *The Sacred Officials of the Eleusinian Mysteries*. Philadelphia: American Philosophical Society.

Clinton, K. 1992. *Myth and Cult: The Iconography of the Eleusinian Mysteries*. Stockholm: Swedish Institute at Athens.

Clinton, K. 2003. "Stages of Initiation in the Eleusinian and Samothracian Mysteries." In *Greek Mysteries: The Archaeology and Ritual of Ancient Greek Secret Cults*, edited by M. B. Cosmopoulos, 50–78. London: Routledge.

Cohen, D. 1989. "Seclusion, Separation, and the Status of Women in Classical Athens." *Greece & Rome* 36: 3–15.
Cohen, D. 1991. *Law, Sexuality, and Society: The Enforcement of Morals in Classical Athens*. Cambridge: Cambridge University Press.
Cohen, D. 1995. *Law, Violence, and Community in Classical Athens*. Cambridge: Cambridge University Press.
Cole, D. K. 2001. "Psychodrama and the Training of Trial Lawyers: Finding the Story." *Northern Illinois University Law Review* 21: 1–40.
Cole, T. 2007. "Who Was Corax?" In *Oxford Readings in the Attic Orators*, edited by E. Carawan, 37–59. Oxford: Oxford University Press.
Connelly, J. B. 1993. "Narrative and Image in Attic Vase Painting: Ajax and Kassandra at the Trojan Palladion." In *Narrative and Event in Ancient Art*, edited by P. J. Holliday, 88–129. Cambridge: Cambridge University Press.
Cooper, C. 1995. "Hyperides and the Trial of Phryne." *Phoenix* 49: 303–318.
Cooper, C. 2004. "Demosthenes Actor on the Political and Forensic Stage." In *Oral Performance and its Context*, edited by C. J. Mackie, 145–161. Leiden: E. J. Brill.
Cooper, G. L., III. 1998. *Attic Greek Prose Syntax*. 2 volumes continuously paginated. Ann Arbor: University of Michigan Press.
Corbeill, A. 2004. *Nature Embodied: Gesture in Ancient Rome*. Princeton: Princeton University Press.
Craik, E. M. 1999. "Mantitheus of Lysias 16: Neither Long-haired nor Simple-minded." *Classical Quarterly* 49: 626–629.
Crawford, R. J., and C. A. Morris. 2011. *The Persuasive Edge*. 2nd edition. Tucson: Lawyers & Judges Publishing Company.
Crichton, A. 1991–1993. "'The Old Are in a Second Childhood': Age Reversal and Jury Service in Aristophanes' *Wasps*." *Bulletin of the Institute of Classical Studies* 38: 59–79.
Csapo, E. 2002. "Kallippides on the Floor-Sweepings: The Limits of Realism in Classical Acting and Performance Styles." In *Greek and Roman Actors: Aspects of an Ancient Profession*, edited by P. Easterling and E. Hall, 127–147. Cambridge: Cambridge University Press.
Csapo, E. 2007. "The Men Who Built the Theatres: *Theatropolai*, *Theatronai*, and *Arkhitektones*." In *The Greek Theatre and Festivals: Documentary Studies*, edited by P. Wilson, 87–121. Oxford: Oxford University Press.
Cutler, B. L., and S. D. Penrod. 1995. *Mistaken Identification: The Eyewitness, Psychology, and the Law*. Cambridge: Cambridge University Press.
Davies, J. K. 1971. *Athenian Propertied Families 600–300 B.C.* Oxford: Clarendon Press.
De Bakker, M. P. 2012. "Demosthenes." In *Space in Ancient Greek Literature*, edited by I. J. F. de Jong, 393–412. Leiden: E. J. Brill.
De Jong, I. J. F. 2012. "Double Deixis in Homeric Speech: On the Interpretation of ὅδε and οὗτος." In *Homer, gedeutet durch ein großes Lexikon: Akten des Hamburger*

Kolloquiums vom 6.–8. Oktober 2010 zum Abschluss des Lexikons des frühgriechischen Epos, edited by M. Meier-Brügger, 63–83. Berlin: Walter De Gruyter.

Decof, L. 2014. *Art of Advocacy: Opening Statement*. Matthew Bender and Co.

Demont, P. 1993. "Die *Epideixis* über die *Techne* im v. und iv. Jh." In *Vermittlung und Tradierung von Wissen in der griechischen Kultur*, edited by W. Kullmann and J. Althoff, 181–209. Tübingen: Gunter Narr Verlag.

Denoyelle, M. 2010. "Comedy Vases from Magna Graecia." In *The Art of Ancient Greek Theater*, by M. L. Hart, et al., 105–111. Los Angeles: Getty Museum.

Denyer, N. 1991. *Language, Thought, and Falsehood in Ancient Greek Philosophy*. Routledge: London.

Dickey, E. 2007. *Ancient Greek Scholarship*. Oxford: Oxford University Press.

Diggle, J. 2004. *Theophrastus: Characters*. Cambridge: Cambridge University Press.

Dillon, M. P. J. 1995. "Payments to the Disabled at Athens: Social Justice or Fear of Aristocratic Patronage?" *Ancient Society* 26: 27–57.

Dobree, P. P. 1831. *Adversaria, Tomus Prior*. Edited by J. Scholefield. Cambridge: Cambridge University Press (typis ac sumptibus academicis excudit J. Smith).

Dodds, E. R. 1951. *The Greeks and the Irrational*. Berkeley: University of California Press.

Dover, K. J. 1968. *Lysias and the* Corpus Lysiacum. Berkeley: University of California Press.

Dover, K. J. 1974. *Greek Popular Morality in the Time of Plato and Aristotle*. Oxford: Basil Blackwell.

Dover, K. J. 1997. *The Evolution of Greek Prose Style*. Oxford: Clarendon Press.

Dozier, C. 2013. "Blinded by the Light: Oratorical Clarity and Poetic Obscurity in Quintilian." In *Synaesthesia and the Ancient Senses*, edited by S. Butler and A. Purves, 141–153. Durham: Acumen.

Duncan, A. 2006. *Performance and Identity in the Classical World*. Cambridge: Cambridge University Press.

Dunn, M. A., P. Salovey, and N. Feigenson. 2006. "The Jury Persuaded (and Not): Computer Animation in the Courtroom." *Law and Policy* 28: 228–248.

Easterling, P. 1999. "Actors and Voices: Reading between the Lines in Aeschines and Demosthenes." In *Performance Culture and Athenian Democracy*, edited by S. Goldhill and R. Osborne, 154–166. Cambridge: Cambridge University Press.

Eden, K. 1986. *Poetic and Legal Fiction in the Aristotelian Tradition*. Princeton: Princeton University Press.

Edwards, M. J. 1995. *Greek Orators IV: Andocides*. Warminster: Aris & Phillips.

Edwards, M. J. 2007. "Lysias." In *Time in Ancient Greek Literature*, edited by I. J. F. de Jong and R. Nünlist, 329–336. Leiden: E. J. Brill.

Edwards, M. J. 2013. "*Hypokritēs* in Action: Delivery in Greek Rhetoric." In *Profession and Performance: Aspects of Oratory in the Greco-Roman World*, edited by C. Kremmydas, J. Powell, and L. Rubinstein, 15–25. London: Institute of Classical Studies.

Edwards, M. J., and S. Usher. 1985. *Greek Orators I: Antiphon and Lysias.* Warminster: Aris & Phillips.
Efstathiou, A. 2004. "The 'Peace of Philokrates': The Assemblies of 18th and 19th Elaphebolion 346 B.C.: Studying History through Rhetoric." *Historia* 53: 385–407.
Emlyn-Jones, C., and W. Preddy. 2013. *Plato: Republic.* 2 volumes. Cambridge, MA: Harvard University Press.
Enfield, N. J. 2009. *The Anatomy of Meaning: Speech, Gesture, and Composite Utterances.* Cambridge: Cambridge University Press.
Esrock, E. J. 1994. *The Reader's Eye: Visual Imaging as Reader Response.* Baltimore: Johns Hopkins University Press.
Eucken, C. 1997. "Der schwache und der starke Logos des Antisthenes." *Hyperboreus* 3: 251–273.
Fantham, E. 1982. "Quintilian on Performance: Traditional and Personal Elements in *Institutio* 11.3." *Phoenix* 36: 243–263.
Fantham, E. 2004. *The Roman World of Cicero's De Oratore.* Oxford: Oxford University Press.
Faraone, C. A. 1999. "Curses and Social Control in the Law Courts of Classical Athens." *Dike* 2: 99–121.
Farenga, V. 1979. "Periphrasis on the Origin of Rhetoric." *MLN* 94: 1033–1055.
Farenga, V. 2006. *Citizen and Self in Ancient Greece: Individuals Performing Justice and the Law.* Cambridge: Cambridge University Press.
Felson, N., ed. 2004. *The Poetics of Deixis in Alcman, Pindar, and Other Lyric. Arethusa* 37.3.
Felson, N., and J. Klein. 2014. "Deixis in Linguistics and Poetics." In *Encyclopedia of Ancient Greek Language and Linguistics*, edited by G. K. Giannakis, Volume 1, 429–433. Leiden: E. J. Brill.
Ferrari, G. R. F. 1989. "Plato and Poetry." In *The Cambridge History of Literary Criticism Volume 1: Classical Criticism*, edited by G. A. Kennedy, 92–148. Cambridge: Cambridge University Press.
Ferrucci, S. 2005. "La ricchezza nascosta: Osservazioni su ἀφανὴς e φανερὰ οὐσία." *Mediterraneo Antico* 8: 145–169.
Feyel, C. 2009. Δοκιμασία: *La place et le rôle de l'examen préliminaire dans les institutions des cités grecques.* Nancy: Association pour la diffusion de la recherche sur l'antiquité.
Fillmore, C. J. 1997. *Lectures on Deixis.* Stanford: Stanford University Press.
Fischer-Lichte, E. 2010. "Performance as Event—Reception as Transformation." In *Theorising Performance: Greek Drama, Cultural History, and Critical Practice*, edited by E. Hall and S. Harrop, 10–28. London: Duckworth.
Fisher, N. 2001. *Aeschines: Against Timarchus.* Oxford: Oxford University Press.
Fisher, R. P., S. J. Ross, and B. S. Cahill. 2010. "Interviewing Witnesses and Victims." In *Forensic Psychology in Context: Nordic and International Approaches*, edited by P. A. Granhag, 56–74. Cullompton, UK: Willan Publishing.

Fögen, T. 2009. "*Sermo corporis*: Ancient Reflections on *gestus*, *vultus*, and *vox*." In *Bodies and Boundaries in Greco-Roman Antiquity*, edited by T. Fögen and M. M. Lee, 15–43. Berlin: Walter de Gruyter.

Fontham, M. R. 2013. *Trial Technique and Evidence*. 4th edition. Boulder, CO: National Institute for Trial Advocacy.

Fontham, M. R., and M. Vitiello. 2013. *Persuasive Written and Oral Advocacy in Trial and Appellate Courts*. 3rd edition. New York: Wolters Kluwer.

Ford, A. 1999. "Reading Homer from the Rostrum: Poems and Laws in Aeschines' *Against Timarchus*." In *Performance Culture and Athenian Democracy*, edited by S. Goldhill and R. Osborne, 231–256. Cambridge: Cambridge University Press.

Fortenbaugh, W. W. 1985. "Theophrastus on Delivery." In *Theophrastus of Eresus: On His Life and Works*, edited by W. W. Fortenbaugh, P. M. Huby, and A. A. Long, 269–288. New Brunswick, NJ: Transaction Books.

Fortenbaugh, W. W. 2005. *Theophrastus of Eresus: Sources for His Life, Writings, Thought, and Influence. Commentary Volume 8: Sources on Rhetoric and Poetics*. Leiden: E. J. Brill.

Foxhall, L. 1996. "The Law and the Lady: Women and Legal Proceedings in Classical Athens." In *Greek Law in Its Political Setting: Justifications not Justice*, edited by L. Foxhall and A. D. E. Lewis, 133–152. Oxford: Clarendon Press.

Frankfurter, F. 1927. *The Case of Sacco and Vanzetti: A Critical Analysis for Lawyers and Laymen*. Boston: Little, Brown and Company.

Frazier, 1994. "À propos de la *dispositio* du *Sur l'ambassade infidèle*: Stratégie rhétorique et analyse politique chez Démosthène." *Revue des Études Grecques* 107: 414–439.

Fredal, J. 1998. *Beyond the Fifth Canon: Body Rhetoric in Ancient Greece*. Unpublished dissertation, The Ohio State University.

Fredal, J. 2001. "The Language of Delivery and the Presentation of Character: Rhetorical Action in Demosthenes' *Against Meidias*." *Rhetoric Review* 20: 251–267.

Fredal, J. 2006. *Rhetorical Action in Ancient Athens: Persuasive Artistry from Solon to Demosthenes*. Carbondale: Southern Illinois University Press.

Frontisi-Ducroux, F. 1996. "Eros, Desire, and the Gaze." Translated by N. Kline. In *Sexuality in Ancient Art: Near East, Egypt, Greece, and Italy*, edited by N. B. Kampen, 81–100. Cambridge: Cambridge University Press.

Furley, W. D. 1996. *Andokides and the Herms: A Study of Crisis in Fifth-century Athenian Religion*. London: Institute of Classical Studies.

Gabrielsen, V. 1986. "φανερά and ἀφανὴς οὐσία in Classical Athens." *Classica et Mediaevalia* 37: 99–114.

Gagarin, M. 1997. *Antiphon: The Speeches*. Cambridge: Cambridge University Press.

Gagarin, M. 1999. "The Orality of Greek Oratory." In *Signs of Orality: The Oral Tradition and its Influence in the Greek and Roman World*, edited by E. A. Mackay, 163–180. Leiden: E. J. Brill.

Gagarin, M. 2001. "Women's Voices in Attic Oratory." In *Making Silence Speak:*

Women's Voices in Greek Literature and Society, edited by A. Lardinois and L. McClure, 161–176. Princeton: Princeton University Press.

Gagarin, M. 2002a. *Antiphon the Athenian: Oratory, Law, and Justice in the Age of the Sophists*. Austin: University of Texas Press.

Gagarin, M. 2002b. "Protagoras' New Fragment: Thirty Years Later." In *Noctes Atticae: 34 Articles on Greco-Roman Antiquity and Its Nachleben: Studies Presented to Jørgen Mejer on His Sixtieth Birthday March 18, 2002*, edited by B. Amden, P. Flensted-Jensen, T. H. Nielsen, A. Schwartz, and C. G. Tortzen, 114–120. Copenhagen: Museum Tusculanum Press.

Gaines, R. N. 2007. "Roman Rhetorical Handbooks." In *A Companion to Roman Rhetoric*, edited by W. Dominik and J. Hall, 163–180. Malden, MA: Blackwell.

Garland, R. 1995. *The Eye of the Beholder: Deformity and Disability in the Graeco-Roman World*. London: Duckworth.

Garvie, A. F. 1986. *Aeschylus: Choephori*. Oxford: Clarendon Press.

Gera, D. L. 2003. *Ancient Greek Ideas on Speech, Language, and Civilization*. Oxford: Oxford University Press.

Ghiggia, P. C. 2002. *Iseo: Contro Leocare 'sulla successione di Diceogene.'* Pisa: ETS.

Gilhuly, K. 2009. *The Feminine Matrix of Sex and Gender in Classical Athens*. Cambridge: Cambridge University Press.

Goldhill, S. 1996. "Refracting Classical Vision: Changing Cultures of Viewing." In *Vision in Context: Historical and Contemporary Perspectives on Sight*, edited by T. Brennan and M. Jay, 17–28. New York: Routledge.

Goldhill, S. 1998. "The Seductions of the Gaze: Socrates and his Girlfriends." In *Kosmos: Essays in Order, Conflict, and Community in Classical Athens*, edited by P. Cartledge, P. Millett, and S. von Reden, 105–124. Cambridge: Cambridge University Press.

Goldhill, S. 1999. "Programme Notes." In *Performance Culture and Athenian Democracy*, edited by S. Goldhill and R. Osborne, 1–29. Cambridge: Cambridge University Press.

Goldhill, S. 2000. "Placing Theatre in the History of Vision." In *Word and Image in Ancient Greece*, edited by N. K. Rutter and B. A. Sparks, 161–179. Edinburgh: Edinburgh University Press.

Goldin-Meadow, S. 2007. "Gesture with Speech and Without It." In *Gesture and the Dynamic Dimension of Language: Essays in Honor of David McNeill*, edited by S. D. Duncan, J. Cassell, and E. T. Levy, 31–49. Amsterdam: John Benjamins.

Gomme, A. W., A. Andrewes, and K. J. Dover. 1970. *A Historical Commentary on Thucydides, Volume 4*. Oxford: Clarendon Press.

Gomme, A. W., A. Andrewes, and K. J. Dover. 1981. *A Historical Commentary on Thucydides, Volume 5*. Oxford: Clarendon Press.

Graham, D. W. 2004. "Was Anaxagoras a Reductionist?" *Ancient Philosophy* 24: 1–18.

Green, R. 2002. "Towards a Reconstruction of Performance Style." In *Greek and*

Roman Actors: Aspects of an Ancient Profession, edited by P. Easterling and E. Hall, 93–126. Cambridge: Cambridge University Press.

Greenwood, E. 2006. *Thucydides and the Shaping of History*. London: Duckworth.

Gribble, D. 2006. "Individuals in Thucydides." In *Brill's Companion to Thucydides*, edited by A. Rengakos and A. Tsakmakis, 439–468. Leiden: E. J. Brill.

Guadagno, R. E., K. v. L. Rhoads, and B. J. Sagarin. 2011. "Figural Vividness and Persuasion: Capturing the 'Elusive' Vividness Effect." *Personality and Social Psychology Bulletin* 37: 626–638.

Gunderson, E. 2000. *Staging Masculinity: The Rhetoric of Performance in the Roman World*. Ann Arbor: University of Michigan Press.

Habinek, T. 2005. *The World of Roman Song: From Ritualized Speech to Social Order*. Baltimore: Johns Hopkins University Press.

Hall, E. 2006. *The Theatrical Cast of Athens: Interactions between Ancient Greek Drama and Society*. Oxford: Oxford University Press.

Hall, J. 2004. "Cicero and Quintilian on the Oratorical Use of Hand Gestures." *Classical Quarterly* 54: 143–160.

Halliwell, S. 1995. *Aristotle: Poetics*. In *Aristotle: Poetics, Longinus: On the Sublime, Demetrius: On Style*, translated by S. Halliwell, W. H. Fyfe, D. C. Innes, and W. R. Roberts; revised by D. A. Russell. Cambridge, MA: Harvard University Press.

Halliwell, S. 2002. *The Aesthetics of Mimesis: Ancient Texts and Modern Problems*. Princeton: Princeton University Press.

Halperin, D. 1986. "Plato and Erotic Reciprocity." *Classical Antiquity* 5: 60–80.

Hamaker, H. G. 1843. *Quaestiones de nonnullis Lysiae orationibus*. Leiden: H. W. Hazenberg.

Hamlin, S. 2008. *Now What Makes Juries Listen*. Thomson/West.

Handrich, R. 2011. "Simple Jury Persuasion: Stand up Straight and Avoid Gesturing with Your Hands in front of the Jury." Keene Trial Consulting: *The Jury Room* blog, February 4, 2011. http://keenetrial.com/blog/2011/02/04/simple-jury-persuasion-stand-up-straight.

Hansen, M. H. 1975. *Eisangelia: The Sovereignty of the People's Court in Athens in the Fourth Century B.C. and the Impeachment of Generals and Politicians*. Odense: Odense University Press.

Hansen, M. H. 1976. Apagoge, Endeixis, *and* Ephegesis *against* Kakourgoi, Atimoi, *and* Pheugontes: *A Study in the Athenian Administration of Justice in the Fourth Century B.C*. Odense: Odense University Press.

Hansen, M. H. 1979. "How Often Did the Athenian *Dicasteria* Meet?" *Greek, Roman, and Byzantine Studies* 20: 243–246.

Hansen, M. H. 1989. *The Athenian Ecclesia II: A Collection of Articles 1983–1989*, by M. H. Hansen. Copenhagen: Museum Tusculanum Press.

Hansen, M. H. 1991a. "Response to Douglas MacDowell." In *Symposion 1990: Vorträge zur griechischen und hellenistischen Rechtsgeschichte*, edited by M. Gagarin, 199–201. Cologne: Böhlau.

Hansen, M. H. 1991b. *The Athenian Democracy in the Age of Demosthenes: Structures, Principles, and Ideology.* Translated by J. A. Crook. Oxford: Basil Blackwell.

Hansen, M. H., and L. Pedersen. 1990. "The Size of the Council of the Areopagos and Its Social Composition in the Fourth Century B.C." *Classica et Mediaevalia* 41: 73–78.

Harris, E. M. 1989. "Demosthenes' Speech Against Meidias." *Harvard Studies in Classical Philology* 92: 117–136.

Harris, E. M. 1995. *Aeschines and Athenian Politics.* Oxford: Oxford University Press.

Harris, E. M. 2001. "Lycurgus." In *Dinarchus, Hyperides, and Lycurgus,* edited by I. Worthington, C. R. Cooper, and E. M. Harris, 153–218. Austin: University of Texas Press.

Harris, E. M. 2006. *Democracy and the Rule of Law in Classical Athens.* Cambridge: Cambridge University Press.

Harris, E. M. 2008. *Demosthenes, Speeches 20–22.* Austin: University of Texas Press.

Harris, E. M. 2013. *The Rule of Law in Action in Democratic Athens.* Oxford: Oxford University Press.

Harris, W. V. 1997. "Lysias III and Athenian Beliefs about Revenge." *Classical Quarterly* 47: 363–366.

Harrison, A. R. W. 1968–1971. *The Law of Athens.* 2 volumes. Oxford: Clarendon Press.

Haydock, R., and J. Sonsteng. 2011. *Trial Advocacy before Judges, Jurors, and Arbitrators.* 4th edition. St. Paul, MN: West.

Hays, A. G. 1937. *Let Freedom Ring.* Revised edition. New York: Liveright Publishing Corporation.

Heath, M. 1995. *Hermogenes On Issues: Strategies of Argument in Later Greek Rhetoric.* Oxford: Clarendon Press.

Heath, M. 2004. *Menander: A Rhetor in Context.* Oxford: Oxford University Press.

Henderson, Jeffrey. 1987. *Aristophanes: Lysistrata.* Oxford: Clarendon Press.

Henderson, John. 2009. "The Runaround: A Volume Retrospect on Ancient Rhetorics." In *The Cambridge Companion to Ancient Rhetoric,* edited by E. Gunderson, 278–290. Cambridge: Cambridge University Press.

Hendren, T. G. 2015. "Meidias Tyrannos: Meidias' Tyrannical Attributes in Demosthenes 21." *Illinois Classical Studies* 40: 21–43.

Henrichs, A. 1994. "Anonymity and Polarity: Unknown Gods and Nameless Altars at the Areopagos." *Illinois Classical Studies* 19: 27–58.

Hesk, J. 1999. "The Rhetoric of Anti-rhetoric in Athenian Oratory." In *Performance Culture and Athenian Democracy,* edited by S. Goldhill and R. Osborne, 201–230. Cambridge: Cambridge University Press.

Hibbitts, B. J. 1994. "Making Sense of Metaphors: Visuality, Aurality, and the Reconfiguration of American Legal Discourse." *Cardozo Law Review* 16: 229–356.

Hobden, F. 2007. "Imagining Past and Present: A Rhetorical Strategy in Aeschines 3, *Against Ctesiphon.*" *Classical Quarterly* 57: 490–501.

Hornblower, S. 2004. *Thucydides and Pindar: Historical Narrative and the World of Epinikian Poetry.* Oxford: Oxford University Press.

Hughes, A. 2012. *Performing Greek Comedy.* Cambridge: Cambridge University Press.

Humphreys, S. 2007. "Social Relations on Stage: Witnesses in Classical Athens." In *Oxford Readings in the Attic Orators,* edited by E. Carawan, 140–213. Oxford: Oxford University Press.

Ierodiakonou, K. 2011. "The Notion of Enargeia in Hellenistic Philosophy." In *Episteme, etc.: Essays in Honour of Jonathan Barnes,* edited by B. Morison and K. Ierodiakonou. Oxford: Oxford University Press.

Innocenti, B. 1994. "Towards a Theory of Vivid Description as Practiced in Cicero's Verrine Orations." *Rhetorica* 12: 355–381.

Isaac, B. 2004. *The Invention of Racism in Classical Antiquity.* Princeton: Princeton University Press.

Jay, M. 1993. *Downcast Eyes: The Denigration of Vision in Twentieth-century French Thought.* Berkeley: University of California Press.

Johnston, S. I. 1999. *Restless Dead: Encounters between the Living and the Dead in Ancient Greece.* Berkeley: University of California Press.

Johnstone, C. L. 1996. "Greek Oratorical Settings and the Problem of the Pnyx: Rethinking the Athenian Political Process." In *Theory, Text, Context: Issues in Greek Rhetoric and Oratory,* edited by C. L. Johnstone, 97–127. Albany: State University of New York Press.

Johnstone, C. L. 2001. "Communicating in Classical Contexts: The Centrality of Delivery." *Quarterly Journal of Speech* 87: 121–143.

Johnstone, S. 1999. *Disputes and Democracy: The Consequences of Litigation in Ancient Athens.* Austin: University of Texas Press.

Johnstone, S. 2005. "Women, Property, and Surveillance in Classical Athens." *Classical Antiquity* 22: 247–274.

Jones, N. F. 2008. *Politics and Society in Ancient Greece.* Westport, CT: Praeger.

Jouanna, J. 1999. *Hippocrates.* Translated by M. B. DeBevoise. Baltimore: Johns Hopkins University Press.

Jouanna, J. 2012. "Rhetoric and Medicine in the Hippocratic Corpus: A Contribution to the History of Rhetoric in the Fifth Century." In *Greek Medicine from Hippocrates to Galen: Selected Papers by Jacques Jouanna,* translated by N. Allies and edited by P. van der Eijk, 39–53. Leiden: E. J. Brill.

Kamen, D. 2013. *Status in Classical Athens.* Princeton: Princeton University Press.

Kapparis, K. A. 1999. *Apollodoros "Against Neaira" [D. 59].* Berlin: Walter de Gruyter.

Kassel, R. 1976. *Aristotelis Ars rhetorica.* Berlin: Walter de Gruyter.

Katsouris, A. 1989. *Rhētorikē Hypokrisē.* Iōannina: Philosophikē Scholē Panepistēmiou Iōanninōn.

Kelly, D. 1996. "Oral Xenophon." In *Voice into Text: Orality and Literacy in Ancient Greece,* edited by I. Worthington, 149–163. Leiden: E. J. Brill.

Kemmer, E. 1903. *Die polare Ausdrucksweise in der griechischen Literatur.* Würzburg: A. Stuber's Verlag.
Kendon, A. 2004. *Gesture: Visible Action as Utterance.* Cambridge: Cambridge University Press.
Kennedy, G. A. 1983. *Greek Rhetoric under Christian Emperors.* Princeton: Princeton University Press.
Kennedy, G. A. 2007. *Aristotle On Rhetoric: A Theory of Civic Discourse.* 2nd edition. New York: Oxford University Press.
Kerényi, C. 1967. *Eleusis: Archetypal Image of Mother and Daughter.* New York: Bollingen Foundation.
Konstan, D. 2003. "Shame in Ancient Greece." *Social Research* 70: 1031–1060.
Lakoff, G., and M. Johnson. 1980. *Metaphors We Live By.* Chicago: University of Chicago Press.
Lampinen, J. M., J. S. Neuschatz, and A. D. Cling. 2014. *The Psychology of Eyewitness Identification.* New York: Psychology Press.
Lanni, A. M. 1997. "Spectator Sport or Serious Politics? οἱ περιεστηκότες and the Athenian Lawcourts." *Journal of Hellenic Studies* 107: 183–189.
Lanni, A. 2006. *Law and Justice in the Courts of Classical Athens.* Cambridge: Cambridge University Press.
Lape, S. 2006. "The Psychology of Prostitution in Aeschines' Speech against Timarchus." In *Prostitutes and Courtesans in the Ancient World*, edited by C. A. Faraone and L. McClure, 139–160. Madison: University of Wisconsin Press.
Lape, S. 2010. *Race and Citizen Identity in the Classical Athenian Democracy.* Cambridge: Cambridge University Press.
Latacz, J. 1985. "Realität und Imagination: Eine neue Lyrik-Theorie und Sapphos φαίνεταί μοι κῆνος-Lied." *Museum Helveticum* 42: 67–94.
Lateiner, D. 2009. "Tears and Crying in Hellenic Historiography: Dacryology from Herodotus to Polybius." In *Tears in the Graeco-Roman World*, edited by T. Fögen, 105–134. Berlin: Walter de Gruyter.
Lausberg, H. 1998. *Handbook of Literary Rhetoric: A Foundation for Literary Study.* Edited by D. E. Orton and R. D. Anderson. Translated by M. T. Bliss. Foreword by G. A. Kennedy. Leiden: E. J. Brill.
Lear, G. R. 2012. "Mimesis and Psychological Change in *Republic* III." In *Plato and the Poets*, edited by P. Destrée and F.-G. Herrmann, 195–216. Leiden: E. J. Brill.
Levene, D. S. 1997. "Pity, Fear, and the Historical Audience: Tacitus on the Fall of Vitellius." In *The Passions in Roman Thought and Literature*, edited by S. M. Braund and C. Gill, 128–149. Cambridge: Cambridge University Press.
Lipsius, J. H. 1905–1915. *Das attische Recht und Rechtsverfahren.* 3 volumes continuously paginated. Leipzig: O. R. Reisland.
Lloyd, G. E. R. 1991. *Methods and Problems in Greek Science*, Cambridge: Cambridge University Press.

Lloyd, G. E. R. 1996. *Adversaries and Authorities: Investigations into Ancient Greek and Chinese Science*. Cambridge: Cambridge University Press.

Loftus, E. F. 1996. *Eyewitness Testimony*. With a new preface by the author. Cambridge, MA: Harvard University Press.

Loftus, E. F., J. M. Doyle, and J. E. Dysart. 2013. *Eyewitness Testimony: Civil and Criminal*. 5th edition. New Providence, NJ: LexisNexis.

Lombardo, G. 2013. "Aspetto verbale e tecniche dell'enargeia: La dimensione <<aoristica>> della descrizione." In *Ekphrasis*, edited by S. Marino and A. Stavru, 23–34. Rome: Aracne.

Loraux, N. 1986. *The Invention of Athens: The Funeral Oration in the Classical City*. Translated by A. Sheridan. Cambridge, MA: Harvard University Press.

Lord, A. B. 2000. *The Singer of Tales*. 2nd edition. Edited by S. Mitchell and G. Nagy. Cambridge, MA: Harvard University Press.

Lossau, M. J. 1964. *Untersuchungen zur antiken Demosthenesexegese*. Bad Homburg: H. M. Gehlen.

Lubet, S. 2006. "Trial Theory and Blind Poetics." *Northeastern University Law Review* 100: 295–302.

Ludwig, P. 2002. *Eros and Polis: Desire and Community in Greek Political Theory*. Cambridge: Cambridge University Press.

Ma, J. 2008. "Chaironeia 338: Topographies of Commemoration." *Journal of Hellenic Studies* 128: 72–91.

MacDowell, D. M. 1962. *Andokides: On the Mysteries*. Oxford: Clarendon Press.

MacDowell, D. M. 1963. *Athenian Homicide Law in the Age of the Orators*. Manchester: Manchester University Press.

MacDowell, D. M. 1978. *The Law in Classical Athens*. Ithaca, NY: Cornell University Press.

MacDowell, D. M. 1990. *Demosthenes: Against Meidias*. Oxford: Clarendon Press.

MacDowell, D. M. 1991. "The Athenian Procedure of *Phasis*." In *Symposion 1990: Vorträge zur griechischen und hellenistischen Rechtsgeschichte*, edited by M. Gagarin, 187–198. Cologne: Böhlau.

MacDowell, D. M. 2000. *Demosthenes: On the False Embassy (Oration 19)*. Oxford: Oxford University Press.

MacDowell, D. M. 2009. *Demosthenes the Orator*. Oxford: Oxford University Press.

Maggiorini, D. 2012. *Sopatro, Demostene e la corona di Alessandro (Diairesis zetematon, VIII.205.5–220.10 Walz)*. Alessandria: Edizioni dell'Orso.

Maidment, K. J. 1941. *Minor Attic Orators, Volume One: Antiphon and Andocides*. Cambridge, MA: Harvard University Press.

Maier-Eichhorn, U. 1989. *Die Gestikulation in Quintilians Rhetorik*. Frankfurt: Peter Lang.

Mann, J. E. 2012. *Hippocrates: On the Art of Medicine*. Leiden: E. J. Brill.

Mariss, R. 2002. *Alkidamas: Über diejenigen, die schriftliche Reden schreiben, oder über die Sophisten*. Münster: Aschendorff.

Markle, M. M. 1990. "Participation of Farmers in Athenian Juries and Assemblies." *Ancient Society* 22: 149–165.

Marr, J. L. 1971. "Andocides' Part in the Mysteries and Hermae Affairs 415 B.C." *Classical Quarterly* 21: 326–338.

Marr, J. L., and P. J. Rhodes. 2008. *The 'Old Oligarch': The Constitution of the Athenians Attributed to Xenophon*. Oxford: Aris & Phillips.

Martin, G. 2009. *Divine Talk: Religious Argumentation in Demosthenes*. Oxford: Oxford University Press.

Martin, R. P. 1989. *The Language of Heroes: Speech and Performance in the* Iliad. Ithaca, NY: Cornell University Press.

McCoskey, D. E. 2012. *Race: Antiquity and Its Legacy*. Oxford: Oxford University Press.

McElhaney, J. W. 1995. "Opening Statements: To Be Effective with the Jury, Tell a Good Story." *ABA Journal* 81.1: 73–74.

McNeill, D. 2005. *Gesture and Thought*. Chicago: University of Chicago Press.

Meijering, R. 1987. *Literary and Rhetorical Theories in Greek Scholia*. Groningen: E. Forster.

Michelakis, P. 2010. "Archiving Events, Performing Documents: On the Seductions and Challenges of Performance Archives." In *Theorising Performance: Greek Drama, Cultural History, and Critical Practice*, edited by E. Hall and S. Harrop, 95–107. London: Duckworth.

Mirhady, D. C. 2002. "Athens' Democratic Witnesses." *Phoenix* 56: 255–274.

Mirhady, D. C. 2004. "Forensic Evidence in Euripides' *Hippolytus*." *Mouseion* 4: 17–34.

Mirhady, D. C. 2007. "The Dikast's Oath and the Question of Fact." In *Horkos: The Oath in Greek Society*, edited by A. H. Sommerstein and J. Fletcher, 48–59. Exeter: Bristol Phoenix Press.

Mirhady, D. C., and C. Schwarz. 2011. "Dikastic Participation." *Classical Quarterly* 61: 744–748.

Missiou, A. 1992. *The Subversive Oratory of Andokides: Politics, Ideology, and Decision-Making in Democratic Athens*. Cambridge: Cambridge University Press.

Momigliano, A. 1980. *Sesto contributo alla storia degli studi classici e del mondo antico*. Volume 1. Rome: Edizioni di Storia e Letteratura.

Morrison, J. V. 2007. "Thucydides' *History* Live: Reception and Politics." In *Politics of Orality*, edited by C. Cooper, 217–233. Leiden: E. J. Brill.

Muir, J. V. 2001. *Alcidamas: The Works and Fragments*. London: Bristol Classical Press.

Mulvey, L. 2009. *Visual and Other Pleasures*. 2nd edition. Houndmills: Palgrave Macmillan.

Munteanu, D. L. 2012. *Tragic Pathos: Pity and Fear in Greek Philosophy and Tragedy*. Cambridge: Cambridge University Press.

Murray, P. 1996. *Plato: On Poetry*. Cambridge: Cambridge University Press.

Mylonas, G. E. 1961. *Eleusis and the Eleusinian Mysteries.* Princeton: Princeton University Press.
Nagy, G. 1990. *Pindar's Homer: The Lyric Possession of an Epic Past.* Baltimore: Johns Hopkins University Press.
Nagy, G. 1996a. *Homeric Questions.* Austin: University of Texas Press.
Nagy, G. 1996b. *Poetry as Performance: Homer and Beyond.* Cambridge: Cambridge University Press.
Naiden, F. S. 2006. *Ancient Supplication.* Oxford: Oxford University Press.
National Academy of Sciences. 2014. *Identifying the Culprit: Assessing Eyewitness Identification.* Washington, DC: National Academies Press.
Németh, G. 2001. "Metics in Athens." *Acta Antiqua Academiae Scientiarum Hungaricae* 41: 331–348.
Nervegna, S. 2007. "Staging Scenes or Plays? Theatrical Revivals of 'Old' Greek Drama in Antiquity." *Zeitschrift für Papyrologie und Epigraphik* 162: 14–42.
Nightingale, A. 2004. *Spectacles of Truth in Classical Greek Philosophy:* Theoria *in Its Cultural Context.* Cambridge: Cambridge University Press.
Nikolaev, A. 2012. "Showing Praise in Greek Choral Lyric and Beyond." *American Journal of Philology* 133: 543–572.
Nisbett, R., and L. Ross. 1980. *Human Inference: Strategies and Shortcomings of Social Judgment.* Englewood Cliffs, NJ: Prentice-Hall.
Nünlist, R. 2009. *The Ancient Critic at Work: Terms and Concepts of Literary Criticism in Greek Scholia.* Cambridge: Cambridge University Press.
Ober, J. 1989. *Mass and Elite in Democratic Athens: Rhetoric, Ideology, and the Power of the People.* Princeton: Princeton University Press.
Ober, J. 1996. *The Athenian Revolution: Essays on Ancient Greek Democracy and Political Theory.* Princeton: Princeton University Press.
Ober, J. 1998. *Political Dissent in Democratic Athens: Intellectual Critics of Popular Rule.* Princeton: Princeton University Press.
Ober, J. 2008. *Democracy and Knowledge: Innovation and Learning in Classical Athens.* Princeton: Princeton University Press.
Ober, J., and B. Strauss. 1990. "Drama, Political Rhetoric, and the Discourse of Athenian Democracy." In *Nothing to Do with Dionysos? Athenian Drama in Its Social Context*, edited by J. J. Winkler and F. I. Zeitlin, 237–270. Princeton: Princeton University Press.
O'Connell, P. 2013. "Hyperides and *Epopteia*: A New Fragment of the *Defense of Phryne*." *Greek, Roman, and Byzantine Studies* 53: 90–116.
O'Connell, P. A. 2015. "Showing, Knowing and the Existence of Τέχναι in Hippocrates, *On the Art*." *Classical Philology* 110: 215–226.
O'Connell, P. A. 2016. "The Rhetoric of Visibility and Invisibility in Antiphon 5, *On the Murder of Herodes*." *Classical Quarterly* 66: 46–58.
Olson, S. D. 2008. *Athenaeus III: Books 6–7.* Cambridge, MA: Harvard University Press.

Osborne, R. 2011. *The History Written on the Classical Greek Body*. Cambridge: Cambridge University Press.
O'Sullivan, N. 1992. *Alcidamas, Aristophanes, and the Beginnings of Greek Stylistic Theory*. Stuttgart: Franz Steiner Verlag.
Otto, N. 2009. *Enargeia: Untersuchung zur Charakteristik alexandrinischer Dichtung*. Stuttgart: Franz Steiner Verlag.
Palmer, L. R. 1950. "The Indo-European Origins of Greek Justice." *Transactions of the Philological Society* 149–168.
Parker, R. 1983. *Miasma: Pollution and Purification in Early Greek Religion*. Oxford: Clarendon Press.
Parker, R. 1991. "The *Hymn to Demeter* and the *Homeric Hymns*." *Greece & Rome* 38: 1–17.
Parker, R. 2005. *Polytheism and Society at Athens*. Oxford: Oxford University Press.
Parry, A. 1981. Logos and Ergon *in Thucydides*. With a New Introduction by D. Kagan. New York: Arno Press.
Patterson, C. 2000. "The Hospitality of Athenian Justice: The Metic in Court." In *Law and Social Status in Classical Athens*, edited by V. Hunter and J. Edmundson, 93–112. Oxford: Oxford University Press.
Paul, G. M. 1982. "*Urbs Capta*: Sketch of an Ancient Literary Motif." *Phoenix* 36: 144–155.
Pearson, A. C. 1909. "Phrixus and Demodice: A Note on Pindar *Pyth*. IV. 162f." *Classical Review* 23: 255–257.
Pearson, L. 1976. *The Art of Demosthenes*. Meisenheim am Glan: Anton Hain.
Pelling, C. 2000. *Literary Texts and the Greek Historian*. London: Routledge.
Pendrick, G. J. 2002. *Antiphon the Sophist: The Fragments*. Cambridge: Cambridge University Press.
Peters, J. S. 2008. "Legal Performance Good and Bad." *Law, Culture, and the Humanities* 4: 179–200.
Phillips, D. D. 2007. "*Trauma ek Pronoias* in Athenian Law." *Journal of Hellenic Studies* 127: 74–105.
Plett, H. F. 2012. *Enargeia in Classical Antiquity and the Early Modern Age: The Aesthetics of Evidence*. Leiden: E. J. Brill.
Poddighe, E. 2012. "La città dei 'purosangue': Identità e sovranità politica ad Atene tra VI e IV sec. a.C." In *Xenoi: Immagine e parola tra razzismi antichi e moderni*, edited by A. Cannas, T. Cossu, and M. Giuman, 3–15. Naples: Liguori.
Pomeroy, S. B. 1997. *Families in Classical and Hellenistic Greece: Representations and Realities*. Oxford: Clarendon Press.
Power, T. 2010. *The Culture of Kitharôidia*. Washington, DC: Center for Hellenic Studies.
Prince, S. 2006. "Socrates, Antisthenes, and the Cynics." In *A Companion to Socrates*, edited by S. Ahbel-Rappe and R. Kamtekar, 75–92. Malden, MA: Blackwell.

Ramshaw, S. 2010. "Jamming the Law: Improvisational Theatre and the 'Spontaneity' of Judgment." *Law Text Culture* 14: 133–159.

Rapp, C. 2002. *Aristoteles: Rhetorik*. 2 volumes. Berlin: Akademie Verlag.

Rea, J. R. 1975. "Notes on Menander's *Perikeiromene*." *Zeitschrift für Papyrologie und Epigraphik* 16: 125–132.

Resnik, J., and D. Curtis. 2011. *Representing Justice: Invention, Controversy, and Rights in City-states and Democratic Courtrooms*. New Haven: Yale University Press.

Reyes, R. M., W. C. Thompson, and G. H. Bower. 1980. "Judgmental Biases Resulting from Differing Availabilities of Arguments." *Journal of Personality and Social Psychology* 39: 2–12.

Reynolds, B., ed. 2014. *Performance Studies: Key Words, Concepts, and Theories*. London: Palgrave.

Rhodes, P. J. 1981. *A Commentary on the Aristotelian* Athenaion Politeia. Corrected edition 1985. Oxford: Clarendon Press.

Richardson, N. J. 1974. *The Homeric Hymn to Demeter*. Oxford: Clarendon Press.

Riedweg, C. 1987. *Mysterienterminologie bei Platon, Philon und Klemens von Alexandrien*. Berlin: Walter de Gruyter.

Riess, W. 2012. *Performing Interpersonal Violence: Court, Curse, and Comedy in Fourth-century BCE Athens*. Berlin: Walter de Gruyter.

Rijksbaron, A. 2006. *The Syntax and Semantics of the Verb in Classical Greek: An Introduction*. 3rd edition. Chicago: University of Chicago Press.

Roisman, J. 2004. "Speaker-Audience Interaction in Athens: A Power Struggle." In *Free Speech in Classical Antiquity*, edited by R. Rosen and I. Sluiter, 261–278. Leiden: E. J. Brill.

Rose, M. L. 2003. *The Staff of Oedipus: Transforming Disability in Ancient Greece*. Ann Arbor: University of Michigan Press.

Roselli, D. K. 2011. *Theater of the People: Spectators and Society in Ancient Athens*. Austin: University of Texas Press.

Ross, W. D. 1959. *Aristotelis Ars Rhetorica*. Oxford: Clarendon Press.

Roy, J. 1995. "Lysias 29.12: Jurors from the Piraeus." *Electronic Antiquity* 3.3: unpaginated.

Rubinstein, L. 2000. *Litigation and Cooperation: Supporting Speakers in the Courts of Classical Athens*. Stuttgart: Franz Steiner Verlag.

Rubinstein, L. 2005. "Main Litigants and Witnesses in the Athenian Courts: Procedural Variations." In *Symposion 2001: Vorträge zur griechischen und hellenistischen Rechtsgeschichte*, edited by R. W. Wallace and M. Gagarin, 99–120. Vienna: Verlag der Österreichischen Akademie der Wissenschaften.

Rusten, J. S. 1989. *Thucydides: The Peloponnesian War Book II*. Cambridge: Cambridge University Press.

Rydberg-Cox, J. A. 2003. "Oral and Written Sources in Athenian Forensic Rhetoric." *Mnemosyne* 56: 652–665.

Ryder, T. T. B. 1976. "Demosthenes and Philip's Peace of 338–7 B.C." *Classical Quarterly* 26: 85–87.

Sartre, J.-P. 2003. *Being and Nothingness.* Translated by H. E. Barnes. Introduction by M. Warnock. With a new preface by R. Eyre. London: Routledge.

Scafuro, A. C. 1994. "Witnessing and False Witnessing: Proving Citizenship and Kin Identity in Fourth-century Athens." In *Athenian Identity and Civic Ideology*, edited by A. L. Boegehold and A. C. Scafuro, 156–198. Baltimore: Johns Hopkins University Press.

Schechner, R. 2003. *Performance Theory.* Revised and expanded edition. With a new preface by the author. London: Routledge.

Schenkeveld, D. M. 1992. "Prose Usages of ἀκούειν: 'To Read.'" *Classical Quarterly* 42: 129–141.

Schloemann, J. 2002. "Entertainment and Democratic Distrust: The Audience's Attitude towards Oral and Written Oratory in Classical Athens." In *Epea & Grammata: Oral and Written Communication in Ancient Greece*, edited by I. Worthington and J. M. Foley, 133–146. Leiden: E. J. Brill.

Scott, G. 1999. "The Poetics of Performance: The Necessity of Spectacle, Music, and Dance in Aristotelian Tragedy." In *Performance and Authenticity in the Arts*, edited by S. Kemal and I. Gaskell, 15–48. Cambridge: Cambridge University Press.

Sealey, R. 1983. "The Athenian Courts for Homicide." *Classical Philology* 78: 275–296.

Sealey, R. 2006. "Aristotle, *Athenaion Politeia* 57.4: Trial of Animals and Inanimate Objects for Homicide." *Classical Quarterly* 56: 475–485.

Searle, J. R. 1969. *Speech Acts: An Essay in the Philosophy of Language.* Cambridge: Cambridge University Press.

Segal, C. P. 1977. "Synaesthesia in Sophocles." *Illinois Classical Studies* 2: 88–96.

Segal, C. P. 1995. "Spectator and Listener." In *The Greeks*, edited by J.-P. Vernant, 184–217. Chicago: University of Chicago Press.

Sevier, J. 2011–2012. "The Unintended Consequences of Local Rules." *Cornell Journal of Law and Public Policy* 21: 291–345.

Shapiro, H. A. 1993. *Personifications in Greek Art: The Representation of Abstract Concepts, 600–400 B.C.* Zürich: Akanthus.

Shedler, J., and M. Manis. 1986. "Can the Availability Heuristic Explain Vividness Effects?" *Journal of Personality and Social Psychology* 51: 26–36.

Sheppard, A. 2014. *The Poetics of Phantasia: Imagination in Ancient Aesthetics.* London: Bloomsbury.

Sifakis, G. M. 2002. "Looking for the Actor's Art in Aristotle." In *Greek and Roman Actors: Aspects of an Ancient Profession*, edited by P. Easterling and E. Hall, 148–164. Cambridge: Cambridge University Press.

Sissa, G. 1999. "Sexual Bodybuilding: Aeschines Against Timarchus." In *Constructions of the Classical Body*, edited by J. I. Porter, 147–168. Ann Arbor: University of Michigan Press.

Sittl, C. 1890. *Die Gebärden der Griechen und Römer.* Leipzig: B. G. Teubner.

Skinner, M. B. 2014. *Sexuality in Greek and Roman Culture.* 2nd edition. Malden, MA: Wiley-Blackwell.

Slater, W. J. 1988. "The Epiphany of Demosthenes." *Phoenix* 42: 126–130.

Smith, M. R. 2008. *Advanced Legal Writing: Theories and Strategies in Persuasive Writing.* 2nd edition. Austin, TX: Wolters Kluwer.

Smith, S. 1999. "Pity and the Polis." In *Rhetoric, The Polis, and the Global Village: Selected Papers from the 1998 Thirtieth Anniversary Rhetoric Society of America Conference,* edited by C. J. Swearington and D. Pruett, 65–74. Mahwah, NJ: Lawrence Erlbaum.

Sourvinou-Inwood, C. 2003. "Festival and Mysteries: Aspects of the Eleusinian Cult." In *Greek Mysteries: The Archaeology and Ritual of Ancient Greek Secret Cults,* edited by M. B. Cosmopoulos, 25–49. London: Routledge.

Spatharas, D. G. 2006. "Λυσίας, *Κατὰ Τείσιδος* (απ. 17 Gernet-Bizos): μια ερμηνευτική προσέγγιση." *Ariadne* 12: 47–67.

Spengel, L. 1867. *Aristotelis Ars Rhetorica.* 2 volumes. Leipzig: B. G. Teubner.

Squire, M. 2013. "Apparitions Apparent: Ekphrasis and the Parameters of Vision in the Elder Philostratus's *Imagines.*" *Helios* 40: 97–140.

Stanford, W. B. 1936. *Greek Metaphor: Studies in Theory and Practice.* Oxford: Basil Blackwell.

Steel, C. 2009. "Divisions of Speech." In *The Cambridge Companion to Ancient Rhetoric,* edited by E. Gunderson, 77–91. Cambridge: Cambridge University Press.

Stevens, B. 2008. "The Scent of Language and Social Synaesthesia at Rome." *Classical World* 101: 159–171.

Storey, I. 2012. "Comedy and the Crises." In *Crisis on Stage: Tragedy and Comedy in Fifth-century Athens,* edited by A. Markantonatos and B. Zimmermann, 303–319. Berlin: Walter de Gruyter.

Sutton, R. F., Jr. 1992. "Pornography and Persuasion on Attic Pottery." In *Pornography and Representation in Ancient Greece and Rome,* edited by A. Richlin, 3–35. Oxford: Oxford University Press.

Symposium: Using Metaphor in Legal Analysis and Communication. 2007. *Mercer Law Review* 58: 835–1112.

Taplin, O. 1992. *Homeric Soundings: The Shaping of the* Iliad. Oxford: Clarendon Press.

Taplin, O. 1993. *Comic Angels and Other Approaches to Greek Drama through Vase Paintings.* Oxford: Clarendon Press.

Tarrant, D. 1960. "Greek Metaphors of Light." *Classical Quarterly* 10: 181–187.

Thomas, R. 1989. *Oral Tradition and Written Record in Classical Athens.* Cambridge: Cambridge University Press.

Thomas, R. 1992. *Literacy and Orality in Ancient Greece.* Cambridge: Cambridge University Press.

Thomas, R. 2000. *Herodotus in Context: Ethnography, Science, and the Art of Persuasion.* Cambridge: Cambridge University Press.

Thomas, R. 2003. "Prose Performance Texts: *Epideixis* and Written Publication in the Late Fifth and Early Fourth Centuries." In *Written Texts and the Rise of Literate Culture in Ancient Greece,* edited by H. Yunis, 162–188. Cambridge: Cambridge University Press.

Thompson, H. A. 1996. "Greetings to the Colloquium." In *The Pnyx in the History of Athens: Proceedings of an International Colloquium Organized by the Finnish Institute at Athens, 7–9 October, 1994*, edited by B. Forsén and G. Stanton, v–vi. Helsinki: Foundation of the Finnish Institute at Athens.

Thompson, W. E. 1976. *De Hagniae Hereditate: An Athenian Inheritance Case*. Leiden: E. J. Brill.

Thür, G. 2005. "The Role of the Witness in Athenian Law." In *The Cambridge Companion to Ancient Greek Law*, edited by M. Gagarin and D. Cohen, 146–169. Cambridge: Cambridge University Press.

Todd, S. C. 1990. "The Purpose of Evidence in Athenian Courts." In *Nomos: Essays in Athenian Law, Politics, and Society*, edited by P. Cartledge, P. Millett, and S. Todd, 19–39. Cambridge: Cambridge University Press.

Todd, S. C. 1993. *The Shape of Athenian Law*. Oxford: Clarendon Press.

Todd, S. C. 2000. *Lysias*. Austin: University of Texas Press.

Todd, S. C. 2004. "Revisiting the Herms and Mysteries." In *Law, Rhetoric, and Comedy in Classical Athens: Essays in Honour of Douglas M. MacDowell*, edited by D. L. Cairns and R. A. Knox, 87–102. Swansea: Classical Press of Wales.

Todd, S. C. 2007a. *A Commentary on Lysias, Speeches 1–11*. Oxford: Oxford University Press.

Todd, S. C. 2007b. "*Lady Chatterley's Lover* and the Attic Orators." In *Oxford Readings in the Attic Orators*, edited by E. Carawan, 312–358. Oxford: Oxford University Press.

Todorov, T. 1977. *The Poetics of Prose*. Translated by R. Howard. With a new foreword by J. Culler. Ithaca, NY: Cornell University Press.

Travlos, J. 1971. *Pictorial Dictionary of Ancient Athens*. New York: Praeger.

Tréheux, J. 1984. "Les cosmes à Latô." In *Aux origines de l'Hellénisme: La Crète et la Grèce. Hommage à Henri van Effenterre présenté par le Centre G. Glotz*, 329–342. Paris: Publications de la Sorbonne.

Trenary, A. D. 2013. "State v. Henderson: A Model for Admitting Eyewitness Identification Testimony." *University of Colorado Law Review* 84: 1257–1303.

Turner, V. 1969. *The Ritual Process: Structure and Anti-Structure*. Chicago: Aldine Publishing Company.

Turner, V. 1982. *From Ritual to Theatre: The Human Seriousness of Play*. New York: Performance Arts Journal Publications.

Turner, V. 1986. *The Anthropology of Performance*. With a preface by R. Schechner. New York: Performance Arts Journal Publications.

Turner, V. 1990. "Are There Universals of Performance in Myth, Ritual, and Drama?" In *By Means of Performance: Intercultural Studies of Theatre and Ritual*, edited by R. Schechner and W. Appel, 8–18. Cambridge: Cambridge University Press.

Usher, S. 1974. *Dionysius of Halicarnassus: Critical Essays, Volume 1*. Cambridge, MA: Harvard University Press.

Usher, S. 1976. "Lysias and His Clients." *Greek, Roman, and Byzantine Studies* 17: 31–40.

Usher, S. 1999. *Greek Oratory: Tradition and Originality*. Oxford: Oxford University Press.
Usher, S., and D. Najock. 1982. "A Statistical Study of Authorship in the Corpus Lysiacum." *Computers and the Humanities* 16: 85–105.
Vamvouri Ruffy, M. 2004. "Visualization and *Deixis am Phantasma* in Aeschylus' *Persae*." *Quaderni Urbinati di Cultura Classica* 78: 11–28.
Vasaly, A. 1993. *Representations: Images of the World in Ciceronian Oratory*. Berkeley: University of California Press.
Vine, P. 2004. *One Man's Castle: Clarence Darrow in Defense of the American Dream*. New York: Amistad/HarperCollins.
Walker, A. D. 1993. "*Enargeia* and the Spectator in Greek Historiography." *Transactions of the American Philological Association* 123: 353–377.
Wallace, R. W. 1989. *The Areopagos Council, to 307 B.C.* Baltimore: Johns Hopkins University Press.
Wallace, R. W. 2003. "*Phainein* in Athenian Laws and Legal Procedure." In *Symposion 1999: Vorträge zur griechischen und hellenistischen Rechtsgeschichte*, edited by G. Thür and F. J. Fernández Nieto, 167–181. Cologne: Böhlau.
Walters, K. R. 1993. "Women and Power in Classical Athens." In *Woman's Power, Man's Game: Essays on Classical Antiquity in Honor of Joy K. King*, edited by M. DeForest, 194–214. Wauconda, IL: Bolchazy-Carducci.
Webb, R. 1997. "Imagination and the Arousal of the Emotions in Greco-Roman Literature." In *The Passions in Roman Thought and Literature*, edited by S. M. Braund and C. Gill, 112–127. Cambridge: Cambridge University Press.
Webb, R. 2009. *Ekphrasis, Imagination, and Persuasion in Ancient Rhetorical Theory and Practice*. Farnham, UK: Ashgate.
Weißenberger, M. 1987. *Die Dokimasiereden des Lysias (orr. 16, 25, 26, 31)*. Frankfurt: Athenäum.
Wells, G. L., R. C. L. Lindsay, and T. J. Ferguson. 1979. "Accuracy, Confidence, and Juror Perceptions in Eyewitness Identification." *Journal of Applied Psychology* 64: 440–448.
West, M. L. 1978. *Hesiod: Works & Days*. Oxford: Clarendon Press.
West, M. L. 1990. *Studies in Aeschylus*. Stuttgart: B. G. Teubner.
Whitehead, D. 1977. *The Ideology of the Athenian Metic*. Cambridge: Cambridge Philological Society.
Whitehead, D. 2000. *Hypereides: The Forensic Speeches*. Oxford: Oxford University Press.
Whitehead, D. 2006. "Absentee Athenians: Lysias Against Philon and Lycurgus Against Leocrates." *Museum Helveticum* 63: 132–151.
Wiater, N. 2011. *The Ideology of Classicism: Language, History, and Identity in Dionysius of Halicarnassus*. Berlin: Walter de Gruyter.
Wilamowitz-Moellendorff, U. von. 1893. *Aristoteles und Athen*. 2 volumes. Berlin: Weidmann.
Willetts, R. F. 1967. *The Law Code of Gortyn*. Berlin: Walter de Gruyter.

Williams, B. 1993. *Shame and Necessity*. Berkeley: University of California Press.
Wilson, M. G., G. B. Northcraft, and M. A. Neale. 1989. "Information Competition and Vividness Effects in On-Line Judgments." *Organizational Behavior and Human Decision Processes* 44: 132–139.
Wilson, P. 2000. *The Athenian Institution of the Khoregia: The Chorus, the City, and the Stage*. Cambridge: Cambridge University Press.
Wilson, P. 2002. "The Musicians among the Actors." In *Greek and Roman Actors: Aspects of an Ancient Profession*, edited by P. Easterling and E. Hall, 39–68. Cambridge: Cambridge University Press.
Wohl, V. 2010a. *Law's Cosmos: Juridical Discourse in Athenian Forensic Oratory*. Cambridge: Cambridge University Press.
Wohl, V. 2010b. "A Tragic Case of Poisoning: Intention between Tragedy and the Law." *Transactions of the American Philological Association* 140: 33–70.
Woodruff, P. 1992. "Aristotle on *Mimēsis*." In *Essays on Aristotle's Poetics*, edited by A. O. Rorty, 73–95. Princeton: Princeton University Press.
Worman, N. 2002. *The Cast of Character: Style in Greek Literature*. Austin: University of Texas Press.
Worman, N. 2008. *Abusive Mouths in Classical Athens*. Cambridge: Cambridge University Press.
Worthington, I. 1991. "Greek Oratory, Revision of Speeches, and the Problem of Historical Reliability." *Classica et Mediaevalia* 42: 55–74.
Worthington, I. 1992. *A Historical Commentary on Dinarchus: Rhetoric and Conspiracy in Late Fourth-century Athens*. Ann Arbor: University of Michigan Press.
Worthington, I. 1996. "Greek Oratory and the Oral/Literate Division." In *Voice into Text: Orality and Literacy in Ancient Greece*, edited by I. Worthington, 165–177. Leiden: E. J. Brill.
Worthington, I. 2004. *Alexander the Great: Man and God*. Harlow, UK: Pearson Education Limited.
Worthington, I. 2008. *Philip II of Macedonia*. New Haven: Yale University Press.
Worthington, I. 2010. "Intentional History: Alexander, Demosthenes, and Thebes." In *Intentional History: Spinning Time in Ancient Greece*, edited by L. Foxhall, H.-J. Gehrke, and N. Luraghi, 239–246. Stuttgart: Franz Steiner Verlag.
Worthington, I. 2013. *Demosthenes of Athens and the Fall of Classical Greece*. New York: Oxford University Press.
Wyse, W. 1904. *The Speeches of Isaeus with Critical and Explanatory Notes*. Cambridge: Cambridge University Press.
Yunis, H. 2001. *Demosthenes: On the Crown*. Cambridge: Cambridge University Press.
Yunis, H. 2005. *Demosthenes, Speeches 18 and 19*. Austin: University of Texas Press.
Zanker, G. 1981. "Enargeia in the Ancient Criticism of Poetry." *Rheinisches Museum für Philologie* 124: 297–311.
Zanker, P. 1995. *The Mask of Socrates: The Image of the Intellectual in Antiquity*. Translated by A. Shapiro. Berkeley: University of California Press.

INDEX OF ANCIENT TEXTS

Aelian
Historical Miscellany
14.22: 202n1

Aelius Theon
2.62.21–63.15 Spengel = 5–6 Patillon: 222n40
2.118.7–8 Spengel = 66 Patillon: 124, 220n11
2.119.31–32 Spengel = 66 Patillon: 220n11

Aeneas Tacticus
11.7: 211n52
29.12: 211n52

Aeschines
1.25: 76, 207n94, 207n95
1.26: 60, 74–75, 204n35
1.33–35: 76, 207n91
1.34: 76, 207n92
1.89: 216n29
2.49: 60, 73, 204n34, 206n81
2.93: 201n85
2.111: 217n40
2.119–120: 222n42
2.122: 216n29
2.152: 194n46
2.179: 11, 194n46
3.1: 200n62
3.40: 217n41
3.46: 109, 216n25
3.49: 128, 221n34
3.51: 201n85
3.52: 41, 200n64
3.56: 207n83
3.59: 71, 206n74
3.72: 70, 206n72
3.97: 70, 206n71
3.125: 217n41
3.149: 70, 206n71
3.153: 127, 221n31
3.156: 221n36
3.157: 127, 221n31, 221n32
3.157–158: 128–129
3.159: 70, 206n71
3.167: 71, 72, 204n33, 206n77
3.171–173: 74, 197n11, 207n85
3.212: 201n85
3.221: 217n41
3.239–240: 221n36
3.244: 127, 221n31
3.252: 224n70
3.255–258: 170, 230n4

Scholia to Aeschines
1.25: 77, 207n98, 207n102

Aeschines the Socratic
fr. 92 Giannantoni: 206n70

Aeschylus

Libation Bearers
61–65: 214n4
973–1006: 83, 208n2
980: 84, 208n5
983–989: 83–84
1012–1013: 84, 208n4

Persians
179–180: 124, 220n10

Seven against Thebes
136: 220n9

Suppliants
197–199: 11, 194n47
496–498: 197n6

Life of
test. 1.15 *TrGF*: 205n57

Agatharcides
fr. 21 *GGM* = Photius, *Bibliotheca* 445b38–447b5: 221n32

Agathon
fr. 22 *TrGF*: 193n36

Alcidamas

Odysseus
22: 217n40

On the Sophists
13: 6, 193n29
16: 6, 193n28
31: 112–113, 218n46

Anaxagoras
fr. 63 [F23] Graham = B21a Diels-Kranz: 101, 213–214n83

Andocides
1.12: 229n85
1.14: 209n20
1.17: 194n53
1.18: 209n26
1.29: 227n55
1.31: 163, 227n55, 229n88
1.32: 163, 227n55, 229n88
1.33: 164, 229n89
1.37: 216n29
1.112: 209n26
1.123: 209n26
1.142: 230n97
1.146: 166, 230n103
1.146–147: 164, 229n90
1.147: 164, 165, 229n91, 229n92
1.148: 164
1.148–149: 194n46
1.149: 165, 229nn93–95
1.150: 166, 230n98
2.14: 92, 211n44

Anonymous Seguerianus
7: 155, 227n43
96: 220n11
111: 220n11

Antiphon
1.1: 203n19
2.2.3: 93, 211n51
2.3.9: 217n41
3.3.3: 217n37
3.4.1–2: 106
4.2.8: 166, 230n100
4.3.2: 35, 199n43
4.3.6: 217n41
4.4.9: 217n41
5.1–7: 203n19
5.11: 15, 195n68
5.27: 208n8
5.81: 108, 215n21
5.83: 209n26
5.84: 209n26
6.15–16: 215n20
6.29: 88

6.32: 215n20
6.41: 215n20
6.45: 94
fr. 71 Thalmheim = 6.1 Gernet: 87, 209n24

Antisthenes
Ajax
1: 122, 219n2
4: 122, 219n3
7: 122, 219n2
8: 122, 123, 219n2, 219n3, 219n4

Odysseus
5: 123, 219n7
6: 123, 219n5
9: 123, 219n5

Fragments
151 Giannantoni: 219n2

Apollodoros
fr. 110b *FGrH*: 228n75

Aquila Romanus
De figuris
30: 193n27

Aristophanes
Acharnians
911–912: 97, 212n64
914: 97, 212n65
917: 97, 212n66
926: 208n11

Assemblywomen
681–686: 194–195n56

Birds
1031: 208n11

Clouds
494–496: 208n11

776–782: 87, 209n21
1222–1223: 208n11
1297: 208n11
1399–1439: 54, 202n6

Frogs
528: 208n11

Knights
278: 92, 211n45
280: 92, 211n46
345–350: 58, 204n26
797–800: 195n58

Scholia to *Knights*
979: 227n41

Lysistrata
624–625: 195n59

Peace
1119: 208n11

Wasps
89–90: 195n63
662: 194n54
962–966: 84, 208n7, 209n20
975–978: 194n46
1435–1440: 208n11

Scholia to *Wasps*
88a: 195n58
300b: 195n58

Wealth
932: 208n11

Aristotle
On Dreams
459b: 10, 194n43

History of Animals
3.1 510a9: 211n52

Aristotle

History of Animals (continued)
4.8 533a4: 211n52
8.48 631a15–20: 212n54

On Memory
450a30–32: 223n51

Metaphysics
1 980a21–27: 12, 194n48

Poetics
11 1452b12: 211n52
17 1455a22–32: 66–67, 205n59
26 1461b27–32: 64–65
26 1461b34–35: 66, 205n57
26 1462a1–6: 66, 205n58
26 1462a8–11: 66

Politics
3 1287a26: 228n58
4 1300b24–30: 195n69
4 1300b29–30: 195n73

Rhetoric
1.3.2 1358b2–8: 112, 218n44
1.12.5 1372a21–26: 30, 198n21
1.15.19 1376a29–33: 209n22
1.15.21 1376b2–5: 208n12
2.4.15 1381b1–2: 31, 198n28
2.6.18 1384a34–38: 9, 193n35
2.8.14 1386a28–1386b1: 30, 198n23
2.8.14 1386a32–33: 31, 59, 198n26, 204n28
2.8.15 1386b2–8: 30–31, 59 198n25, 204n29
2.13.13–14 1390a11–19: 35, 199n42
2.23.11 1398a32–b5: 100, 213n82
2.23.15 1399a17–28: 202n4
2.24.2 1400b37–1401a12: 32, 199n34
3.1.5 1403b35–1404a8: 2, 191n6
3.2.3 1404b14–15: 57, 203n21
3.2.4 1404b18–21: 57, 203n22
3.7.6 1408a25–30: 31, 198n29
3.7.7 1408a31–32: 31, 199n32,
3.7.7 1408a32–36: 110, 216n33
3.10–11 1410b6–1413b2: 124, 220n12
3.12.2 1413b19–21: 6, 193n27
3.15.5 1416a21–24: 31, 198n27
3.16 1417a36–38: 69, 206n69
3.16 1417a38–1417b3: 69, 206n70

Fragments (Gigon)
128: 8, 193n32
963: 228n60

Pseudo-Aristotle

Constitution of the Athenians
24.3: 194n54
28.3: 77
49.4: 201n88
53.3: 194n52
57.3: 195n69
57.4: 195n68, 196n76
63.3: 194n55
63–69: 195n61
68.1: 194n52

Rhetoric for Alexander
15.1–6 1431b20–1432a3: 87, 209n22
36.7 1442a23–24: 30, 198n20
36.7–15 1442a20–1442b28: 30, 198n22
36.11 1442b4–5: 30, 198n19
36.37–42 1444a16–1444b7: 192n13

Arrian

Anabasis
1.7–8: 221n35

Athenaeus
12.552d: 29, 197n14
13.590d–f: 1, 191n1

Autolycus

Risings and Settings
2.1: 212n54

INDEX OF ANCIENT TEXTS

Chariton
Khaireas and Kallirhoe
5.7.10–5.8.3: 201n81

Cicero
Brutus
141: 56, 203n13

Divisions of Oratory
20: 220n13

On Invention
1.9: 203n17
1.104: 220n13
2.78: 220n13

Orator
24: 79, 208n105
55–56: 2, 191n3
55–60: 191n4
59–60: 203n12

On the Orator
1.142: 56, 203n17, 203n18
3.202: 220n13
3.213–227: 191n4
3.220: 56, 203n14

Demades
fr. 75 de Falco: 204n34

Demetrius
On Style
217: 221n28
222: 129, 222n38

Demosthenes
6.2: 217n40
6.19: 220n20
7.36: 217n40
12.18: 217n40
14.4: 220n20

17.20: 220n20
18.131: 217n40
18.135: 209n26
18.136: 217n41
18.137: 209n26
18.172–173: 170, 230n2
18.180: 170, 230n3
18.232: 206n75, 206n80
18.235: 211n52
18.258–262: 207n84
18.280: 113, 218n50
18.300: 169, 220n20, 230n1
19.8: 222n41
19.19–24: 222n42
19.27–28: 222n44
19.30: 222n41
19.34–63: 222n42
19.53–54: 222n43
19.59–61: 222n43
19.61–64: 222n47
19.64: 133, 222n45, 222n49
19.64–65: 132
19.66: 131, 222n46
19.72: 222n46
19.115: 220n20
19.146: 209n26
19.176: 217n41
19.213: 209n26
19.251: 75, 207n87
19.251–255: 78, 207n102
19.252: 76, 207n95
19.255: 76, 78, 207n95, 207n103
19.263: 220n2019.281: 194n46
19.286: 207n89
19.310: 194n46
19.314: 204n34
19.325: 222n43
20.118: 228n58
21.18: 216n29
21.72: 126, 220n17, 223n50
21.82: 200n67, 209n26
21.83–92: 200n64

Demosthenes (*continued*)
21.87: 200n68
21.93: 200n67, 209n26
21.96–96: 42
21.99: 194n46
21.107: 200n67, 209n26
21.115: 220n20
21.121: 200n67, 209n26
21.167: 209n26
21.174: 200n67, 209n26
21.182: 194n46
21.186–188: 194n46
21.195: 206n66
21.217: 216n29
22.53: 68, 141–142, 206n62
23.63–78: 195n69
23.78: 195n73
23.96: 228n58
23.168: 216n29
23.206: 217n41
25.11: 105, 214n5
25.62: 2, 46, 191n2, 201n82
26.1: 217n40
27.2: 203n19
27.18: 215n20
27.19: 213n73
27.47: 108, 215n21
27.62: 98
28.7: 213n68
28.9: 217n41
29.3: 217n41
29.5: 217n41
29.26: 209n26
29.33: 215n20
29.42: 107, 215n12
29.53: 209n26
30.5: 217n41
30.14–17: 215n20
30.25: 215n20
33.3: 107, 215n12
33.35–36: 217n35
34.29: 210n39
35.29: 227n41
36.1: 36
36.2: 199n49, 199n53
36.8: 199n49
36.9: 199n49
36.11: 199n49
36.12: 199n49
36.14: 199n49
36.15: 199n49
36.22: 199n49
36.31: 199n49
36.32: 199n49
36.36: 199n50
36.47: 199n49
36.53: 199n49
36.53–54: 199n50
36.55–57: 199n51
36.56: 37, 199n49, 199n52
36.57: 37, 199n53
36.61: 199n49, 199n50, 200n54
37.2: 215n20
37.8: 209n26
37.15: 201n80
37.17: 215n20
37.23–24: 201n79
37.31: 209n26
37.39: 201n77
37.44: 44–45
37.48: 45, 201n78
37.55–56: 29, 197n15
38.9–11: 111, 217n38
38.22: 217n40
39.24: 209n26
39.40–41: 228n58
40.7: 209n26
40.19: 215n20
40.32: 201n85
40.33: 201n86
40.38–39: 217n35
40.60: 108, 215n21
41.2: 203n19
41.13: 217n41
41.14–15: 111–112, 217n42
41.15: 217n41

41.20: 217n37
42.5: 91, 210n40, 210n41
42.29: 217n41
43.18: 107, 215n16
43.70: 210n39
44.15: 215n20
45.8: 215n20
45.68–69: 206n65
46.6: 209n19
46.7: 210n35
47.24: 209n26
47.27: 209n26
47.31–32: 215n20
47.36: 208n11
47.38: 208n11
47.41: 47, 201n83
47.60: 208n11
47.67: 90–91
48.1: 203n19
48.39: 110, 216–217n35, 217n40
48.46: 215n20
49.18: 209n26
50.24: 227n41
50.29: 215n20
52.2: 228n59
52.20: 217n35
52.21: 209n26
52.31: 209n26
53.16: 208n11
53.18: 209n26
53.20: 209n26
53.21: 209n26
53.25: 209n26
53.26: 109, 216n26
53.28: 213n73
54.9: 209n26
54.30: 217n40
55.2: 217n41
55.12: 209n26, 217n35
55.14: 217n41
57.4: 210n35
57.17: 215n20
57.27: 209n26

57.46: 215n20
57.62: 215n20, 217n35
57.63: 228n58
58.54: 217n41
59.25: 209n26
59.32: 209n26
59.34: 88, 209n26, 209n27
59.40: 209n26
59.48: 209n26
59.53: 209n26
59.61: 209n26
59.62: 215n20
59.70: 209n26
59.84: 209n26
59.111: 217n40
60.12: 219n68
60.18: 219n68
61.20: 220n20
letter 2.1: 217n40

Scholia to Demosthenes
19.64–65: 134–135, 223n50, 223–224nn52–61
20.75: 216n29
21.95: 43–44, 200n70, 200n71, 200n72
21.96: 200–201n72
22.53: 68, 142, 143, 206n63, 224n2, 224n3

Dinarchus
1.1: 216n27, 217n41
1.18–21: 221n36
1.95: 216n29
1.111: 199n48
3.3: 51, 202n100

Diodorus Siculus
1.48.6: 105, 214n7
16.60.1–3: 222n47
17.8.3–14: 221n35

Diogenes Laertius
1.70: 55, 202n8
6.3: 122, 219n2

Dionysius
fr. 5 *TrGF*: 214n4

Dionysius of Halicarnassus
Demosthenes
11: 153, 226n37
53–54: 58, 204n27
57: 206n75

On Imitation
Epitome 5.5 (=39.23–25 Aujac): 221n31

Isocrates
18: 8, 193n32

Lysias
7: 124–125, 220n13
21: 226n25
23–27: 226n24

Epicharmus
fr. 214 *PCG* (=fr. B12 Diels-Kranz): 220n12

Euripides
Andromache
103–116: 222n39

Electra
771: 105, 214n3
909–910: 58, 204n26

Hecuba
814–819: 210n34

Herakles
613: 161, 228n67

Hippolytos
1022–1024: 87, 209n21

Trojan Women
474–499: 222n39
647–650: 224n67

Fragments (TrGF)
fr. 223.86–87: 214n4
fr. 255: 214n4

Eustathius
Commentary on the Iliad 4.235.1–6 van der Valk: 202–203n9

Gorgias
Helen
8–14: 29, 210n34

Defense of Palamedes
7: 96, 212n57
8: 96, 212n58
9: 96, 212n59
10: 96, 212n60
12: 96
15: 216n29

Heraclitus
fr. 34 [F21] Graham = B101a Diels-Kranz: 89, 210n31

Hermogenes
On Invention
4.6: 202n4

On Issues
5.20–21: 202n4

Scholia to *On Issues*
7.374.9–29 Walz: 222n44

Pseudo-Hermogenes
On the Method of Forceful Speaking
33: 222n40

Progymnasmata
10.1: 220n11

Pseudo-Herodian
De Figuris
47 Hajdú = 8.603 Walz: 221n32

Herodotus
proem: 113, 218n47
1.8: 89, 210n31
1.8–12: 10, 194n44
1.136: 100, 213n81
5.45.1–2: 215n20
8.84.2: 226n22
8.94.2–3: 226n22

Hesiod
Catalogue of Women
fr. 165.5 Merkelbach-West:
   220n9

Melampodia
fr. 273 Merkelbach-West: 220n20

Theogony
27: 89, 210n32

Works and Days
256–273: 105, 214n2

Hippocrates
On the Art
1.1: 114, 218n55
9–12: 101, 214n84
11.2: 101, 214n85, 228n57
11.4: 115, 218n57, 218n58
11.5: 115, 218n59
12.4: 115, 219n60
13.1: 114, 218n53

On Breaths
3.2–3: 115, 219n62
3.3: 116, 219n63
5.2: 116, 219n64
7.2: 116, 219n63
9.1: 219n63
14.2: 116, 219n65

On Fleshes
614: 171, 230n6

Hippolytus
Refutation of all Heresies
5.8.39: 229n78
5.8.40: 162, 229n76

Hipponax
fr. 36 West: 214n6

Homer
Iliad
1.194–200: 212n54
1.245–246: 55, 203n10
3.218–219: 55, 202n9
20.131: 220n9

Scholia to Iliad
14.226–227: 126, 220–221n21
18.506b: 202–203n9

Odyssey
3.420: 220n9
4.841: 220n9
7.201: 220n9
8.499: 107, 215n14
11.563: 200n70
16.161: 220n9
16.155–163: 212n54
16.470: 171, 230n6

Hymn to Demeter
470–482: 229n79
473–482: 161

Hymn to Hermes
190–211: 84, 208n6
354–355: 84, 208n6

Hyperides
1.10: 33, 199n38
2.9: 194n46
3.3: 28, 197n7
4.11–13: 199n38, 199n39
4.41: 194n46

Hyperides (*continued*)
5.6: 216n27
6.16: 219n68
6.24: 219n68
6.29: 219n68
p. 57 Jensen = p. 103 fr. 15b Colin: 29, 197n14

Inscriptions
IC IV 47.21–22: 211n47
IC IV 72 col. 1 39–46: 211n47
IE 28a.59–60: 216n27
IE 641: 228n74
IG I³ 35.16–18: 216n27
IG I³ 78a: 216n27
IG I³ 104.18–19: 196n76
IG I³ 104. 24–25: 196n76
IG II² 2318.119: 205n57
IG II² 2319.82–83: 205n57
IG II² 2325.24: 205n57
IG II² 2325.251: 205n57
IG II² 2325.252: 205n57
IG II² 3661: 2228n74
IG II² 3764.3–4: 228n75
IG II² 3811.1–2: 228n75
IG IX, 2 521.5–18: 211n48
IG XI, 2 145.37–38: 195n63
IG XI, 2 287 A 81: 195n63
IG XII, 6.1 155.11–13: 215n20

Isaeus
1.1–2: 203n19
2.17: 215n20
2.38: 217n37
3.6–7: 215n20
3.19: 208n11
3.30: 99
3.40: 216n29
3.55: 215n20
5.7–8: 27–28, 197n6
5.20: 194n53
6.5–7: 215n20
6.10: 215n20
6.12: 215n20
6.22: 99, 213n75
6.23: 99, 213n76
6.41: 91, 210n39
6.62: 215n20
6.64: 215n20
6.65: 215n20
7.1: 100, 213n78
7.2: 100, 213n79, 213n80
8.6: 215n20
8.9: 217n40
8.28: 215n20
8.35: 213n68
9.7–13: 208n12
9.35: 215n20
10.15: 109, 215n20, 216n28
11.4: 217n41
11.43: 213n68
11.48: 109, 216n31, 216n33
12.7: 215n20

Isocrates
2.30: 211n52
4.15: 217n40
4.28: 161, 228n65, 229n79
5.90: 207n87
8.73: 220n20
8.104: 217n40
9.65: 217n40
9.65–69: 199n34
10.4: 217n40
10.61: 220n9
15.53: 214n8
15.102: 217n40
15.321: 194n46
17.7–9: 213n70
17.54: 217n40
18.52–54: 2, 191n2
18.53–54: 46, 201n81
18.54: 194n53
18.56: 217n40
18.65: 217n37
20.4: 217n40

letter 2.8: 207n87

Justin
11.3.6–4.8: 221n35

Lycurgus
1.14–19: 136, 224n64
1.21–27: 136, 224n64
1.40–41: 136–137
1.42: 138, 224n66
1.44: 139, 224n69
1.58: 136, 224n64

Lysias
1.21: 89
1.26: 90, 210n37
2.8: 219n68
2.10: 219n68
2.34: 147, 225n14, 225n16
2.35: 147, 225n18
2.35–37: 147, 226n19
2.37: 147, 226n20
2.38: 147, 226n21
2.39: 147, 225n14, 226n22
2.40: 225n14
2.41: 219n68
2.42: 225n14
2.43: 219n68
2.55: 219n68
2.56: 219n68
2.58: 219n68
2.63: 219n68
2.64: 219n68
2.67: 219n68
2.69: 219n68
3.4: 35, 199n44
3.6: 224n67
3.14: 208n11
3.20: 208n11, 209n26
4.12: 108, 215n21
6.3: 220n9
6.50: 229n87
6.50–51: 159
6.54: 229n87
6.55: 163, 229n86, 229n87
7.11: 217n41
7.25: 216n29
7.30: 217n37
7.42: 215n20
8.5–6: 211n52
8.12: 217n41
9.9–10: 95, 212n55
10.1: 216n29
10.5: 209n26
10.19: 93–94, 212n53
10.28–30: 202n102
10.29: 29, 198n18
11.10–11: 202n102
12.56: 217n40
12.74: 216n29
12.100: 12, 194n50, 229n87
13.35: 194n53
13.37: 211n52
13.42: 209n26
13.66: 209n26
13.68: 209n26
13.81: 209n26
14.28: 210n39
16.19: 29, 197n16
17.1: 203n19
19.1: 203n19
19.4: 217n41
19.23: 209n26
19.27: 209n26
20.1: 34, 199n40
20.2: 34, 199n37, 199n40
20.3: 34
20.4: 199n37
20.6: 199n41
20.8: 199n41
20.8–9: 199n37
20.14: 199n41
20.16: 199n41
20.22: 199n41
20.26: 215n20
20.28: 215n20

Lysias (*continued*)
20.34: 35, 194n46, 199n46
20.35: 35–36
21.10: 209n26
21.25: 194n46
22.12: 109, 216n30
23.1: 109, 216n23
23.8: 209n26
23.14: 209n26
24.2: 202n96
24.4–5: 201n90
24.6: 201n92
24.7: 202n96
24.10–12: 201n92, 202n95
24.13: 202n95
24.14: 48, 202n95
24.18: 49
24.19–20: 201n92, 202n95
24.22–23: 202n98
24.27: 49
25.14: 217n40
28.17: 227n42
29.12: 195n60
30.8: 217n41
30.23–24: 227n42
30.33: 200n62
31.5–14: 200n58
31.11: 38
31.12: 38, 170, 230n5
31.14: 200n59, 209n26
31.15: 39
31.16: 110, 200n59, 215n20, 217n36
31.17–19: 40, 200n60
31.23: 209n26
31.32: 40, 200n61, 200n63
32.2: 217n41, 226n27
32.4–7: 226n25
32.6: 213n73
32.12–17: 226n29
32.14: 98, 213n72
32.18: 151
32.20: 213n73
32.22: 213n72
32.23: 213n68
32.25: 213n73
32.27: 213n73
fr. A3a col. 4.9–12 Carey: 209n18
fr. 114 Carey: 215n20
fr. 118 Carey: 200n62
fr. 172 Carey: 213n68
fr. 194 Carey: 208n11, 209n18
fr. 208 Carey: 202n101
fr. 278 Carey: 155, 227n43
fr. 279 Carey 1: 154
fr. 279 Carey 1–4: 226n40
fr. 279 Carey 4: 155
fr. 279 Carey 6: 153
fr. 287: 213n70
fr. 425 Carey: 215n10

Menander
Perikeiromene
384–385: 208n11

Menander Rhetor
443.16–18: 44, 201n74

Orphica
Hymn 62.1–5: 214n4
fr. 33 Bernabé: 105, 214n5
fr. 144 Bernabé: 214n6
test. 713 T 4 Bernabé: 228n74

Palatine Anthology
7.357: 214n4
11.42: 228n74

Papyri
P. Mil. Vogl. I 20.18–32: 228n74
POxy 410 col. 1.1–12: 193n29
POxy 410 col. 4.114–123: 192n13
POxy 2537.6–15 (=Lys. fr. 208 Carey): 202n101

Pausanias
1.15.3: 230n96
1.32.5: 230n96

INDEX OF ANCIENT TEXTS

Philodemus
Rhetoric
4 col. 18.18–19.16, 1.200–201 Sudhaus: 2–3, 191–192n8

Pindar
fr. 137 Snell-Maehler: 228n66

Plato
Apology
34c: 11, 194n46

Cratylus
420b: 10, 194n42

Hippias Minor
304d: 217n40

Laws
745a: 211n52
816a: 55, 202n7
917d–e: 93, 211n50
927b: 166, 230n102

Menexenos
237b: 117, 219n67
241a: 219n68
242d: 219n68
242e: 219n68

Phaedrus
228a–c: 58, 204n26
250b–c: 101, 214n86
251c: 10, 194n42

Protagoras
320b–c: 113, 218n51

Republic
327b2–4: 205n53
360a–d: 211n52
389a–b: 63, 205n49
392c: 61, 204n37

393c: 62, 204n39
395b–c: 62, 204n38
395c: 62, 204n41
395d: 62, 204n42
395d–396a: 62, 205n43
396c: 63, 205n51
396d: 62, 205n44
397a: 62, 205n45, 206n46
397b: 63, 205n47
398a–b: 63, 205n49
439a–441c: 10, 194n45
495e: 28–29, 197n12
514a–517c: 214n86
603c–d: 10, 194n45

Timaeus
45b-d: 194n42

Plutarch
Alexander
11.9–12: 221n35

Demosthenes
11.3: 72, 206n79
15.5: 207n104, 224n70
23.1–2: 221n35
24.2–3: 224n70

Isis and Osiris
355a: 105, 214n7

Nikias
8.6: 60, 77–78, 204n31, 207n99

Perikles
32.4: 194n53

On Progress in Virtue
81e: 228n75

Solon
8.1: 207n95

On Talkativeness
504c: 5, 192n21

Theseus
35.5: 230n96

Whether the Athenians Were More Famous When It Came to War or When It Came to Wisdom
347b: 144, 225n5

Pseudo-Plutarch
Lives of the Ten Orators
840c: 207n104, 224n70
840d–e: 140, 192n20, 224n71
849e: 191n1

Pollux
8.49: 211n43
9.34: 227n41

Proclus
Ilioupersis summary: 222n39
Hymn 1.38: 214n4

Protagoras
fr. 21 [F2] Graham: 102–103, 214n88

Quintilian
Orator's Education
2.15.9: 191n1
6.2.26–36: 127, 221n26
8.3.63–72: 221n28
8.3.64–65: 222n39
8.3.67–70: 221n33
11.3: 191n4
11.3.65: 56, 203n15
11.3.65–184: 57, 203n23
11.3.67: 203n20
11.3.88–91: 203n14
11.3.180–184: 203n12

Rhetoric for Herennius
3.1: 203n17
3.19: 2, 191n5
3.19–3.27: 191n4
4.51: 221n32
4.68–69: 220n13

Sextus Empiricus
Against the Professors
2.4: 191n1

Solon
fr. 11.7 West: 107, 215n15

Sophocles
Ajax
462–465: 193n36

Antigone
263: 126, 220n18

Electra
877–878: 220n18

Oedipus Tyrannus
122–123: 209n25
535: 220n18

Women of Trachis
889: 171, 230n6

Fragments (TrGF)
fr. 12: 214n4
fr. 837: 228n66

Tacitus
Histories
3.68.1: 225n17

Theocritus
10.19–20: 214n6

Theophrastus
Characters
4.4: 206n68
5.6: 206n68
26.4: 29, 197n13

History of Plants
7.4.3: 212n54

Fragments (Fortenbaugh)
666.24: 2, 191n7
696: 129, 222n38
712: 2, 191n7
713: 2, 191n7

Thucydides
1.22.1: 226n34
1.22.3: 87, 209n23
3.37–40: 210n33
3.38.4: 113, 218n49
3.42.3: 113, 218n48
5.77.8: 216n27
6.27–29: 227n53
6.53: 227n53
6.55: 208n9
6.60: 227n53
7.71.2–3: 145, 225n7
7.71.4: 145, 225n9
7.71.5: 145–146, 225n10, 225n11

Tragic Fragments (Anonymous)
161 *TrGF*: 197
421 *TrGF*: 214n4

Valerius Maximus
8.10 ext. 1: 208n107

Virgil
Aeneid
2.29–30: 227n51

Xenophon
Agesilaus
7.2: 212n54

Cavalry Commander
5.7: 211n52

Cyropaedia
7.5.55: 211n52
8.1.31: 211n52

Hellenica
1.2.6–13: 226n25
2.3.43: 211n52
5.1.21: 227n41
5.3.16: 211n52
6.4.16: 211n52

Memorabilia
1.1.10: 211n52
3.4.1: 47, 201n84

Pseudo-Xenophon
Constitution of the Athenians
1.10: 28, 197n9

GENERAL INDEX

ability, physical, 37–40. *See also* disability, physical; strength, physical; weakness, physical
account books, 98
Achilles, 55; arms of, 122–123
acting/actors, 2, 4, 18, 59, 66, 77, 170, 193n25, 198n26, 204n39, 205n57, 206n78
actio, 2
adoption, 100
adultery, 30, 31, 32, 50, 89–90, 101
adverbs, deictic, 42, 227n51. *See also* deixis; pronouns, deictic
Aegisthus, 83
Aelius Theon, 124
Aeschines: imitation of Solon, 76, 78–79
—Works: *Against Timarkhos* (1), 60, 69, 74–79, 175, 206n76; *On the Dishonest Embassy* (2), 11, 60, 73, 175–176; *Against Ktesiphon* (3), 60, 69, 70–74, 109, 128–131, 170, 176, 192n20; scholia, 77
Aeschines of Sphettos, 69
Aeschylus: *Life of*, 205n57
—Works: *Eumenides*, 18; *Libation Bearers*, 83–85; *Persians*, 124; *Suppliants*, 11
agōn, 9, 193n27
air, power of, 115
Ajax, 121–123, 139, 200n70

Alcidamas, *On the Sophists*, 6, 112–113, 192n15
Alexander the Great, 60, 71, 73, 128
Alkibiades, 163, 229n80
alpha privative, 38
American Bar Association Journal, 126–127
Amphiktiony, Delphic, 131 132, 222n47
Amphitryon, 161
Amsterdam, Anthony G., 20–22
Anakeia, festival of, 153, 226n39
anaphora, 156, 160. *See also* deixis; pronouns, deictic
Anaxagoras, 101
ancestors, 164–167
Andocides, 157–167, 227–228n56; *On the Mysteries* (1), 163–167, 176; *On His Return* (2), 91–92, 176
"Anonymous Seguerianus," 155
Antenor, 55
Antiphon, 102; *First Tetralogy* (2), 93, 176–177; *Second Tetralogy* (3), 106–107, 177; *Third Tetralogy* (4), 35, 166, 177; *On the Murder of Herodes* (5), 208n1; *On the Chorus Boy* (6), 87–88, 94–95, 177
Antisthenes, *Ajax*, 121–123, 139, 177
apodeixis, 113, 114, 117, 169, 216n27
Apollo, 15, 84, 131
Apollodoros, 37, 47, 69, 88, 90, 179, 181, 182

GENERAL INDEX

aporrhēxai, 70–72
appearance, physical: and ability, 37–40, 45–46; versus actions, 29; Aristotle on, 30–32; and assumptions about behavior, 34–35; of Athenian slaves, 28; and biases, 27–33; as complement to language, 1, 2, 6, 11, 31–32; and forensic strategy, 29–33; as form of proof, 27, 46–50; *genos* and *hexis*, 31, 32; and moral qualities, 61, 69, 74–75, 204n36; non-Greek, 27–28; readers' reaction to, 51–52; as sign of internal illness, 115; and supplication in court, 11; and Sweet trial, 25–26; theatrical aspects of, 27; in *Against Meidias* (Dem. 21), 41–44; in *For Phormion* (Dem. 36), 36–37; in *Against Pantainetos* (Dem. 37), 44–46; in *Against Simon* (Lys. 3), 35; in *For Polystratos* (Lys. 20), 33–37, 172; in *Against Philon* (Lys. 31), 37–40
archons, 16, 188
Areopagos, 15, 16, 18, 196n77, 216n27
Aristeides, 76, 170
Aristophanes: *Acharnians*, 97; *Clouds*, 54, 87, 102; *Knights*, 58, 92; *Wasps*, 14, 18, 84; *Wealth*, 214n6; scholia, 207n98
Aristotle: 8; *On Dreams*, 10; *Metaphysics*, 12; *Poetics*, 61, 64–68, 70, 72, 77; *Rhet.*, 1, 2, 6, 9, 30–33, 35, 57, 59, 61, 69, 87, 100, 110, 112, 124, 193n27, 198n23
Arkhippos, 152–157
Aspasia, 117
assumptions, cultural, 30, 32, 33, 37, 40, 46, 50, 67
Athenaeus, *The Scholars at Dinner*, 1, 51
Athens, Classical: after battle of Chaeronea, 136–139; legal system of, 13–17, 86–90, 121–122; as performance culture, 3–4; racial prejudice in, 27–28, 197n8

attractiveness, 26, 32
audience: of assembly, 59; and Athenian citizenship, 9; and emotions, 127, 134–135, 137, 138–139, 143; and *enargeia*, 124, 126, 129; and gestures, 55–56, 61, 64–68, 69, 70, 71, 72, 74, 75, 78, 79; and language of demonstration and/or visibility, 92, 94, 109, 112, 114, 115, 116, 117, 118; and performance, 4, 6, 8, 16, 18, 21, 51–52; of theater, 83–84, 92. *See also* jurors (*dikastai*)
audience, "external" and "internal," 142–143, 167; in *Against Diogeiton* (Lys. 32), 150–152; in *Against Teisis* (Lys. fr. 278–279 Carey), 152–157; in forensic oratory, 148–150; in funeral oratory, 146–148; in Thucydides, 144–146
aulētai, 65–66, 67, 70, 72
Austin, J. L., 3, 4

Balkin, Jack M., 18
bēma, 14, 36, 41, 70, 71, 77, 149, 166, 170
Benveniste, Emile, 108
Blanshard, Alastair, 173
blindness, 105, 162, 209n25, 214n1, 214n6
Boegehold, Alan, 57
bookkeepers, 97
boulē and *bouleutai*, 15, 37–40, 47–50, 91–92, 94, 110, 178, 187, 188, 211n52. *See also dokimasia*
bouleutērion, 94
Bourdieu, Pierre, 31
bribery, 43, 70, 71, 72, 78, 113, 128, 131, 175, 178, 182, 218n48, 222n44
Brown v. Board of Education, 22
Bruner, Jerome, 21–22
Bühler, Karl, 156
Burkert, Walter, 162
Butler, Judith, 3

cap, felt (*pilidion*), 76, 207n95
Carey, Christopher, 50, 197n17

GENERAL INDEX

Chaeronea, battle of, 128, 136, 139, 172, 182, 224n64, 224n68
childbirth, 171
children: acknowledgement of, 85, 86, 98–100, 103; display of in court, 11, 35–36, 152, 165, 194n46; in suffering cities, 129, 131, 132
Cicero: *Brutus*, 56; *On the Orator*, 56; *Orator*, 2, 79
cities, conquered or threatened, 127–139, 222n39
citizens, ideal, 78
citizenship, Athenian, 9, 27, 28, 41–43, 74–75, 84, 138–139, 142, 158, 176, 182, 183, 186, 188, 206n76, 210–211n42
city, ideal, 61–62
civic suffering: in *Against Ktesiphon* (Aeschin. 3), 128–131; in *On the Dishonest Embassy* (Dem. 19), 131–136; in *Against Leokrates* (Lycurgus 1), 136–139
cloak (*himation*), 29, 60, 64, 75, 76, 77, 78
clothing, 28, 30–31, 69, 198n25, 198n26
Clytemnestra, 83–84
Cole, Dana, 127
communication, formal registers of, 58, 79
conspiracy, antidemocratic, 158
constructions, grammatical, 21–22; impersonal, 132, 137
contracts, written, 86
convictions, wrongful, 89, 210n30
counterfeit goods, 93
courtroom television dramas, 17–18
courts, Athenian, 13–14, 118, 148–149. See also Athens, Classical: legal system of
cowardice, 51, 72, 73, 136, 139, 185
Cratylus, 69
cross-examination, 87
Csapo, Eric, 67
curses and curse tablets, 159, 166, 230n101. *See also* dead

Danaids, 11
dead: cooperation of the living and the, 165–166; power of the, 166–167
death: burial ceremonies, 148; concealment of Euktemon's, 91
De Bakker, M. P., 149
debt collection, 68, 90, 111, 141–142, 178, 182, 185. *See also* mortgage stone
Decof, Leonard, 126, 128
deigma (samples market), 153, 154, 156, 172, 227n41
*deik- (Proto-Indo-European Root), 93, 108
deiknumi (demonstrate) and compounds, 51, 84–86, 89–90, 90–93, 97, 98, 100, 101, 107–111, 112–114, 116, 117, 153–154, 159, 161, 162, 170, 215n11, 215n14, 216n27; and *dikē*, 93. *See also apodeixis*; deixis; demonstration, vocabulary of
deixis, 197n3, 227n48; *am Phantasma*, 156–157, 227n51; ocular, 156, 157. *See also* adverbs, deictic; anaphora; pronouns, deictic
Delphinion, 15, 16, 197n77
Demeter, 160–161, 162, 163, 164, 166
Demetrius, *On Style*, 129
demonstratio ad oculos, 156, 157. *See also* deixis
demonstration: in funeral oratory, 117; in Hippocratic texts, 114–117
demonstration, vocabulary of, 85–86, 90–93; authoritative connotations in epideictic contexts, 112–118; authoritative connotations in forensic contexts, 108–112, 117–118. *See also deiknumi*
dēmos, 34, 35, 36, 60, 77, 110, 128, 137, 138, 139, 166
Demosthenes, 6, 58–59, 128–131, 149, 204n34; gestures of, 60, 70–74; nickname, 170

273

Demosthenes (*continued*)
—Works: *On the Crown* (18), 113, 169–170, 178; *On the Dishonest Embassy* (19), 75, 78–79, 131–136, 138, 147, 178; *Against Meidias* (21), 41–44, 50, 69, 125–126, 172, 178; *Against Androtion* (22), 68, 141–143, 178; *First Speech Against Aristogeiton* (25), 46–47, 105, 179; *First Speech Against Aphobos* (27), 97–98, 179; *For Phormion* (36), 36–37, 179; *Against Pantainetos* (37), 29, 44–46, 179–180; *Against Nausimakhos and Xenopeithes* (38), 111, 180; *Second Speech Against Boiotos* (40), 47; *Against Spoudias* (41), 111–112, 180; *Against Phainippos* (42), 91, 180; *Against Makartatos* (43), 107, 181; *First Speech Against Stephanos* (45), 69, 181; *Against Euergos and Mnesiboulos* (47), 47, 90–91, 92, 181; *Against Olympiodorus* (48), 110, 181–182; *Against Nikostratos* (53), 109, 182; *Against Neaira* (59), 88, 182; scholia, 43–44, 68, 134–135, 142–143
descriptions, incomplete, 129
diatupōsis (impression), 134. See also *enargeia*
Didymus the Blind, *Commentary on the Psalms*, 102–103
dikē, etymology of, 93. See also Justice
dikē pseudomarturiōn, 87, 89
Dinarchus, *Against Philokles* (3), 51, 182
Diodoros, 68, 141–143
Diogeiton, daughter of, 150–152
Dionysia, 41, 43, 178, 205n57
Dionysius of Halicarnassus: *Demosthenes*, 58, 153; *Isocrates*, 8; *Lysias*, 124–126, 139
disability, physical, 38, 47–50, 172, 188, 201n89, 202n97. See also ability, physical
diseases, 115, 116. See also illnesses, internal
disenfranchisement, 41–43, 44. See also citizenship, Athenian
dokimasia, 15, 25, 37–38, 40, 49, 110, 187, 188, 200n56
doubt, reasonable, 122–123
Drakon's legislation, 16
drunkenness, 88, 177
dunatos/adunatos, 38–40, 48. See also ability, physical

Eden, Kathy, 126
Egyptians, 27–28, 105
eikos arguments, 122–123, 125
ekphrasis, 124, 125, 128, 221n32, 223n56. See also *enargeia*
elderly, the, 14, 40, 128, 130, 131, 132, 136, 138. See also old age
Eleusinian Mysteries, 158–164, 166, 228n61
elites, biases of Athenian, 28–29, 61, 64, 67–68, 70, 72, 73, 74, 79, 204n36
emendation, textual, 197–198n17, 198n26
emotions, transfer of, 123, 127, 131–136, 137, 143, 144–148, 152, 154, 167
enargeia (vividness), 121, 124–127, 134, 139, 142, 144, 148, 156, 157, 167, 219–220n8, 220n14. See also deixis
enargēs (vivid), 113, 124, 125–126, 221n31
endeixis, 91–92, 97, 210–211n42, 212n62
energeia, 220n12
enthymeme, 32, 100, 209n22
epideixis and the epideictic genre, 5, 112–114, 116–118, 192n18, 192n20, 218n43
epiphany, 124, 170, 212n54
Euripides: *Electra*, 58, 105; *Herakles*, 161–162; *Hippolytos*, 87
evidence: false, 47, 87, 89; hearsay, 89; written documents as, 86, 98
evidence, visual: ability, 37–40; age, 34–35, 36, 172; Athenian preference for, 7, 86–90, 106; clothing, 30–31,

274

198n25; disability, 48–50, 172; and *enargeia*, 133; in *Libation Bearers*, 83–84; in *On the Murder of Eratosthenes* (Lys. 1), 89–90; in *For the Soldier* (Lys. 9), 95; silence, 41–44; and vocabulary of demonstration and visibility, 107, 108–112, 114–115, 116, 118; wounds, 46–47, 156
excellence (*aretē*), 113–114
exile, 15, 130, 158, 171, 176, 177, 210–211n42
eyes, as witnesses, 89
eyewitness testimony: in American judicial system, 88–89; as guarantee of truth, 87–89, 209n26; inaccuracy of, 209n25; and jurors' decision, 121–122, 126; language associated with, 85–86; in *Libation Bearers*, 83–85, 91. *See also* witness

farmers, 25, 31, 32, 195n60
fastidiousness, 31, 32
fear, 132–135, 147, 166–167
fees, payment of, 54, 201n87
foreigners (*xenoi*), 15, 27, 137, 138, 153, 197n5
Four Hundred, the, 33, 91, 172, 176, 187–188, 199n35
Freeman v. Pitts, 22

Gagarin, Michael, 6, 150
gaze, the jurors' 9–12
genos and *hexis*, 31, 32
Genos Dikanikon (Victor Bers), 59
gestures: appropriate versus inappropriate, 55–61; in assembly versus court, 59–60; on Athenian vases, 57; in Classical Athens, 54–55, 56–61; and the deaf, 53–54; of Demosthenes, 70–74; distracting effects of, 55–56; ethical interpretations of (Plato and Aristotle), 61–68; in Homer, 55–56, 61; instinctive nature of, 58–59; of Kleon, 60, 77–78; and Korax's invention of rhetoric, 53–54; modern use of, 53–54, 55, 56; "overdoing" of, 66–67; and pleas for pity, 59; restraint from, 64, 76, 78; in Roman oratory, 57; and social status, 63–64, 66–68, 72–74; of Timarkhos, 74–79. *See also* mimesis; *skhēma*
Gorgias: *Defense of Palamedes*, 95–96, 102, 182–183; *Helen*, 89, 102; *On Not Being*, 102
Gortyn, Law Code of, 93, 211n47
grain, 92, 109, 188
grief, 58, 133, 134, 135, 138, 139, 143
Gyges, 10

Hall, Edith, 3, 11, 27
handbooks: ancient rhetorical, 2, 3, 59, 87, 128, 155; modern trial, 55–56, 61, 126
hands, covering of, 64, 76, 78
Harris, Edward, M., 192n14
Hays, Arthur Garfield, 25, 26, 32, 33, 50
hearing, 6–7, 89, 145–148; as seeing, 106–108
Helios, 84
Heraclitus, 89
Herakles, 161–162
herms, mutilation of, 158–159, 176, 186, 227–228n56
Herodotus, 10, 89, 100, 113
Hertz, Randy, 20–21
Hesiod: *Theogony*, 89; *Works and Days*, 105
Hesk, John, 69
hexis. *See genos* and *hexis*
Hibbitts, Bernard, 20, 215n17
hierophant, 162–163, 228n68
Hippocrates: *On Breaths*, 114, 115–116, 118, 171; *On Fleshes*, 171; *On the Art*, 101, 114–115, 116–117, 118. *See also* medicine, Hippocratic
hissing, 69

historiography, 144, 171
Homer: *Iliad*, 55, 58; interpretation of, 206n76; *Odyssey*, 107; performance of, 5, 192n16; scholia, 126; and shame, 9
Homeric Hymn to Demeter, 160–162, 163, 228n61
Homeric Hymn to Hermes, 84
homicide, 2, 20, 25–26, 46, 83–84, 89–90, 90–91, 93, 94, 166, 176, 177, 186, 187. *See also* trials: homicide
houses, destruction of, 132, 134–135
houtos/houtosi. *See* pronouns, deictic
hubris, 20, 34, 49, 126, 135
Hughes, Alan, 57
humor, 49, 50, 202n95
Humphreys, Sally, 86–87
hupokrisis, 2
Hyperides: and the trial of Phryne, 1–2, 51; *In Defense of Lykophron* (1), 33, 183; *Against Philippides* (2), 29, 51; *Against Athenogenes* (3), 28; *Funeral Oration* (6), 117

illnesses, internal, 101, 115, 118
images, transference of mental, 126–127. *See also enargeia*
imagination, appeals to, 8, 127–128, 148–150; of Athenians, 168; in *Against Ktesiphon* (Aeschin. 3), 128–131; in *On the Mysteries* (Andoc. 1), 163–167; in *On the Dishonest Embassy* (Dem. 19), 131–136, 138–139, 143; in *Against Leokrates* (Lycurgus 1), 136–139, 172; in Lysias' funeral oration (2), 146–148; in *Against Andocides* (Lys. 6), 158–163; in *Against Diogeiton* (Lys. 32), 150–152; in *Against Teisis* (Lys. fr. 278–279 Carey) 152–157; in Thucydides, 144–146. *See also* deixis: *am Phantasma*; *enargeia*
impiety, 1, 131, 158, 160, 163, 164, 176, 212n63

inexperience, forensic, 36, 57, 58, 150
inheritance, 20, 51, 109, 111, 150, 175, 180, 181–182, 183, 184–185, 202n95
initiates: jurors in Andocides' trial as, 158, 159, 160, 163, 164, 166, 167; *mustai* and *epoptai*, 162
injury, display of, 46, 47, 153–154, 156
Innocence Project, the, 210n30
inscriptions, 13, 93, 148, 192n18, 197n5, 208n9, 211n47
Isaeus, 51, 99–100; *On the Estate of Pyrrhos* (3), 99, 183; *On the Estate of Dikaiogenes* (5), 27–28, 183–184; *On the Estate of Philoktemon* (6), 91, 99, 184; *On the Estate of Apollodoros* (7), 100, 184; *On the Estate of Aristarkhos* (10), 109, 184–185; *On the Estate of Hagnias* (11), 109, 185
Isocrates, 8, 31; *Panegyrikos* (4), 161, 163; *Evagoras* (9), 32; *Against Kallimakhos* (18), 2, 46, 185
isomorphism, 27

Jouanna, Jacques, 114
"judgmental capacity" (*gnōmē*), 159–160
juries, size of, 13, 194n53, 194n54
jurors (*dikastai*): appeals to imaginations of, 127–140, 148–167; as audience, 4, 11; belief in witnesses, 88–89; commiseration with Straton, 42–44; and "common knowledge," 110; demographic composition of, 14, 195n60; as "external audience," 142, 150, 154; as initiates in Eleusinian mysteries, 158, 159, 160, 163, 164, 166, 167; as judges, 13, 112; as "knowers," 12; as listeners, 106; memories of, 160, 164–165; payment of, 14; power of, 10–12, 20, 171–172; selection of, 13–14; visual biases of, 29–32; and vocabulary of demonstration and visibility, 108–112; as witnesses, 107–108, 109–110, 118, 128–131, 143

276

"Jury Room" blog, 55
Justice (*Dikē*), personified, 105

Kallippides, 66, 67, 77, 205n57
kalokagathia, 204n36
Katsouris, Andreas, 57
Kennedy, George, 31
Khilon of Sparta, 55
khorēgos, 41, 178
Kleon, 14, 60, 77–78, 113, 207n98, 210n33
knowing: Greek verbs of, 12, 101, 212n54; and presence, 87, 88, 102–103; 123, 125, 131; and seeing, 12, 101–103, 113–114, 114–117, 132
knowledge: common, 110; unspeakable, 161
Korax, 53–54

language: Aeschines' criticism of Demosthenes', 70–71; and cultural values, 19–22; as means of determining truth, 123; of performative prose, 6, 8; unreliability of, 89; and witness testimony, 85–86. *See also* demonstration, vocabulary of; *logos* (word) versus *ergon* (deed); visibility, vocabulary of
law: against disorderly speakers, 76; against insulting generals, 95; and literature, 21; as performance, 18; regulating prostitution, 94; verbal arguments based on, 109; witnesses in Athenian, 86–87; written, role of in Athenian legal decisions, 171, 172, 196n82
legal terminology, Athenian, 20, 92, 103–104
Leokrates. *See* Lycurgus
Levinson, Sanford, 18
lexis (speaking style), 31, 57, 63, 205n50
litigants as actors, 4, 206n78
logos (word) versus *ergon* (deed), 89, 110, 114, 122, 217n37

Love: and the gaze, 10; (*Erōs*), personified, 105, 214n6
Lubet, Steven, 126
lust, 35
Lycurgus, *Against Leokrates* (1), 136–139, 147, 172, 185
Lysias, 5, 6; *On the Murder of Eratosthenes* (1), 89–90, 93, 101, 186; *Funeral Oration* (2), 117, 146–148, 186; *Against Simon* (3), 35, 186; *Against Andocides* (6), 158–163, 164, 166–167, 186; *For the Soldier* (9), 95, 186–187; *Against Theomnestos* (10), 29–30, 51–52, 93–94, 187; *Against Theomnestos* (11), 51–52; *Against Eratosthenes* (12), 12, 187; *For Mantitheos* (16), 29, 50, 187, 197–198n17; *For Polystratos* (20), 33–37, 172, 187–188; *Against the Grain Retailers* (22), 109, 188; *Against Pankleon* (23), 108–109, 188; *For the Disabled Man* (24), 47–50, 172, 188; *Against Philon* (31), 37–40, 48, 110, 170, 188; *Against Diogeiton* (32), 98, 150–152, 167, 189; *Against Teisis* (fr. 278–279 Carey), 152–157, 167, 172, 189

Marathon, battle of, 165
Marcus Antonius, 56
marriage, Athenian, 28–29, 99, 142–143, 180, 182, 183, 189
McElhaney, James, 126–127
medicine, Hippocratic, 101, 114–117, 118, 171
Meidias, 41–44
memory, idealized, 165; as canon of rhetoric, 5, 56; as mind-imprint, 223n51; of past oratorical performances, 60, 73, 78; of ritual experience, 158–160, 163, 164; selective, 87
Menander Rhetor, 44
metastasis (transfer of responsibility), 135–136

277

metics, 15, 27, 28, 38, 136, 186, 187, 188, 197n5, 200n58
mimesis, 61–67, 77; tragic versus epic, 64–65, 66. *See also* gestures
Mirhady, David, 87, 159
mise en abyme, 145, 146
moderation, 35, 37, 62, 78, 203n12; and the gaze, 10
moneylenders, 29
mortgage stone, 91, 180, 184
movements, sacred, 162. *See also* gestures
murder. *See* homicide
Murray, Penelope, 62
musical productions, 65, 205n47, 205n56
Mynniskos, 66, 205n57
Mytilene Debate, 113, 210n33

noselessness, 2, 46–47
nudity, 1–2, 75, 77, 78

Ober, Josiah, 110
Odeion, 14
Odysseus, 55, 56, 58, 61, 95, 122, 123, 177, 182
old age, 34–35, 36, 37, 40, 41, 45, 99, 129, 130, 133, 137, 172. *See also* elderly, the
Old Oligarch, the. *See* Pseudo-Xenophon
oligarchs, 29, 33, 34, 35, 36, 38, 92, 187, 188, 199n35
oratory, forensic, 3; appeals to imagination in, 8, 121–167; concealing weakness in, 110–111; and drama, 4, 27; impersonal constructions in, 132, 137; insults in, 197n11; "internal audiences" in, 141–143, 148–156; parts of, 5–6; physiognomic arguments in, 68–78; visual rhetoric in, 25–52; vocabulary of demonstration and visibility in, 108–112

oratory, funerary, 117, 146–148, 186
oratory, Roman, 56, 57
Orestes, 18, 83–84, 85, 91

Palamedes, 95–96, 102, 182–183
Palladion, 15, 16
pankration (fighting competition), 60, 75, 78
Pantainetos, 44–46
Parabyston, 14
paternity, acknowledgment of, 86, 98–100
pathos, 49, 50, 134
patriotism, 38, 40, 136, 139, 170
peace guardian (*eirēnophulax*), 70
Peace of Philokrates, 70, 222n41
Peloponnesian War, 131, 150, 158
pension, 48–50
performance: culture, 4; decline in standards of, 76–77; ethical interpretation of, 70–71; mimetic, 62, 63; theories of, 3–4
performance, forensic: conditions of, 13–17, 149; definition of, 4; ephemeral nature of, 5, 192n18, 193n26; Greek verbs for, 3–4; law as, 18; as legal discourse, 19–21; and manipulation of the audience's seeing and hearing, 6–7; in modern courtrooms, 17–22; of poetry, 5, 192n16; reliant upon language, 21–22; as representation of reality, 18–19
performance, oratorical: formal instruction in, 2–3; handbooks on, 2–3; in modern scholarship, 3
Perikles, 76, 77, 78
Persians, 100, 128, 147, 165
persuasion, and appearance, 1, 28–32, 50–51, 52; and clothing, 30–31; in courts, 118; and *enargeia*, 124–125, 156; in epideictic contexts, 112, 118; and gestures, 79; and mental images, 163, 164, 167; and oratorical perfor-

mance, 2, 6, 8, 17, 18, 20, 22, 27, 53–54, 78, 149, 150; and rhetoric of seeing, 170–172; and sophists, 102; and speaking style (*lexis*), 57
phainō (make visible) and compounds, 85, 97–100, 101, 104, 107, 162, 212n63, 215n14
phainomai (become visible), 30–31, 85–86, 95, 102–103, 112, 126, 198n23, 208n9, 212n54
phaneros (visible), 85–86, 89–90, 93–96, 97–98, 100, 101, 108, 110, 111–112, 113, 115–116, 126, 169, 211n52, 212n54
phasis, 97, 212n62
Philip of Macedon, 70, 71, 73, 78, 131, 132, 135, 169, 175, 178
Philodemus, 2–3
Philon, 37–40
Phokis, destruction of, 131–136
Phormion, 36–37
Phryne, trial of, 1–2, 51
physicians, 25–26, 47, 90. *See also* Hippocrates; medicine, Hippocratic
"physiognomic interpretation," 69, 78, 79
pity, 1, 11, 30–31, 35–36, 43–44, 49, 59, 132–135, 138–139, 172, 198n23, 198n25, 202n97
Plato: *Apology*, 11; *Cratylus*, 10; *Laws*, 55, 93, 166; *Menexenus*, 117; *Phaedrus*, 10, 58, 101; *Protagoras*, 113–114; *Republic*, 10, 28–29, 61–64, 66, 67, 70, 102; *Timaeus*, 10
Plutarch: *Isis and Osiris*, 105; *Life of Demosthenes*, 72; *Life of Nikias*, 60, 77–78; *On Talkativeness*, 5; *Whether the Athenians Were More Famous When It Came to War or When It Came to Wisdom*, 144–145, 148, 149
Pnyx, 14, 60
poetry, Greek, 2, 5, 7, 57, 59, 113, 124, 157, 192n16, 206n76, 215n14. *See also* Aristotle: *Poetics*

Polystratos, 33–37
Potnia, 162
poverty, 26, 30, 38–39, 42, 43, 142, 171
precedent, 18, 31, 32, 186n82
prejudice. *See* appearance, physical: and assumptions about behavior; appearance, physical: and biases; assumptions, cultural; elites, biases of Athenian; racism: in Classical Athens
presence. *See enargeia*; imagination, appeals to; knowing: and presence
Pre-Socratic philosophers, 101
Prigg v. Pennsylvania, 21
probability. *See eikos* arguments
pronouns, deictic, 27, 34, 35, 36, 37, 45, 92, 127, 152, 154–157, 160, 197n3, 227nn48–49. *See also* adverbs, deictic; deixis
pronouns, indefinite, 147
property, visible versus invisible, 97–98, 213n68
prose style, Greek, 6
prostitution, 74, 78, 94, 175, 178, 182, 224n67
Protagoras, 102–104, 113–114
proving, Greek verbs of, 111–112
Prytaneion, 16
Pseudo-Longinus, 127
Pseudo-Plutarch, *Lives of the Ten Orators*, 140, 192n20
Pseudo-Xenophon (the "Old Oligarch"), 28, 199n37
psychodrama, 127

questions, rhetorical, 6, 146–147, 148
Quintilian, 56, 57, 127, 215n13

racism: in Classical Athens, 27–28, 197n8; in twentieth-century Detroit, 26
Ramshaw, Sara, 18
reading aloud, 146, 225n12

reason, compared to sight in Hippocratic thought, 115–116
religion, Athenian, 4, 101, 166. *See also* Eleusinian Mysteries
revenge, 11, 84, 90, 153, 166–167, 171, 230n100
rhetoric, canons of, 5, 56
Rhetoric for Alexander, 30, 87
Rhetoric for Herennius, 2
ring composition, 6, 36, 193n31
ritual experience, 158, 160, 163, 164, 167
Rose, Martha, 48
Rubinstein, Lene, 87
running, 60, 64

Salamis, battle of, 146–148, 226n22; statue of Solon on, 76, 78
Sartre, John-Paul, 9–10
saying, Greek and Latin verbs for, 108
sea battles, 144–148
Searle, John, 3, 4
seeing, 6–7; and being seen, 9–11; and believing, 114, 171; and Eleusinian mysteries, 160–162; emotional response to, 10–11, 138–139; Greek words for, 12, 27, 101, 106–107, 132–133; language of sight in *enargeia*, 127, 129, 132–133, 136–137, 145; and power, 9, 10–11; rhetoric of, 7, 169, 170, 171. *See also enargeia*; gaze, the jurors'; hearing: as seeing; imagination, appeals to; knowing: and seeing; visibility
segregation, 22, 26
self-control, 35, 76, 78. *See also* moderation
self-injury, 47. *See also* injury, display of
shame: before wife, 142, 143; and being seen, 9–10, 193n34, 193n36, 194n40; caused by Aeschines' policy towards Philip, 131–132, 222n46; of Demosthenes' guardians, 98; at lack of knowledge, 110; and mimesis, 62, 63; and Timarkhos' nudity, 75

sight, imaginary. *See* imagination, appeals to
sight, physical. *See* seeing
"sight of the mind," 101, 115
silence, of Antigenes, 45; of internal audience in Lys. 32, 151–152; of Phokians, 133; of Phormion, 36; of Straton, 41–44, 50, 172
singing, 4, 5, 41, 55, 65, 107, 147, 172
skhēma, 53–54, 62–63, 68, 202n4, 204n39, 206n66. *See also* gestures
skopeō/skeptomai (look into), 106–107
slaves, 21, 25, 28, 44, 45, 46, 48, 57, 142, 176, 179, 180, 181, 188, 211n47
Socrates, 11, 28–29, 47, 61–64, 66, 102, 113–114, 116, 117
soldiers, 47, 63, 84, 95, 96, 101, 117, 137, 186, 207n87
Sopatros, *Division of Questions*, 135–136
sophists and sophistic discourse, 7 32, 101–102, 112, 116
Sophocles: *Antigone*, 126; *Oedipus Tyrannos*, 209n25; *Women of Trachis*, 171
space, 13, 16, 30, 130, 149, 160
spectacle: (*thea*), 145; (*theama*), 132, 133
spectatorship, 225n6; and Athenian citizenship, 9; and epideictic oratory, 112, 113; imagined, 123; and performance, 65–66; in scholia to *Against Meidias*, 44; shared, 167; and trials, 16, 74, 103
speeches, forensic: composition of, 17; editing and revision of, 7, 51–52, 193n31; purposes of, 56–57; rehearsals of, 58; sold as books, 8; spatial references in, 17; surviving texts of, 4–5, 7; vocabulary choice in, 21–22. *See also* performance, forensic
spinning, in dance or oratory, 65, 66, 67, 68, 70, 72, 73
statements, authoritative, 71, 85, 108–112, 113–114, 116, 118, 169, 171, 172
State v. Henderson, 209–210n29

statue: of Anakreon, 204n36; of cult figure in Mysteries ritual, 162, 229n80; of judge in Thebes, 105; of Solon, 76, 78
stichomythia, 92
Stoa Poikile, 14, 165, 221n31
stratēgos, 47
Straton, 41–44
strength, physical, 29, 37–40, 45, 46
style. *See* language
sunēgoroi (supporting speakers), 33, 35, 36, 78, 130, 199n39
supplication. *See* children: display of in court; Phryne, trial of
Sweet trial, 25–26, 27, 32, 33, 50
syllogisms, false, 32
synaesthetic metaphors in Greek, 107
Syracuse, battle in harbor of, 144–146, 148; as birthplace of rhetoric, 53–54

Tacitus, 224n1, 225n8, 225n17
Teisias, 53–54
Teisis, 149, 152–157
theater, 2, 5; similarity to courtroom, 4, 9, 16, 18, 27, 168
Thebes, destruction of, 128–131, 133, 137, 140, 221n35
Themistokles, 76
Theophrastus, 129; *Characters*, 29, 69; *On Delivery*, 2
theorists, ancient rhetorical, 2, 5, 6, 124, 127, 135
Thesmophoria, 228n61
thinness, 29, 51
Thirty, the, 150, 165, 187, 211n52
Thomas, Rosalind, 6, 114
Thucydides, 87, 89, 113, 144–146, 147, 148, 151, 171, 207n98
Timarkhos, 60, 69, 74–79, 172, 175, 207n86
Todd, Stephen, 86
Todorov, Tzvetan, 19
trials: fairness of, 121–122; homicide, 15–16; interest in, 18; personnel and locations of, 14–15. *See also dokimasia*
Trigonion, 14
Trojan War, 95, 222n39
truth: jurors' responsibility to determine, 106–107; witnesses and, 87–90

underworld, the, 161–162, 166. *See also* dead

values, cultural: and forensic discoure, 19–21. *See also* assumptions, cultural
vase paintings, 7, 10, 28, 57, 205n53, 222n39
violence, physical, 35, 41, 43, 46–47, 54, 65–66, 67, 72, 76, 90, 92, 93, 153, 154, 155, 178, 186, 189
Virgil, *Aeneid*, 227n51
visibility, 6–7; between juror and litigant, 14–15, 157; as personal experience, 8. *See also* knowing: and seeing; shame: and being seen; women: visibility of
visibility, vocabulary of, 85–86, 93–100, 215n17; authoritative connotations in forensic contexts, 108–112; in medicine and philosophy, 101–104, 114–117. *See also phainō*; *phainomai*; *phaneros*
vividness. *See enargeia*
vocabulary, importance of, 21–22
voting. *See* jurors: power of
voting urns, 14

Walker, Andrew, 145
water-clock (*klepsudra*), 14, 17
weakness, physical, 30, 34, 37, 38–40, 45, 46, 49, 50, 138. *See also* disability, physical
wealth 35, 39, 42, 43, 109, 180; (*Ploutos*), personified, 105, 214n6
Webb, Ruth, 135–136

wheat, 162. *See also* grain
whipping, 153, 155, 156, 189
witness(es) (*martus*): 86–90; absence of, 48, 87, 95–96; alternative Greek words for, 208n8; bystander as, 86, 97; credibility of, 87–89; formulaic testimony of, 87; function of, 86–87; Helios as, 83–84; in Homeric scholia, 126; as "internal audience," 143; jurors as, 107, 109–110, 118, 129–130, 143; language associated with, 83–86; and vocabulary of demonstration, 90–93; and vocabulary of visibility, 93–100. See also *apodeixis*; demonstration, vocabulary of; eyewitness testimony; visibility, vocabulary of
wives, 4, 26, 68, 89, 90, 99, 101, 109, 141–143, 165, 183, 186. *See also* marriage, Athenian
women: forensic voice of, 150–151; as microcosm of polis, 138; visibility of, 224n67
"word picture," 126–127. See also *enargeia*
Worman, Nancy, 31
Wyse, William, 99–100

Xenophon, *Memorabilia*, 47